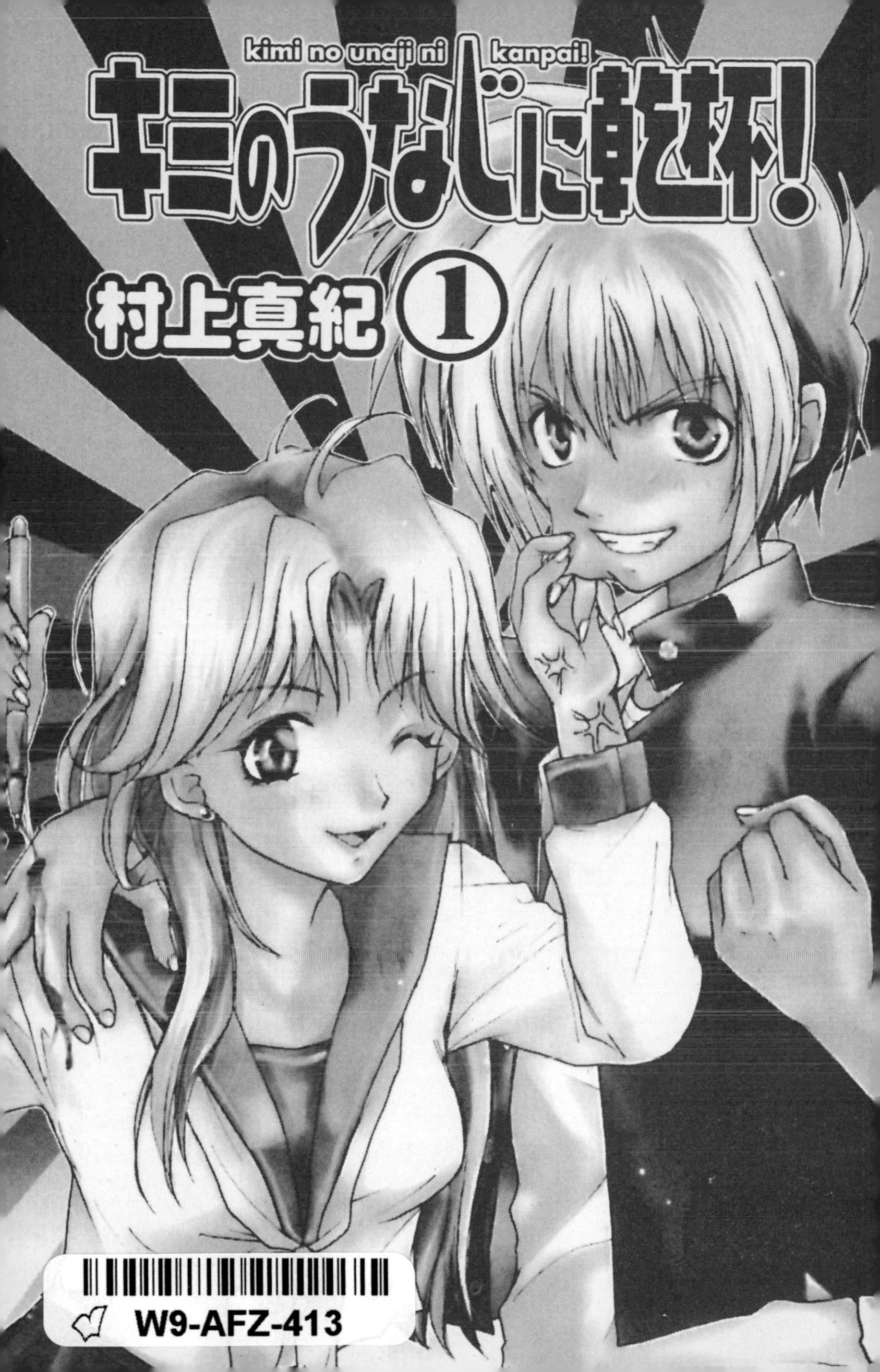
kimi no unaji ni kanpai!
キミのうなじに乾杯!
村上真紀
1

Kanpai! Vol. 1
created by Maki Murakami

Translation - Christine Schilling
English Adaptation - Aaron Sparrow
Copy Editor - Emily Wing
Retouch and Lettering - Jose Macasocol, Jr.
Production Artists - Chris Anderson and James Lee
Cover Design - Al-Insan Lashley

Editor - Lillian Diaz-Przybyl
Digital Imaging Manager - Chris Buford
Production Managers - Jennifer Miller and Mutsumi Miyazaki
Managing Editor - Jill Freshney
VP of Production - Ron Klamert
Publisher and E.I.C. - Mike Kiley
President and C.O.O. - John Parker
C.E.O. - Stuart Levy

A **TOKYOPOP** Manga

TOKYOPOP Inc.
5900 Wilshire Blvd. Suite 2000
Los Angeles, CA 90036

E-mail: info@TOKYOPOP.com
Come visit us online at www.TOKYOPOP.com

ISBN: 1-59532-317-1

First TOKYOPOP printing: September 2005
10 9 8 7 6 5 4 3 2
Printed in the USA

VOLUME ONE

by Maki Murakami

HAMBURG // LONDON // LOS ANGELES // TOKYO

CONTENTS

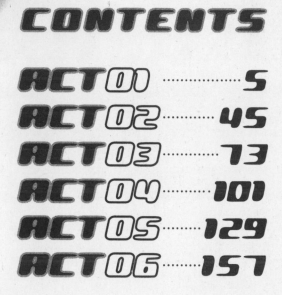

ACT 01

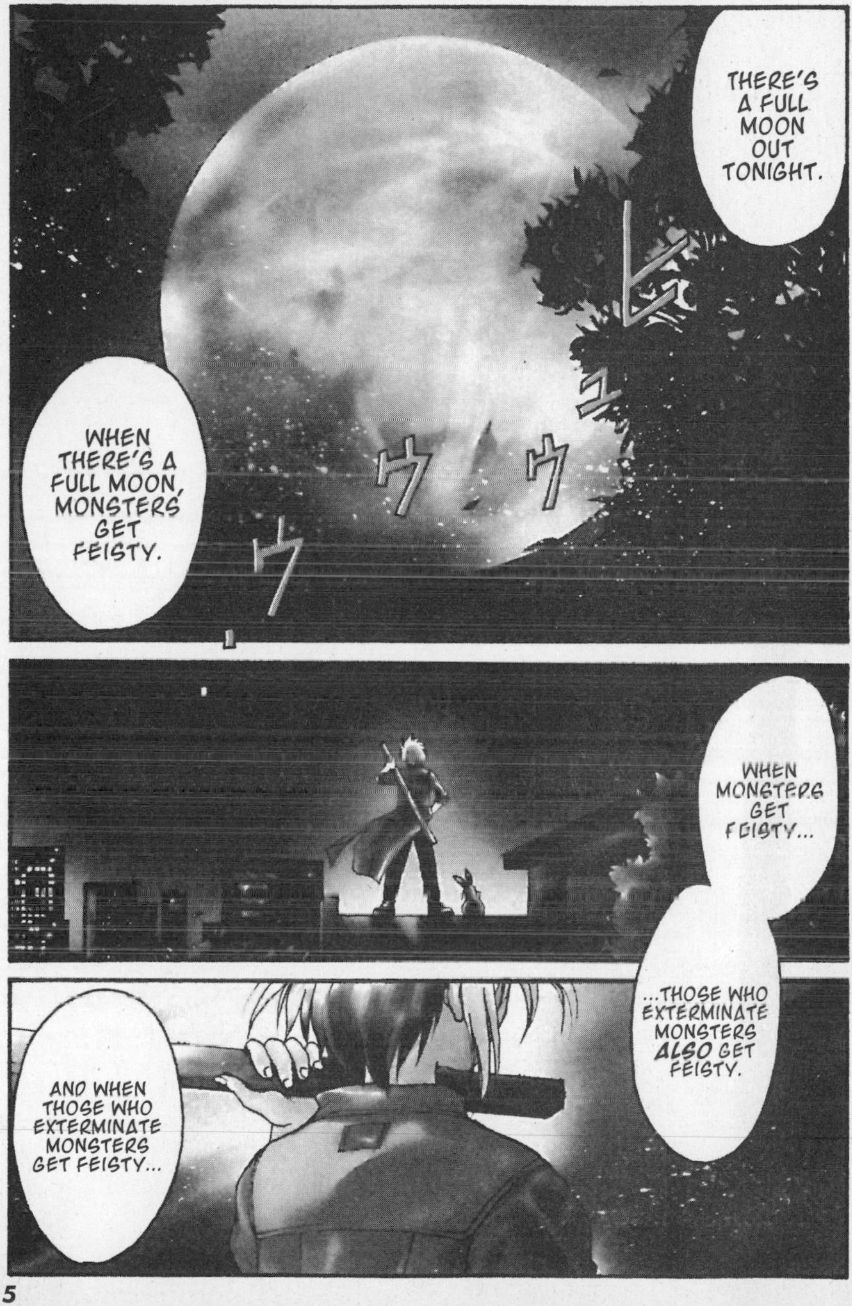
THERE'S A FULL MOON OUT TONIGHT.
ヒュウウウ
WHEN THERE'S A FULL MOON, MONSTERS GET FEISTY.
WHEN MONSTERS GET FEISTY...
...THOSE WHO EXTERMINATE MONSTERS *ALSO* GET FEISTY.
AND WHEN THOSE WHO EXTERMINATE MONSTERS GET FEISTY...

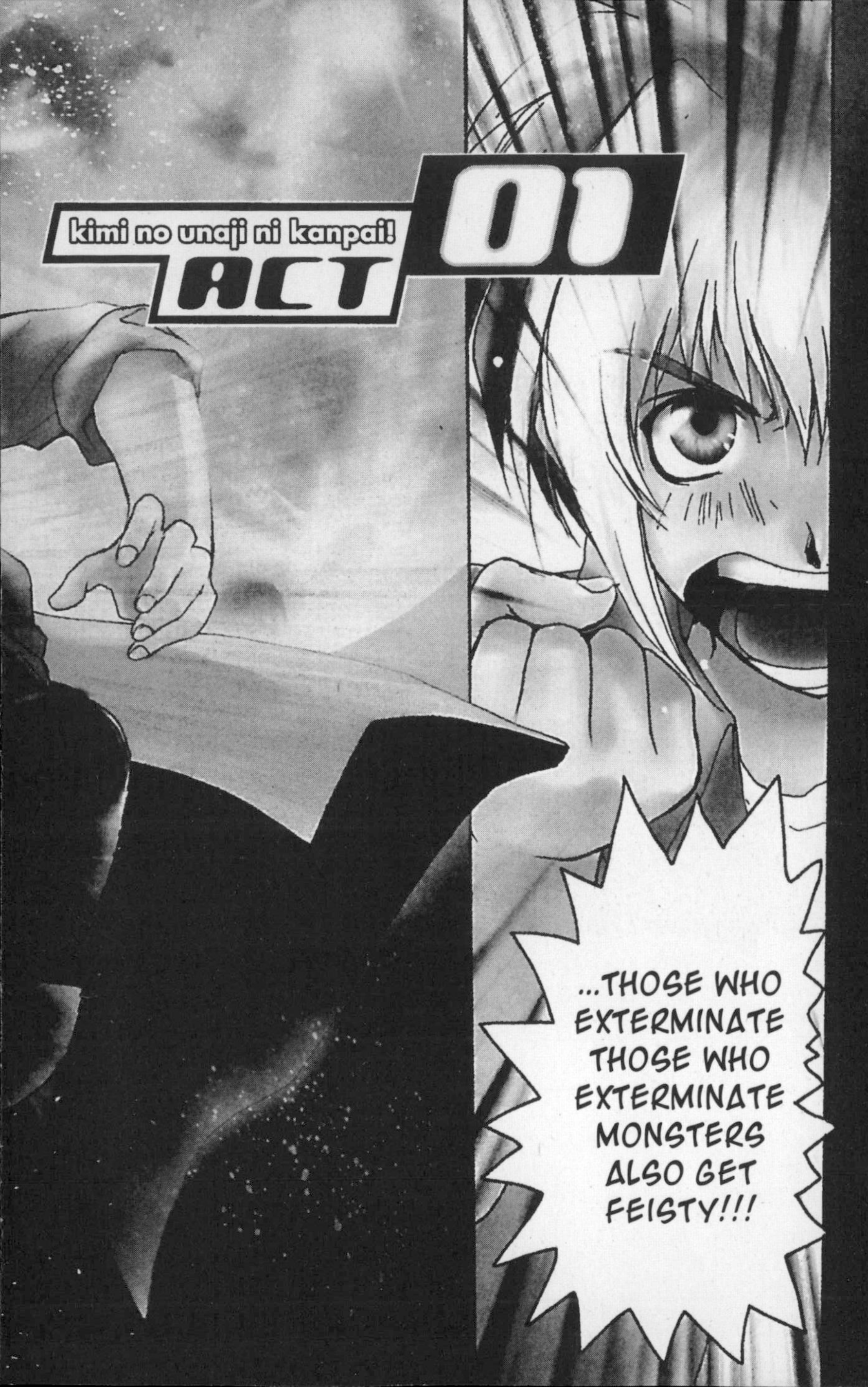
kimi no unaji ni kanpai!
ACT 01
...THOSE WHO EXTERMINATE THOSE WHO EXTERMINATE MONSTERS ALSO GET FEISTY!!!

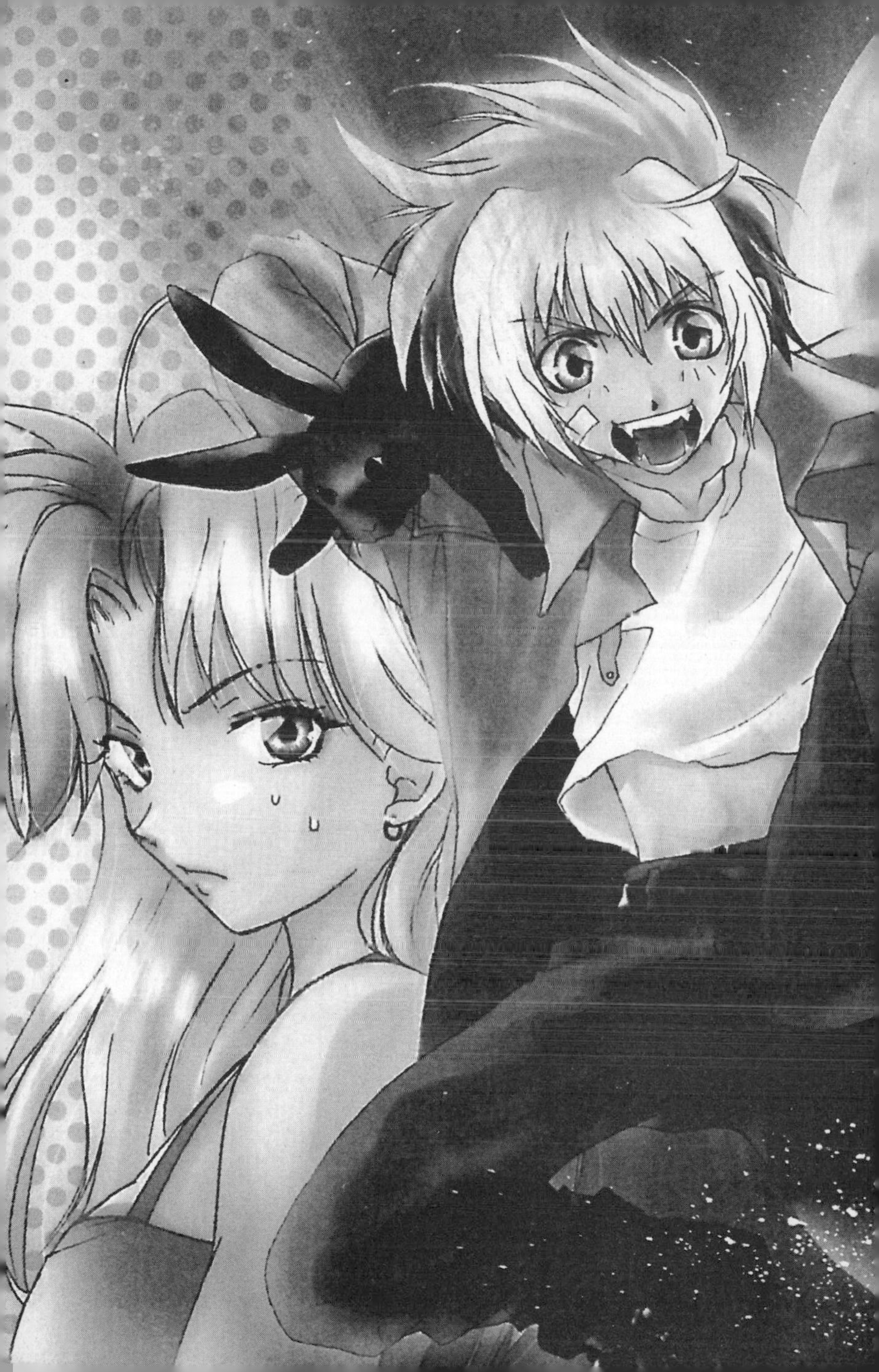

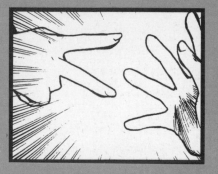

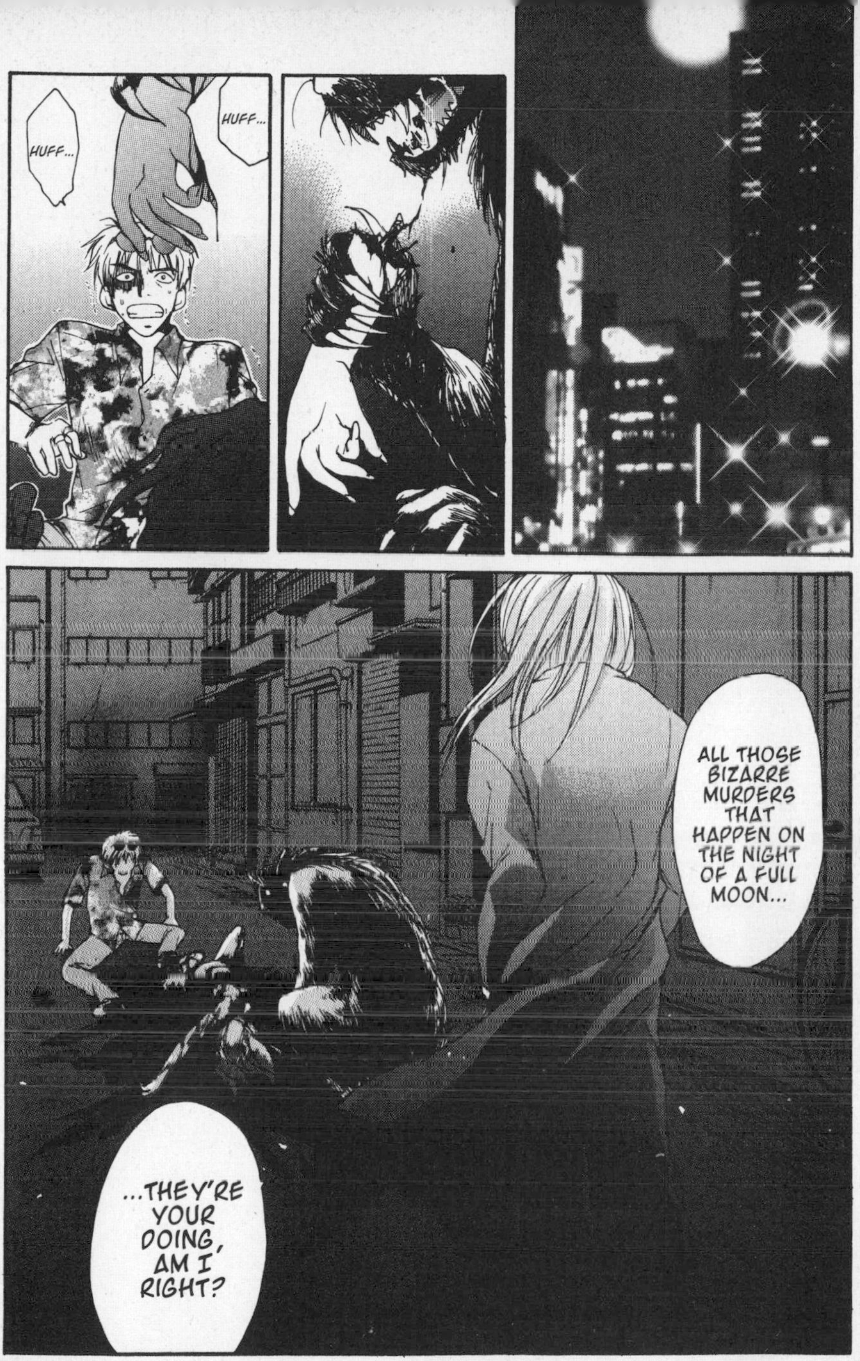
HUFF...
HUFF...
ALL THOSE BIZARRE MURDERS THAT HAPPEN ON THE NIGHT OF A FULL MOON...
...THEY'RE YOUR DOING, AM I RIGHT?

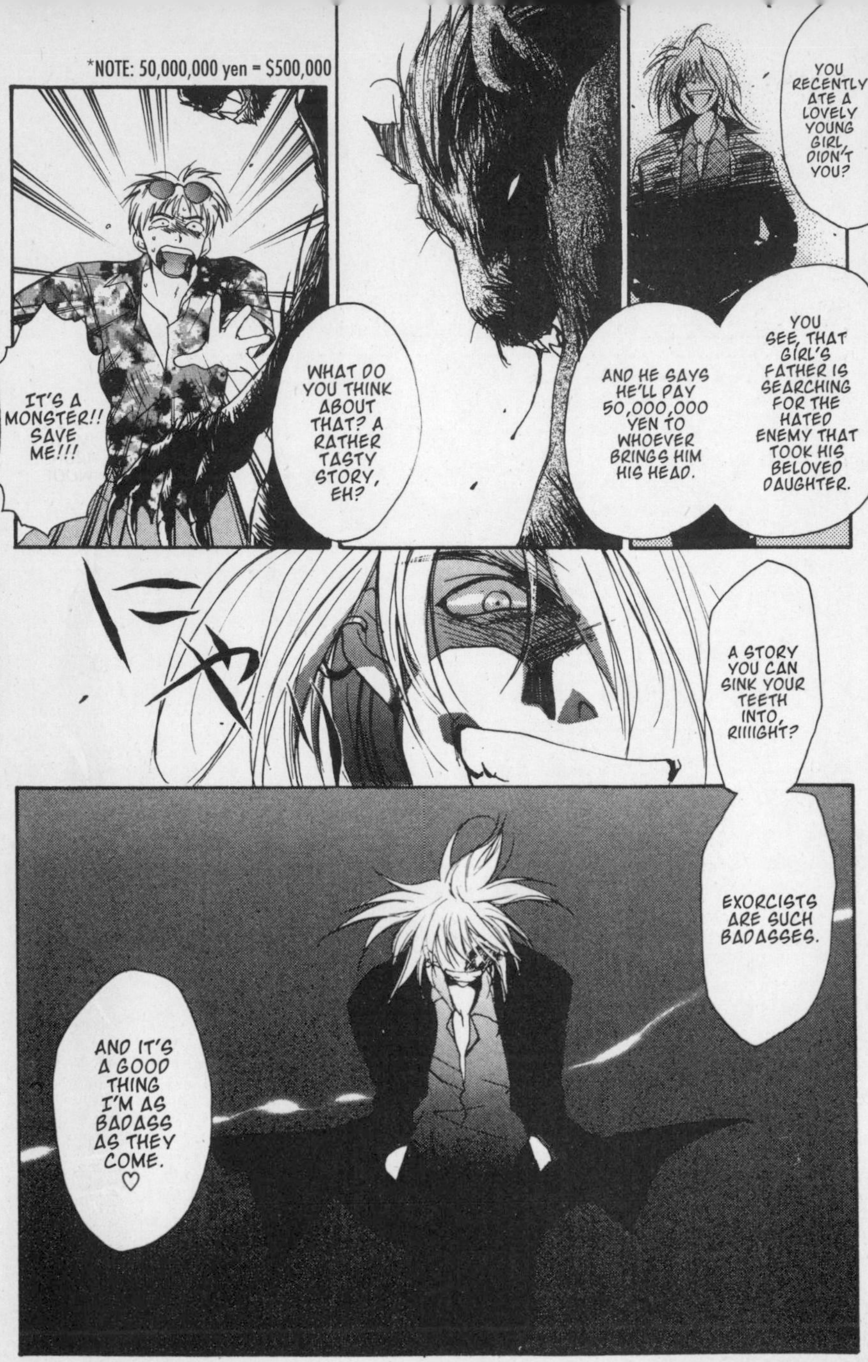
YOU RECENTLY ATE A LOVELY YOUNG GIRL, DIDN'T YOU?
YOU SEE, THAT GIRL'S FATHER IS SEARCHING FOR THE HATED ENEMY THAT TOOK HIS BELOVED DAUGHTER.
AND HE SAYS HE'LL PAY 50,000,000 YEN TO WHOEVER BRINGS HIM HIS HEAD.
*NOTE: 50,000,000 yen = $500,000
WHAT DO YOU THINK ABOUT THAT? A RATHER TASTY STORY, EH?
IT'S A MONSTER!! SAVE ME!!!
A STORY YOU CAN SINK YOUR TEETH INTO, RIIIIGHT?
EXORCISTS ARE SUCH BADASSES.
AND IT'S A GOOD THING I'M AS BADASS AS THEY COME. ♡

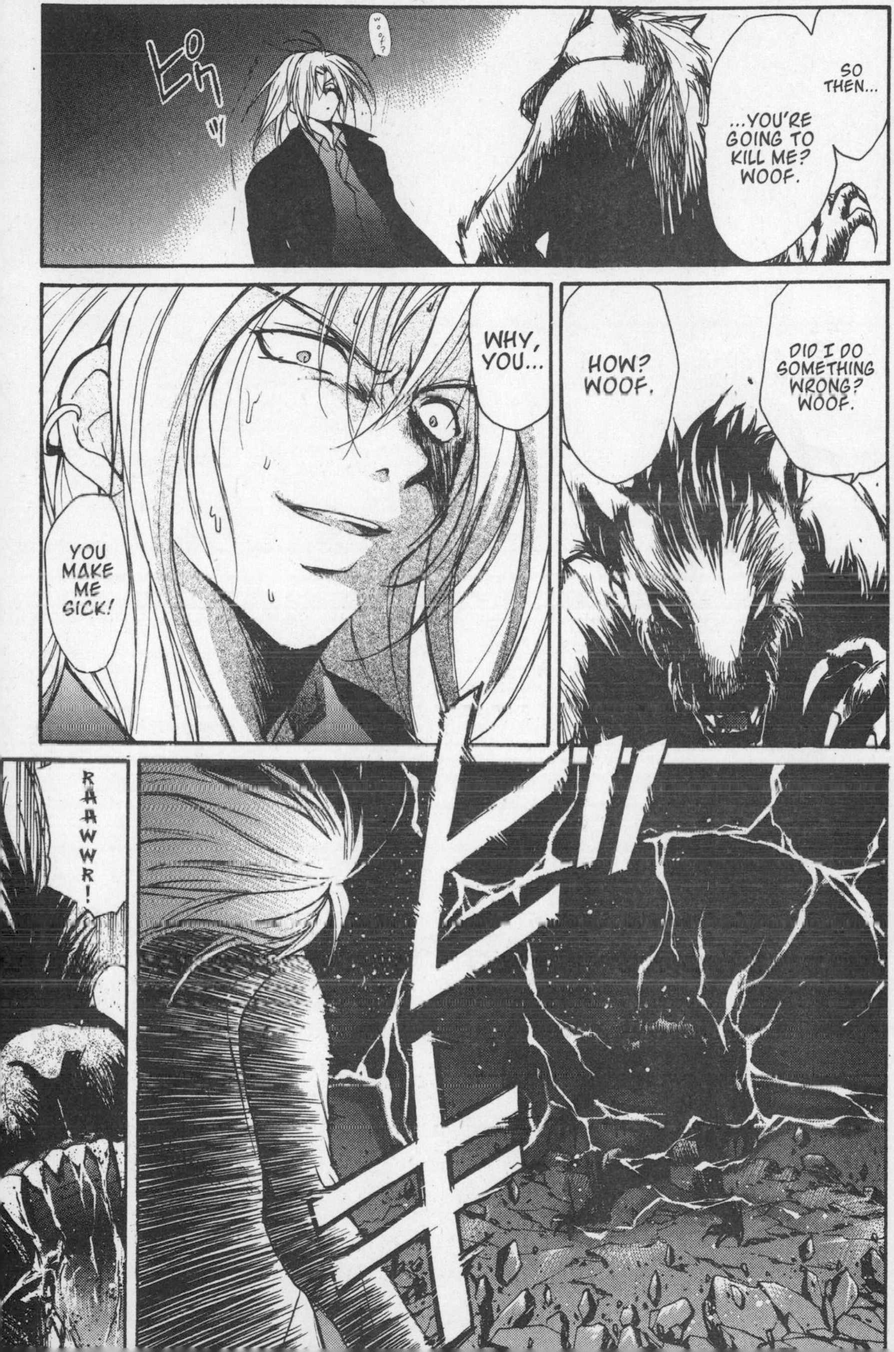
SO THEN...
...YOU'RE GOING TO KILL ME? WOOF.
woof?
ピクッ
DID I DO SOMETHING WRONG? WOOF.
HOW? WOOF.
WHY, YOU...
YOU MAKE ME SICK!
ビキ
RAAWWR!

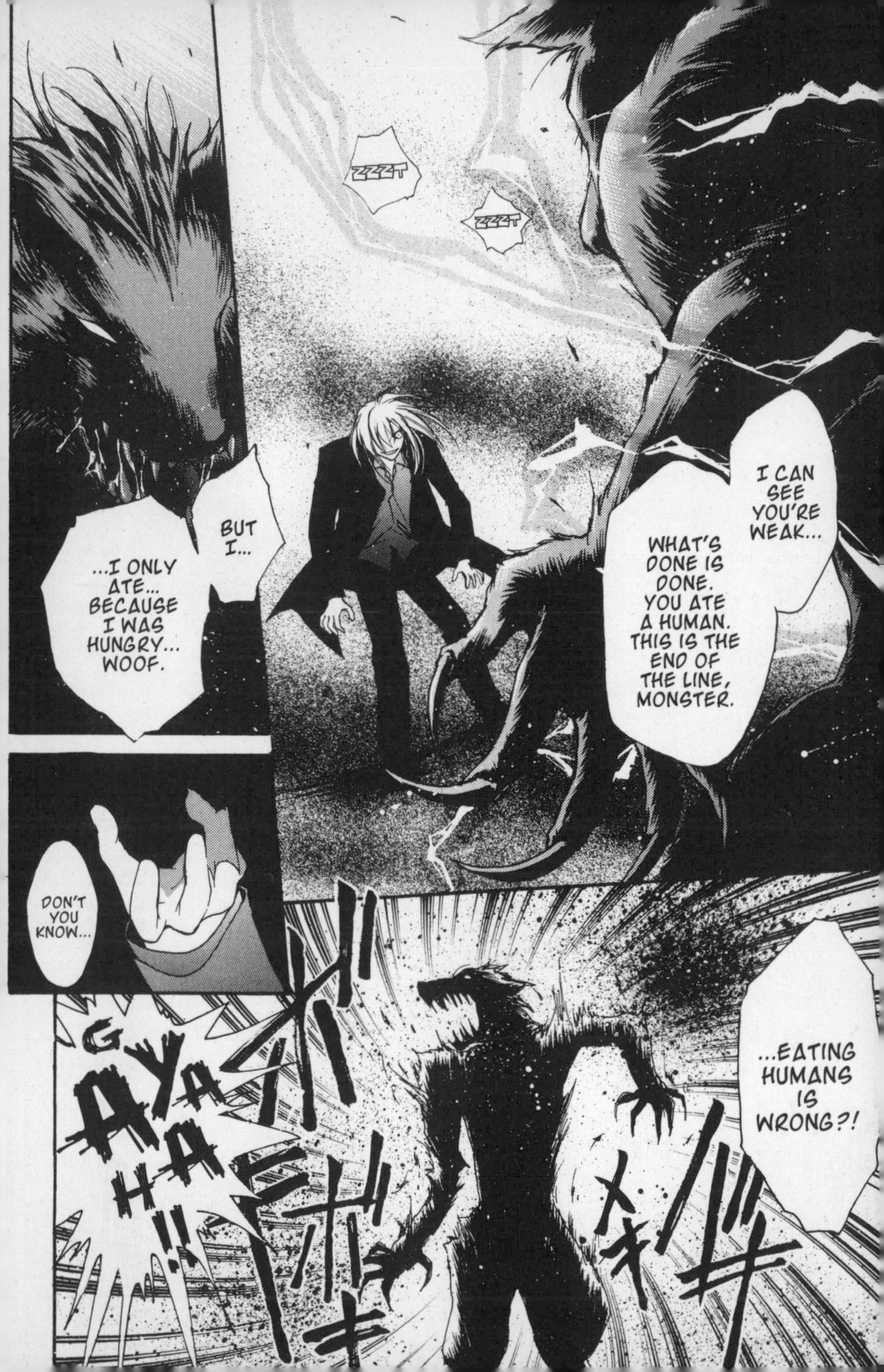
ZZZT
ZZZT
I CAN SEE YOU'RE WEAK...
WHAT'S DONE IS DONE. YOU ATE A HUMAN. THIS IS THE END OF THE LINE, MONSTER.
BUT I...
...I ONLY ATE... BECAUSE I WAS HUNGRY... WOOF.
DON'T YOU KNOW...
...EATING HUMANS IS WRONG?!
GYAHAHA!!

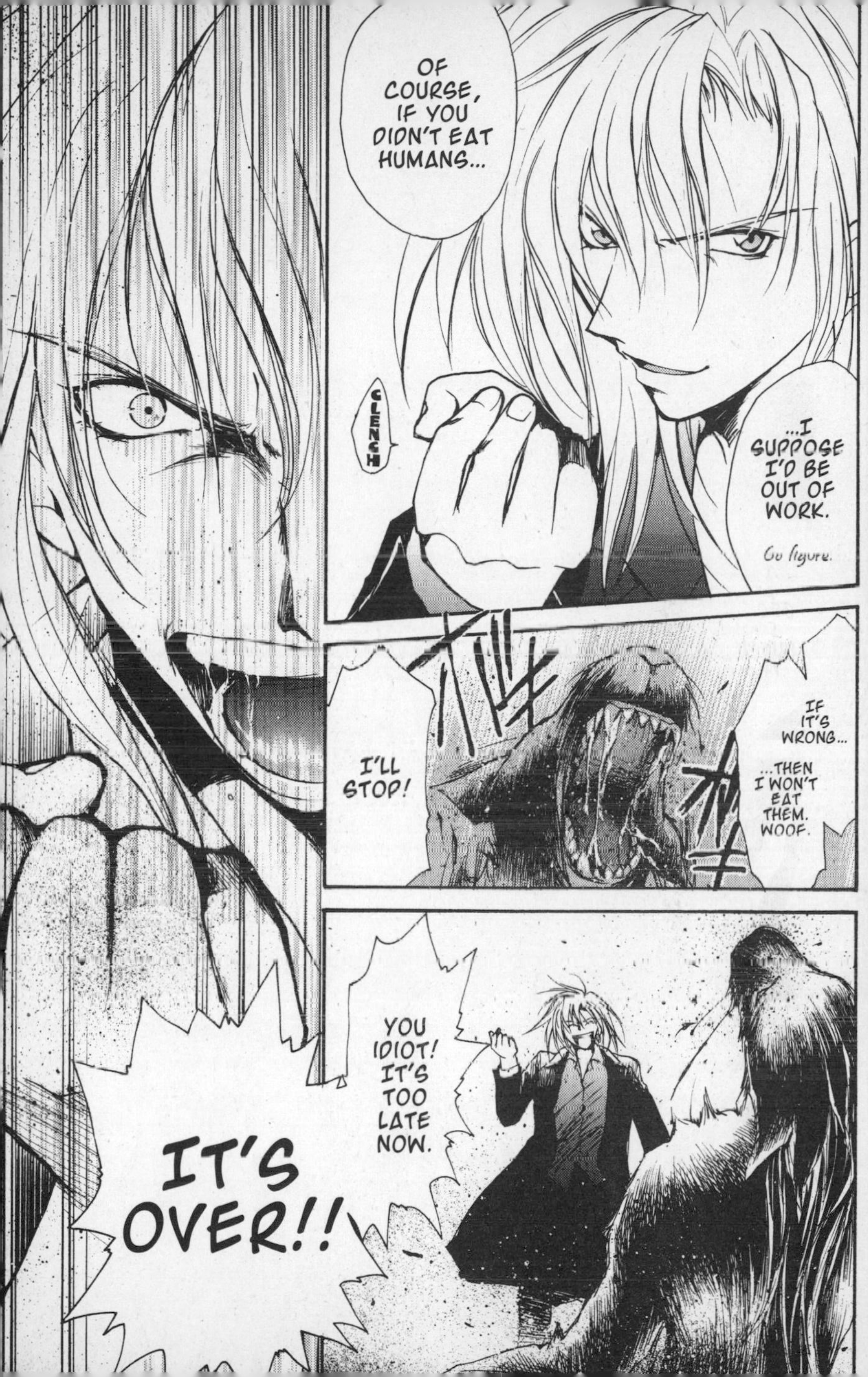
OF COURSE, IF YOU DIDN'T EAT HUMANS...
CLENCH
...I SUPPOSE I'D BE OUT OF WORK.
Go figure.
IF IT'S WRONG...
...THEN I WON'T EAT THEM. WOOF.
I'LL STOP!
YOU IDIOT! IT'S TOO LATE NOW.
IT'S OVER!!

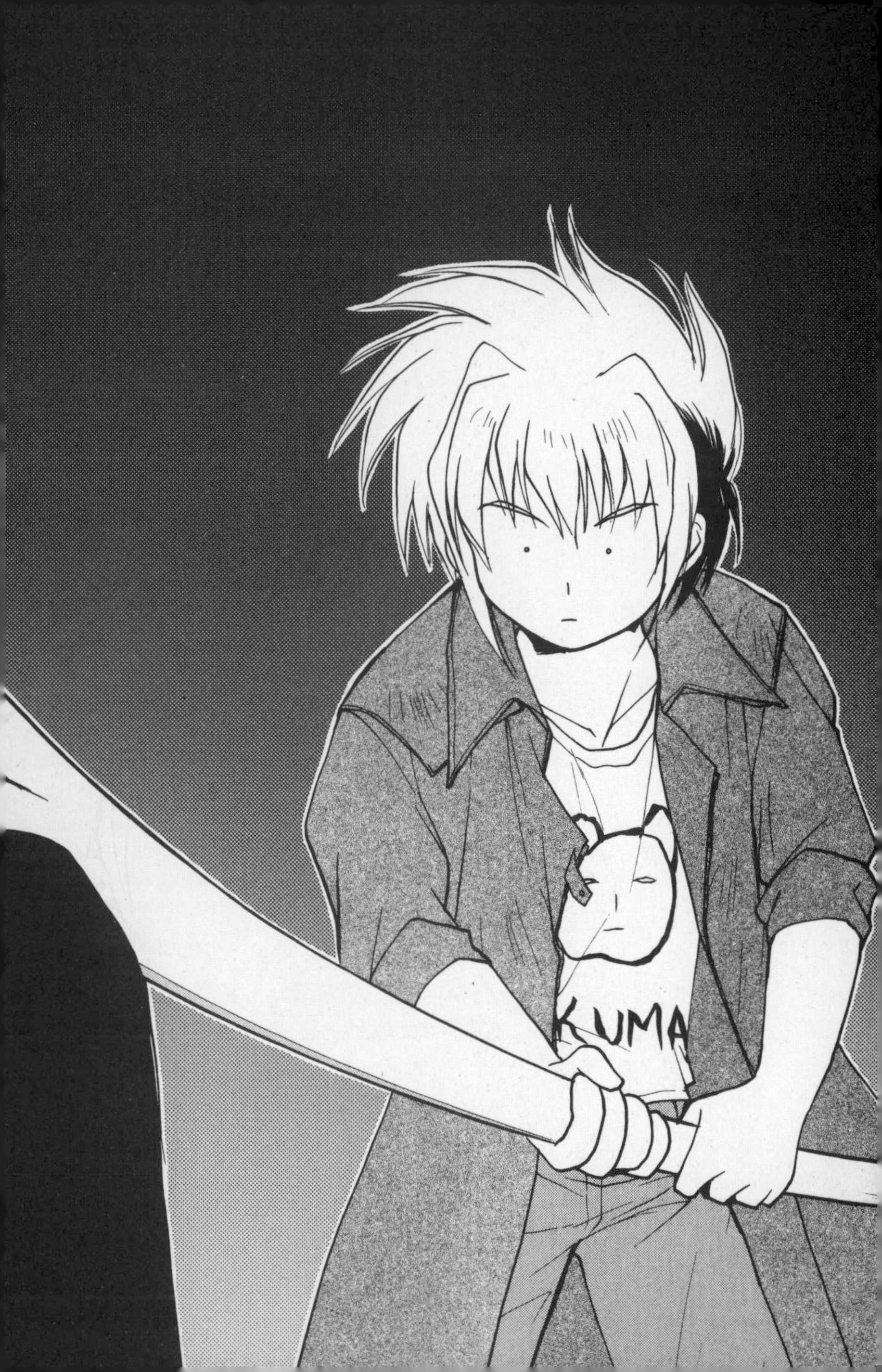
KUMA

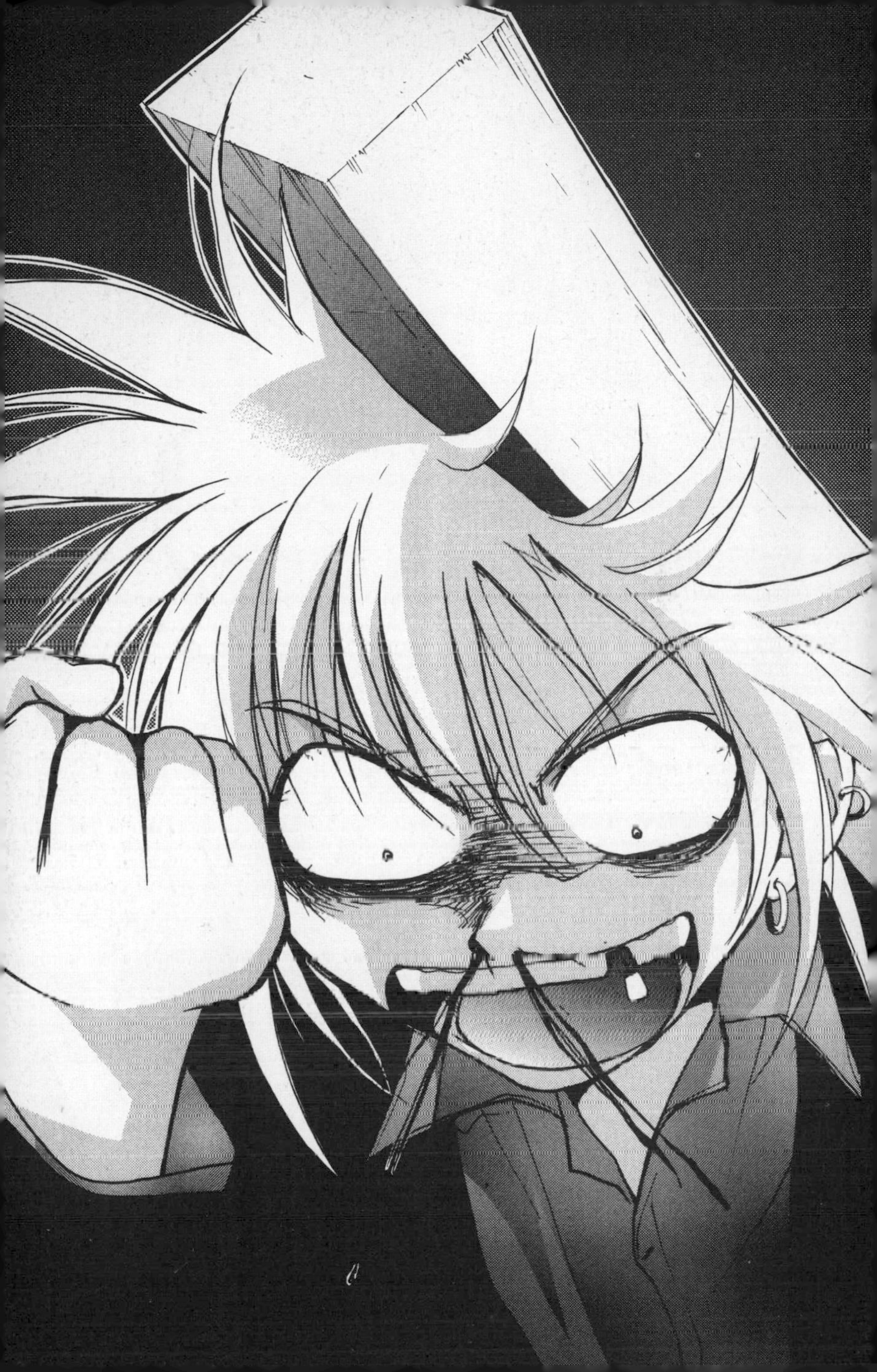

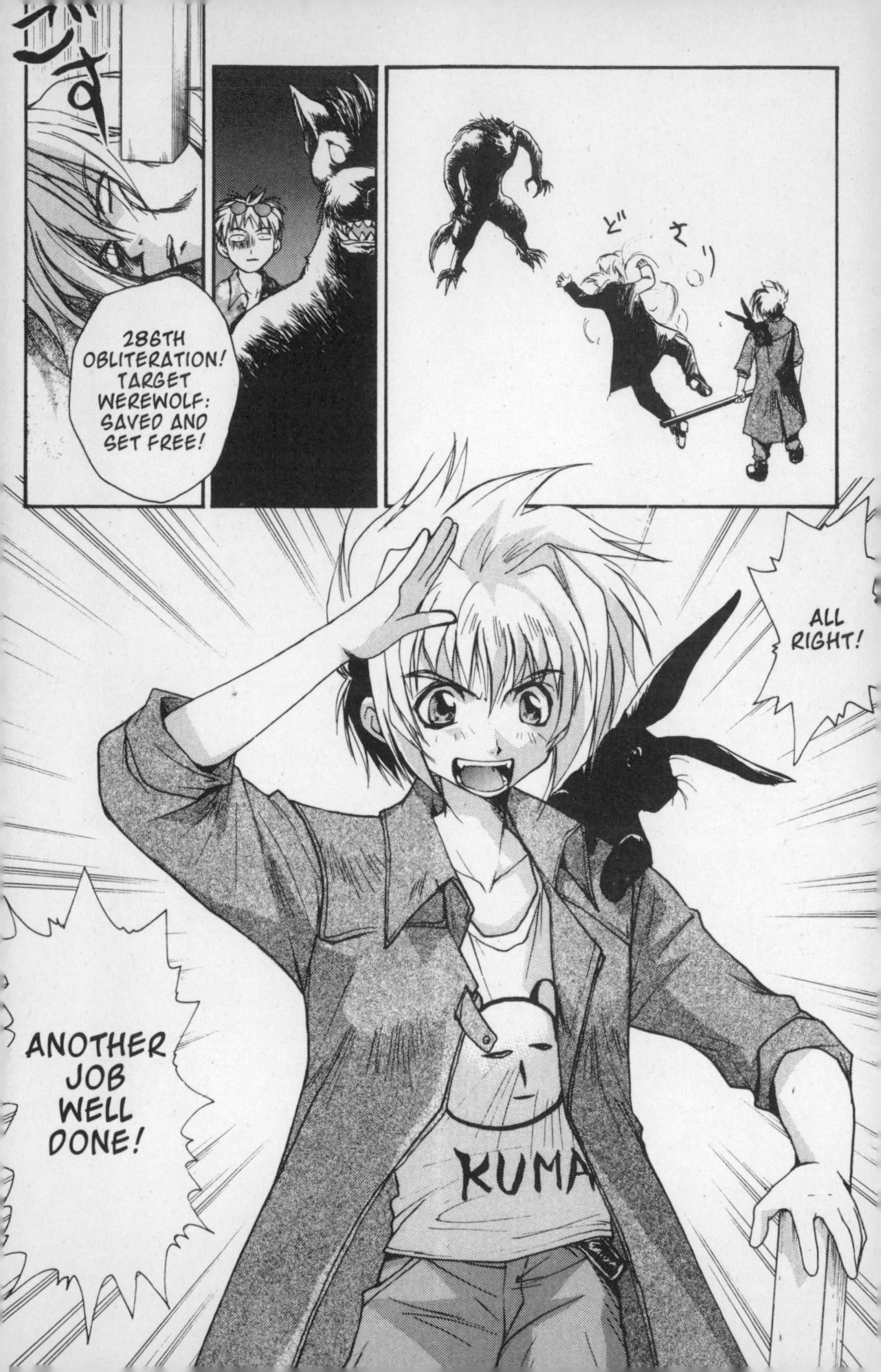
どさり
286TH OBLITERATION! TARGET WEREWOLF: SAVED AND SET FREE!
ごす
ALL RIGHT!
ANOTHER JOB WELL DONE!
KUMA

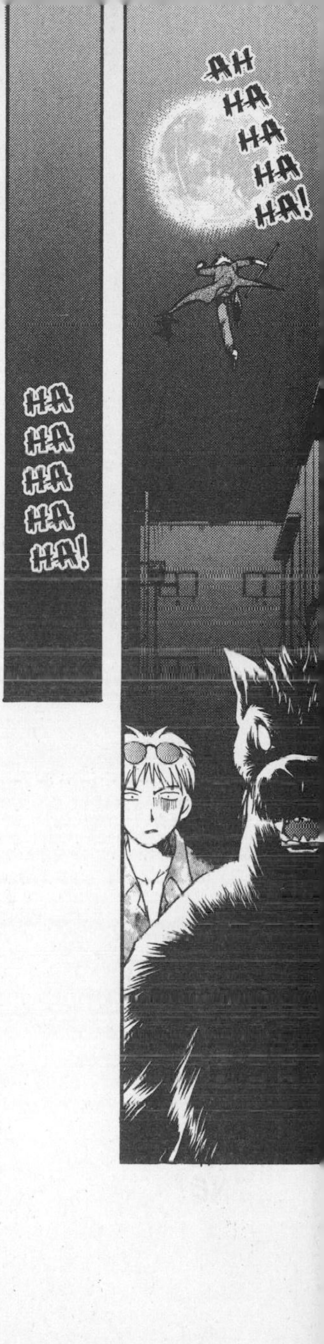
AH HA HA HA HA!
HA HA HA HA HA!

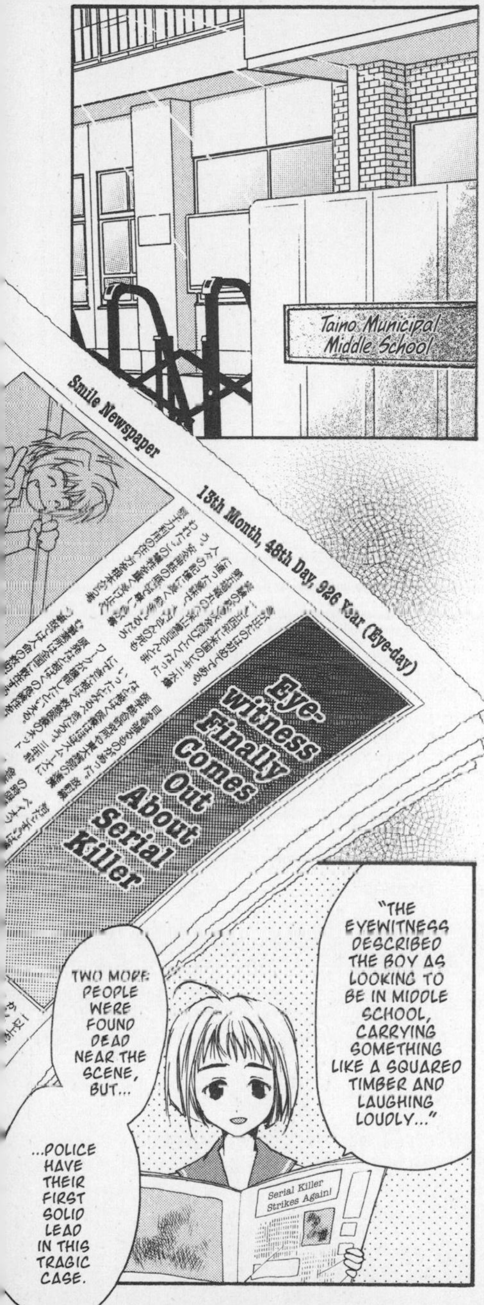
Taino Municipal Middle School
Smile Newspaper
13th Month, 48th Day, 926 Year (Eye-day)
Eye-witness Finally Comes Out About Serial Killer
"THE EYEWITNESS DESCRIBED THE BOY AS LOOKING TO BE IN MIDDLE SCHOOL, CARRYING SOMETHING LIKE A SQUARED TIMBER AND LAUGHING LOUDLY..."
TWO MORE PEOPLE WERE FOUND DEAD NEAR THE SCENE, BUT...
...POLICE HAVE THEIR FIRST SOLID LEAD IN THIS TRAGIC CASE.
Serial Killer Strikes Again!

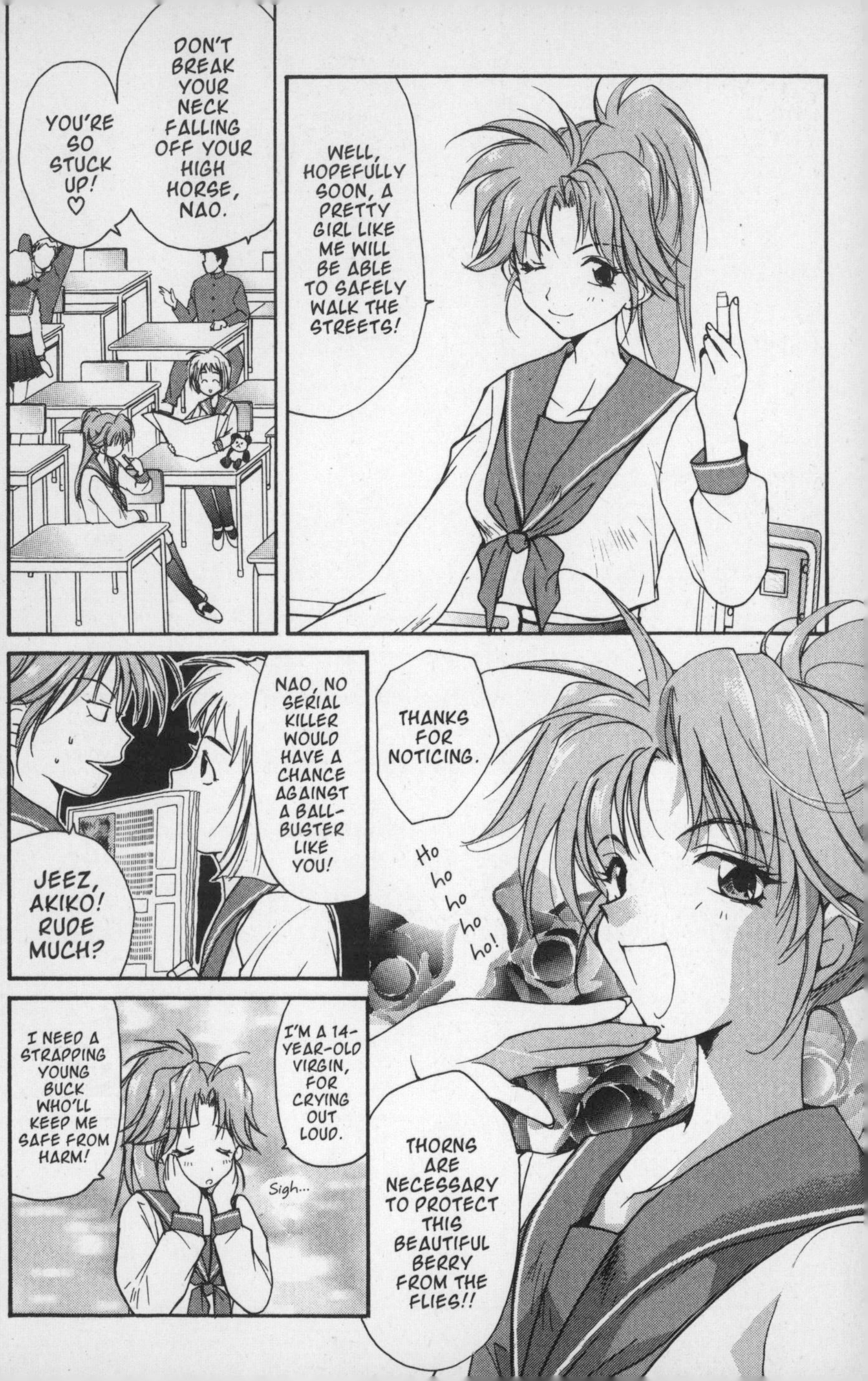
WELL, HOPEFULLY SOON, A PRETTY GIRL LIKE ME WILL BE ABLE TO SAFELY WALK THE STREETS!
DON'T BREAK YOUR NECK FALLING OFF YOUR HIGH HORSE, NAO.
YOU'RE SO STUCK UP! ♡
THANKS FOR NOTICING.
Ho ho ho ho ho!
THORNS ARE NECESSARY TO PROTECT THIS BEAUTIFUL BERRY FROM THE FLIES!!
NAO, NO SERIAL KILLER WOULD HAVE A CHANCE AGAINST A BALL-BUSTER LIKE YOU!
JEEZ, AKIKO! RUDE MUCH?
I'M A 14-YEAR-OLD VIRGIN, FOR CRYING OUT LOUD.
I NEED A STRAPPING YOUNG BUCK WHO'LL KEEP ME SAFE FROM HARM!
Sigh...

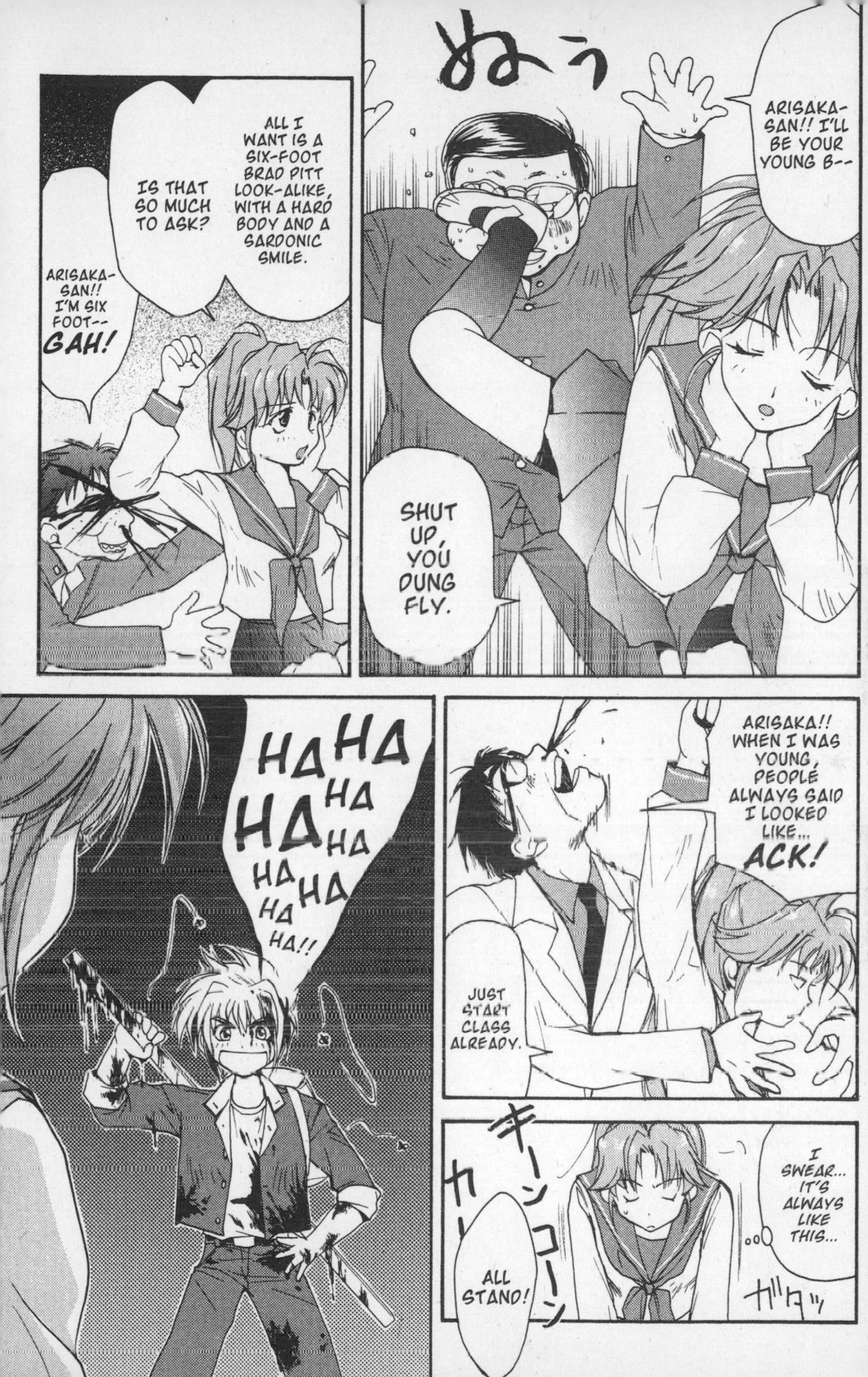
ぬぅ
ARISAKA-SAN!! I'LL BE YOUR YOUNG B--
SHUT UP, YOU DUNG FLY.
ALL I WANT IS A SIX-FOOT BRAD PITT LOOK-ALIKE, WITH A HARD BODY AND A SARDONIC SMILE.
IS THAT SO MUCH TO ASK?
ARISAKA-SAN!! I'M SIX FOOT-- GAH!
ARISAKA!! WHEN I WAS YOUNG, PEOPLE ALWAYS SAID I LOOKED LIKE... ACK!
JUST START CLASS ALREADY.
I SWEAR... IT'S ALWAYS LIKE THIS...
キーンコーン
カー
ALL STAND!
ガタッ
HAHA HA HA HA HA HA HA HA HA HA!!

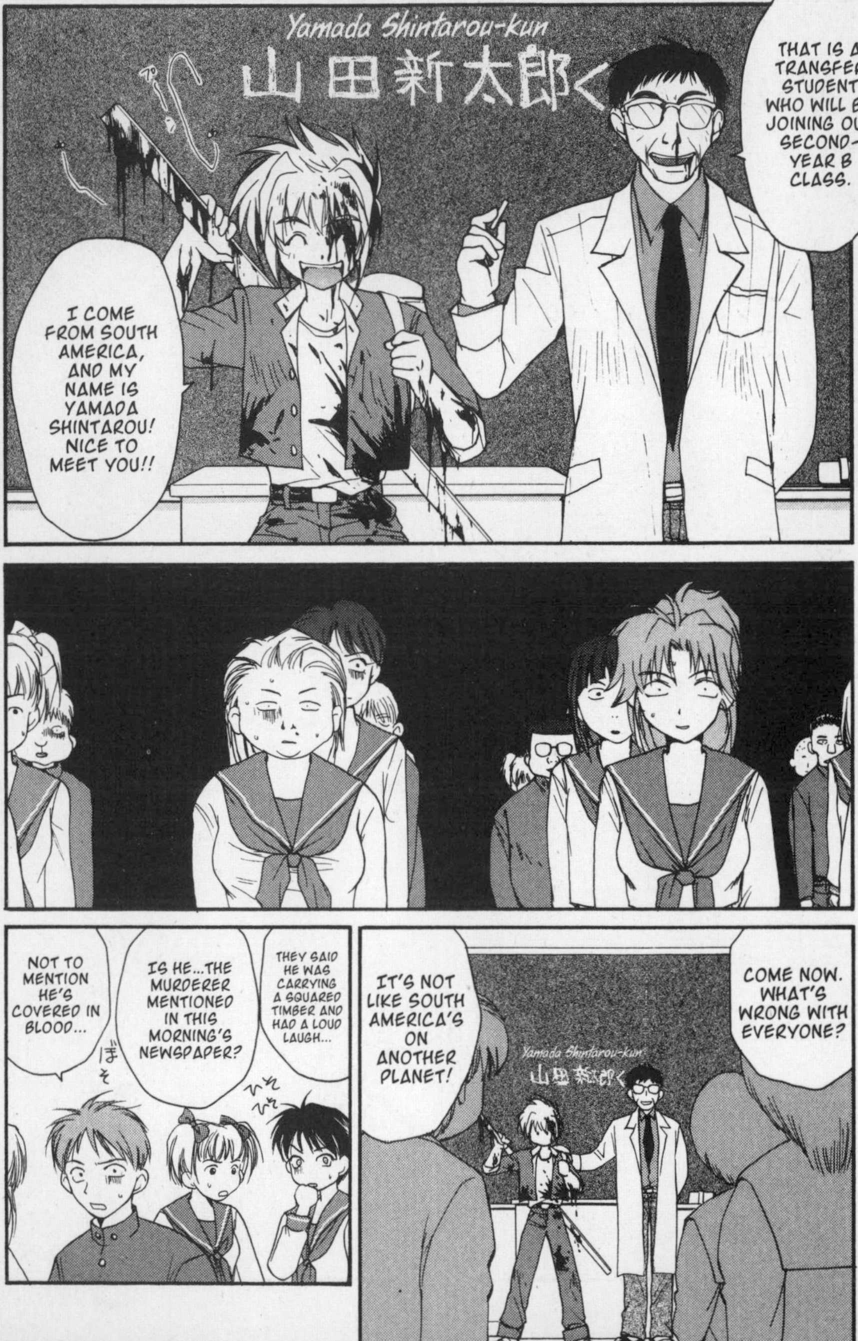
Yamada Shintarou-kun
山田新太郎く
THAT IS A TRANSFER STUDENT WHO WILL BE JOINING OUR SECOND-YEAR B CLASS.
I COME FROM SOUTH AMERICA, AND MY NAME IS YAMADA SHINTAROU! NICE TO MEET YOU!!
COME NOW. WHAT'S WRONG WITH EVERYONE?
Yamada Shintarou-kun
山田新太郎く
IT'S NOT LIKE SOUTH AMERICA'S ON ANOTHER PLANET!
THEY SAID HE WAS CARRYING A SQUARED TIMBER AND HAD A LOUD LAUGH...
ひそひそ
IS HE...THE MURDERER MENTIONED IN THIS MORNING'S NEWSPAPER?
ぼそ
NOT TO MENTION HE'S COVERED IN BLOOD...

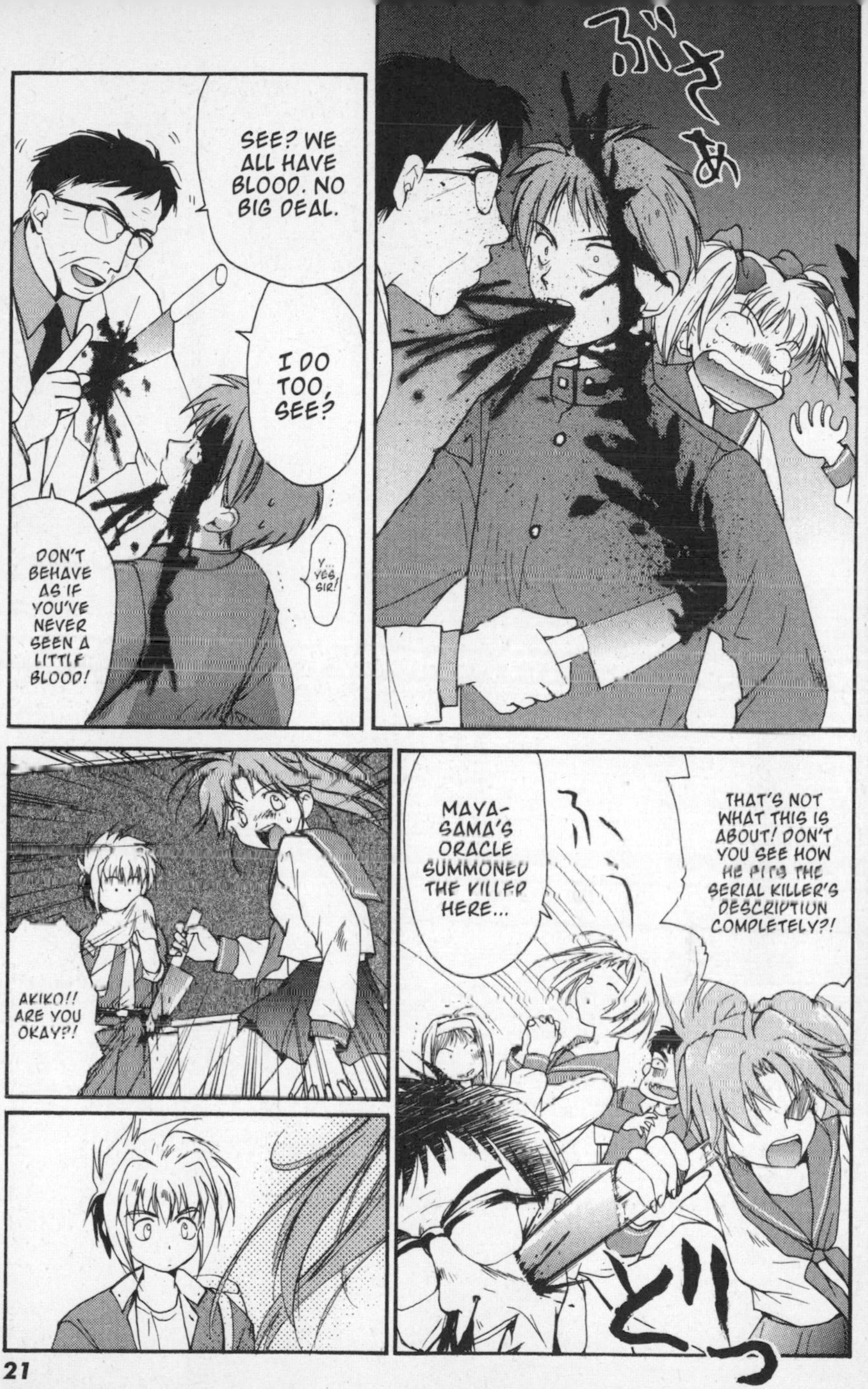
ぶさぁ
SEE? WE ALL HAVE BLOOD. NO BIG DEAL.
I DO TOO, SEE?
DON'T BEHAVE AS IF YOU'VE NEVER SEEN A LITTLE BLOOD!
Y... YES SIR!
THAT'S NOT WHAT THIS IS ABOUT! DON'T YOU SEE HOW HE FITS THE SERIAL KILLER'S DESCRIPTION COMPLETELY?!
ふ
MAYA-SAMA'S ORACLE SUMMONED THE KILLER HERE...
とりっ
AKIKO!! ARE YOU OKAY?!

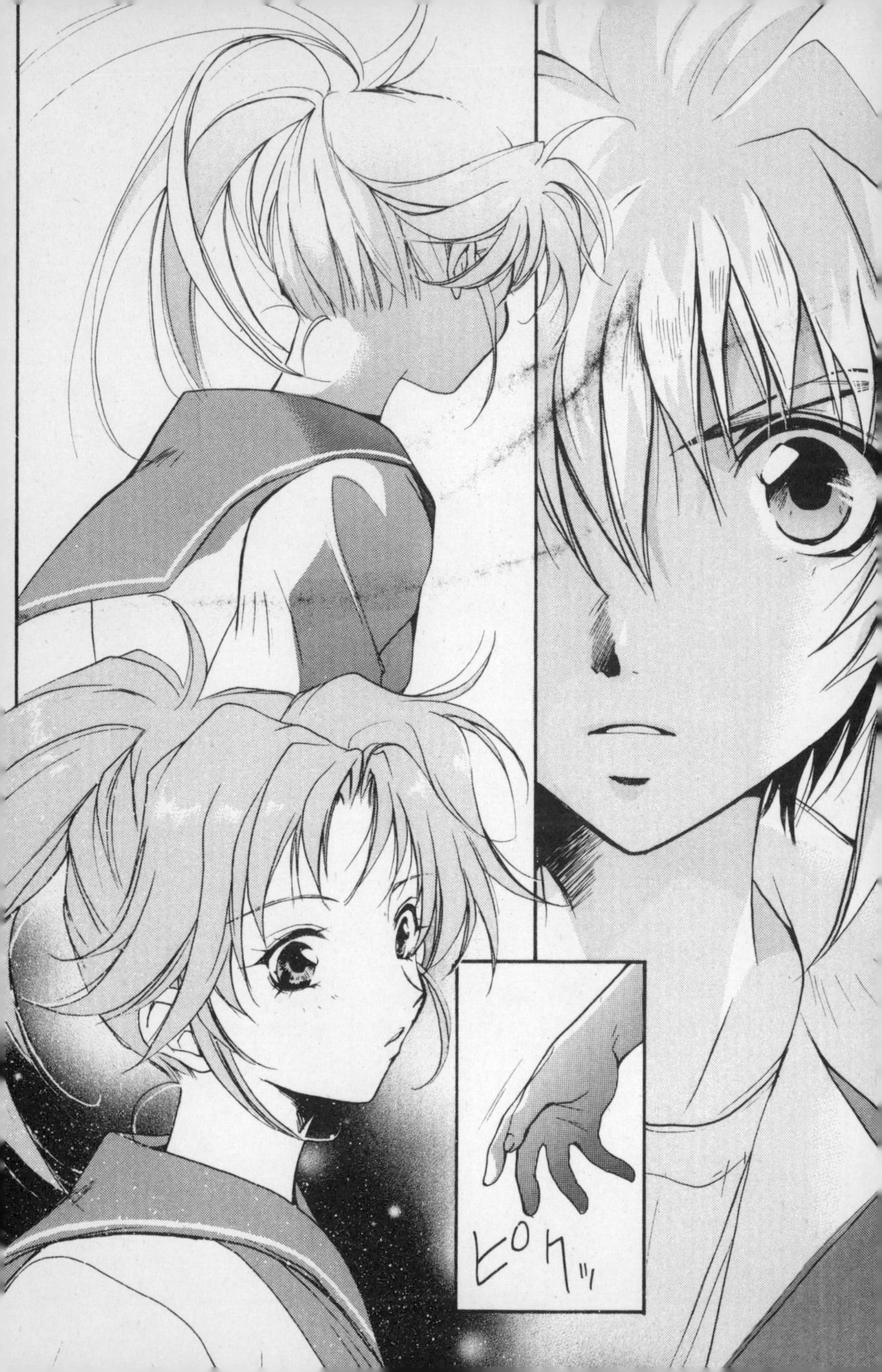
ピクッ

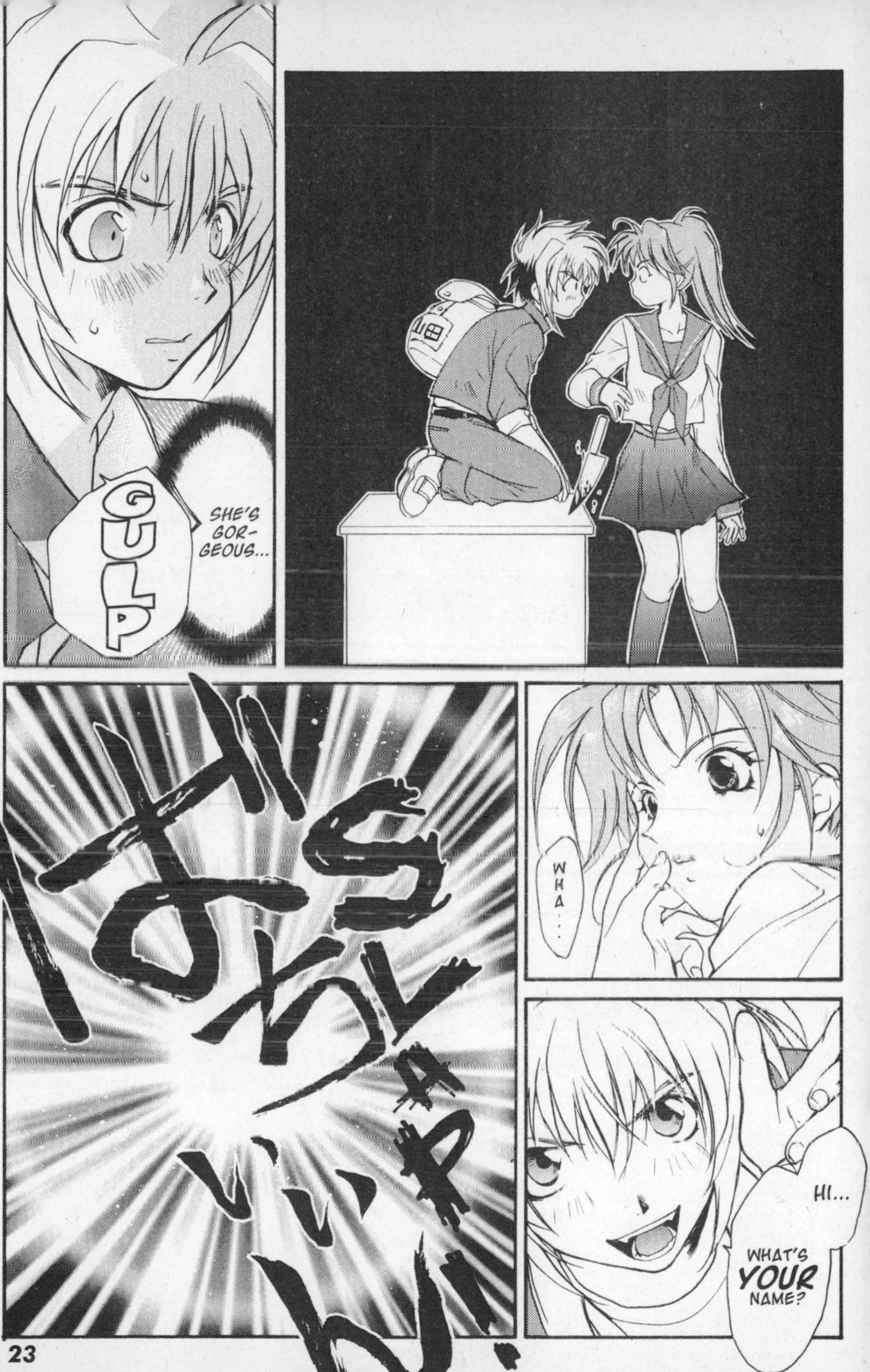
GULP
SHE'S GOR-GEOUS...
WHA...
HI...
WHAT'S YOUR NAME?

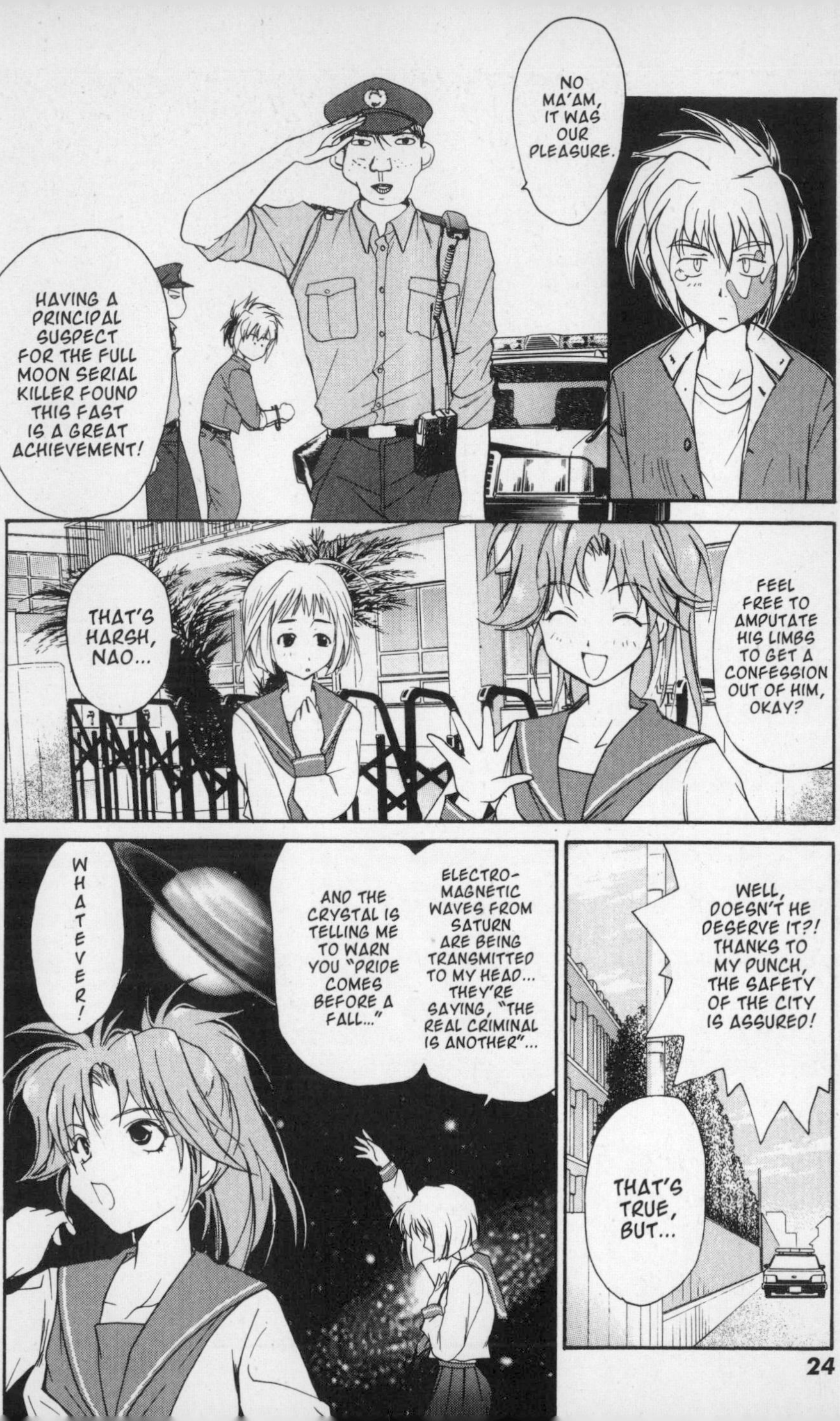
NO MA'AM, IT WAS OUR PLEASURE.
HAVING A PRINCIPAL SUSPECT FOR THE FULL MOON SERIAL KILLER FOUND THIS FAST IS A GREAT ACHIEVEMENT!
FEEL FREE TO AMPUTATE HIS LIMBS TO GET A CONFESSION OUT OF HIM, OKAY?
THAT'S HARSH, NAO...
WELL, DOESN'T HE DESERVE IT?! THANKS TO MY PUNCH, THE SAFETY OF THE CITY IS ASSURED!
THAT'S TRUE, BUT...
ELECTRO-MAGNETIC WAVES FROM SATURN ARE BEING TRANSMITTED TO MY HEAD... THEY'RE SAYING, "THE REAL CRIMINAL IS ANOTHER"...
AND THE CRYSTAL IS TELLING ME TO WARN YOU "PRIDE COMES BEFORE A FALL..."
WHATEVER!

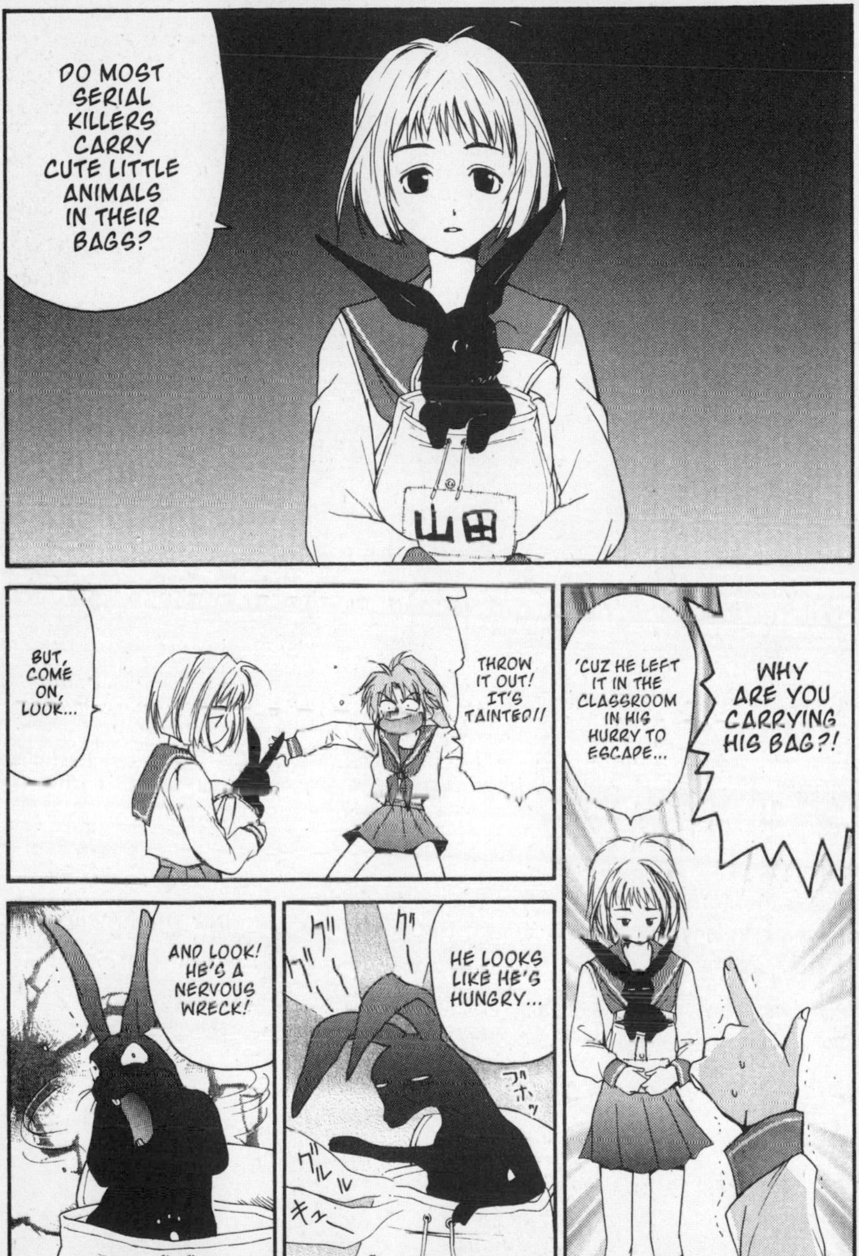
DO MOST SERIAL KILLERS CARRY CUTE LITTLE ANIMALS IN THEIR BAGS?
山田
WHY ARE YOU CARRYING HIS BAG?!
'CUZ HE LEFT IT IN THE CLASSROOM IN HIS HURRY TO ESCAPE...
THROW IT OUT! IT'S TAINTED!!
BUT, COME ON, LOOK...
HE LOOKS LIKE HE'S HUNGRY...
AND LOOK! HE'S A NERVOUS WRECK!

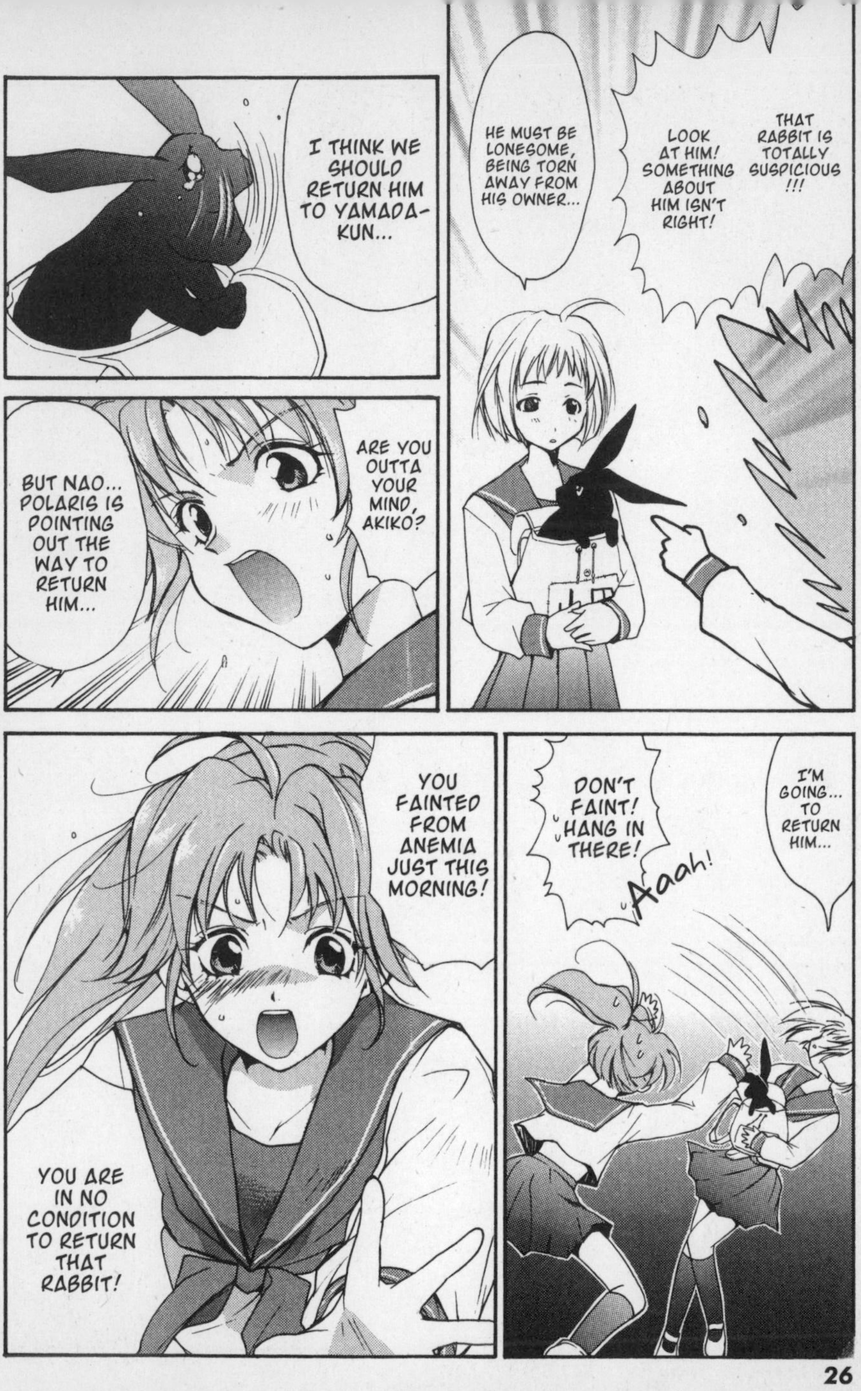
THAT RABBIT IS TOTALLY SUSPICIOUS!!!
LOOK AT HIM! SOMETHING ABOUT HIM ISN'T RIGHT!
HE MUST BE LONESOME, BEING TORN AWAY FROM HIS OWNER...
I THINK WE SHOULD RETURN HIM TO YAMADA-KUN...
ARE YOU OUTTA YOUR MIND, AKIKO?
BUT NAO... POLARIS IS POINTING OUT THE WAY TO RETURN HIM...
I'M GOING... TO RETURN HIM...
DON'T FAINT! HANG IN THERE!
Aaah!
YOU FAINTED FROM ANEMIA JUST THIS MORNING!
YOU ARE IN NO CONDITION TO RETURN THAT RABBIT!

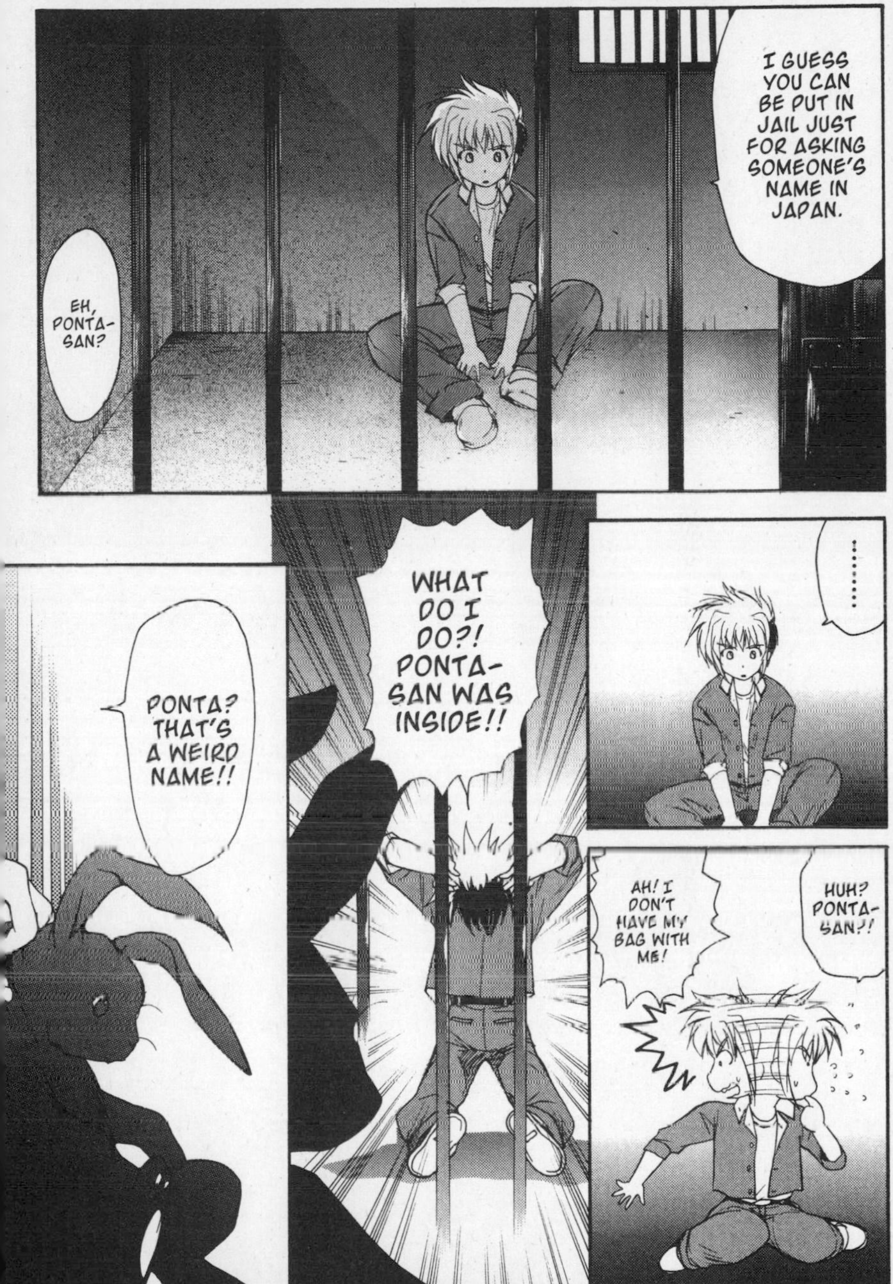
I GUESS YOU CAN BE PUT IN JAIL JUST FOR ASKING SOMEONE'S NAME IN JAPAN.
EH, PONTA-SAN?
......
HUH? PONTA-SAN?!
AH! I DON'T HAVE MY BAG WITH ME!
WHAT DO I DO?! PONTA-SAN WAS INSIDE!!
PONTA? THAT'S A WEIRD NAME!!

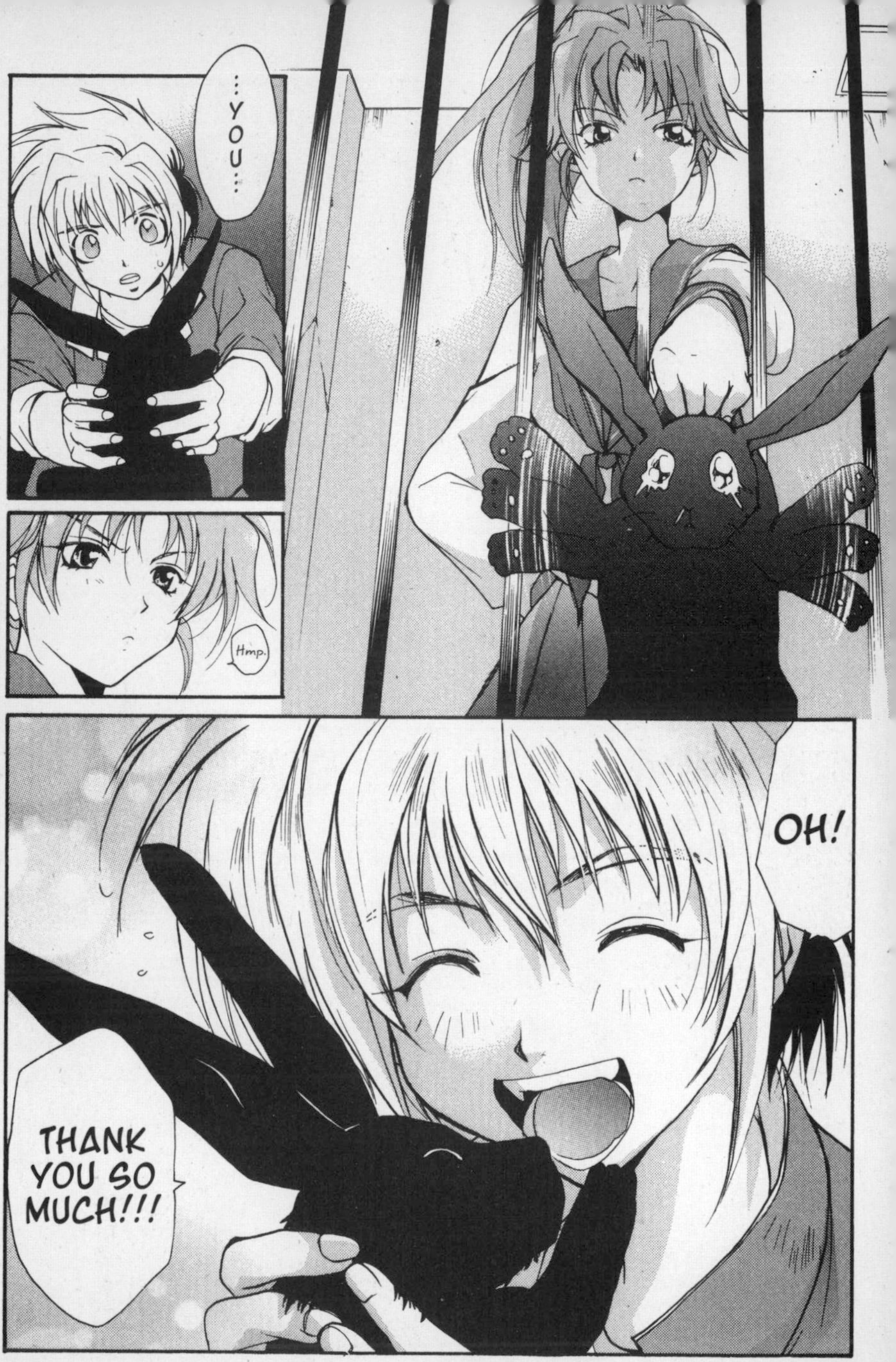
...YOU...
Hmp.
OH!
THANK YOU SO MUCH!!!

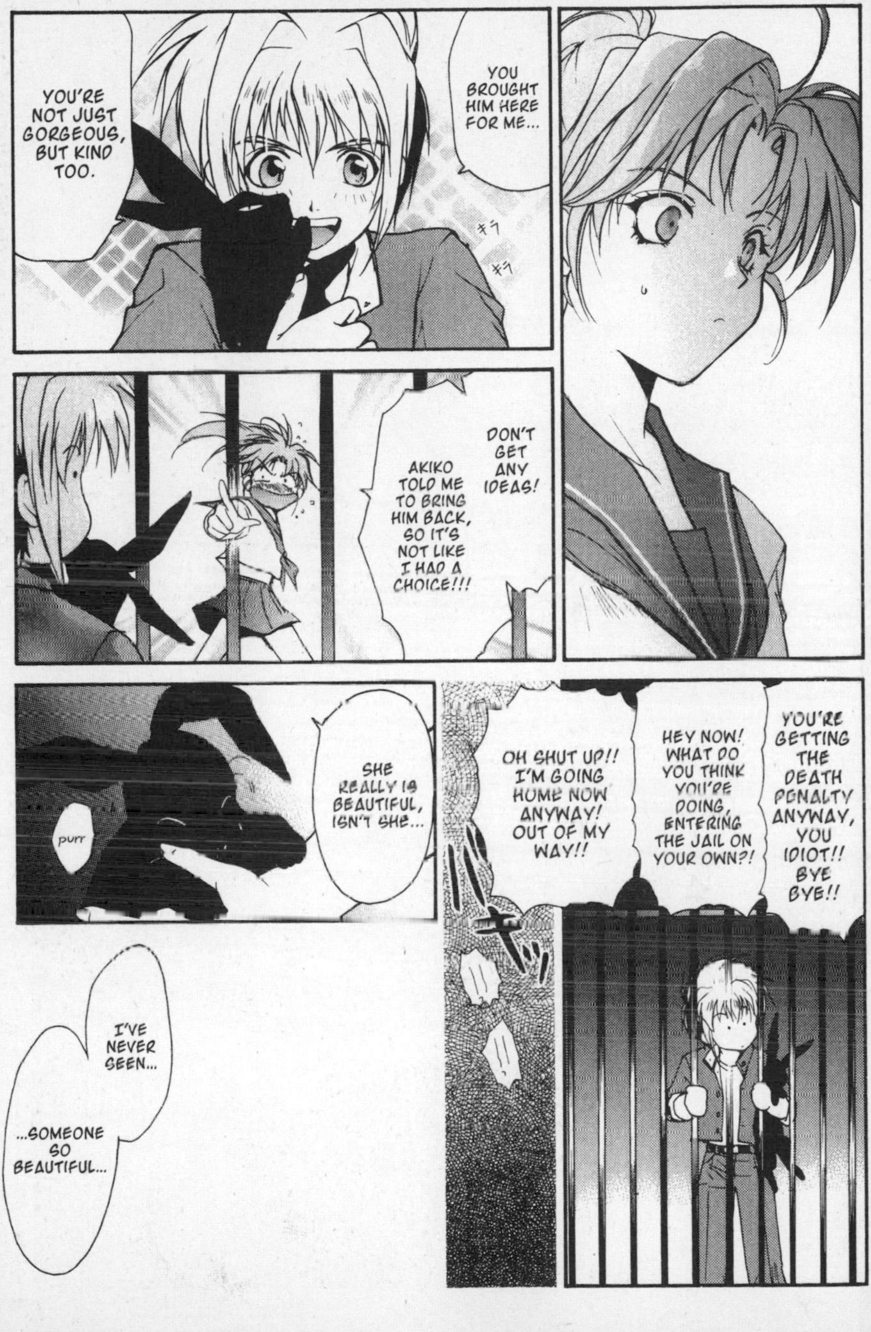
YOU BROUGHT HIM HERE FOR ME...
YOU'RE NOT JUST GORGEOUS, BUT KIND TOO.
キラ
キラ
DON'T GET ANY IDEAS!
AKIKO TOLD ME TO BRING HIM BACK, SO IT'S NOT LIKE I HAD A CHOICE!!!
YOU'RE GETTING THE DEATH PENALTY ANYWAY, YOU IDIOT!! BYE BYE!!
HEY NOW! WHAT DO YOU THINK YOU'RE DOING, ENTERING THE JAIL ON YOUR OWN?!
OH SHUT UP!! I'M GOING HOME NOW ANYWAY! OUT OF MY WAY!!
SHE REALLY IS BEAUTIFUL, ISN'T SHE...
purr
I'VE NEVER SEEN...
...SOMEONE SO BEAUTIFUL...

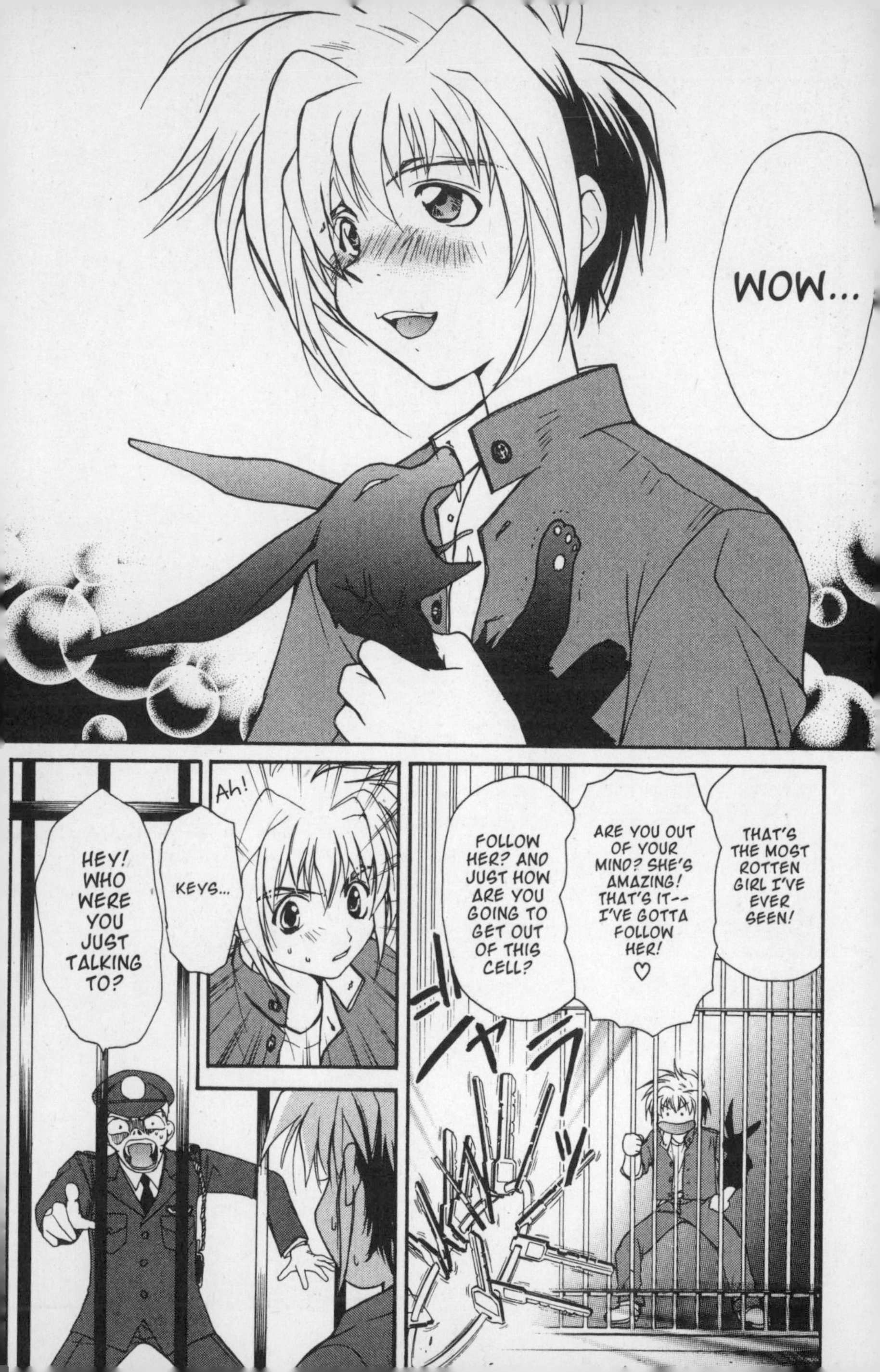
WOW...
THAT'S THE MOST ROTTEN GIRL I'VE EVER SEEN!
ARE YOU OUT OF YOUR MIND? SHE'S AMAZING! THAT'S IT-- I'VE GOTTA FOLLOW HER! ♡
FOLLOW HER? AND JUST HOW ARE YOU GOING TO GET OUT OF THIS CELL?
ジャラ
Ah!
KEYS...
HEY! WHO WERE YOU JUST TALKING TO?

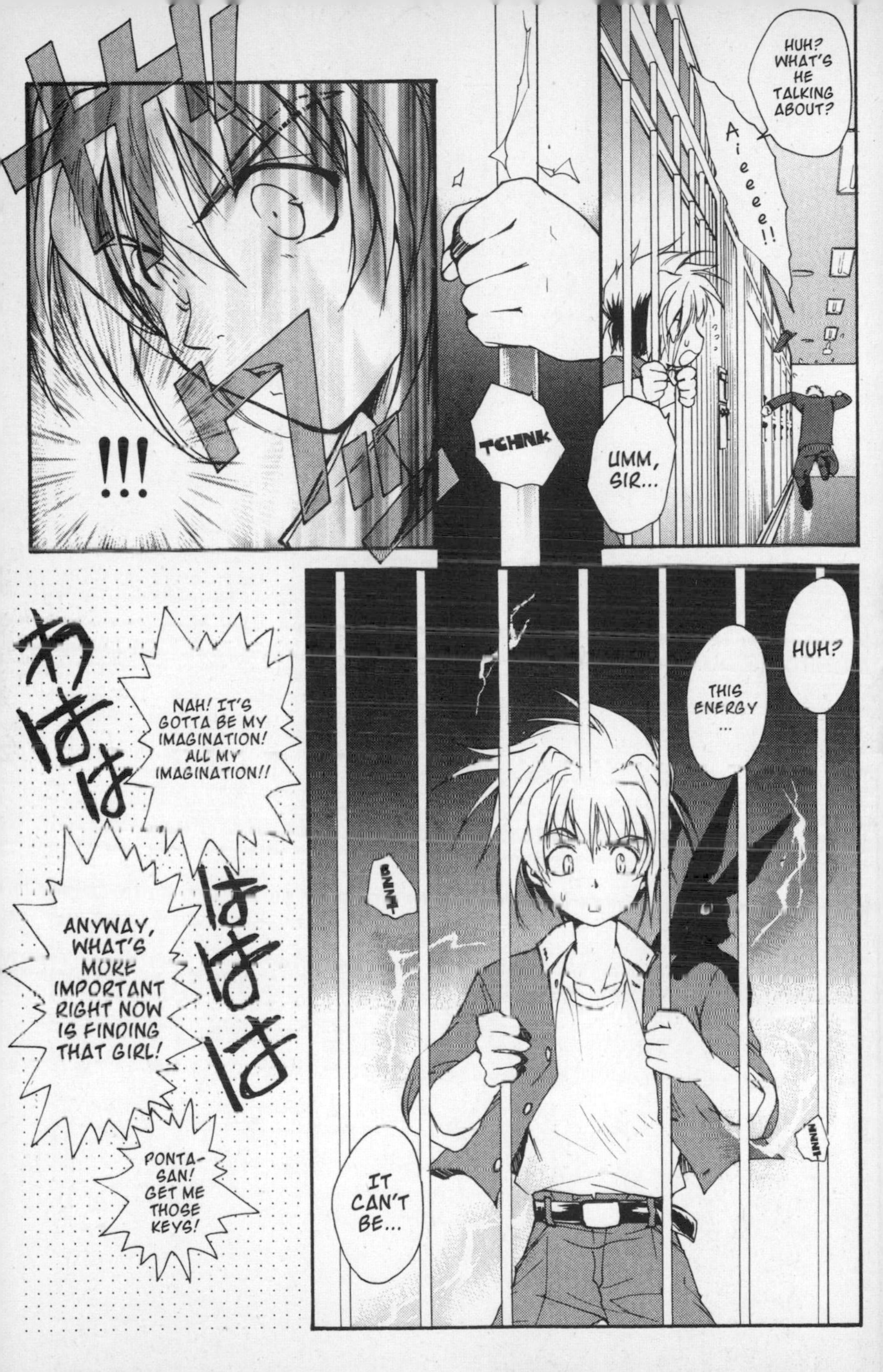

HUH? WHAT'S HE TALKING ABOUT?
Aieeee!!
UMM, SIR...
TCHNK
!!!
HUH?
THIS ENERGY ...
IT CAN'T BE...
わはは
ははは
NAH! IT'S GOTTA BE MY IMAGINATION! ALL MY IMAGINATION!!
ANYWAY, WHAT'S MORE IMPORTANT RIGHT NOW IS FINDING THAT GIRL!
PONTA-SAN! GET ME THOSE KEYS!

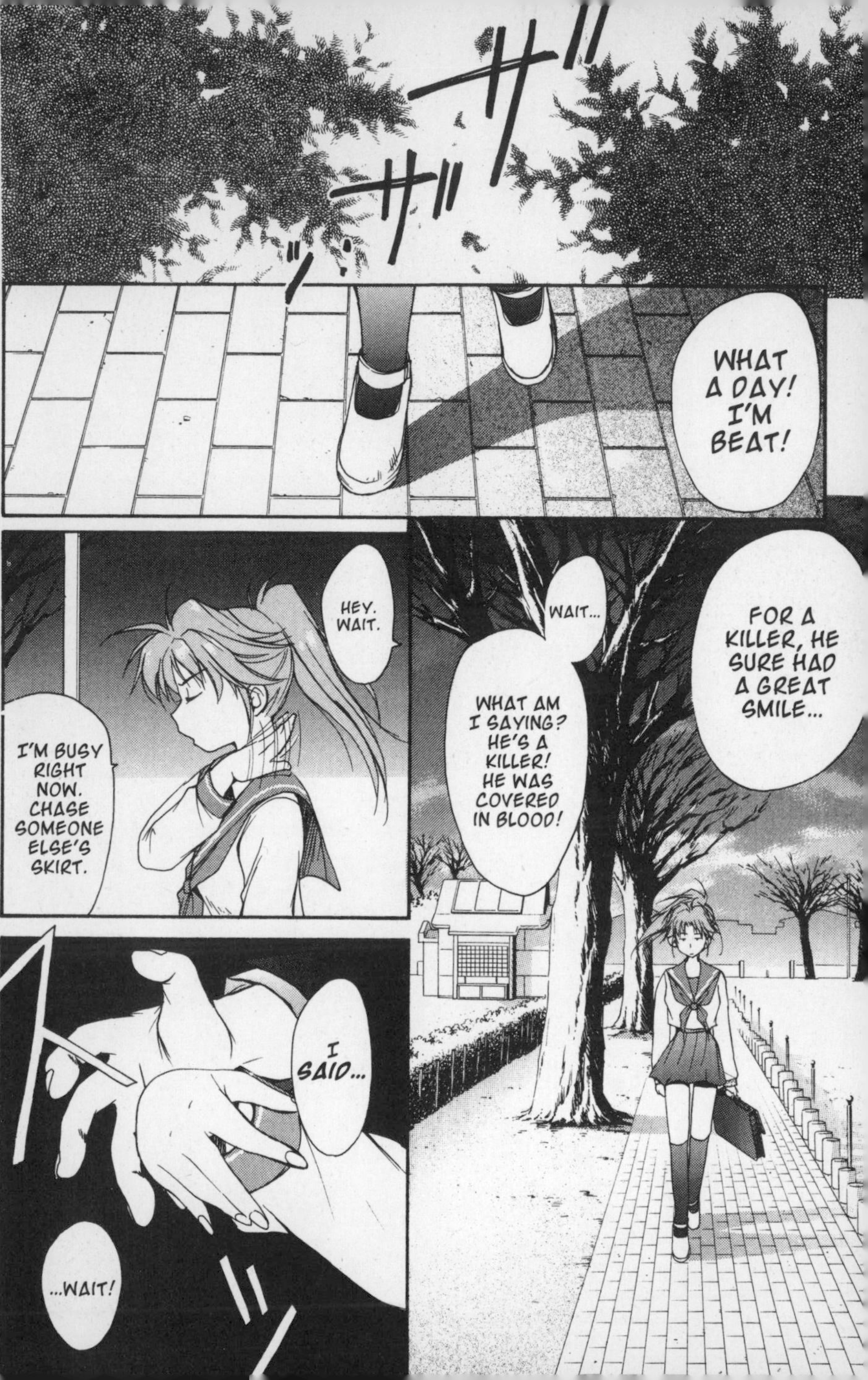
ザザ
WHAT A DAY! I'M BEAT!
FOR A KILLER, HE SURE HAD A GREAT SMILE...
WAIT...
WHAT AM I SAYING? HE'S A KILLER! HE WAS COVERED IN BLOOD!
HEY. WAIT.
I'M BUSY RIGHT NOW. CHASE SOMEONE ELSE'S SKIRT.
I SAID...
...WAIT!

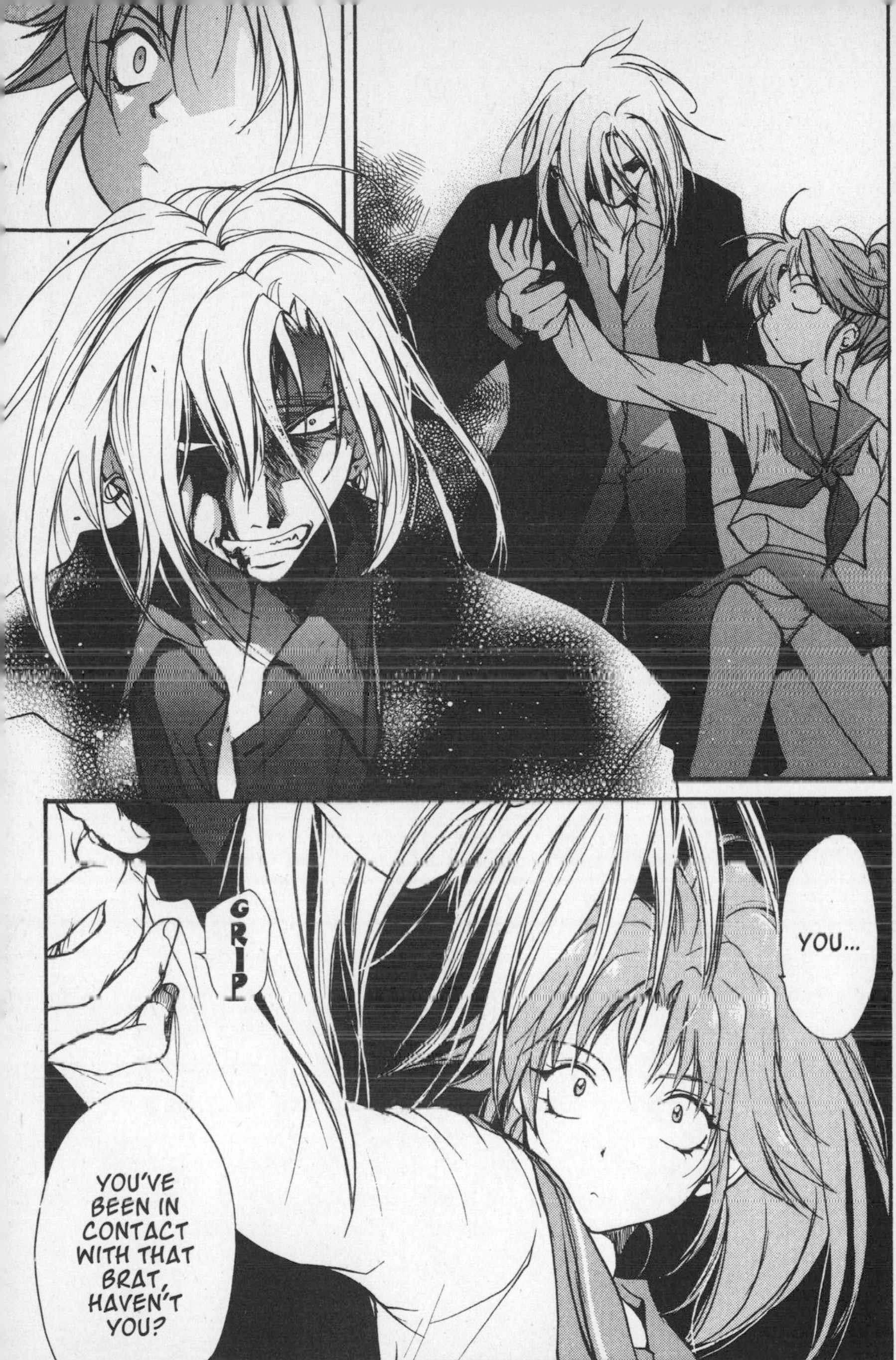
YOU...
GRIP
YOU'VE BEEN IN CONTACT WITH THAT BRAT, HAVEN'T YOU?

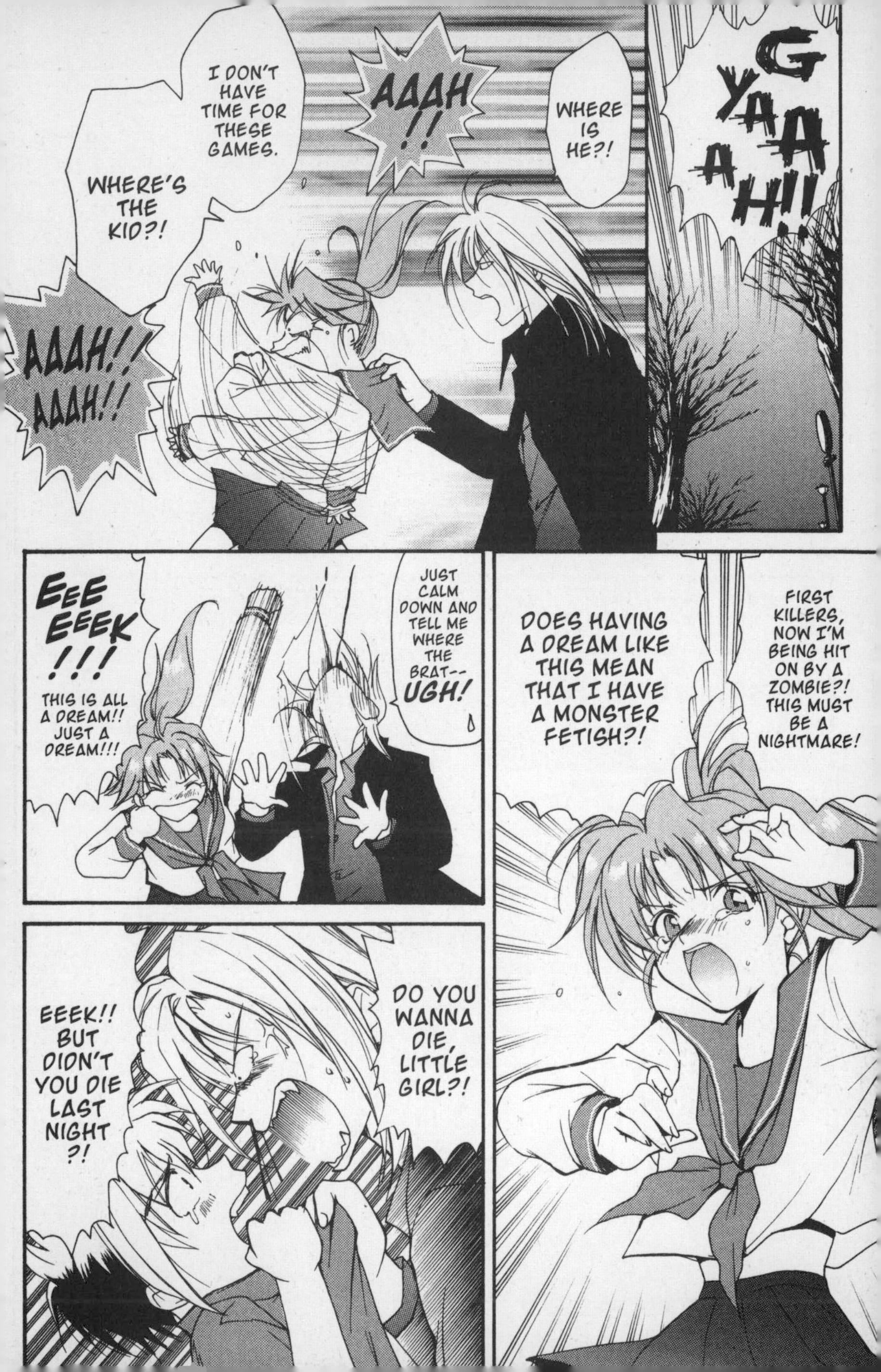
GYAAAAH!!
WHERE IS HE?!
AAAH!!
I DON'T HAVE TIME FOR THESE GAMES.
WHERE'S THE KID?!
AAAH!! AAAH!!
FIRST KILLERS, NOW I'M BEING HIT ON BY A ZOMBIE?! THIS MUST BE A NIGHTMARE!
DOES HAVING A DREAM LIKE THIS MEAN THAT I HAVE A MONSTER FETISH?!
JUST CALM DOWN AND TELL ME WHERE THE BRAT-- UGH!
EEEEEEK!!!
THIS IS ALL A DREAM!! JUST A DREAM!!!
DO YOU WANNA DIE, LITTLE GIRL?!
EEEK!! BUT DIDN'T YOU DIE LAST NIGHT?!

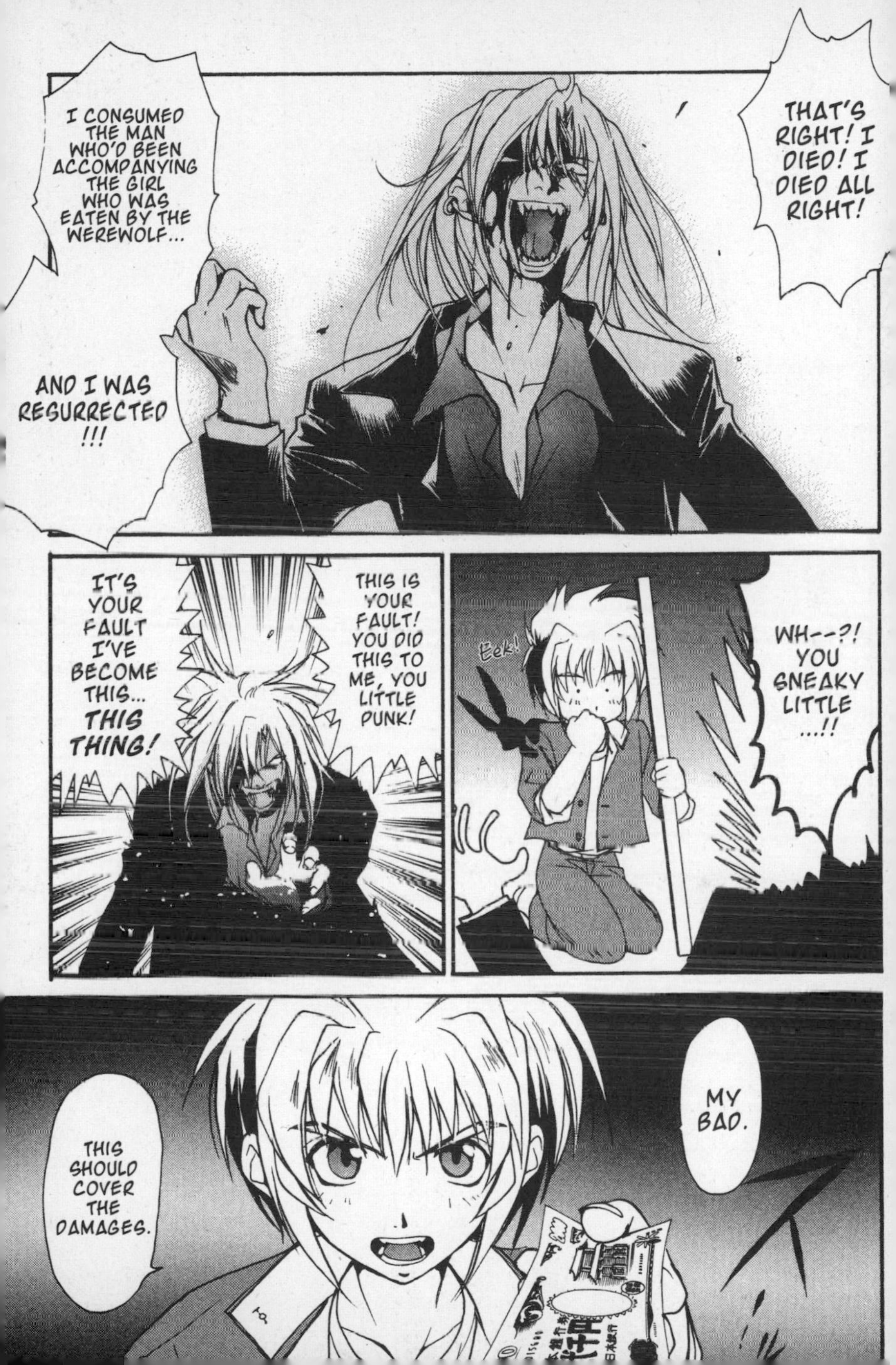
THAT'S RIGHT! I DIED! I DIED ALL RIGHT!
I CONSUMED THE MAN WHO'D BEEN ACCOMPANYING THE GIRL WHO WAS EATEN BY THE WEREWOLF...
AND I WAS RESURRECTED !!!
WH--?! YOU SNEAKY LITTLE ...!!
Eek!
THIS IS YOUR FAULT! YOU DID THIS TO ME, YOU LITTLE PUNK!
IT'S YOUR FAULT I'VE BECOME THIS... **THIS THING!**
MY BAD.
THIS SHOULD COVER THE DAMAGES.

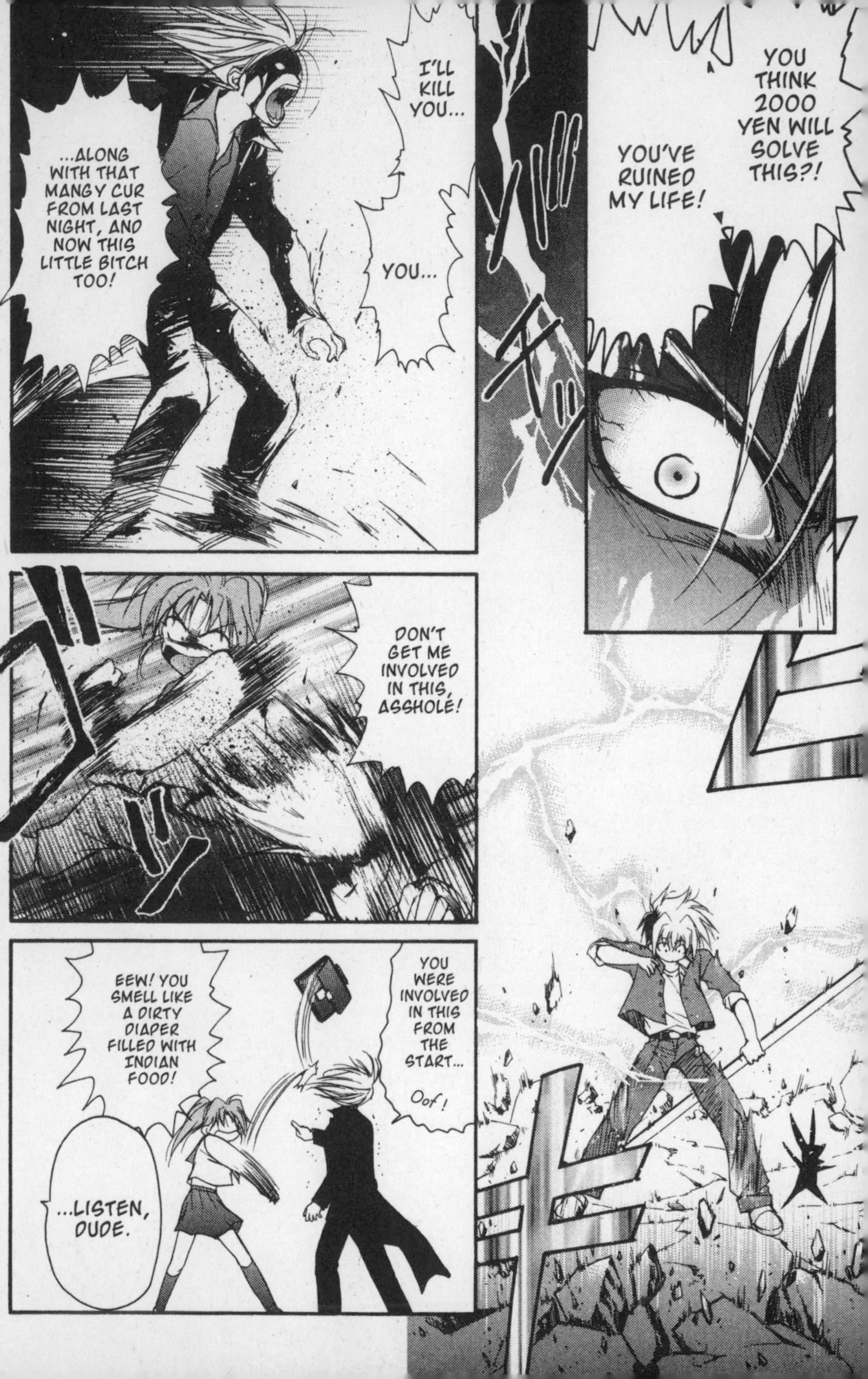
YOU THINK 2000 YEN WILL SOLVE THIS?!
YOU'VE RUINED MY LIFE!
YOU...
I'LL KILL YOU...
...ALONG WITH THAT MANGY CUR FROM LAST NIGHT, AND NOW THIS LITTLE BITCH TOO!
DON'T GET ME INVOLVED IN THIS, ASSHOLE!
YOU WERE INVOLVED IN THIS FROM THE START...
Oof!
EEW! YOU SMELL LIKE A DIRTY DIAPER FILLED WITH INDIAN FOOD!
...LISTEN, DUDE.

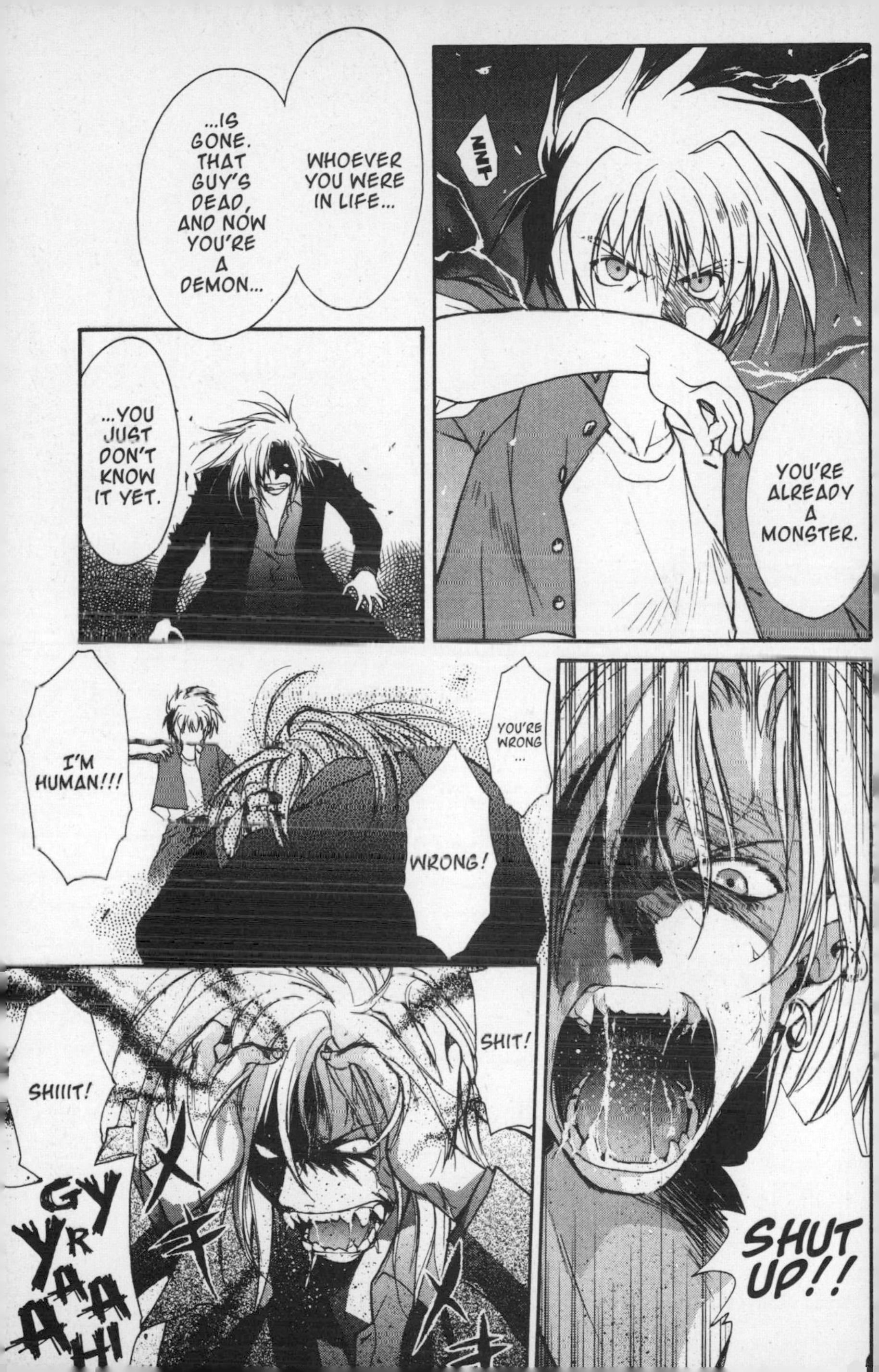
NNT
YOU'RE ALREADY A MONSTER.
WHOEVER YOU WERE IN LIFE...
...IS GONE. THAT GUY'S DEAD, AND NOW YOU'RE A DEMON...
...YOU JUST DON'T KNOW IT YET.
SHUT UP!!
YOU'RE WRONG ...
WRONG!
I'M HUMAN!!!
SHIT!
SHIIIT!

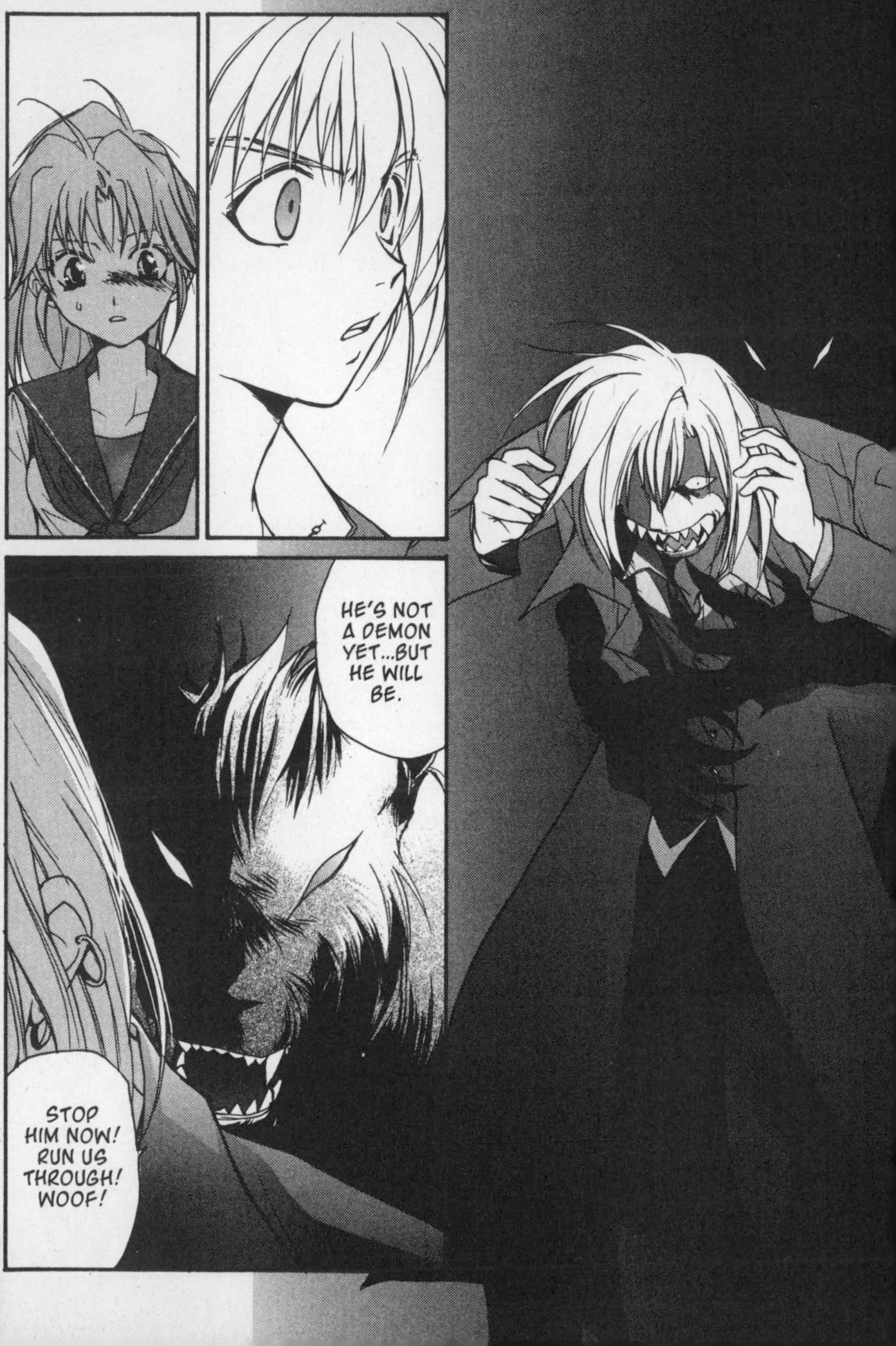
HE'S NOT A DEMON YET...BUT HE WILL BE.
STOP HIM NOW! RUN US THROUGH! WOOF!

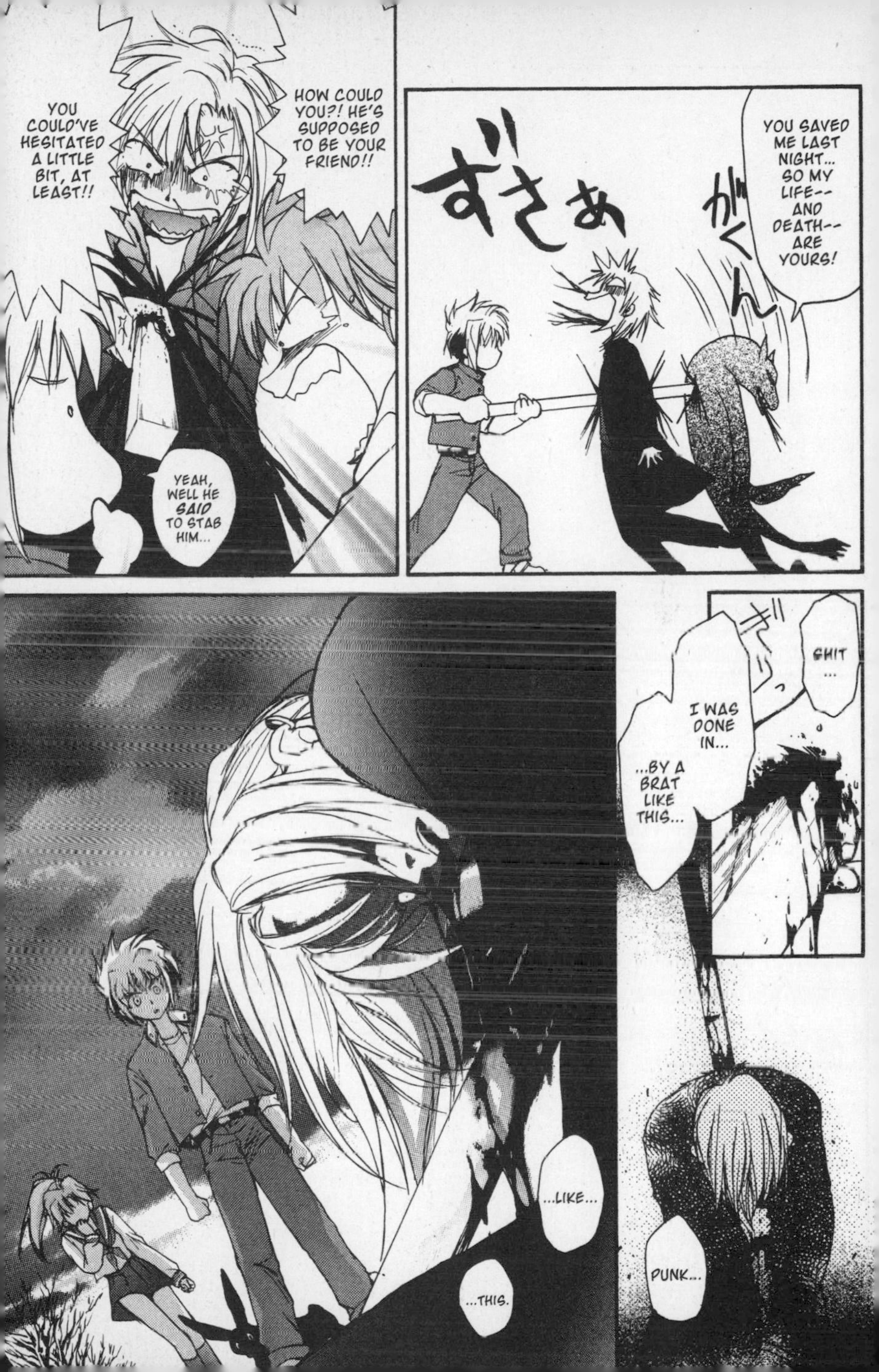

YOU SAVED ME LAST NIGHT... SO MY LIFE-- AND DEATH-- ARE YOURS!
がくん
ずさぁ
HOW COULD YOU?! HE'S SUPPOSED TO BE YOUR FRIEND!!
YOU COULD'VE HESITATED A LITTLE BIT, AT LEAST!!
YEAH, WELL HE *SAID* TO STAB HIM...
SHIT...
ぎりっ
I WAS DONE IN...
...BY A BRAT LIKE THIS...
PUNK...
...LIKE...
...THIS.

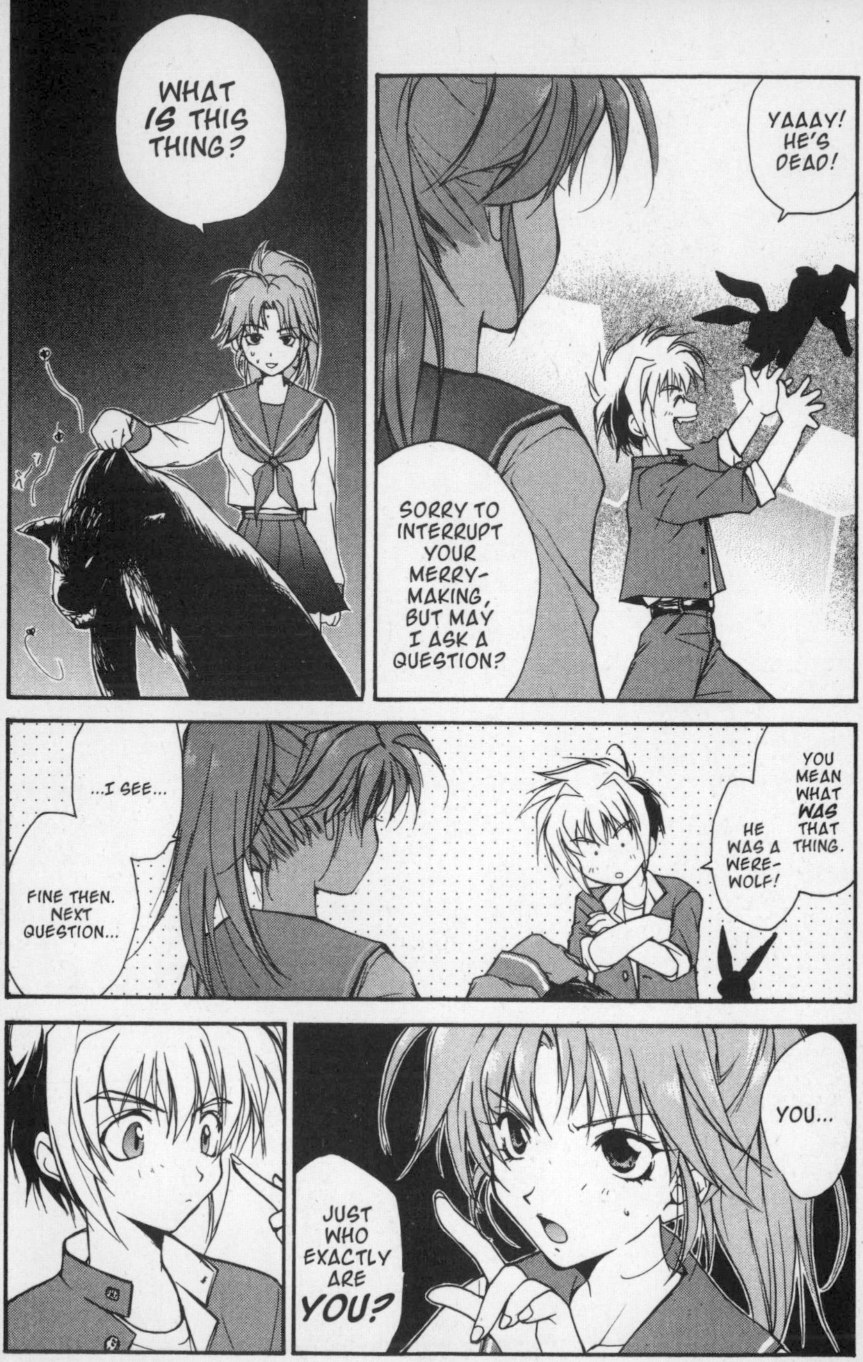
YAAAY! HE'S DEAD!
SORRY TO INTERRUPT YOUR MERRY-MAKING, BUT MAY I ASK A QUESTION?
WHAT *IS* THIS THING?
YOU MEAN WHAT *WAS* THAT THING.
HE WAS A WERE-WOLF!
...I SEE...
FINE THEN. NEXT QUESTION...
YOU...
JUST WHO EXACTLY ARE *YOU?*

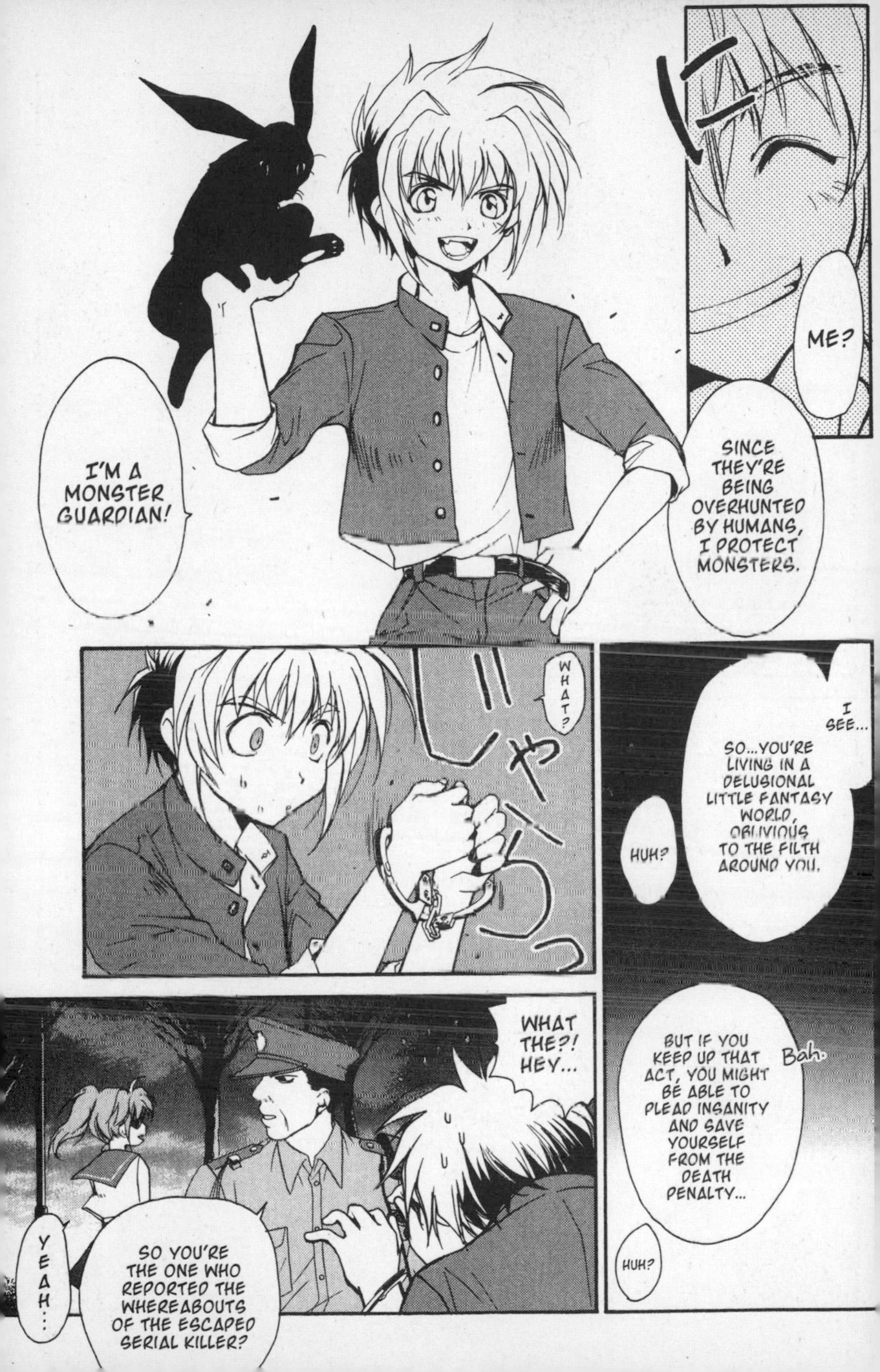
ME?
I'M A MONSTER GUARDIAN!
SINCE THEY'RE BEING OVERHUNTED BY HUMANS, I PROTECT MONSTERS.
I SEE...
SO...YOU'RE LIVING IN A DELUSIONAL LITTLE FANTASY WORLD, OBLIVIOUS TO THE FILTH AROUND YOU.
HUH?
BUT IF YOU KEEP UP THAT ACT, YOU MIGHT BE ABLE TO PLEAD INSANITY AND SAVE YOURSELF FROM THE DEATH PENALTY...
Bah.
HUH?
WHAT?
WHAT THE?! HEY...
SO YOU'RE THE ONE WHO REPORTED THE WHEREABOUTS OF THE ESCAPED SERIAL KILLER?
YEAH...

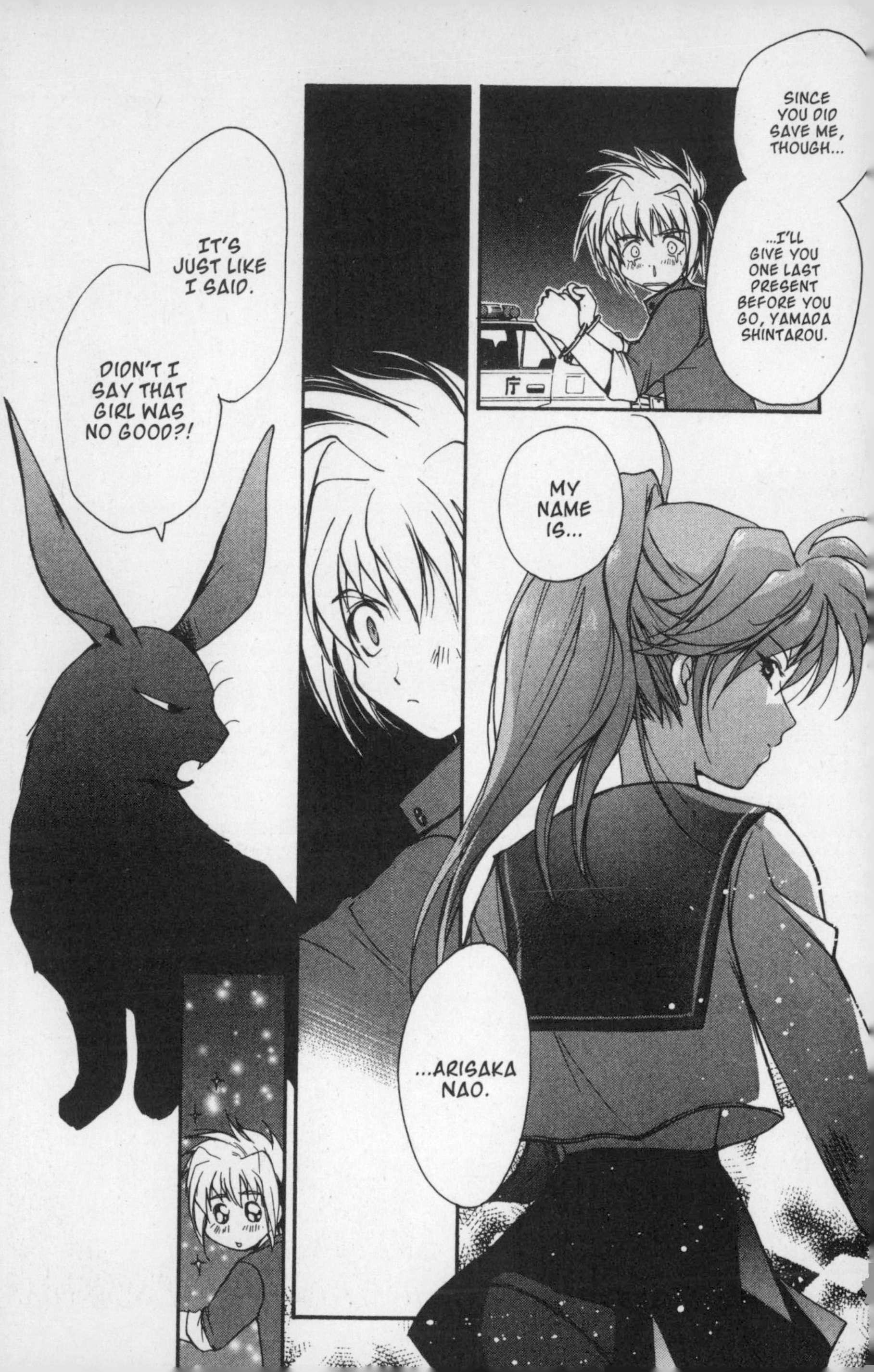
SINCE YOU DID SAVE ME, THOUGH...
...I'LL GIVE YOU ONE LAST PRESENT BEFORE YOU GO, YAMADA SHINTAROU.
MY NAME IS...
...ARISAKA NAO.
IT'S JUST LIKE I SAID.
DIDN'T I SAY THAT GIRL WAS NO GOOD?!

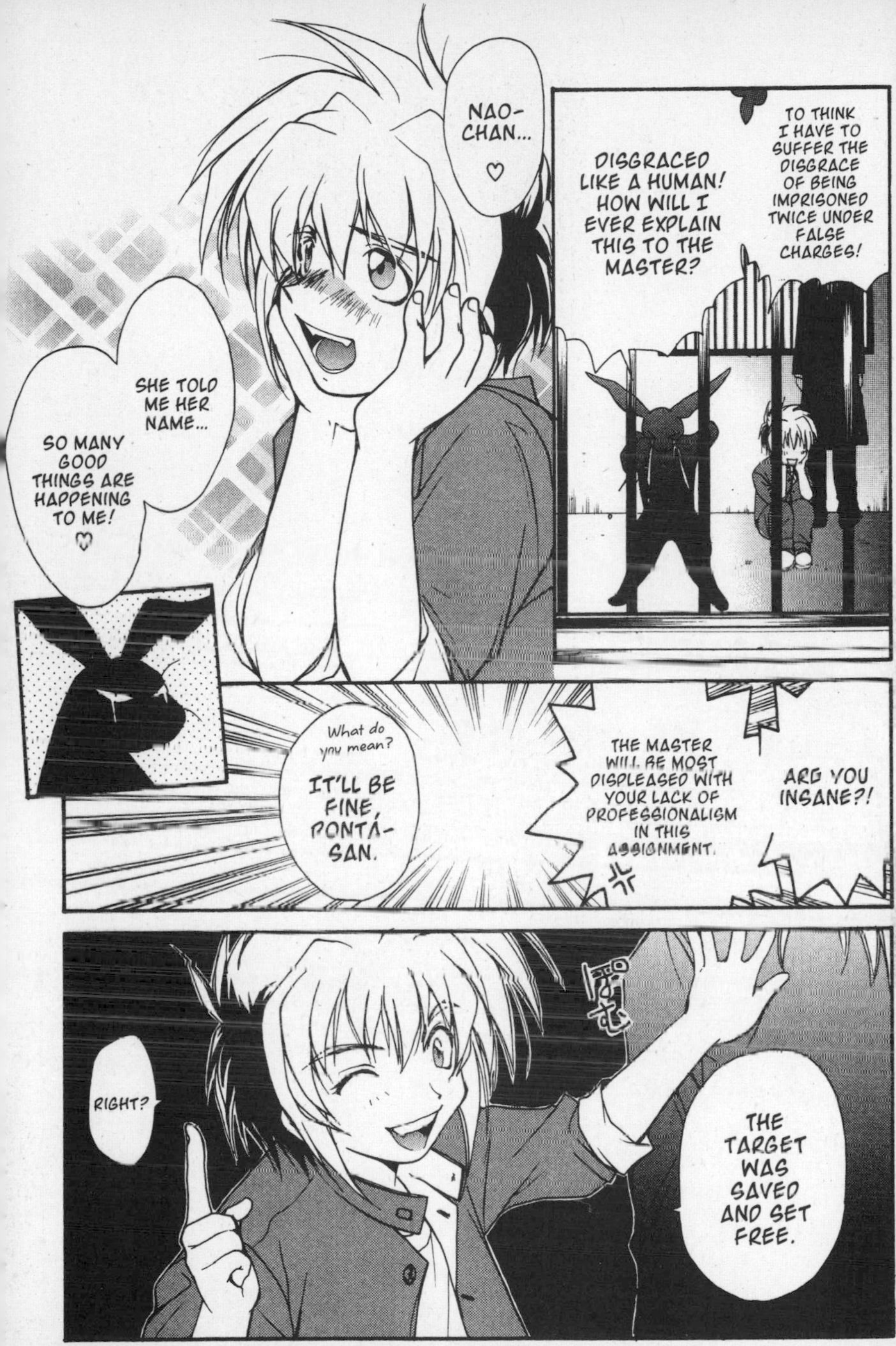

TO THINK I HAVE TO SUFFER THE DISGRACE OF BEING IMPRISONED TWICE UNDER FALSE CHARGES!
DISGRACED LIKE A HUMAN! HOW WILL I EVER EXPLAIN THIS TO THE MASTER?
NAO-CHAN... ♡
SHE TOLD ME HER NAME...
SO MANY GOOD THINGS ARE HAPPENING TO ME! ♡
ARE YOU INSANE?!
THE MASTER WILL BE MOST DISPLEASED WITH YOUR LACK OF PROFESSIONALISM IN THIS ASSIGNMENT.
What do you mean?
IT'LL BE FINE, PONTÁ-SAN.
THE TARGET WAS SAVED AND SET FREE.
RIGHT?

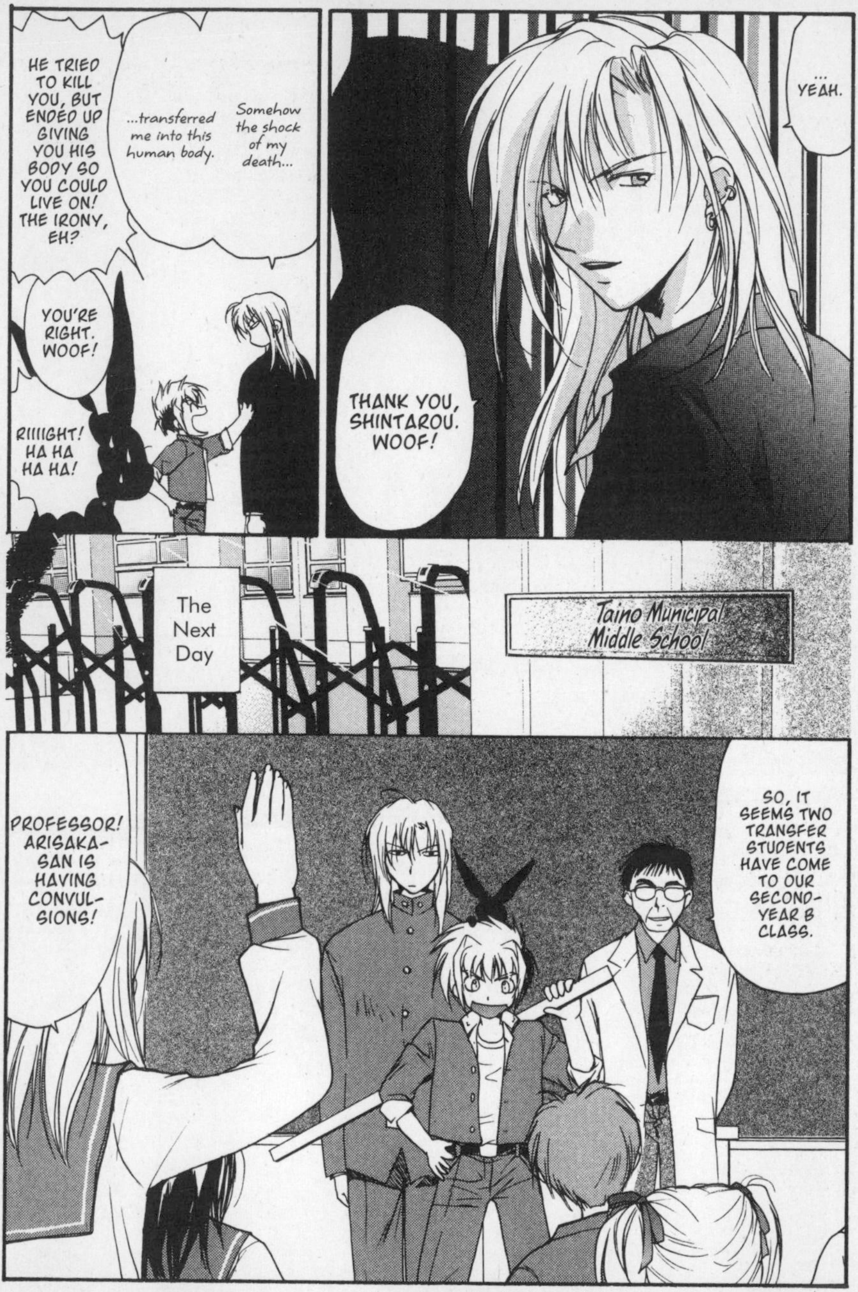
... YEAH.
THANK YOU, SHINTAROU. WOOF!
Somehow the shock of my death...
...transferred me into this human body.
HE TRIED TO KILL YOU, BUT ENDED UP GIVING YOU HIS BODY SO YOU COULD LIVE ON! THE IRONY, EH?
YOU'RE RIGHT. WOOF!
RIIIIGHT! HA HA HA HA!
Taino Municipal Middle School
The Next Day
SO, IT SEEMS TWO TRANSFER STUDENTS HAVE COME TO OUR SECOND-YEAR B CLASS.
PROFESSOR! ARISAKA-SAN IS HAVING CONVUL-SIONS!

ACT 01 END

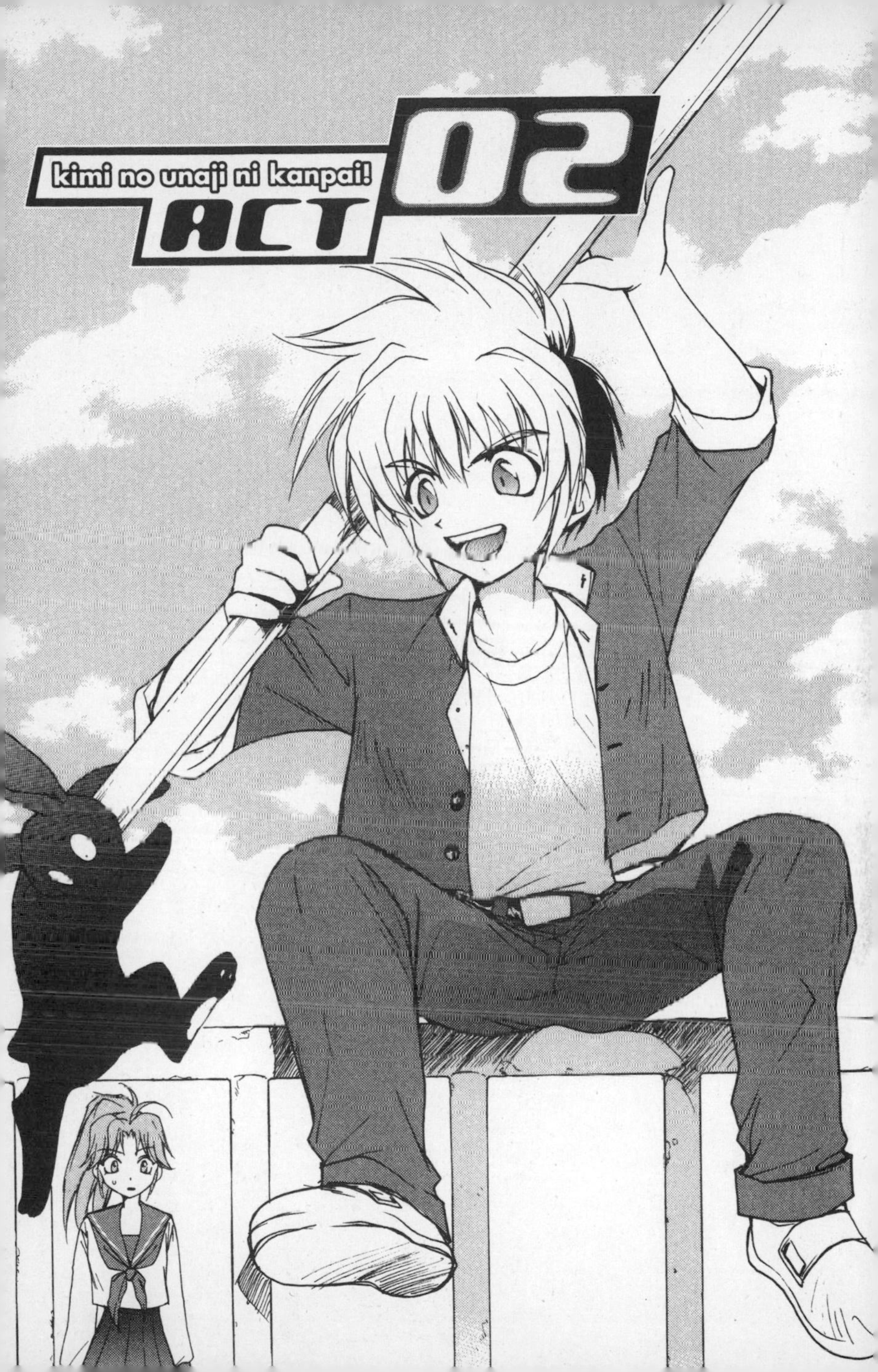
kimi no unaji ni kanpai!
ACT 02

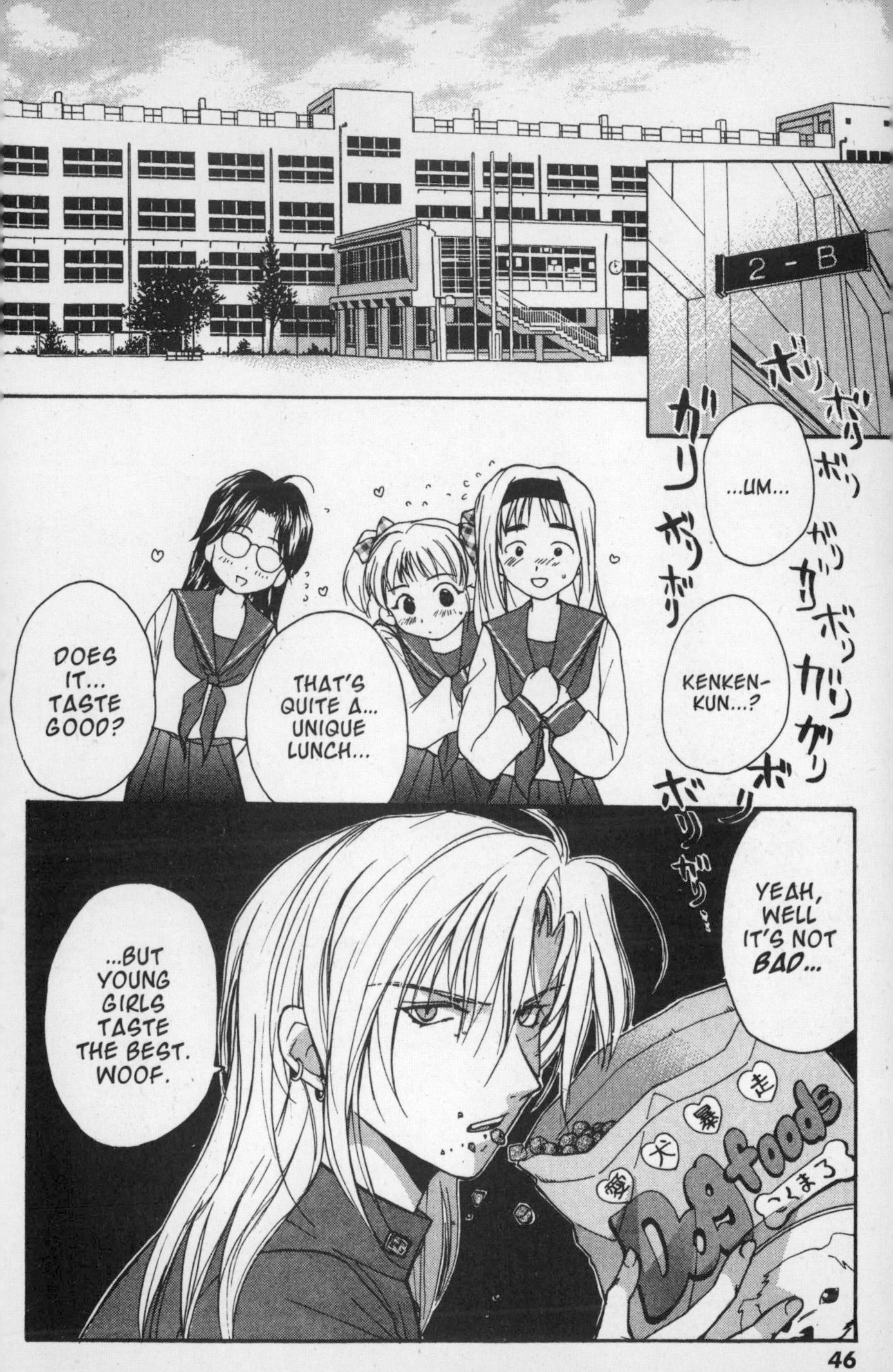
2 - B
...UM...
KENKEN-KUN...?
THAT'S QUITE A... UNIQUE LUNCH...
DOES IT... TASTE GOOD?
YEAH, WELL IT'S NOT *BAD*...
...BUT YOUNG GIRLS TASTE THE BEST. WOOF.

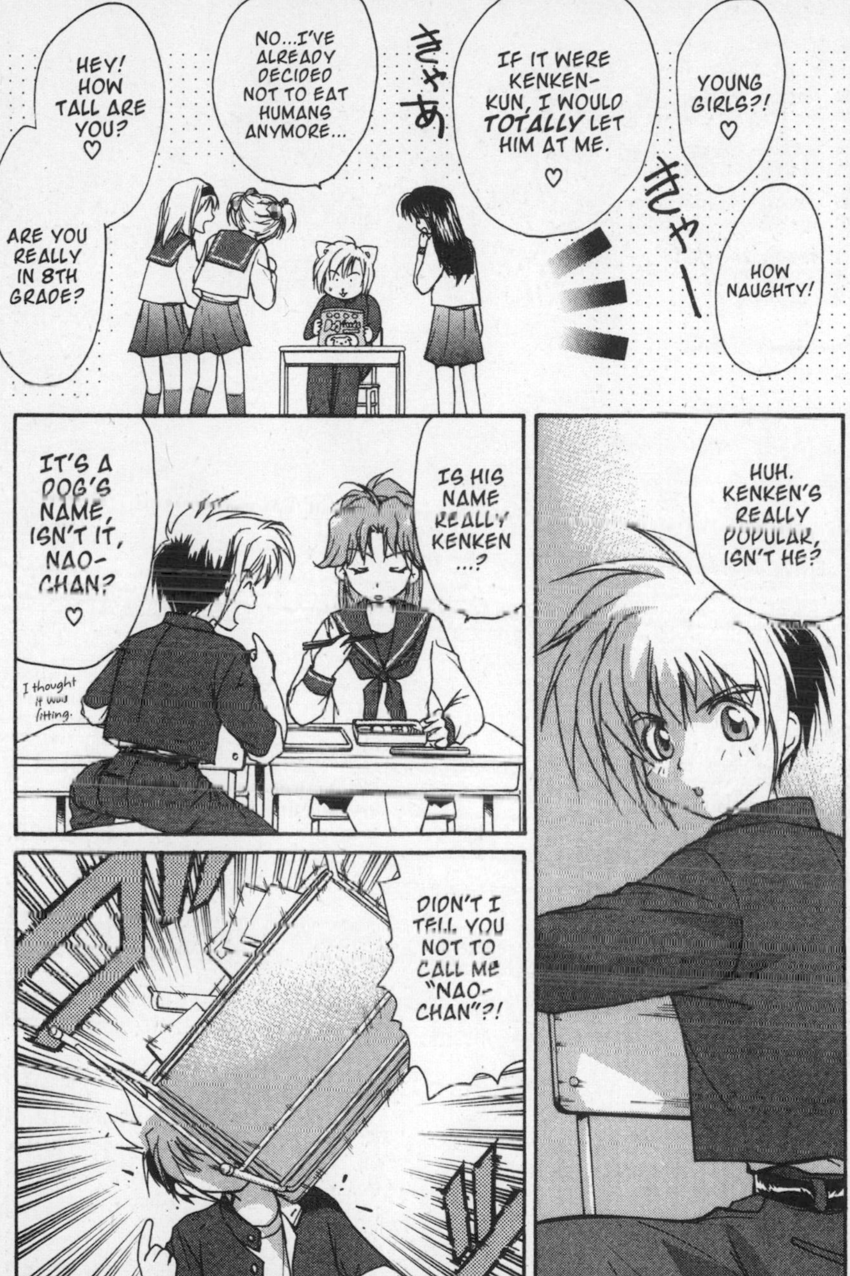
YOUNG GIRLS?! ♡
HOW NAUGHTY!
きゃー
IF IT WERE KENKEN-KUN, I WOULD *TOTALLY* LET HIM AT ME. ♡
きゃあ
NO...I'VE ALREADY DECIDED NOT TO EAT HUMANS ANYMORE...
HEY! HOW TALL ARE YOU? ♡
ARE YOU REALLY IN 8TH GRADE?
HUH. KENKEN'S REALLY POPULAR, ISN'T HE?
IS HIS NAME REALLY KENKEN ...?
IT'S A DOG'S NAME, ISN'T IT, NAO-CHAN? ♡
I thought it was fitting.
DIDN'T I TELL YOU NOT TO CALL ME "NAO-CHAN"?!

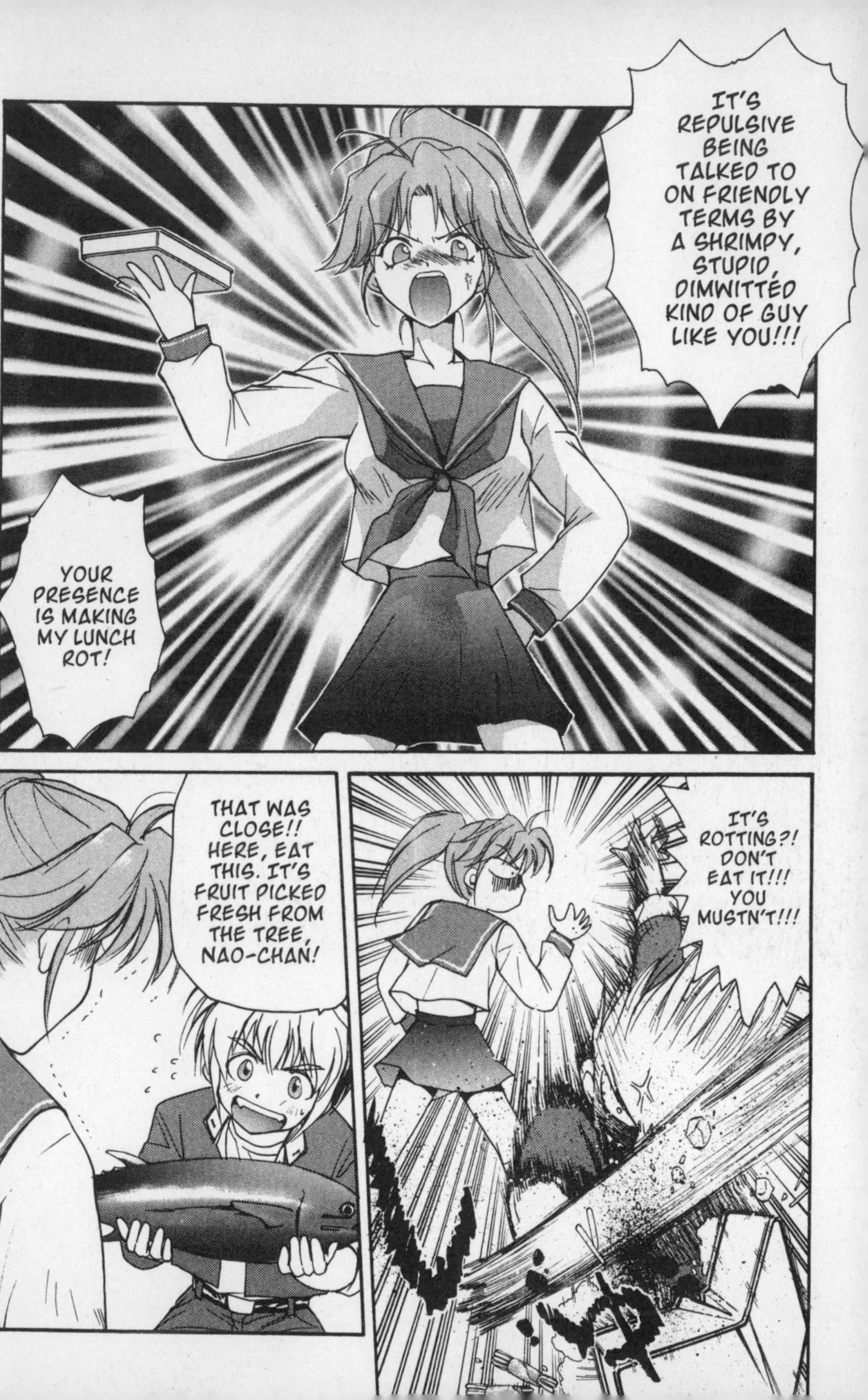
IT'S REPULSIVE BEING TALKED TO ON FRIENDLY TERMS BY A SHRIMPY, STUPID, DIMWITTED KIND OF GUY LIKE YOU!!!
YOUR PRESENCE IS MAKING MY LUNCH ROT!
IT'S ROTTING?! DON'T EAT IT!!! YOU MUSTN'T!!!
THAT WAS CLOSE!! HERE, EAT THIS. IT'S FRUIT PICKED FRESH FROM THE TREE, NAO-CHAN!

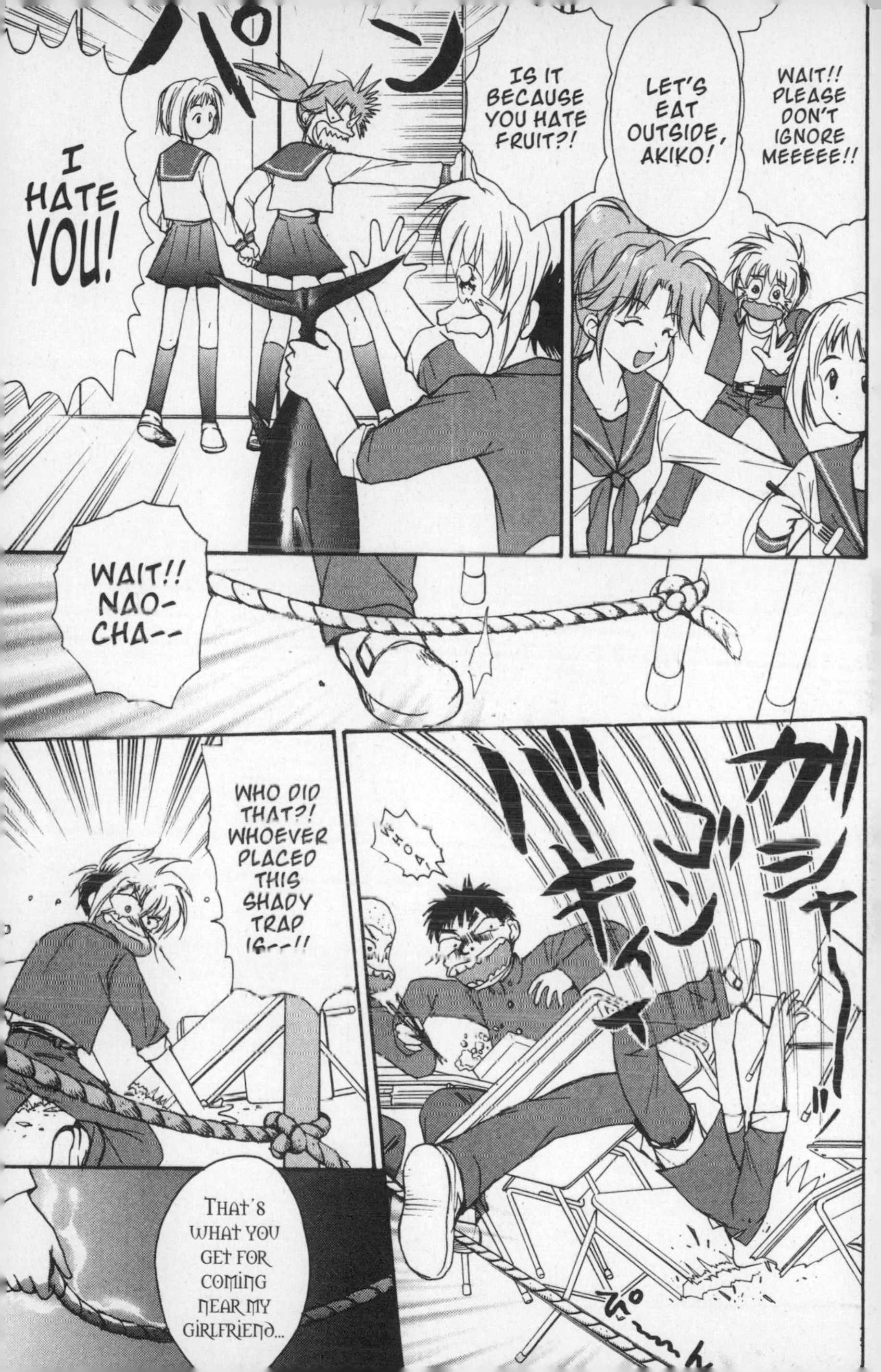
WAIT!! PLEASE DON'T IGNORE MEEEEE!!
LET'S EAT OUTSIDE, AKIKO!
パーン
IS IT BECAUSE YOU HATE FRUIT?!
I HATE YOU!
WAIT!! NAO-CHA--
WHO DID THAT?! WHOEVER PLACED THIS SHADY TRAP IS--!!
That's what you get for coming near my girlfriend...

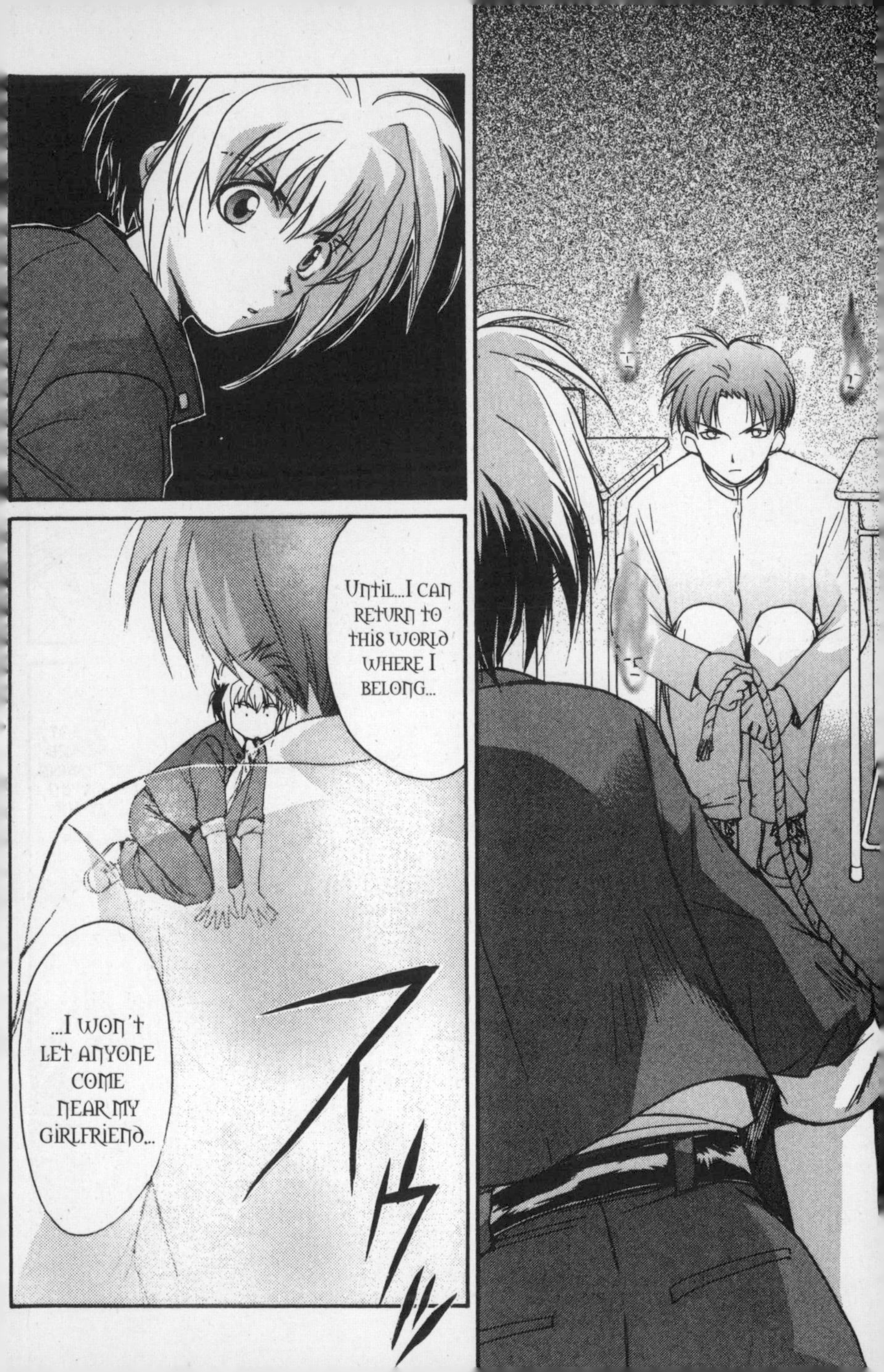
Until...I can return to this world where I belong...
...I won't let anyone come near my girlfriend...

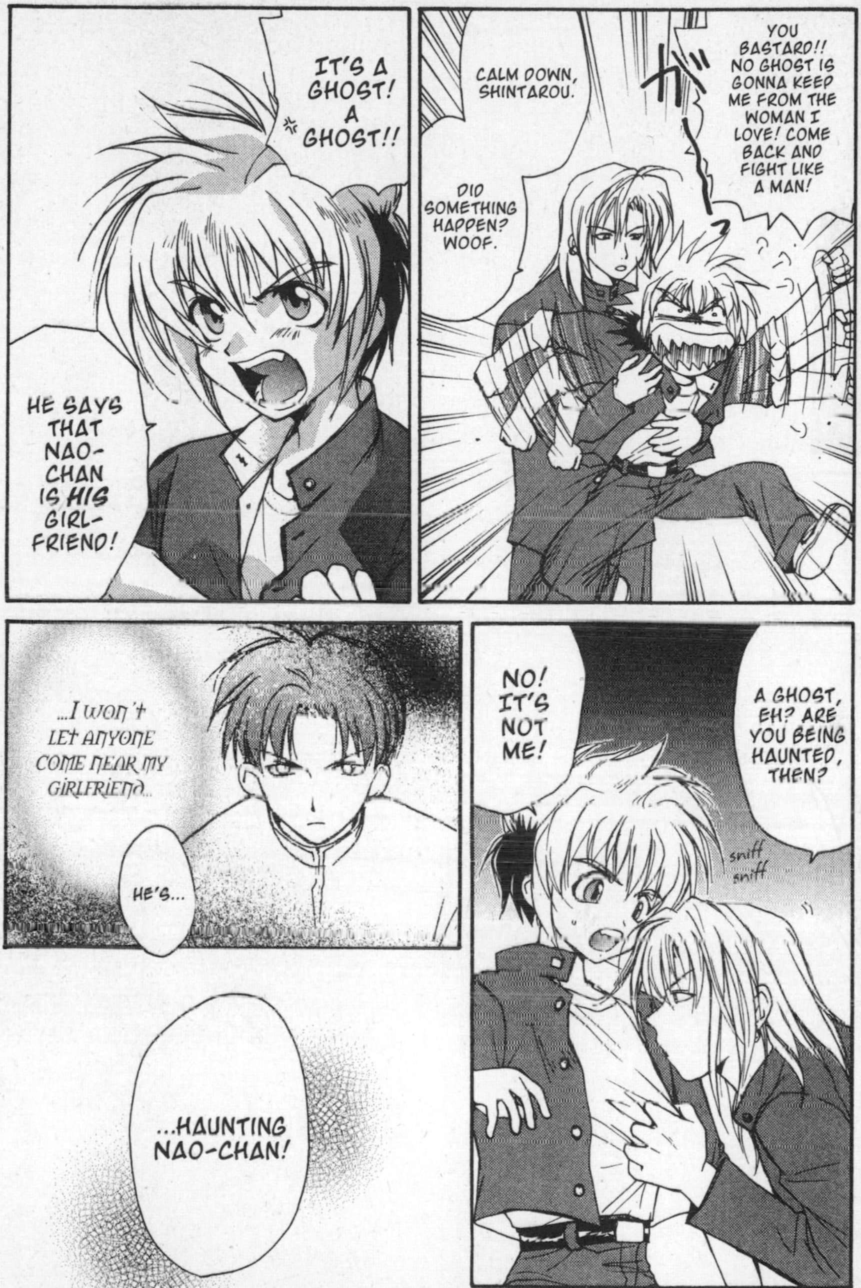
YOU BASTARD!! NO GHOST IS GONNA KEEP ME FROM THE WOMAN I LOVE! COME BACK AND FIGHT LIKE A MAN!
CALM DOWN, SHINTAROU.
DID SOMETHING HAPPEN? WOOF.
IT'S A GHOST! A GHOST!!
HE SAYS THAT NAO-CHAN IS HIS GIRLFRIEND!
A GHOST, EH? ARE YOU BEING HAUNTED, THEN?
NO! IT'S NOT ME!
sniff sniff
...I won't let anyone come near my girlfriend...
HE'S...
...HAUNTING NAO-CHAN!

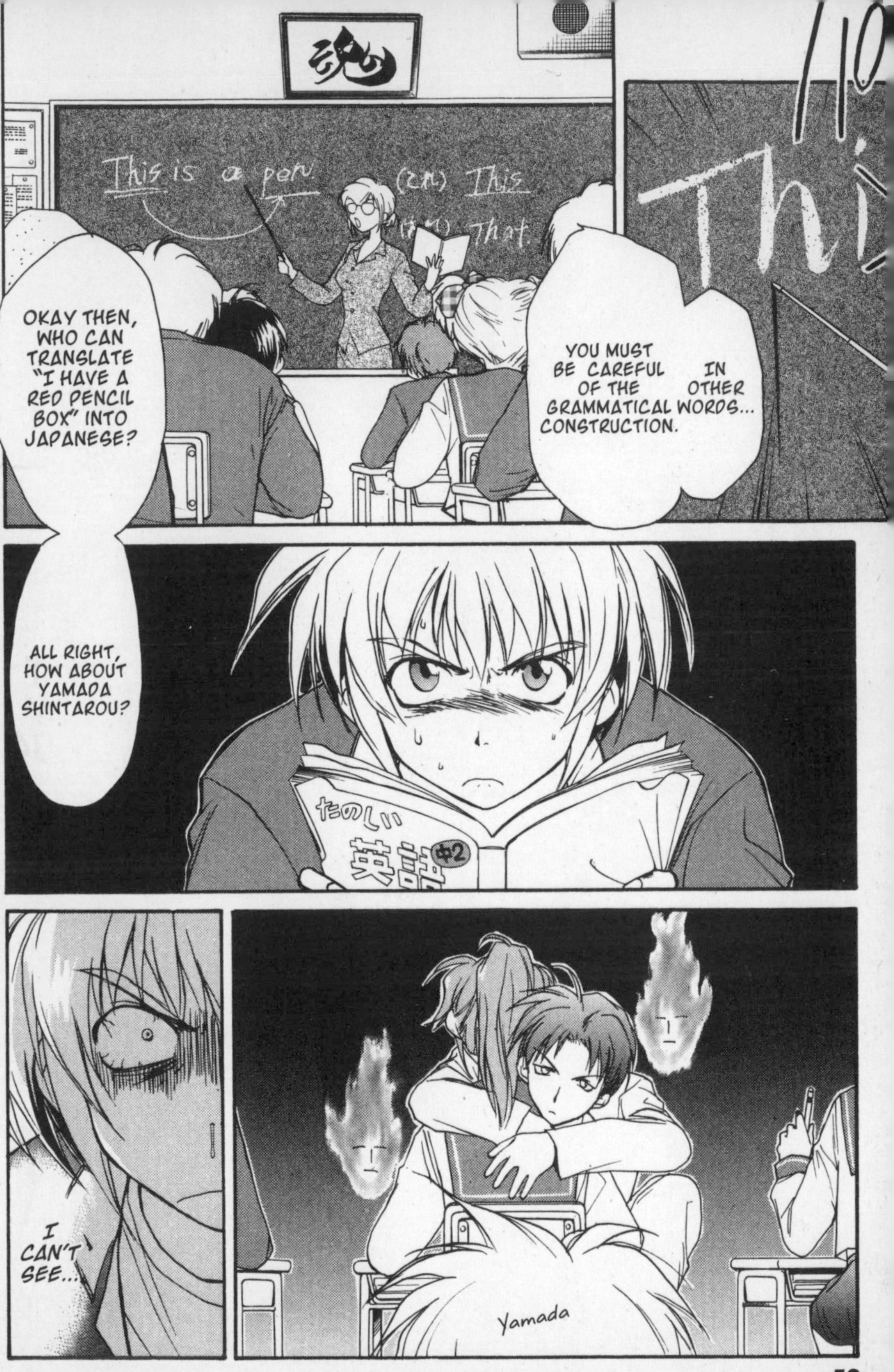
YOU MUST BE CAREFUL OF THE GRAMMATICAL CONSTRUCTION.
IN OTHER WORDS...
魂
This is a pen.
This
That.
OKAY THEN, WHO CAN TRANSLATE "I HAVE A RED PENCIL BOX" INTO JAPANESE?
ALL RIGHT, HOW ABOUT YAMADA SHINTAROU?
たのしい 英語 中2
Yamada
I CAN'T SEE...

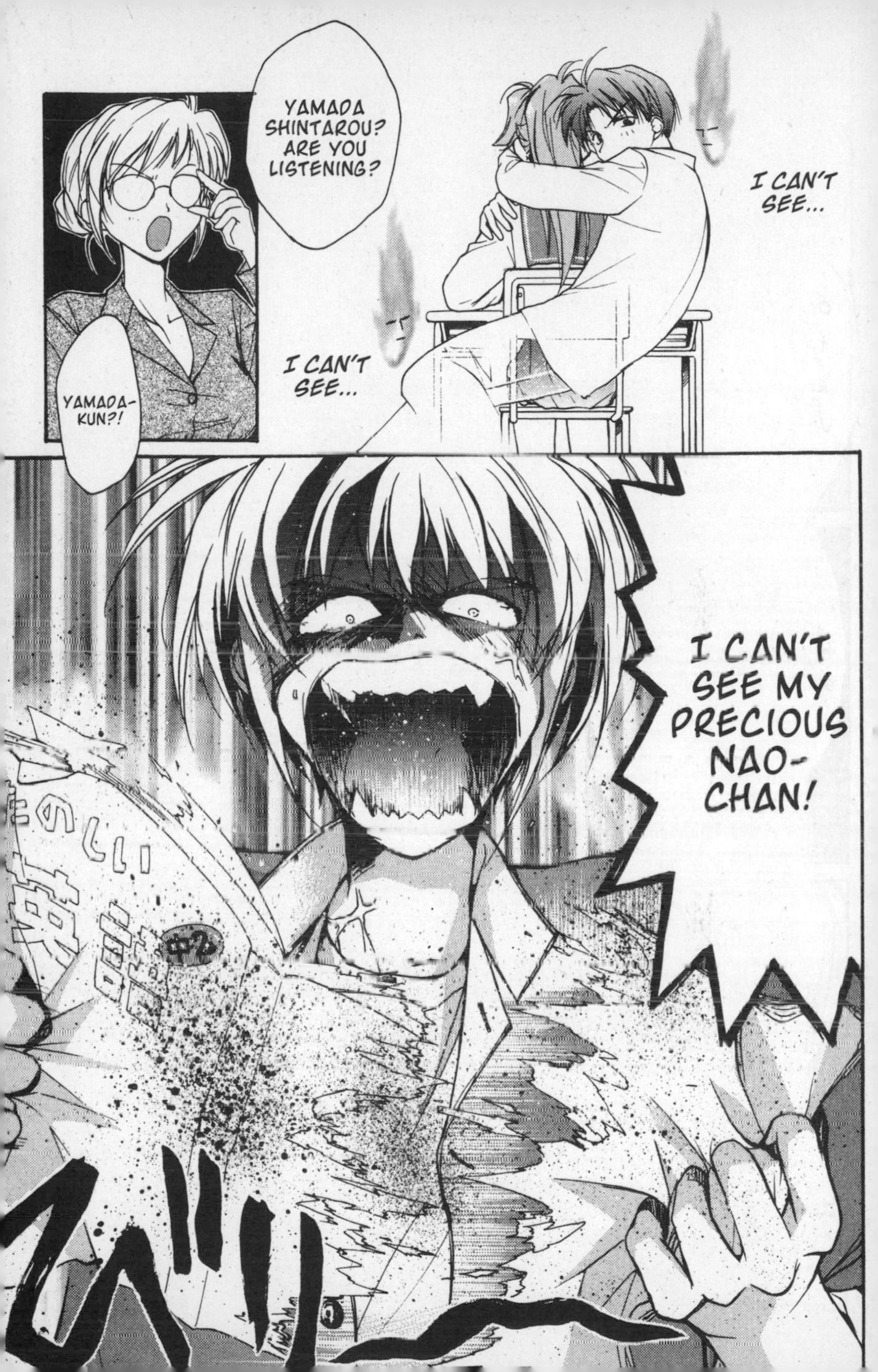
I CAN'T SEE...
I CAN'T SEE...
YAMADA SHINTAROU? ARE YOU LISTENING?
YAMADA-KUN?!
I CAN'T SEE MY PRECIOUS NAO-CHAN!

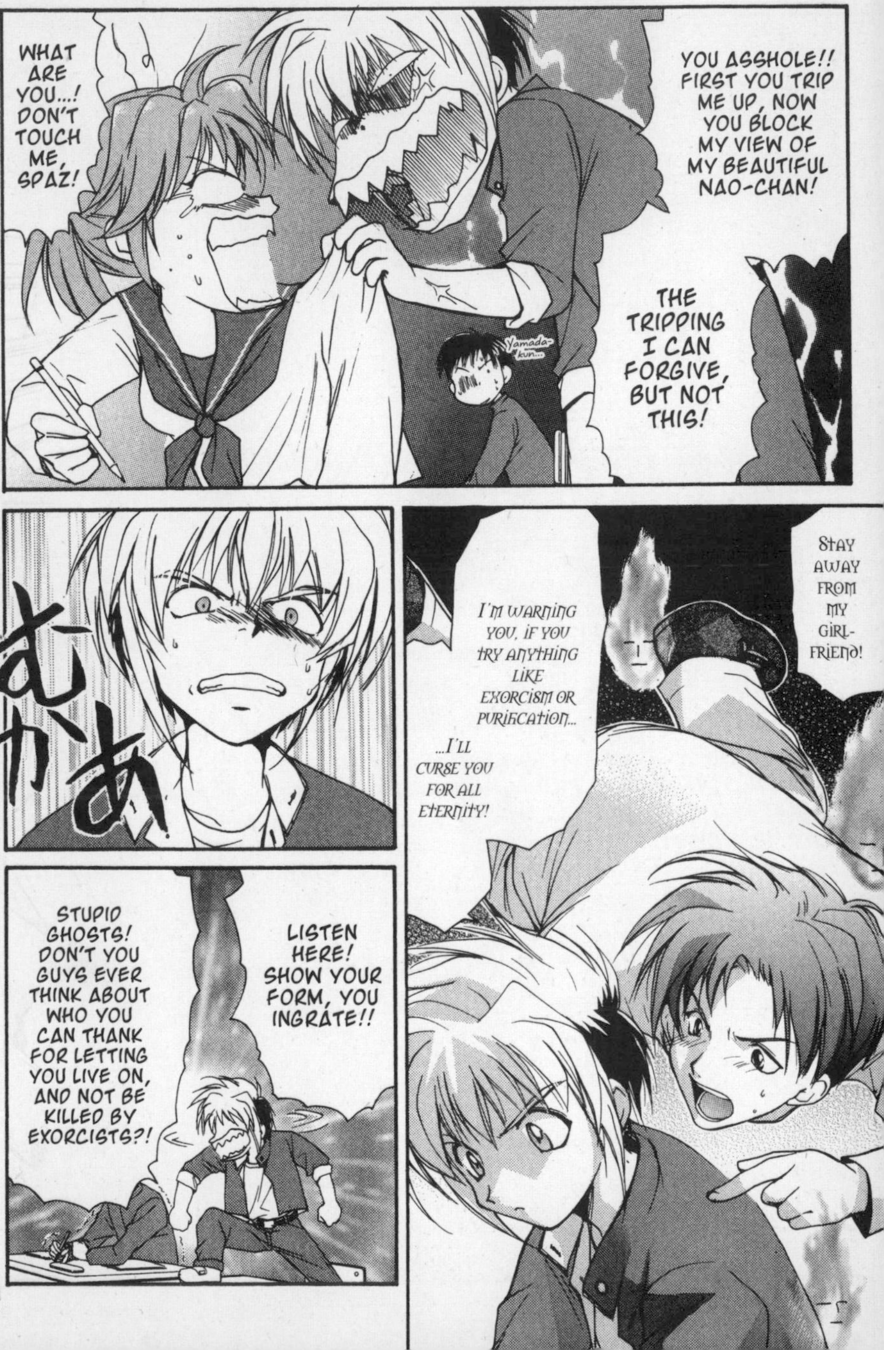
YOU ASSHOLE!! FIRST YOU TRIP ME UP, NOW YOU BLOCK MY VIEW OF MY BEAUTIFUL NAO-CHAN!
WHAT ARE YOU...! DON'T TOUCH ME, SPAZ!
THE TRIPPING I CAN FORGIVE, BUT NOT THIS!
Yamada-kun...
STAY AWAY FROM MY GIRL-FRIEND!
I'M WARNING YOU, IF YOU TRY ANYTHING LIKE EXORCISM OR PURIFICATION...
...I'LL CURSE YOU FOR ALL ETERNITY!
むかあ
LISTEN HERE! SHOW YOUR FORM, YOU INGRATE!!
STUPID GHOSTS! DON'T YOU GUYS EVER THINK ABOUT WHO YOU CAN THANK FOR LETTING YOU LIVE ON, AND NOT BE KILLED BY EXORCISTS?!

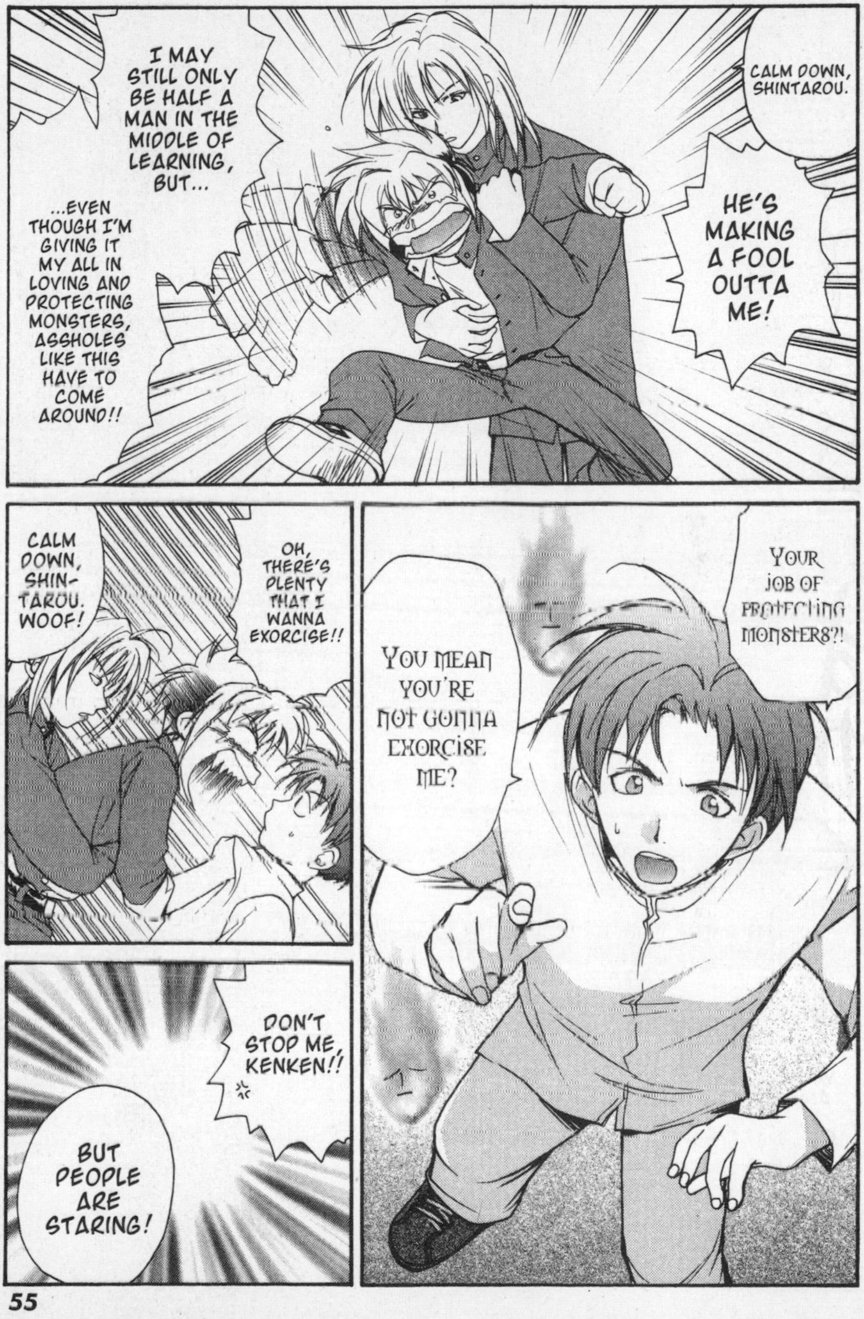
CALM DOWN, SHINTAROU.
HE'S MAKING A FOOL OUTTA ME!
I MAY STILL ONLY BE HALF A MAN IN THE MIDDLE OF LEARNING, BUT...
...EVEN THOUGH I'M GIVING IT MY ALL IN LOVING AND PROTECTING MONSTERS, ASSHOLES LIKE THIS HAVE TO COME AROUND!!
YOUR JOB OF PROTECTING MONSTERS?!
YOU MEAN YOU'RE NOT GONNA EXORCISE ME?
OH, THERE'S PLENTY THAT I WANNA EXORCISE!!
CALM DOWN, SHIN-TAROU. WOOF!
DON'T STOP ME, KENKEN!!
BUT PEOPLE ARE STARING!

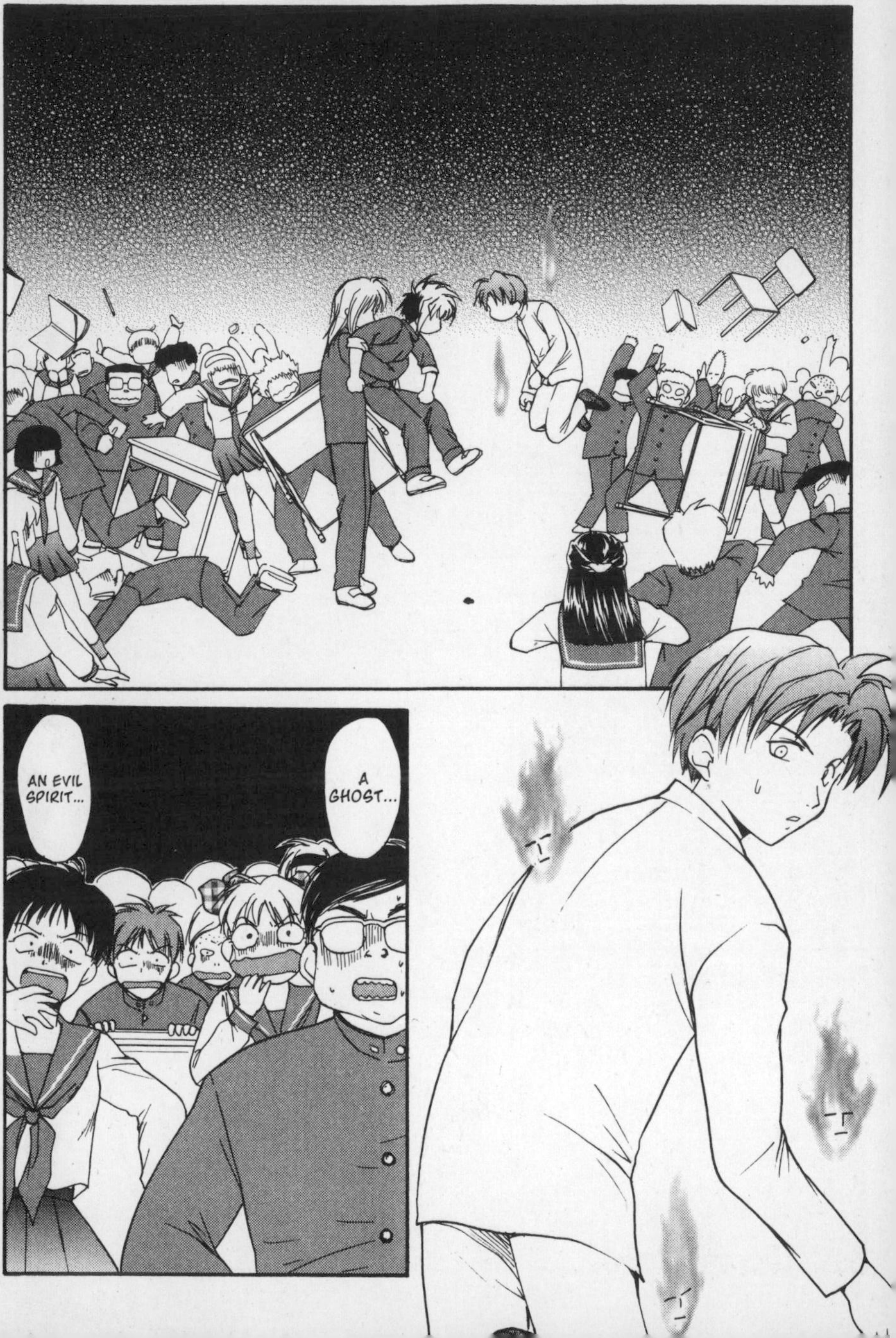
A GHOST...
AN EVIL SPIRIT...

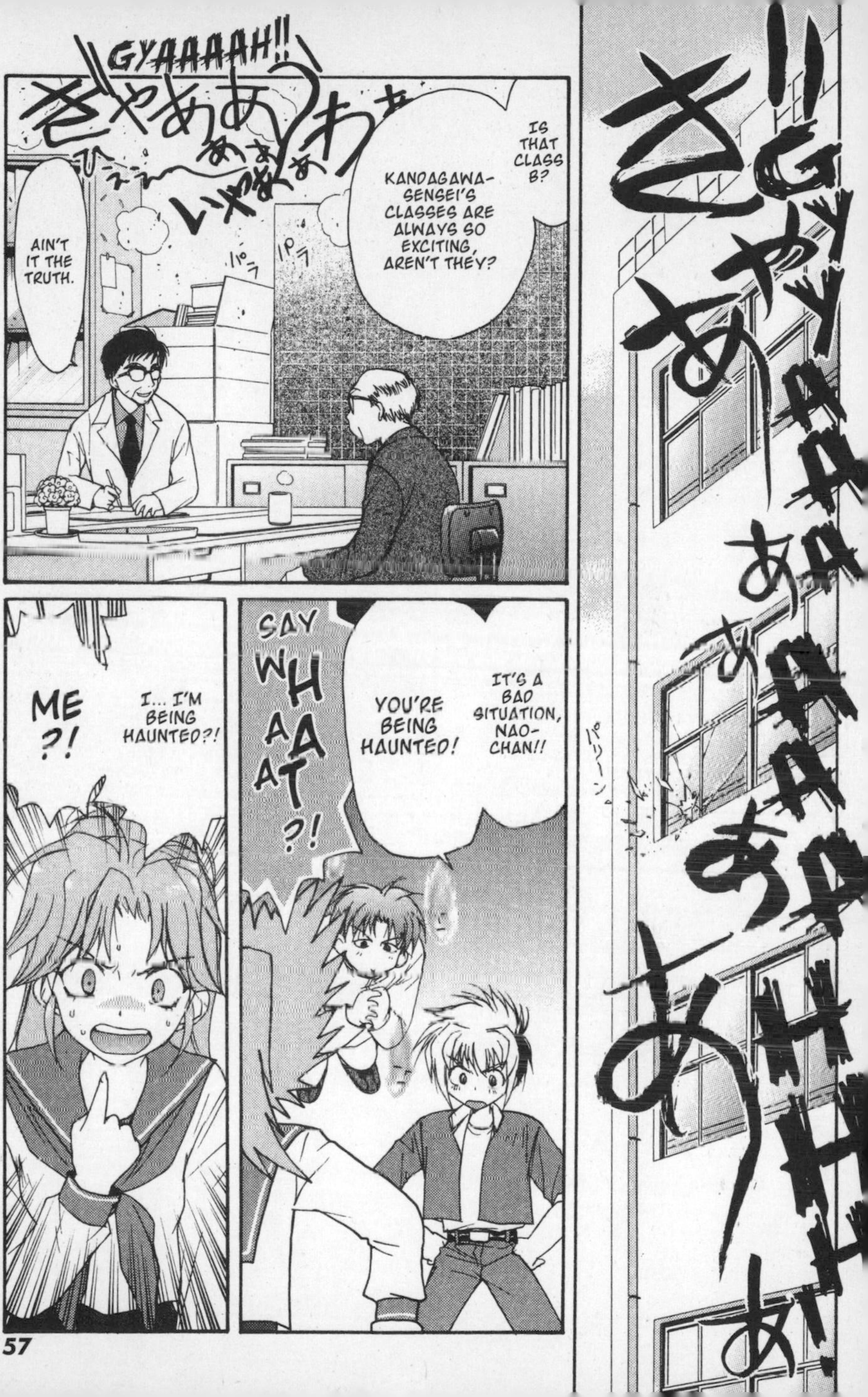
パリーン
GYAAAAH!!
IS THAT CLASS B?
KANDAGAWA-SENSEI'S CLASSES ARE ALWAYS SO EXCITING, AREN'T THEY?
AIN'T IT THE TRUTH.
IT'S A BAD SITUATION, NAO-CHAN!!
YOU'RE BEING HAUNTED!
SAY WHAAAT?!
I... I'M BEING HAUNTED?!
ME?!

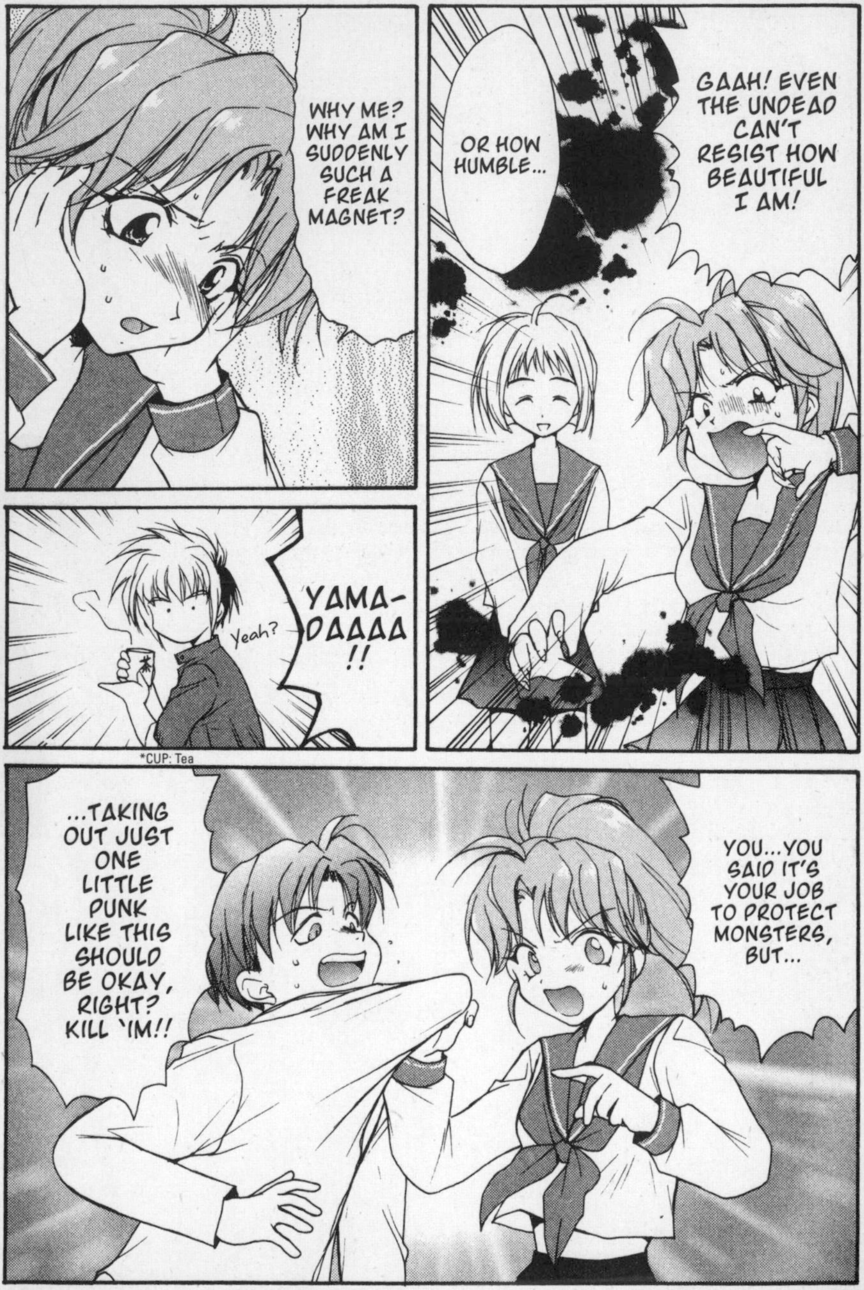
GAAH! EVEN THE UNDEAD CAN'T RESIST HOW BEAUTIFUL I AM!
OR HOW HUMBLE...
WHY ME? WHY AM I SUDDENLY SUCH A FREAK MAGNET?
YAMA-DAAAA!!
Yeah?
YOU...YOU SAID IT'S YOUR JOB TO PROTECT MONSTERS, BUT...
...TAKING OUT JUST ONE LITTLE PUNK LIKE THIS SHOULD BE OKAY, RIGHT? KILL 'IM!!
*CUP: Tea

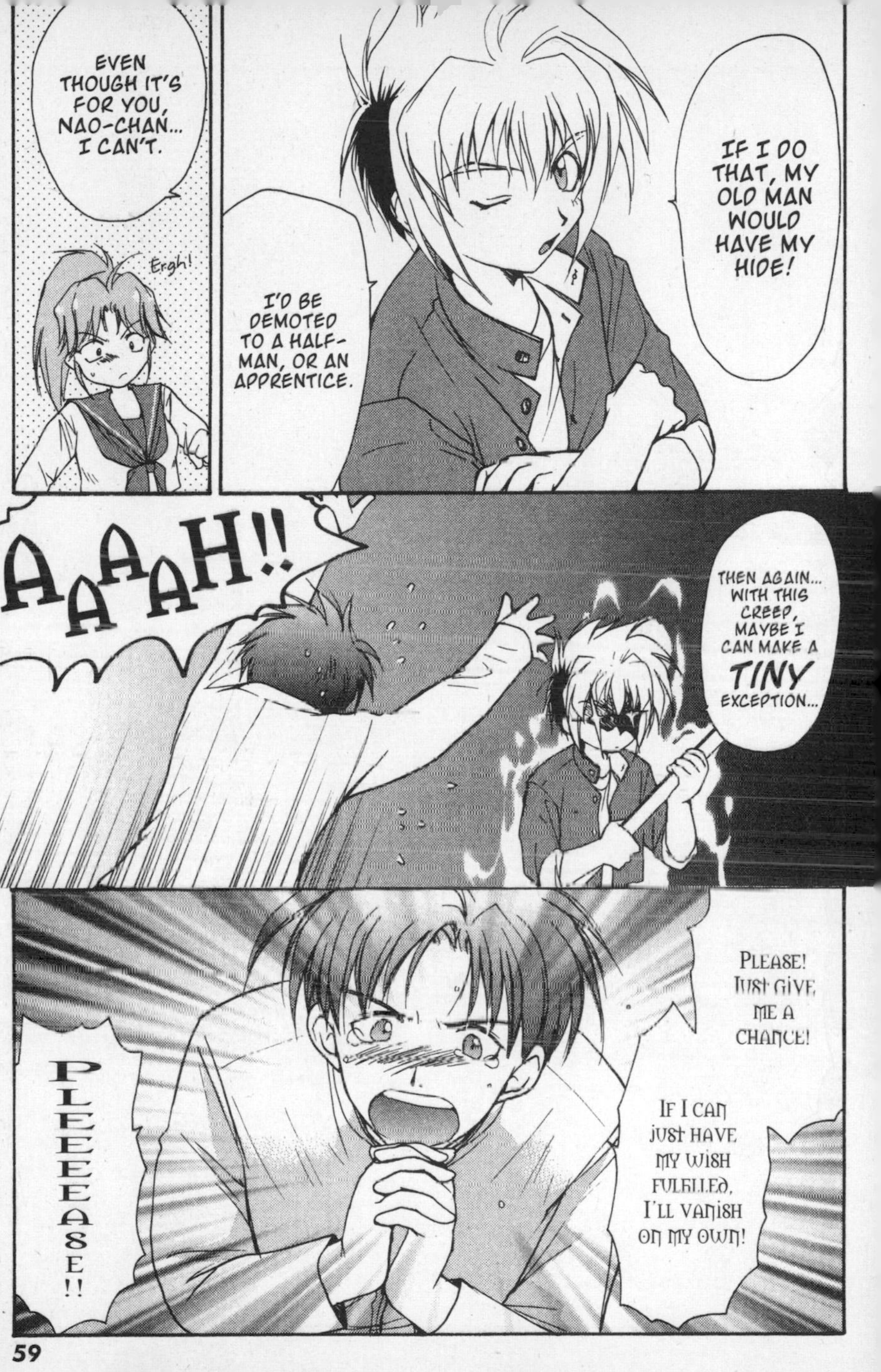
IF I DO THAT, MY OLD MAN WOULD HAVE MY HIDE!
I'D BE DEMOTED TO A HALF-MAN, OR AN APPRENTICE.
EVEN THOUGH IT'S FOR YOU, NAO-CHAN... I CAN'T.
Ergh!
THEN AGAIN... WITH THIS CREEP, MAYBE I CAN MAKE A TINY EXCEPTION...
AAAAH!!
PLEASE! JUST GIVE ME A CHANCE!
IF I CAN JUST HAVE MY WISH FULFILLED, I'LL VANISH ON MY OWN!
PLEEEEEASE!!

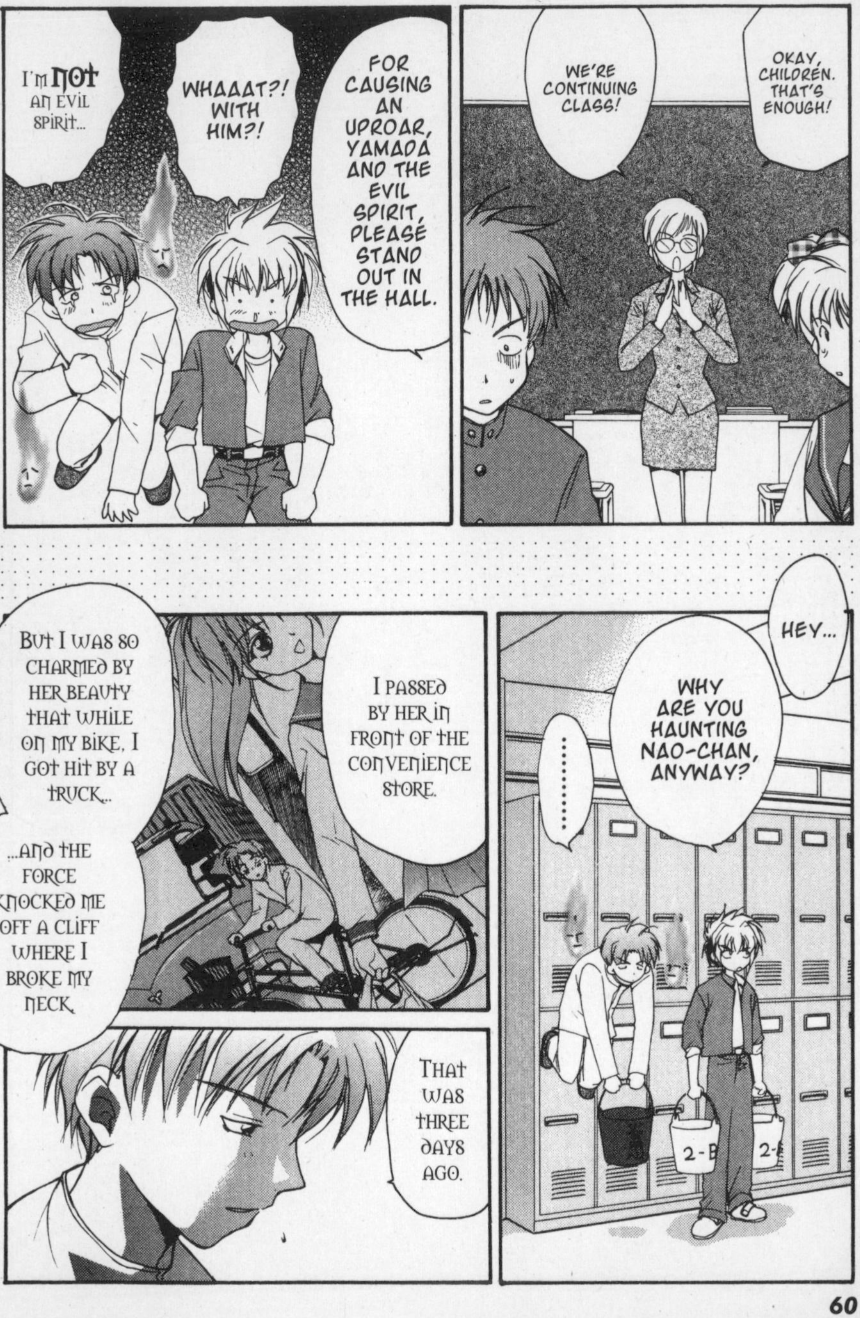
OKAY, CHILDREN. THAT'S ENOUGH!
WE'RE CONTINUING CLASS!
FOR CAUSING AN UPROAR, YAMADA AND THE EVIL SPIRIT, PLEASE STAND OUT IN THE HALL.
WHAAAT?! WITH HIM?!
I'm NOT an evil spirit...
HEY...
WHY ARE YOU HAUNTING NAO-CHAN, ANYWAY?
....
I passed by her in front of the convenience store.
But I was so charmed by her beauty that while on my bike, I got hit by a truck...
...and the force knocked me off a cliff where I broke my neck.
That was three days ago.

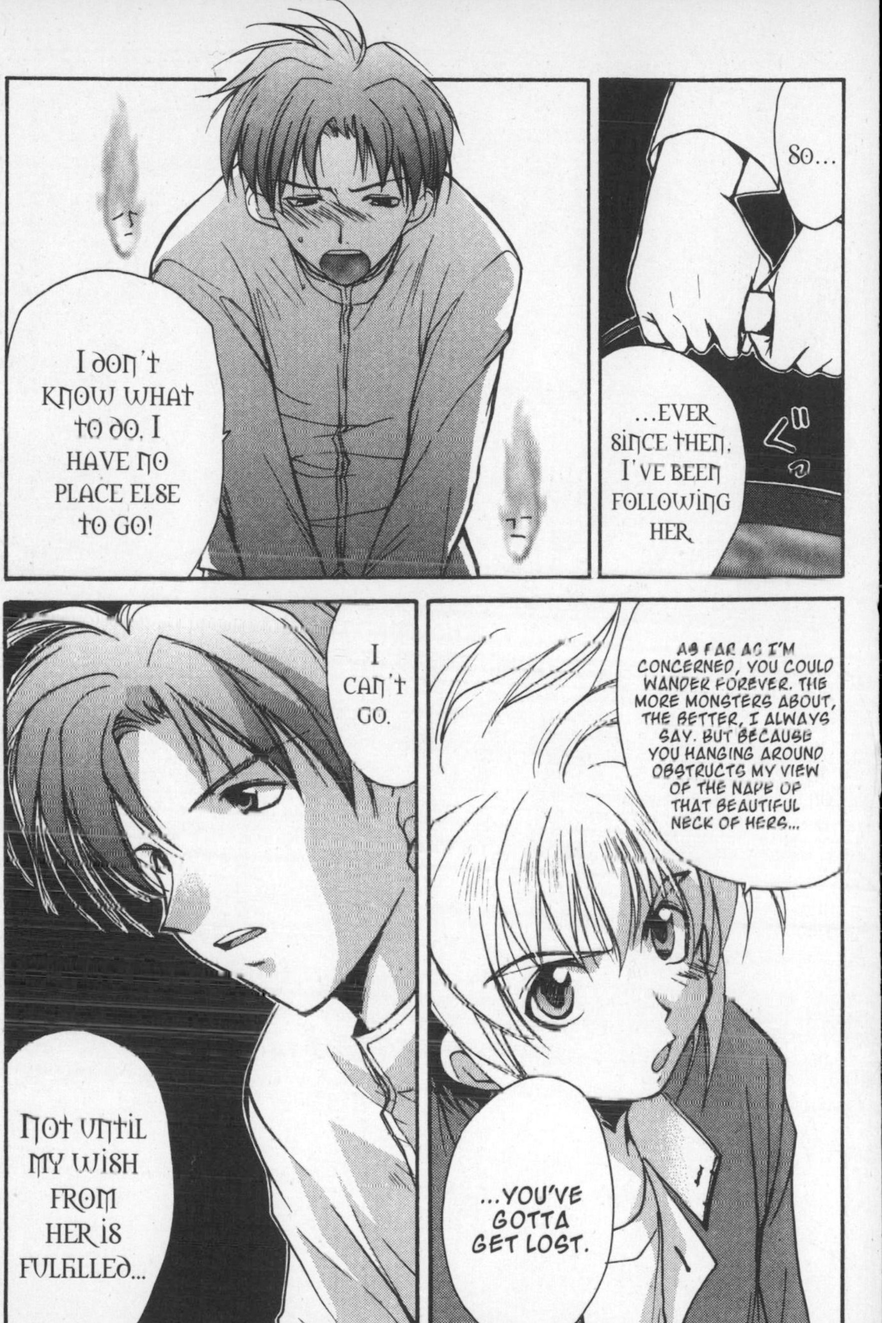
SO...
...EVER SINCE THEN, I'VE BEEN FOLLOWING HER.
I DON'T KNOW WHAT TO DO. I HAVE NO PLACE ELSE TO GO!
AS FAR AS I'M CONCERNED, YOU COULD WANDER FOREVER. THE MORE MONSTERS ABOUT, THE BETTER, I ALWAYS SAY. BUT BECAUSE YOU HANGING AROUND OBSTRUCTS MY VIEW OF THE NAPE OF THAT BEAUTIFUL NECK OF HERS...
...YOU'VE GOTTA GET LOST.
I CAN'T GO.
NOT UNTIL MY WISH FROM HER IS FULFILLED...

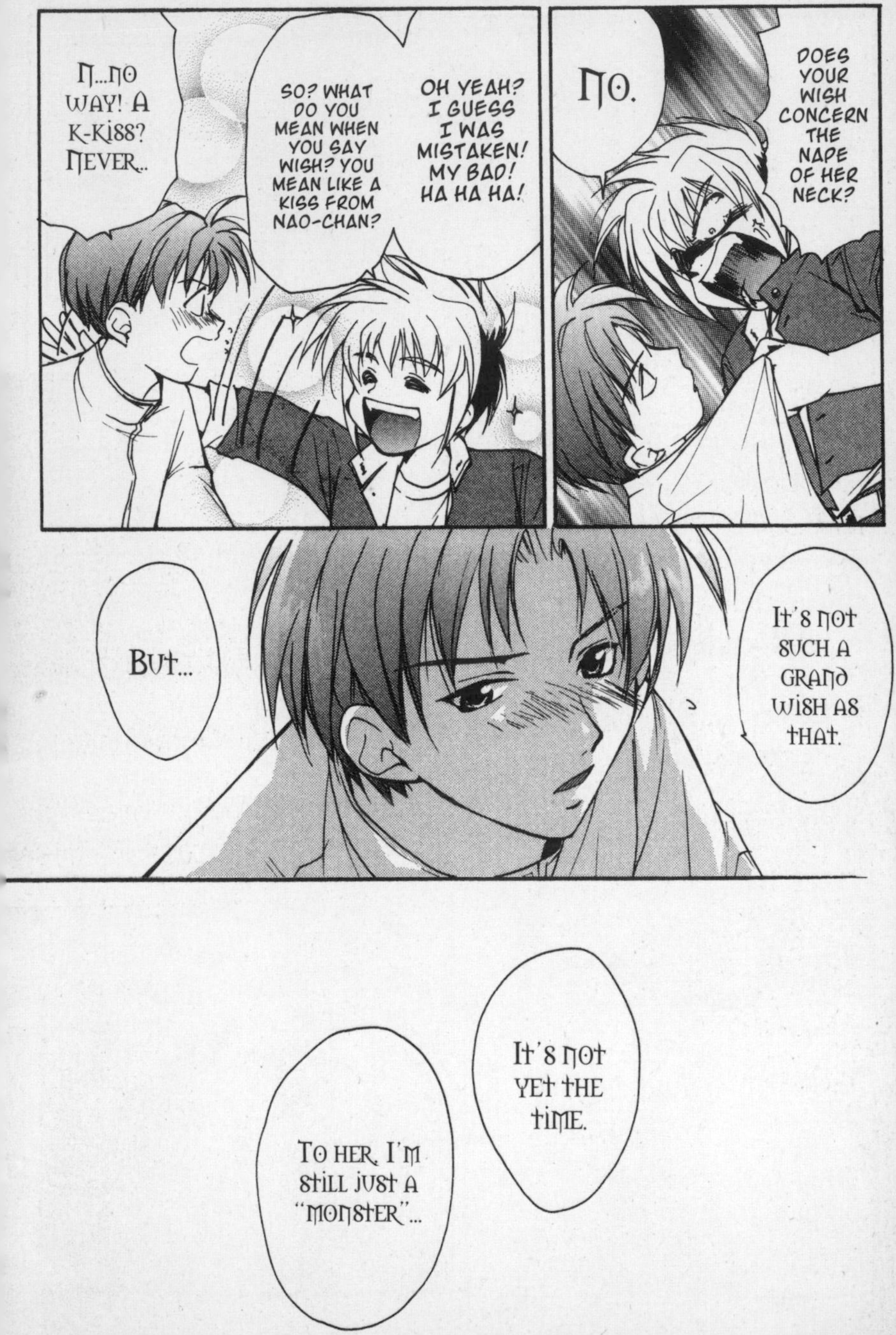
DOES YOUR WISH CONCERN THE NAPE OF HER NECK?
NO.
OH YEAH? I GUESS I WAS MISTAKEN! MY BAD! HA HA HA!
SO? WHAT DO YOU MEAN WHEN YOU SAY WISH? YOU MEAN LIKE A KISS FROM NAO-CHAN?
N...NO WAY! A K-KISS? NEVER...
It's not such a grand wish as that.
But...
It's not yet the time.
To her, I'm still just a "monster"...

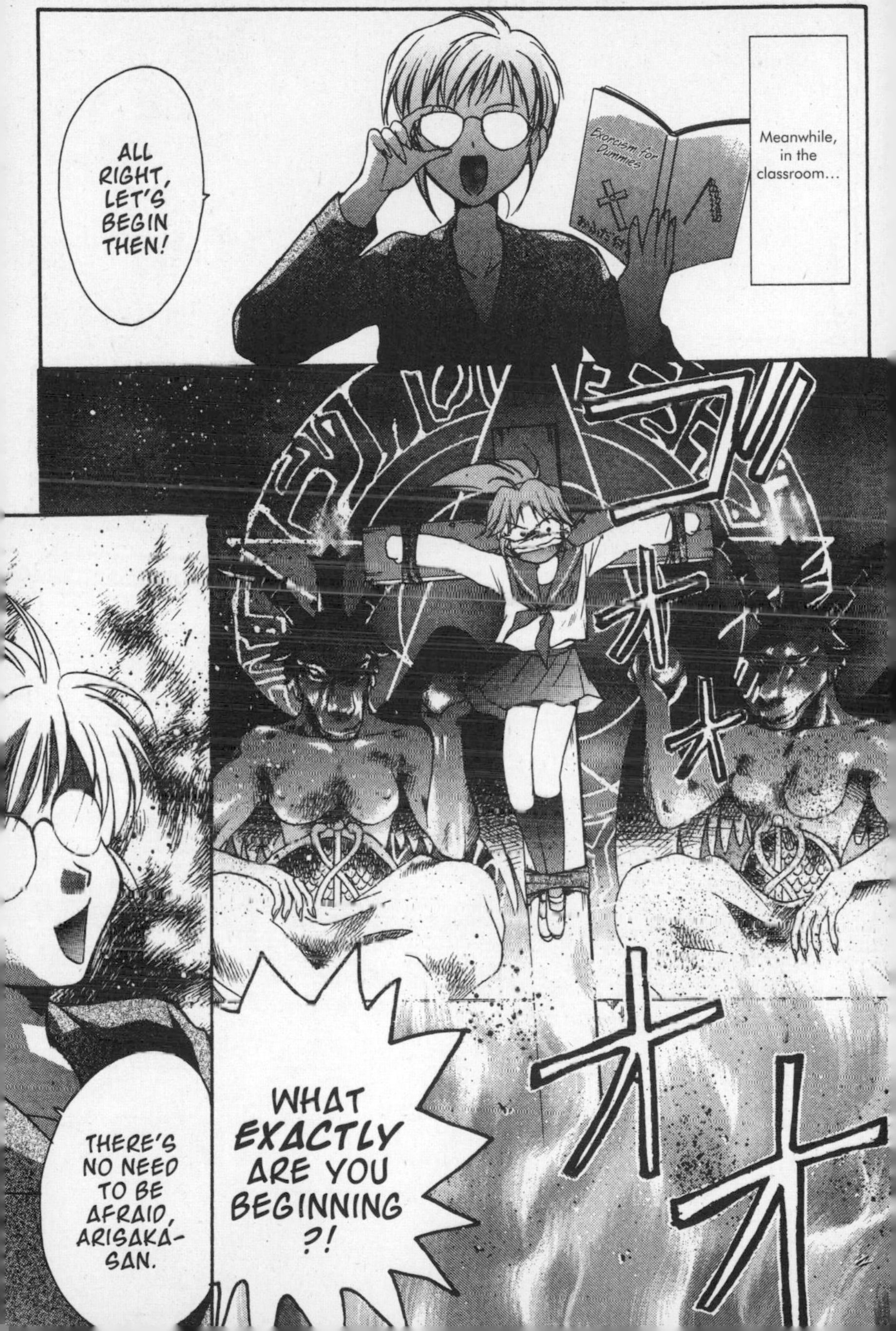
Meanwhile, in the classroom…
ALL RIGHT, LET'S BEGIN THEN!
Exorcism for Dummies
WHAT EXACTLY ARE YOU BEGINNING?!
THERE'S NO NEED TO BE AFRAID, ARISAKA-SAN.

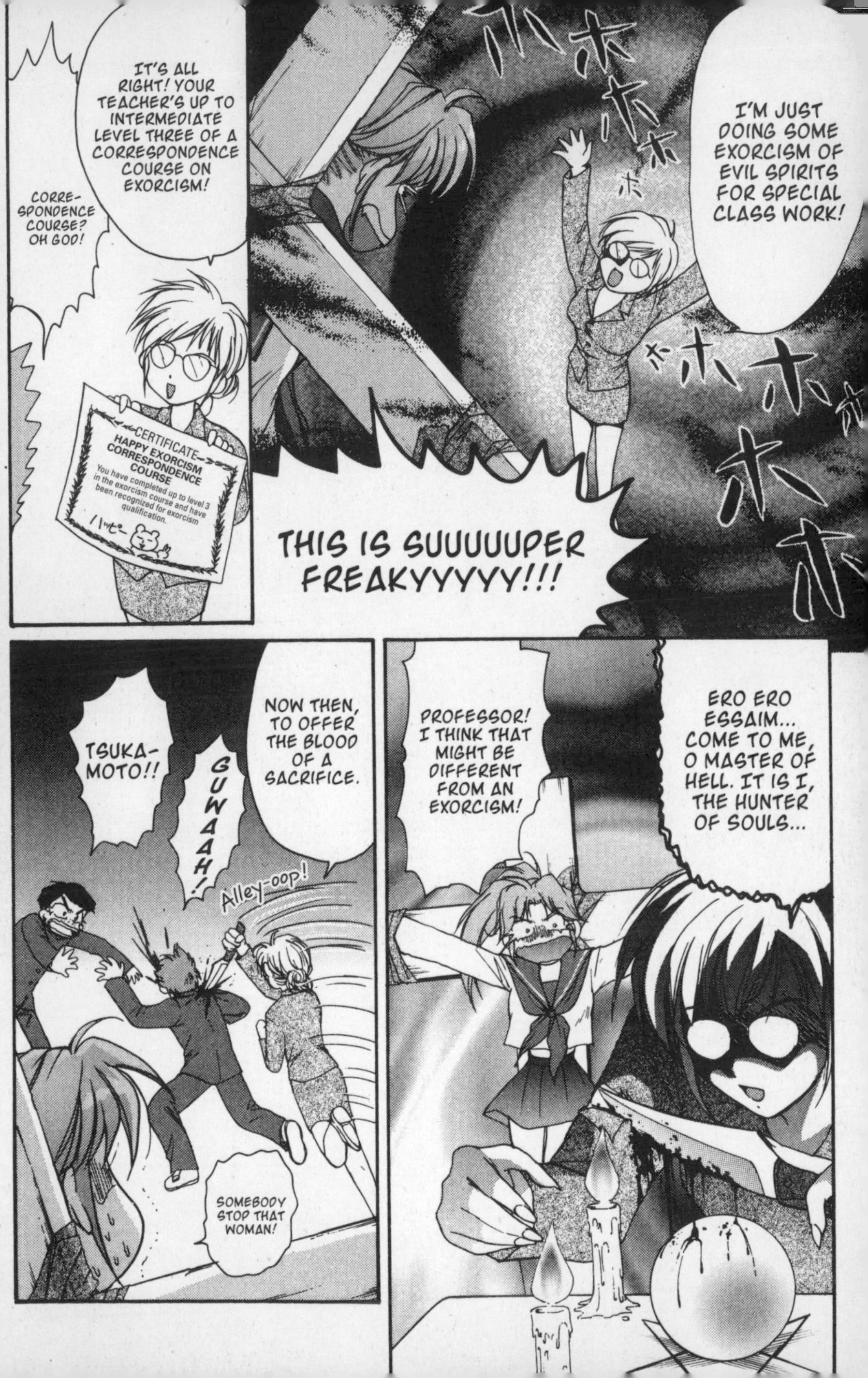
I'M JUST DOING SOME EXORCISM OF EVIL SPIRITS FOR SPECIAL CLASS WORK!
THIS IS SUUUUUPER FREAKYYYYY!!!
IT'S ALL RIGHT! YOUR TEACHER'S UP TO INTERMEDIATE LEVEL THREE OF A CORRESPONDENCE COURSE ON EXORCISM!
CORRE-SPONDENCE COURSE? OH GOD!
CERTIFICATE
HAPPY EXORCISM CORRESPONDENCE COURSE
You have completed up to level 3 in the exorcism course and have been recognized for exorcism qualification.
ERO ERO ESSAIM... COME TO ME, O MASTER OF HELL. IT IS I, THE HUNTER OF SOULS...
PROFESSOR! I THINK THAT MIGHT BE DIFFERENT FROM AN EXORCISM!
NOW THEN, TO OFFER THE BLOOD OF A SACRIFICE.
TSUKA-MOTO!!
GUWAAAH!
Alley-oop!
SOMEBODY STOP THAT WOMAN!

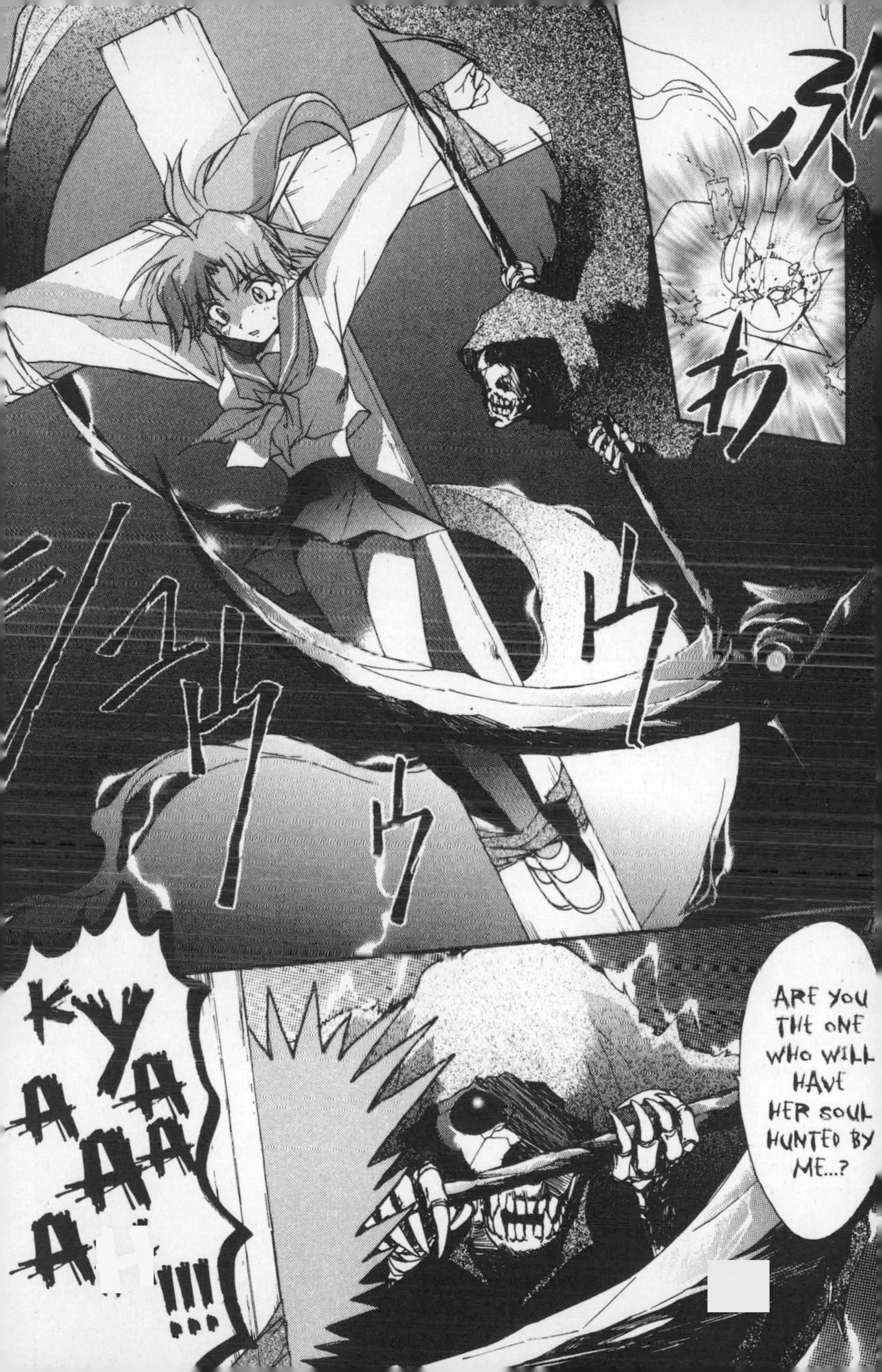
ARE YOU THE ONE WHO WILL HAVE HER SOUL HUNTED BY ME...?
KYAAAAAAH!!!

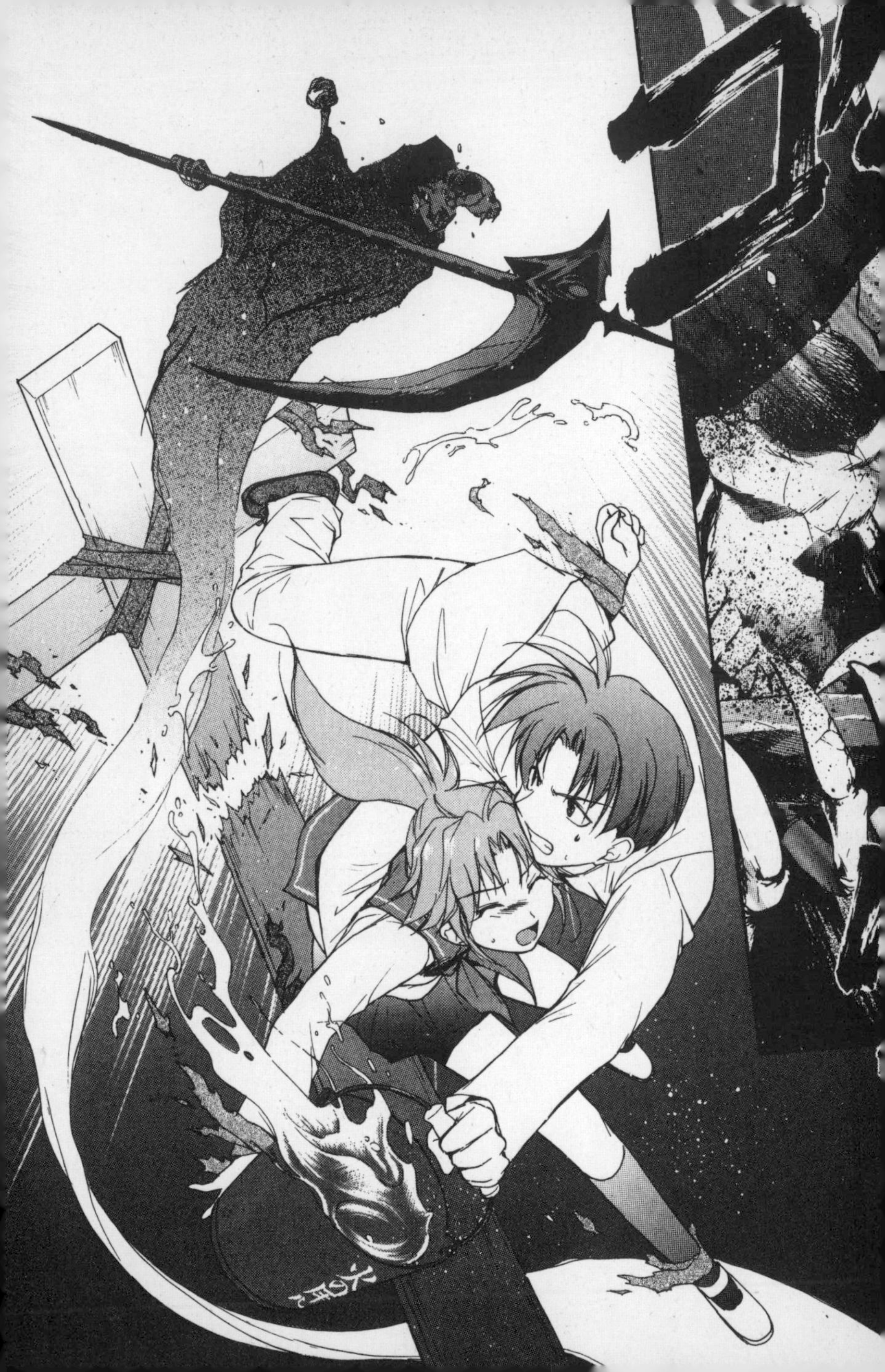
火の用

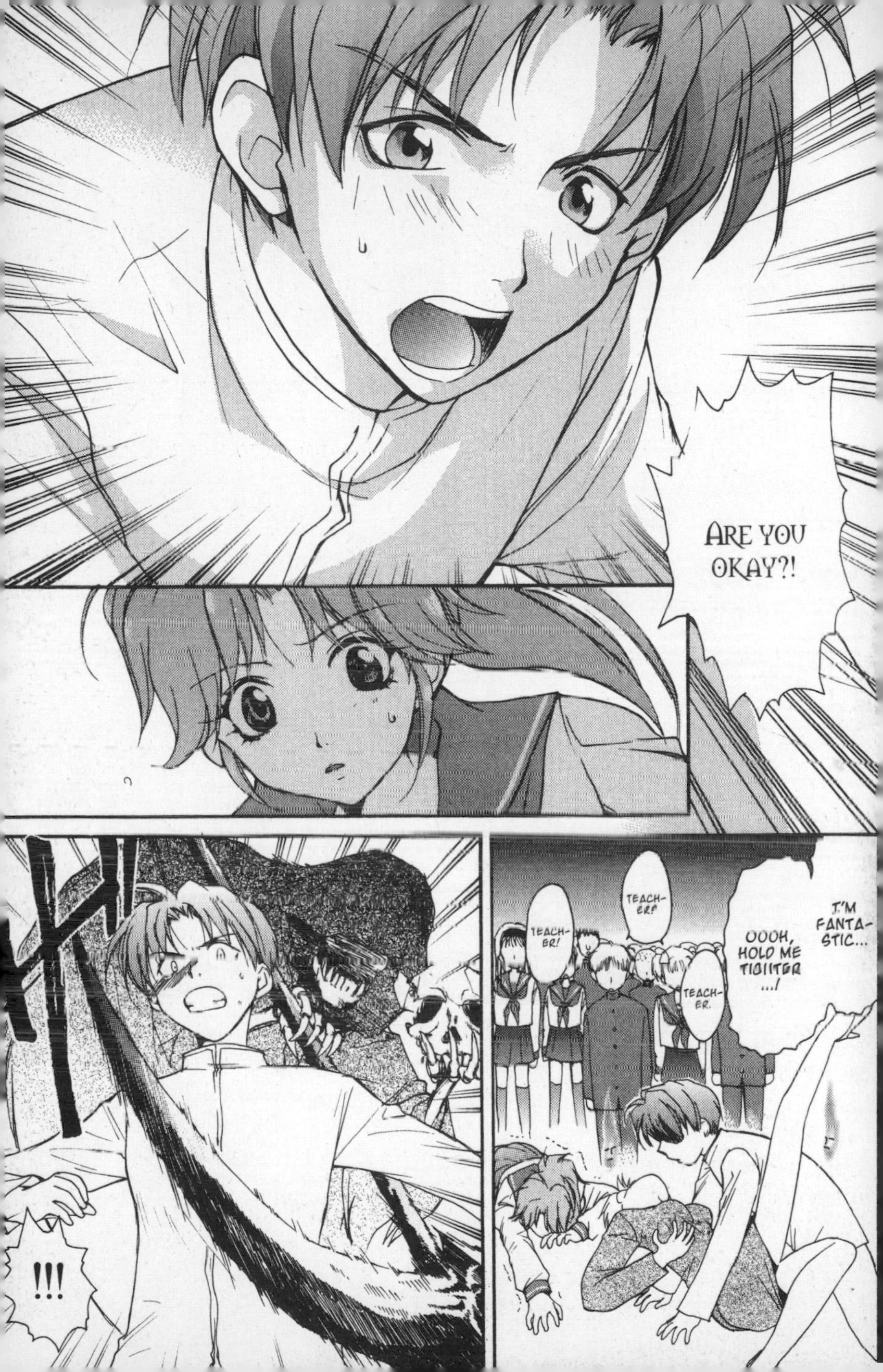
ARE YOU OKAY?!
I'M FANTASTIC...
OOOH, HOLD ME TIGHTER ...!
TEACHER?
TEACHER.
TEACHER!
!!!

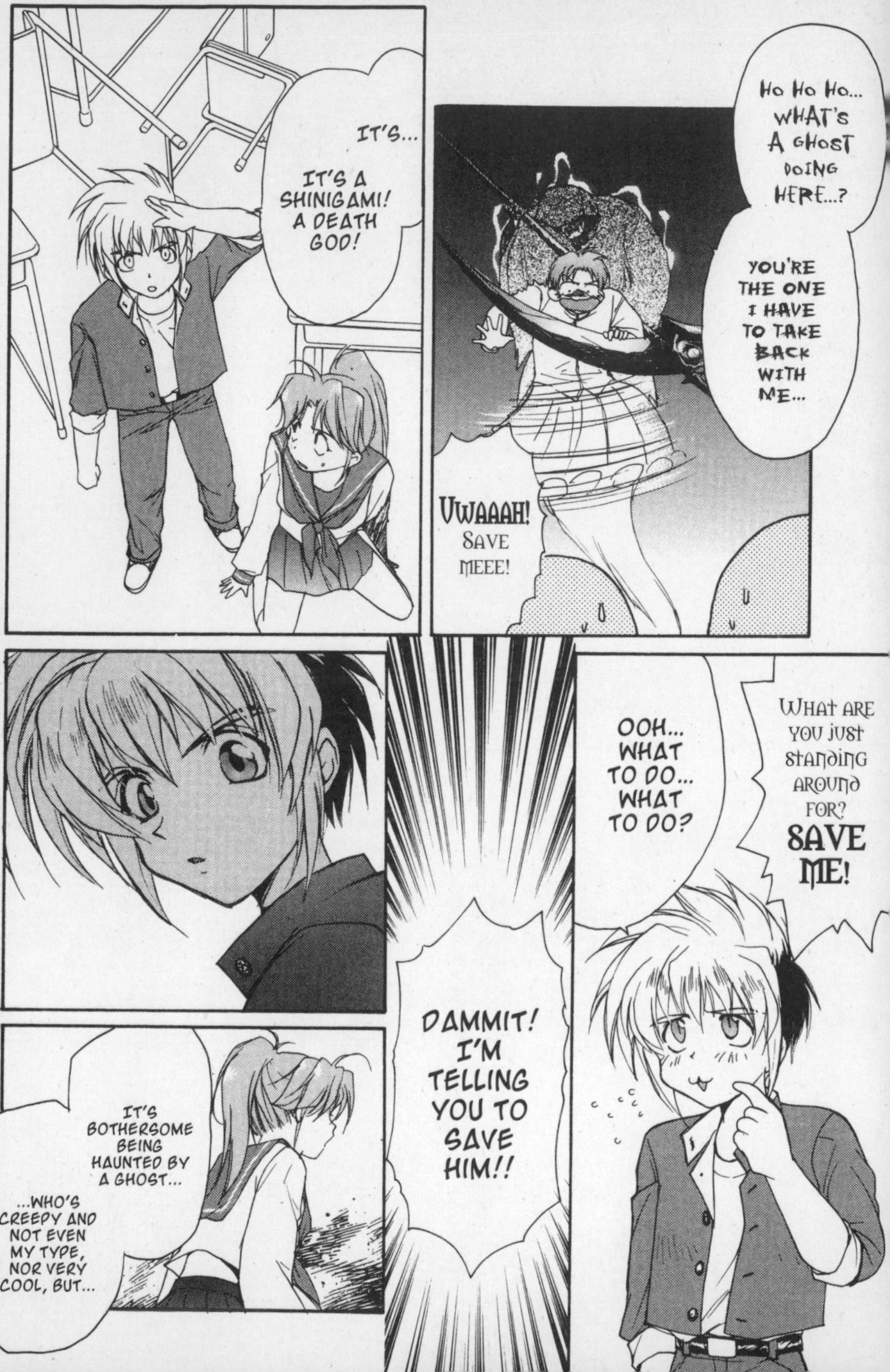
Ho Ho Ho... WHAT's A GHOST DOING HERE...?
YOU'RE THE ONE I HAVE TO TAKE BACK WITH ME...
UWAAAH! SAVE MEEE!
IT'S...
IT'S A SHINIGAMI! A DEATH GOD!
What ARE YOU just standing AROUND FOR? SAVE ME!
OOH... WHAT TO DO... WHAT TO DO?
DAMMIT! I'M TELLING YOU TO SAVE HIM!!
IT'S BOTHERSOME BEING HAUNTED BY A GHOST...
...WHO'S CREEPY AND NOT EVEN MY TYPE, NOR VERY COOL, BUT...

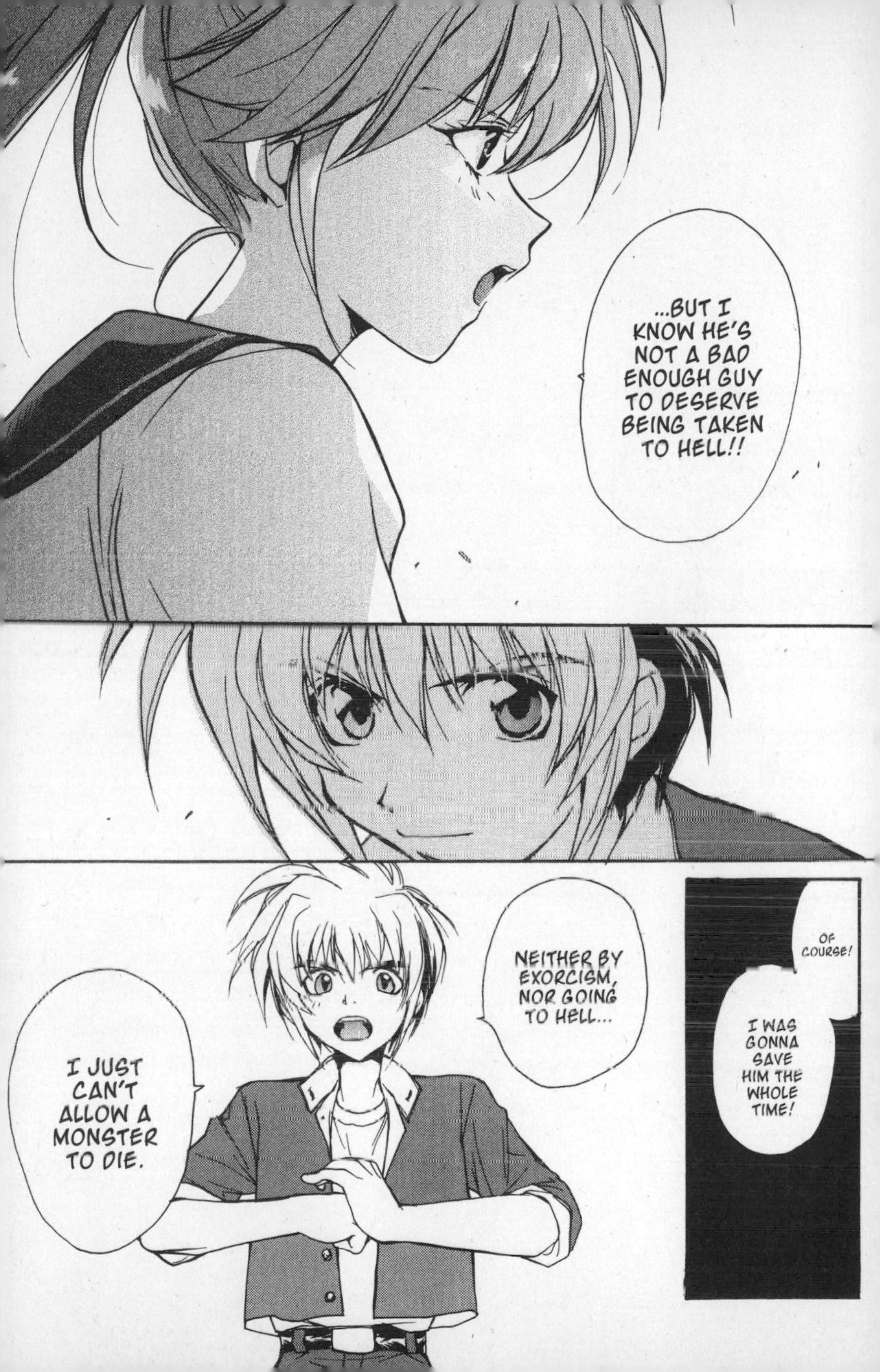
...BUT I KNOW HE'S NOT A BAD ENOUGH GUY TO DESERVE BEING TAKEN TO HELL!!
OF COURSE!
I WAS GONNA SAVE HIM THE WHOLE TIME!
NEITHER BY EXORCISM, NOR GOING TO HELL...
I JUST CAN'T ALLOW A MONSTER TO DIE.

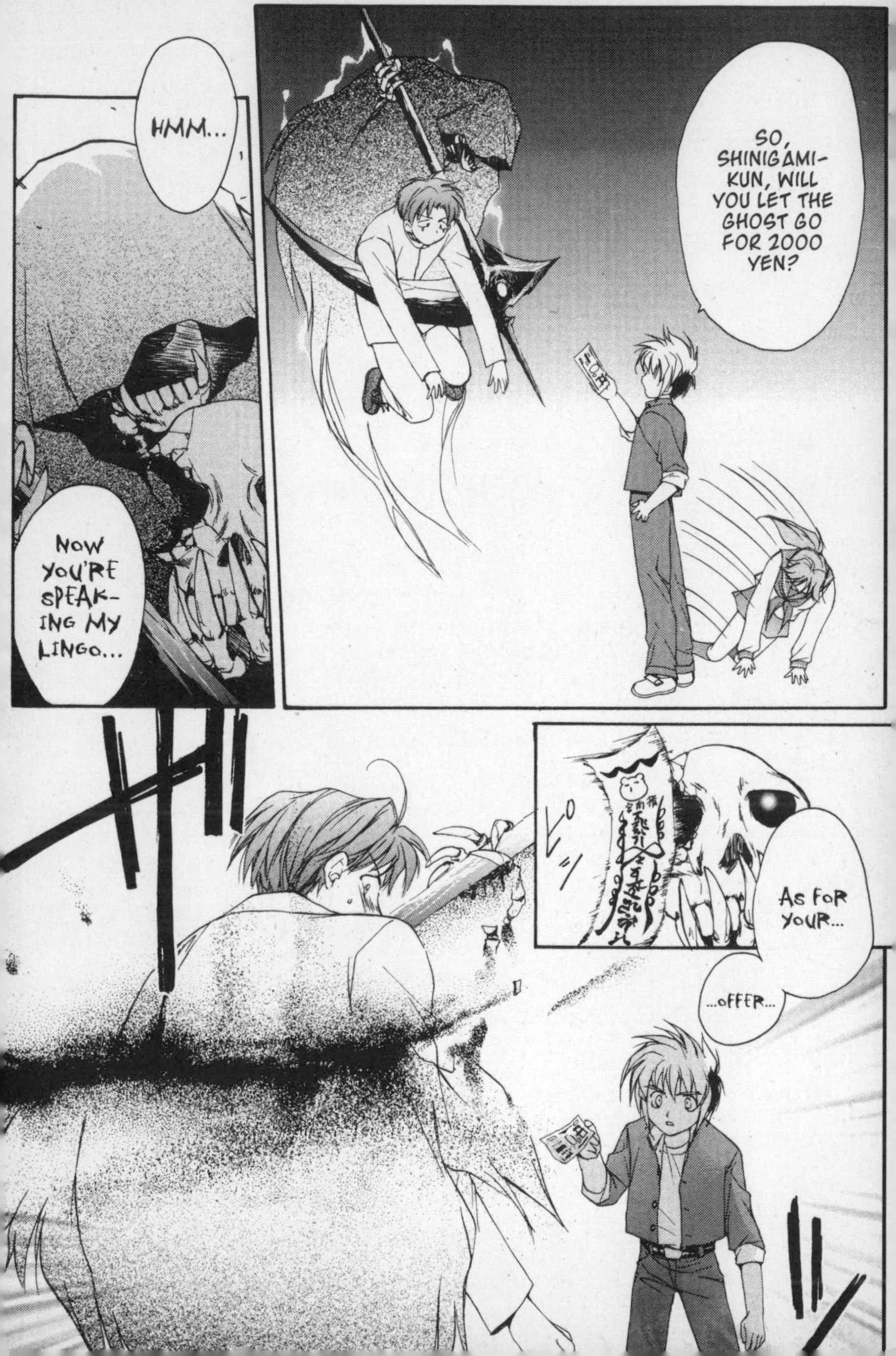
SO, SHINIGAMI-KUN, WILL YOU LET THE GHOST GO FOR 2000 YEN?
HMM...
NOW YOU'RE SPEAKING MY LINGO...
As FOR YOUR...
...OFFER...

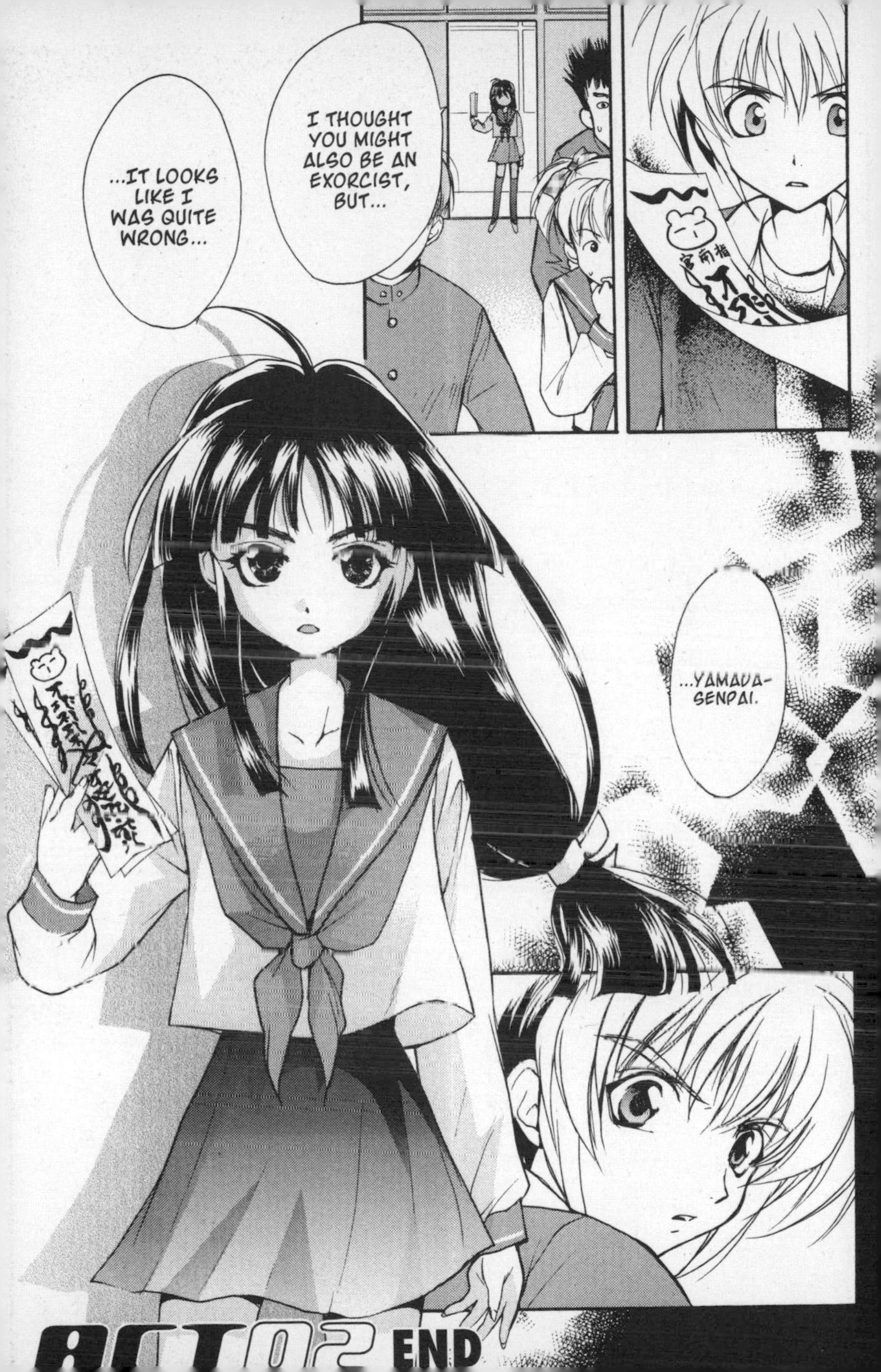
I THOUGHT YOU MIGHT ALSO BE AN EXORCIST, BUT...
...IT LOOKS LIKE I WAS QUITE WRONG...
...YAMADA-SENPAI.
ACT 02 END

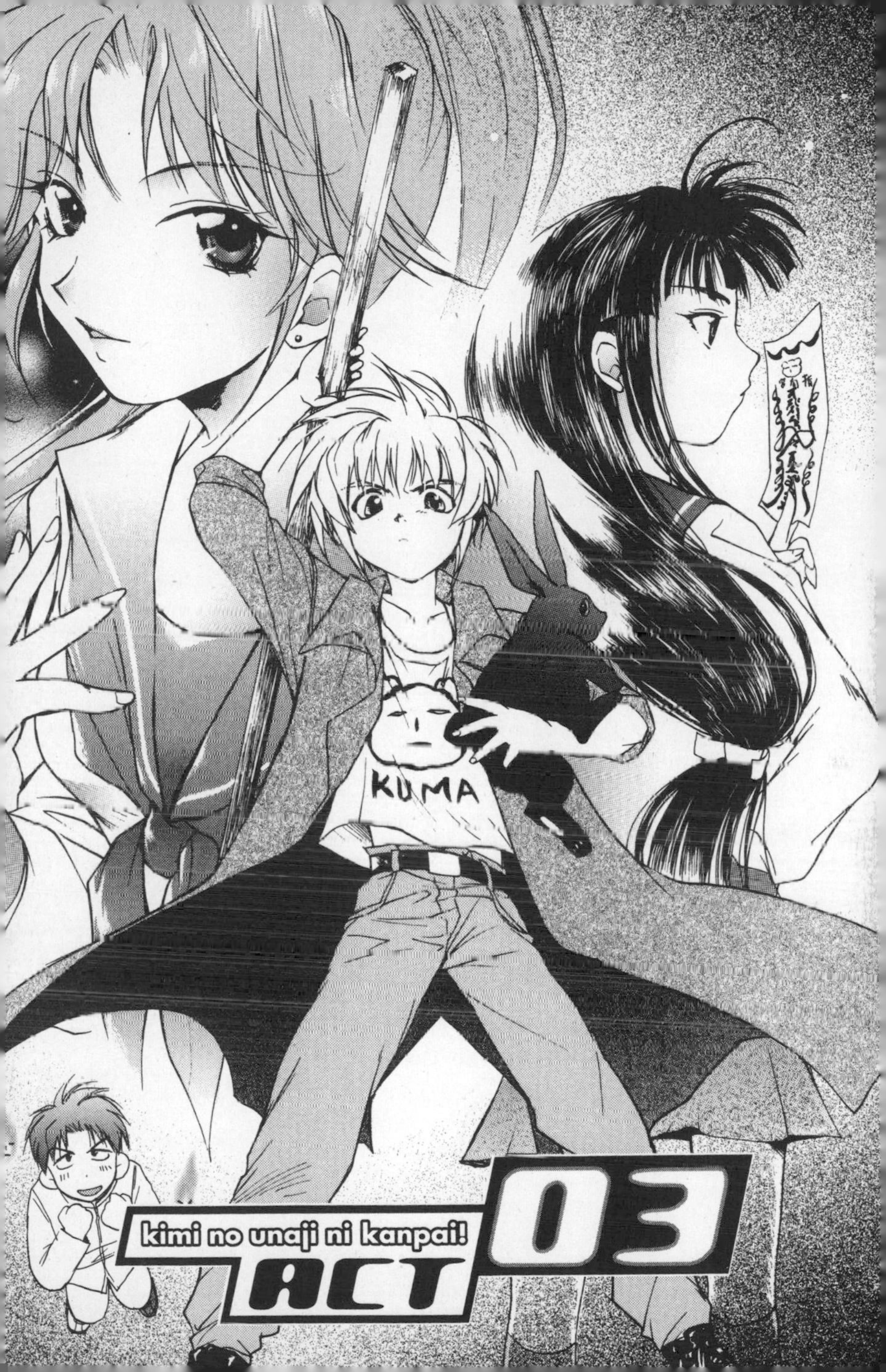
KUMA
kimi no unaji ni kanpai!
ACT 03

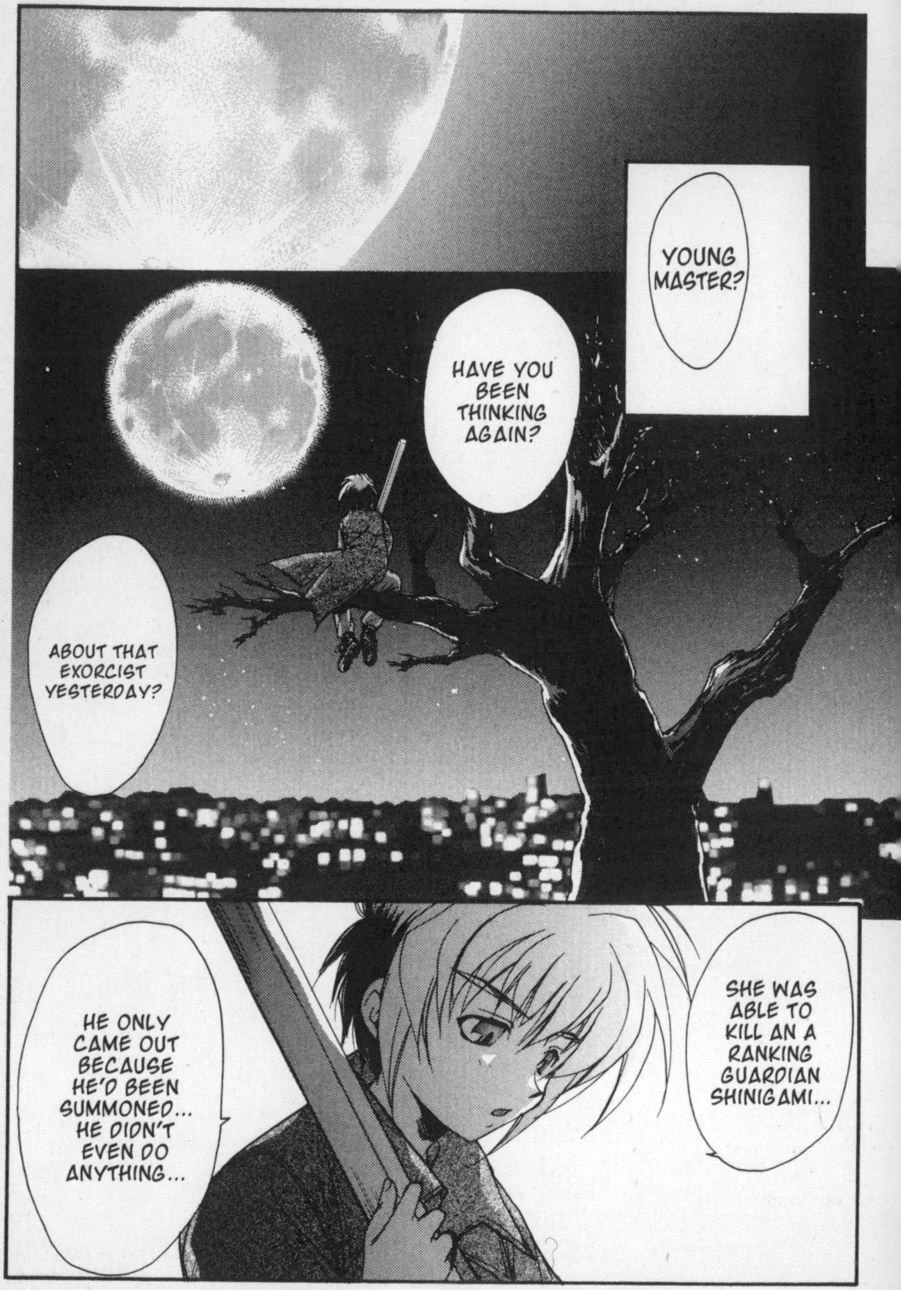
YOUNG MASTER?
HAVE YOU BEEN THINKING AGAIN?
ABOUT THAT EXORCIST YESTERDAY?
SHE WAS ABLE TO KILL AN A RANKING GUARDIAN SHINIGAMI...
HE ONLY CAME OUT BECAUSE HE'D BEEN SUMMONED... HE DIDN'T EVEN DO ANYTHING...

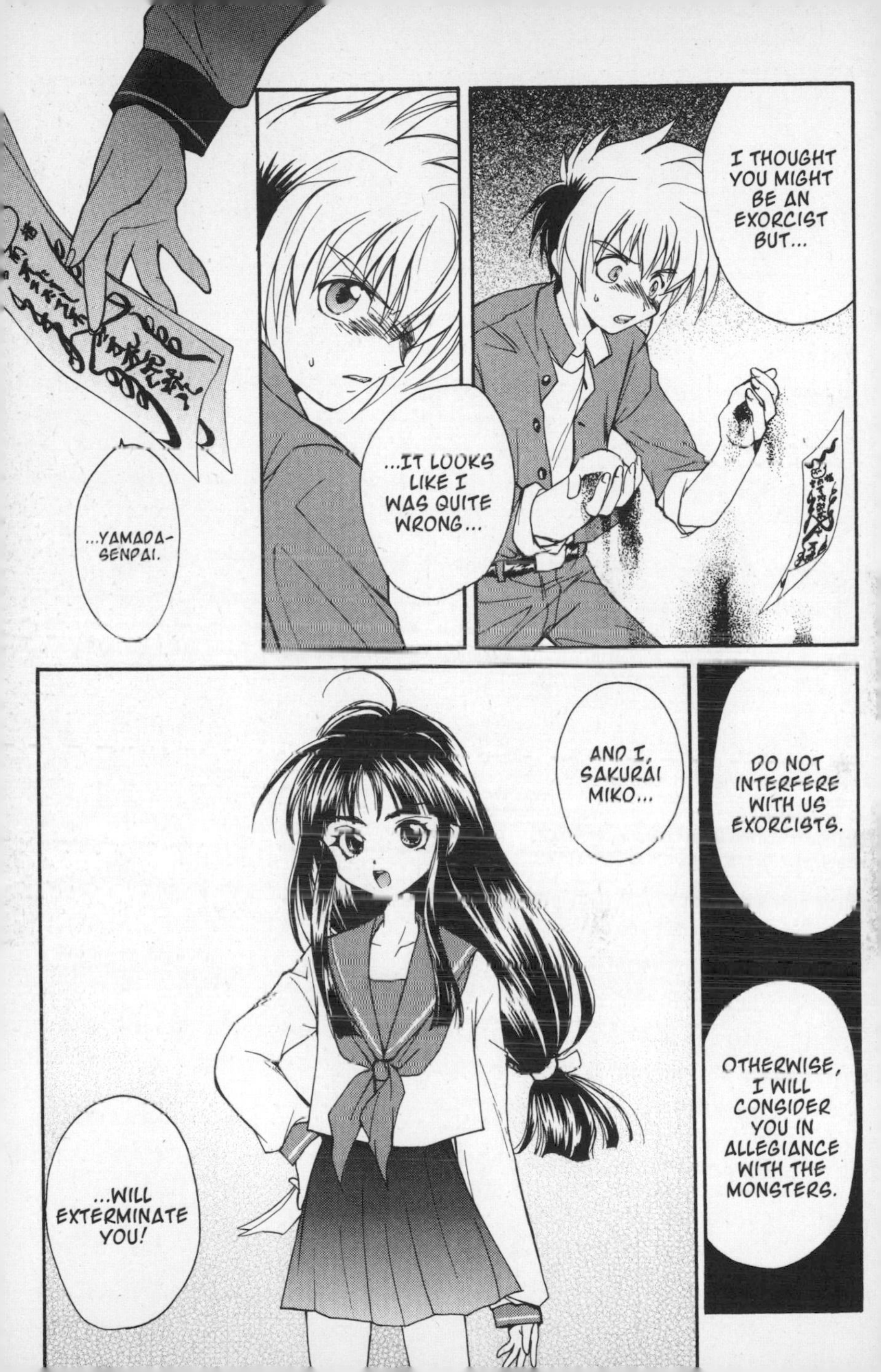
I THOUGHT YOU MIGHT BE AN EXORCIST BUT...
...IT LOOKS LIKE I WAS QUITE WRONG...
...YAMADA-SENPAI.
DO NOT INTERFERE WITH US EXORCISTS.
OTHERWISE, I WILL CONSIDER YOU IN ALLEGIANCE WITH THE MONSTERS.
AND I, SAKURAI MIKO...
...WILL EXTERMINATE YOU!

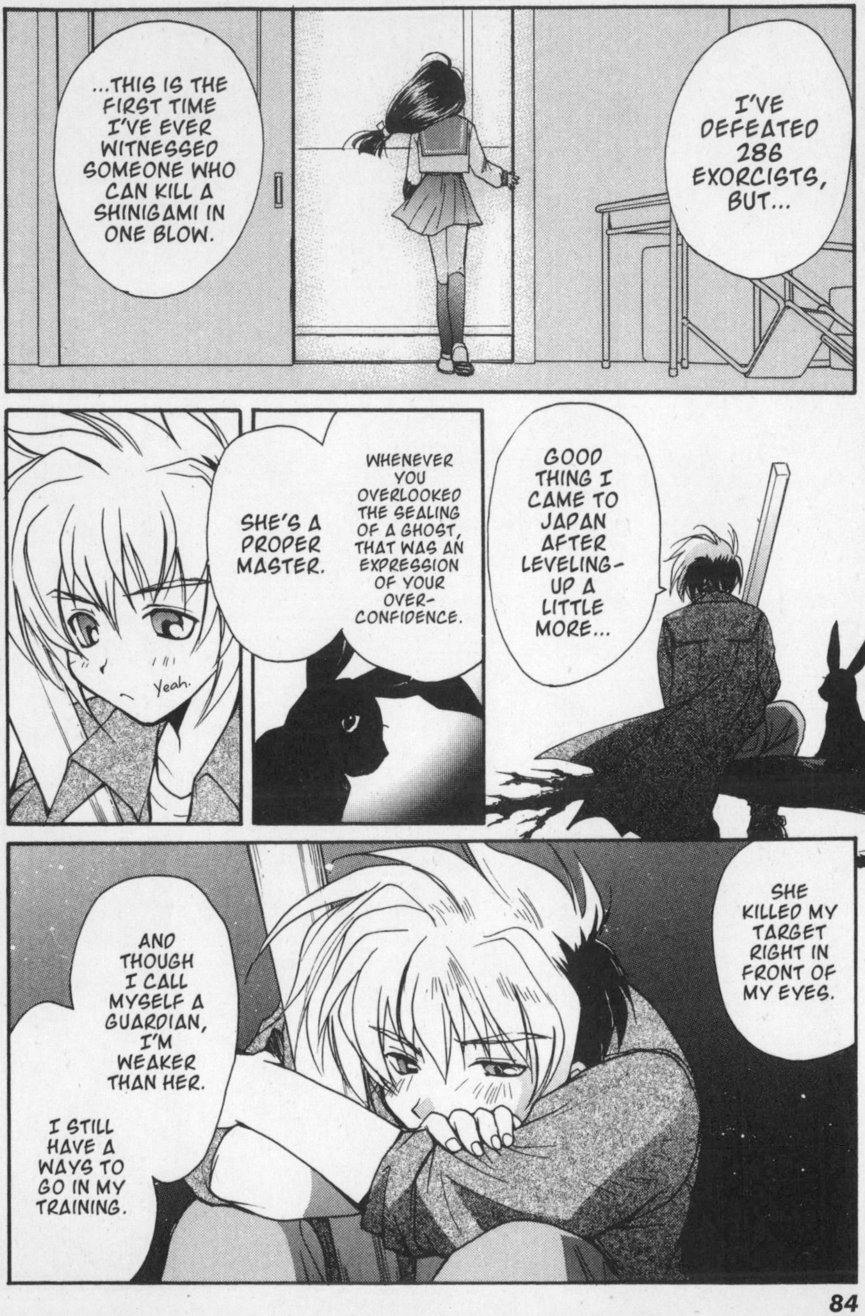
I'VE DEFEATED 286 EXORCISTS, BUT...
...THIS IS THE FIRST TIME I'VE EVER WITNESSED SOMEONE WHO CAN KILL A SHINIGAMI IN ONE BLOW.
GOOD THING I CAME TO JAPAN AFTER LEVELING-UP A LITTLE MORE...
WHENEVER YOU OVERLOOKED THE SEALING OF A GHOST, THAT WAS AN EXPRESSION OF YOUR OVER-CONFIDENCE.
SHE'S A PROPER MASTER.
Yeah.
SHE KILLED MY TARGET RIGHT IN FRONT OF MY EYES.
AND THOUGH I CALL MYSELF A GUARDIAN, I'M WEAKER THAN HER.
I STILL HAVE A WAYS TO GO IN MY TRAINING.

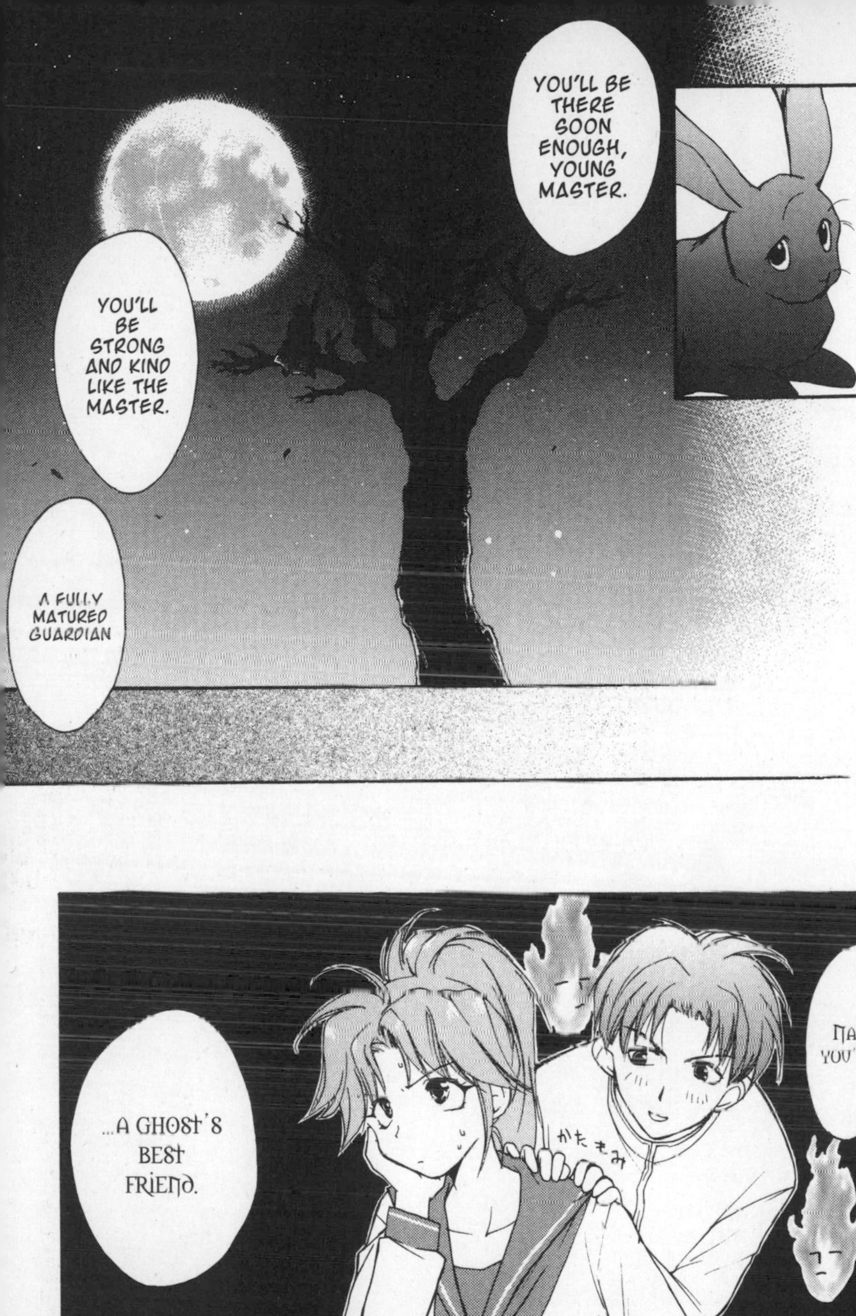
YOU'LL BE THERE SOON ENOUGH, YOUNG MASTER.
YOU'LL BE STRONG AND KIND LIKE THE MASTER.
A FULLY MATURED GUARDIAN
NAO, YOU'RE...
かたもみ
...A GHOST'S BEST FRIEND.

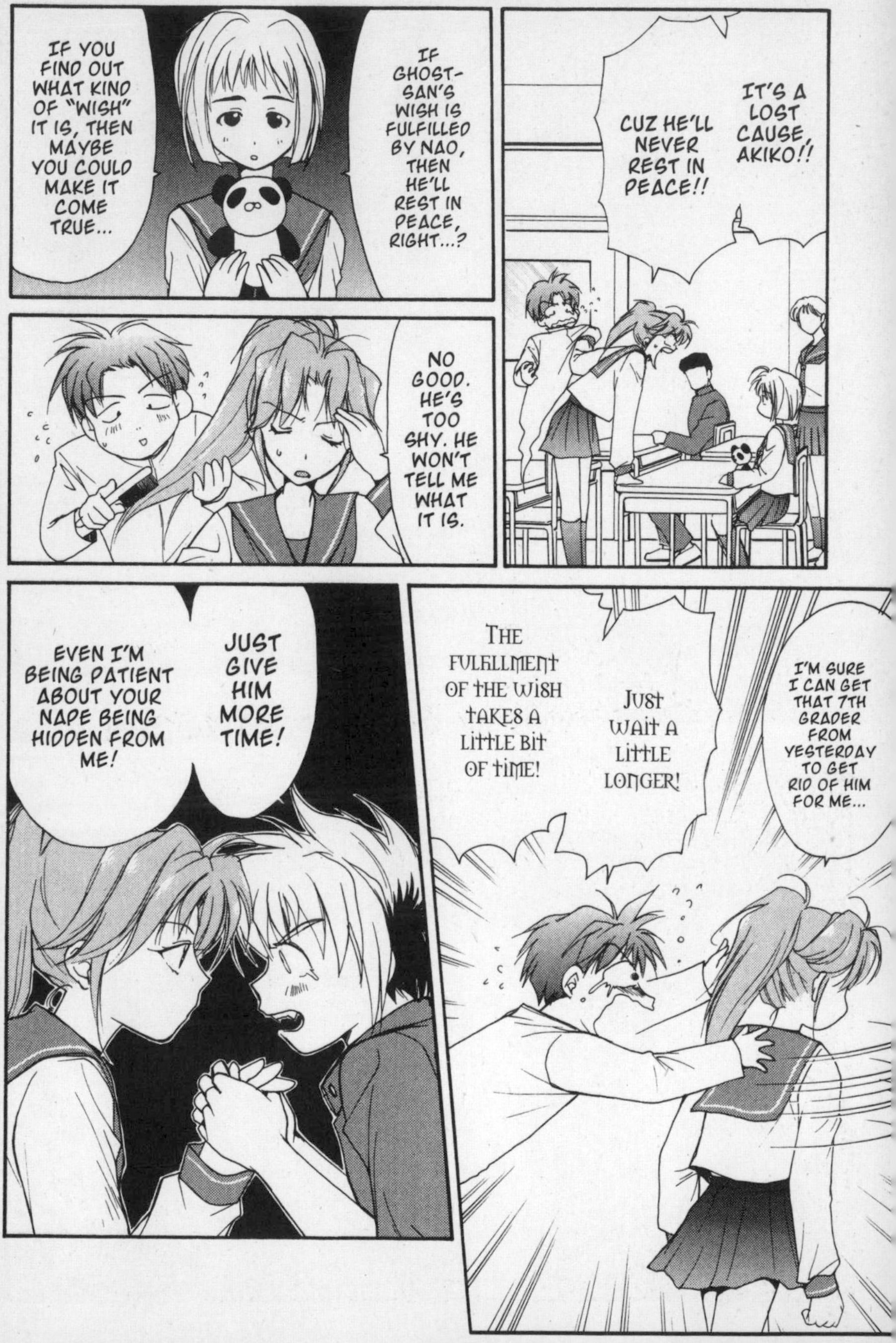
IT'S A LOST CAUSE, AKIKO!!
CUZ HE'LL NEVER REST IN PEACE!!
IF GHOST-SAN'S WISH IS FULFILLED BY NAO, THEN HE'LL REST IN PEACE, RIGHT...?
IF YOU FIND OUT WHAT KIND OF "WISH" IT IS, THEN MAYBE YOU COULD MAKE IT COME TRUE...
NO GOOD. HE'S TOO SHY. HE WON'T TELL ME WHAT IT IS.
I'M SURE I CAN GET THAT 7TH GRADER FROM YESTERDAY TO GET RID OF HIM FOR ME...
Just wait a little longer!
The fulfillment of the wish takes a little bit of time!
JUST GIVE HIM MORE TIME!
EVEN I'M BEING PATIENT ABOUT YOUR NAPE BEING HIDDEN FROM ME!

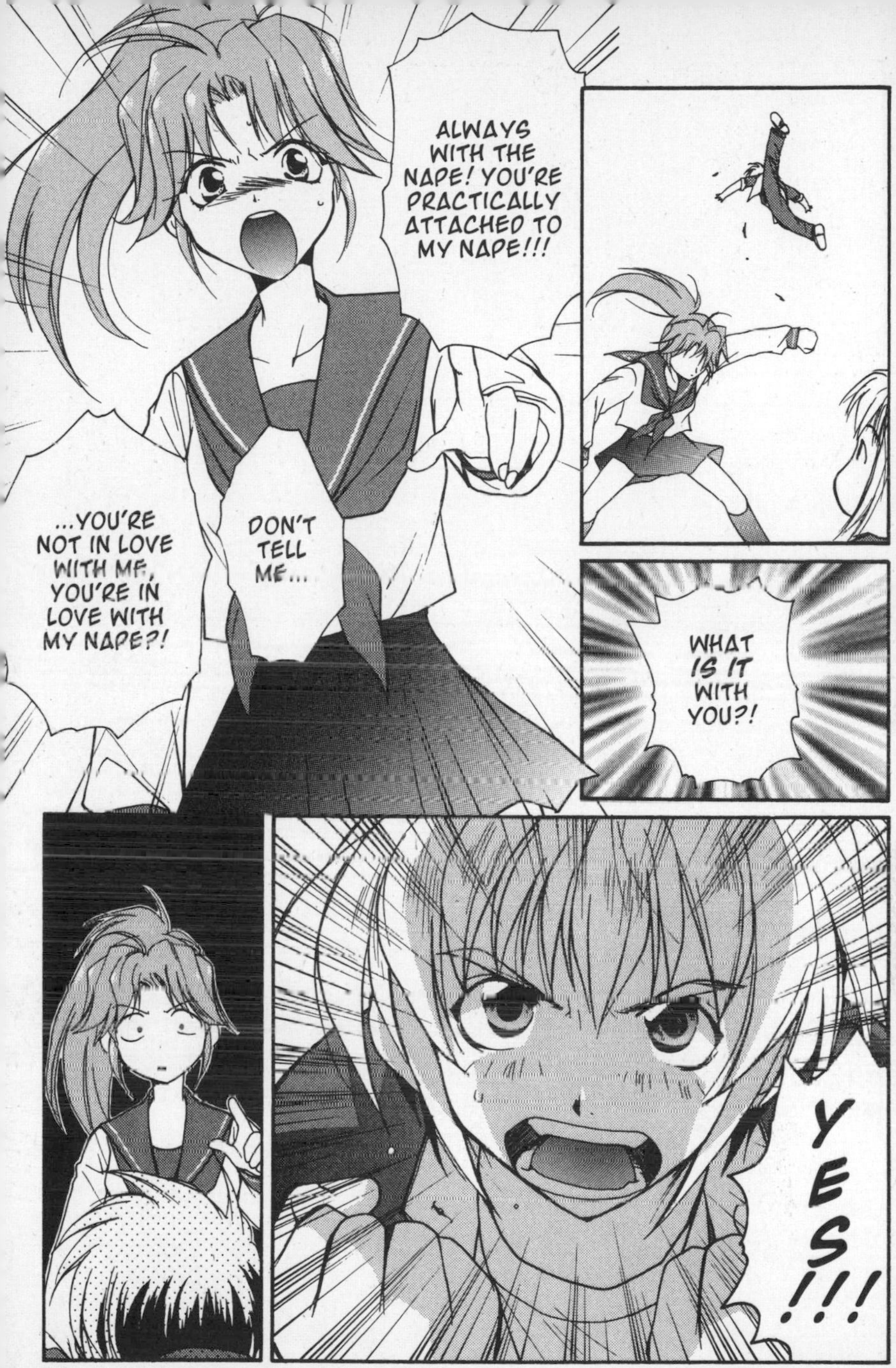
WHAT IS IT WITH YOU?!
ALWAYS WITH THE NAPE! YOU'RE PRACTICALLY ATTACHED TO MY NAPE!!!
DON'T TELL ME...
...YOU'RE NOT IN LOVE WITH ME, YOU'RE IN LOVE WITH MY NAPE?!
YES!!!

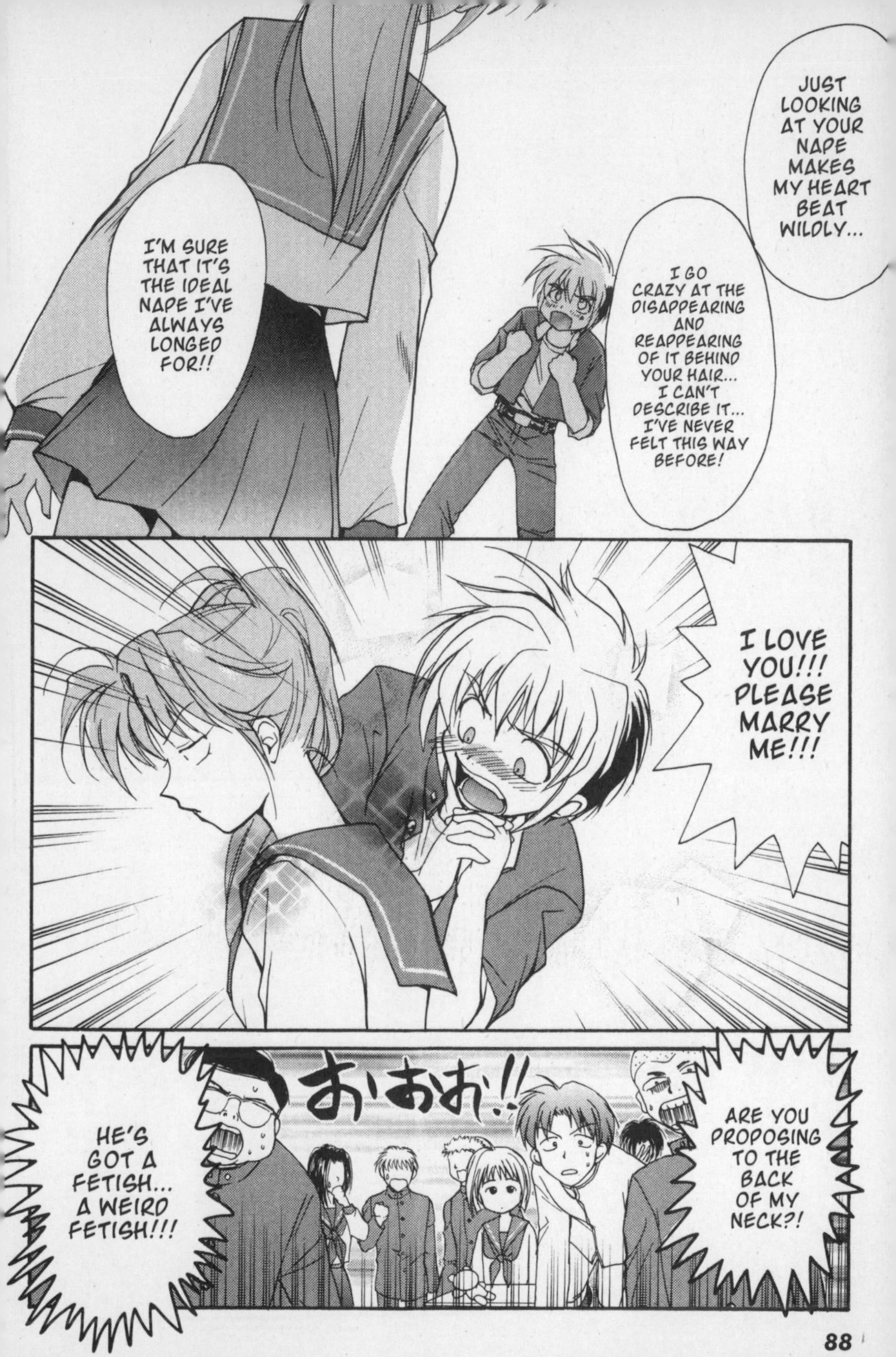
JUST LOOKING AT YOUR NAPE MAKES MY HEART BEAT WILDLY...
I GO CRAZY AT THE DISAPPEARING AND REAPPEARING OF IT BEHIND YOUR HAIR... I CAN'T DESCRIBE IT... I'VE NEVER FELT THIS WAY BEFORE!
I'M SURE THAT IT'S THE IDEAL NAPE I'VE ALWAYS LONGED FOR!!
I LOVE YOU!!! PLEASE MARRY ME!!!
ARE YOU PROPOSING TO THE BACK OF MY NECK?!
おあお!!
HE'S GOT A FETISH... A WEIRD FETISH!!!

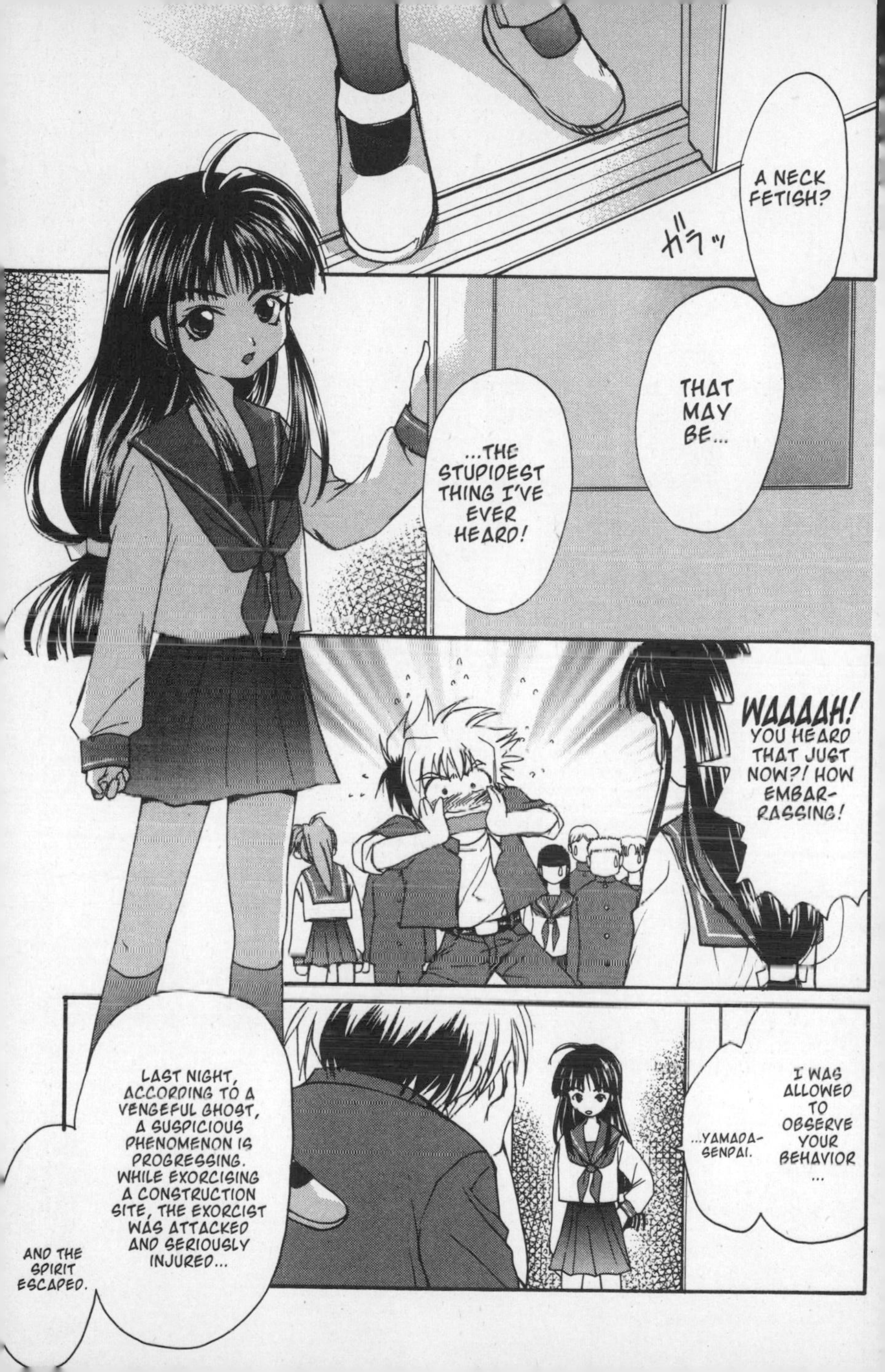
A NECK FETISH?
ガラッ
THAT MAY BE...
...THE STUPIDEST THING I'VE EVER HEARD!
WAAAAH! YOU HEARD THAT JUST NOW?! HOW EMBARRASSING!
I WAS ALLOWED TO OBSERVE YOUR BEHAVIOR ...
...YAMADA-SENPAI.
LAST NIGHT, ACCORDING TO A VENGEFUL GHOST, A SUSPICIOUS PHENOMENON IS PROGRESSING. WHILE EXORCISING A CONSTRUCTION SITE, THE EXORCIST WAS ATTACKED AND SERIOUSLY INJURED...
AND THE SPIRIT ESCAPED.

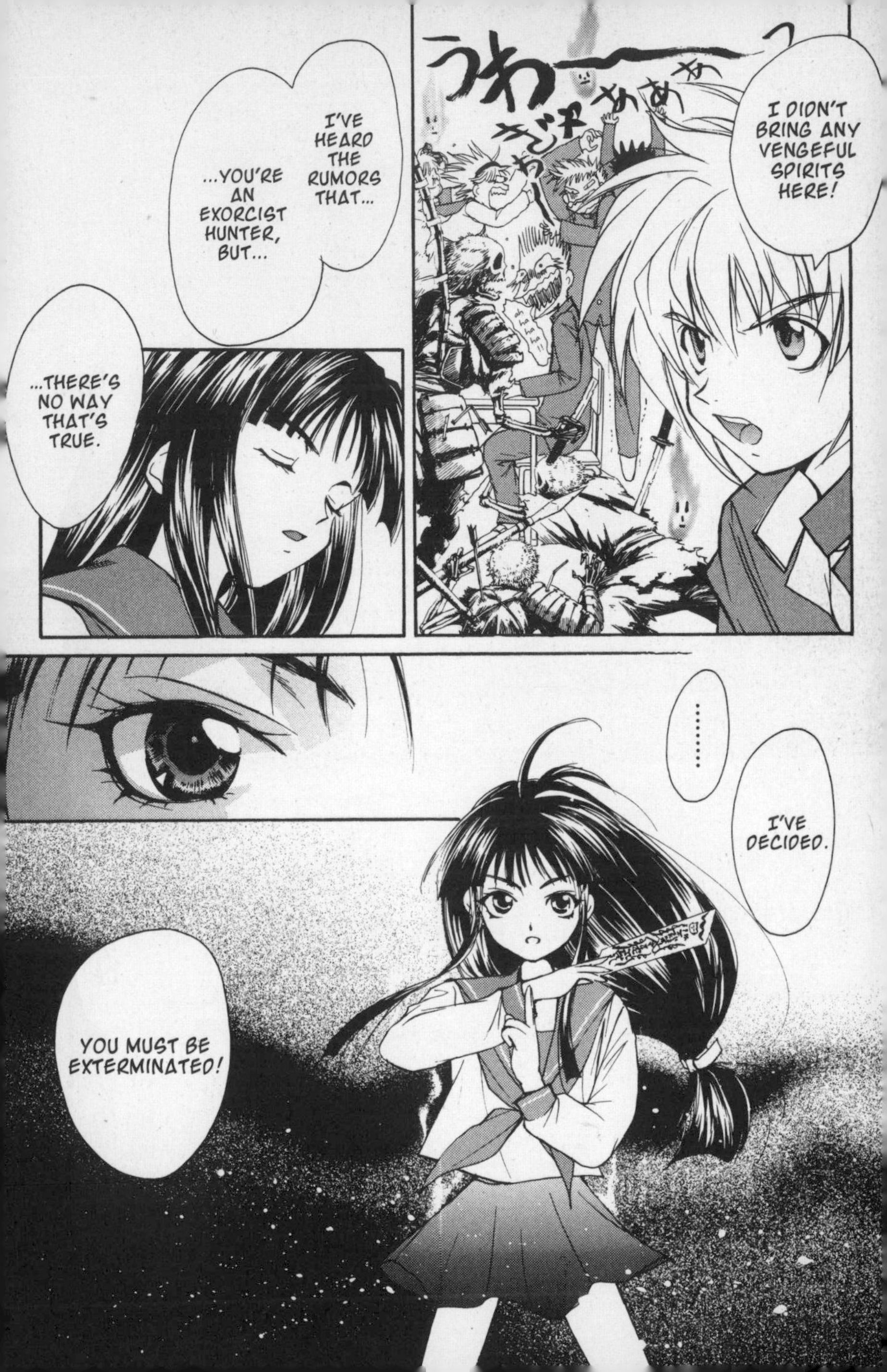

うわーーっ
I DIDN'T BRING ANY VENGEFUL SPIRITS HERE!
I'VE HEARD THE RUMORS THAT...
...YOU'RE AN EXORCIST HUNTER, BUT...
...THERE'S NO WAY THAT'S TRUE.
......
I'VE DECIDED.
YOU MUST BE EXTERMINATED!

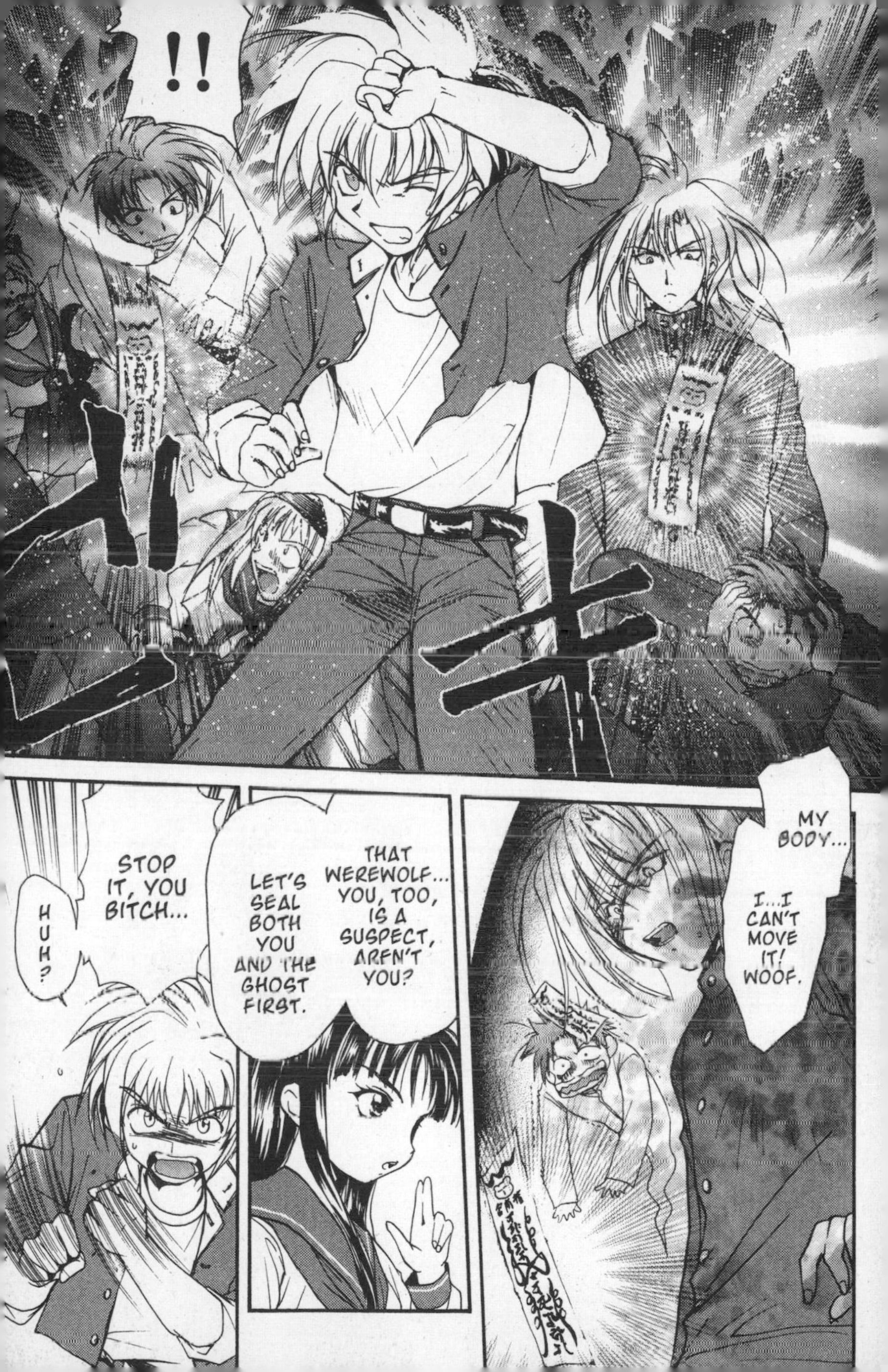
!!
MY BODY...
I...I CAN'T MOVE IT! WOOF.
THAT WEREWOLF... YOU, TOO, IS A SUSPECT, AREN'T YOU?
LET'S SEAL BOTH YOU AND THE GHOST FIRST.
STOP IT, YOU BITCH...
HUH?

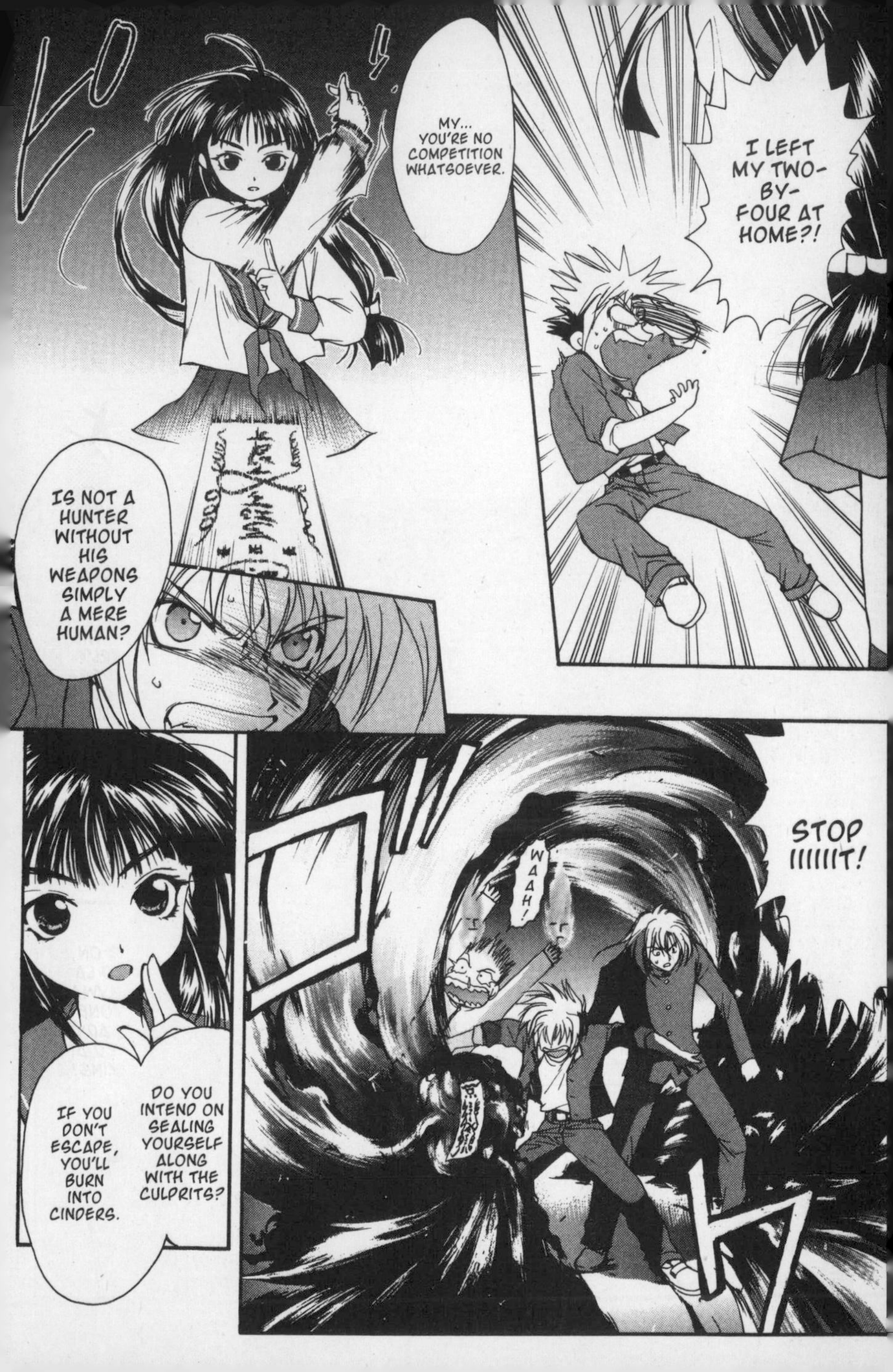
I LEFT MY TWO-BY-FOUR AT HOME?!
MY... YOU'RE NO COMPETITION WHATSOEVER.
IS NOT A HUNTER WITHOUT HIS WEAPONS SIMPLY A MERE HUMAN?
STOP IIIIIIIT!
WAAH!
DO YOU INTEND ON SEALING YOURSELF ALONG WITH THE CULPRITS?
IF YOU DON'T ESCAPE, YOU'LL BURN INTO CINDERS.

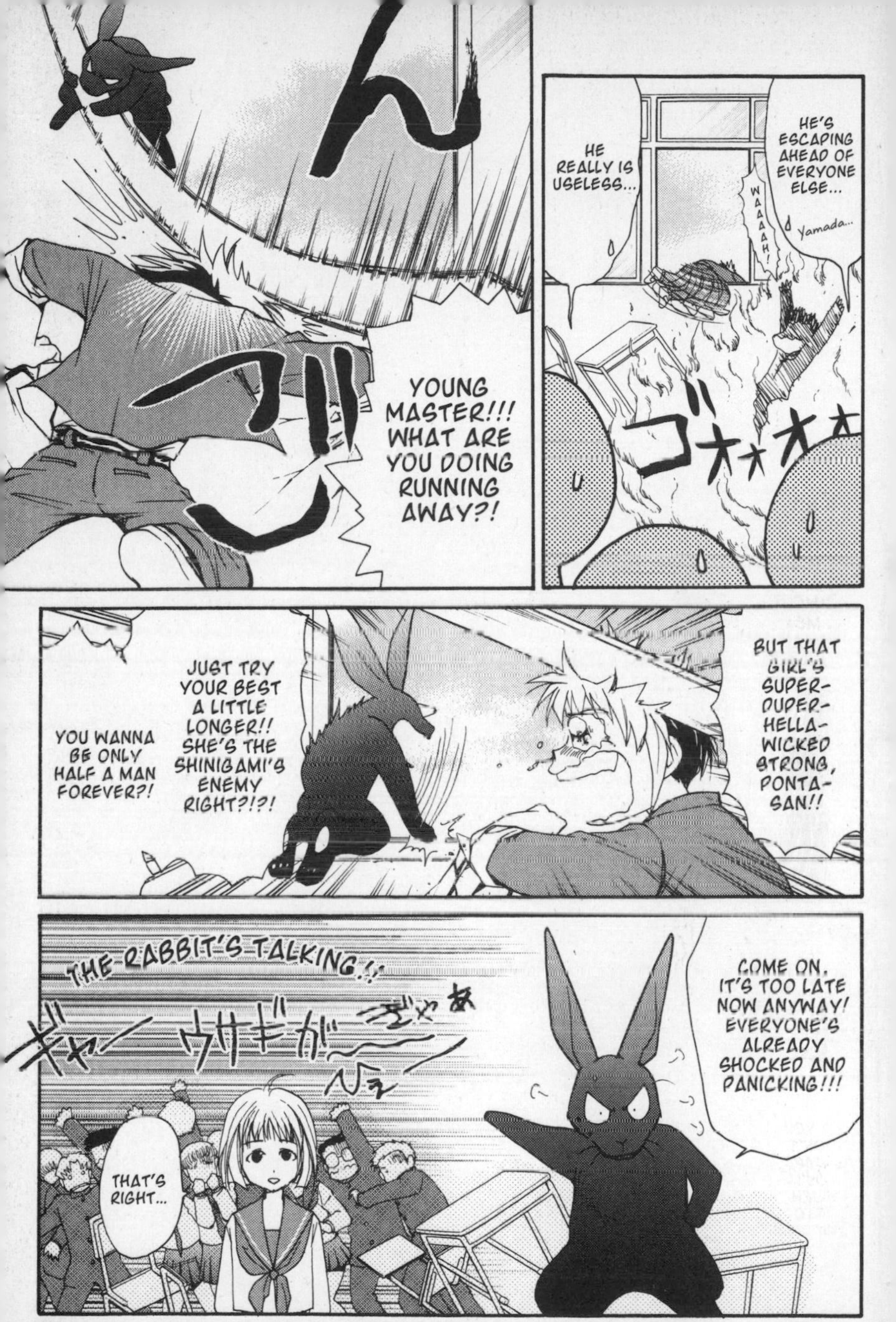
HE'S ESCAPING AHEAD OF EVERYONE ELSE...
WAAAAAH!
Yamada...
HE REALLY IS USELESS...
YOUNG MASTER!!! WHAT ARE YOU DOING RUNNING AWAY?!
BUT THAT GIRL'S SUPER-DUPER-HELLA-WICKED STRONG, PONTA-SAN!!
JUST TRY YOUR BEST A LITTLE LONGER!! SHE'S THE SHINIGAMI'S ENEMY RIGHT?!?!
YOU WANNA BE ONLY HALF A MAN FOREVER?!
COME ON. IT'S TOO LATE NOW ANYWAY! EVERYONE'S ALREADY SHOCKED AND PANICKING!!!
THE RABBIT'S TALKING!!
THAT'S RIGHT...

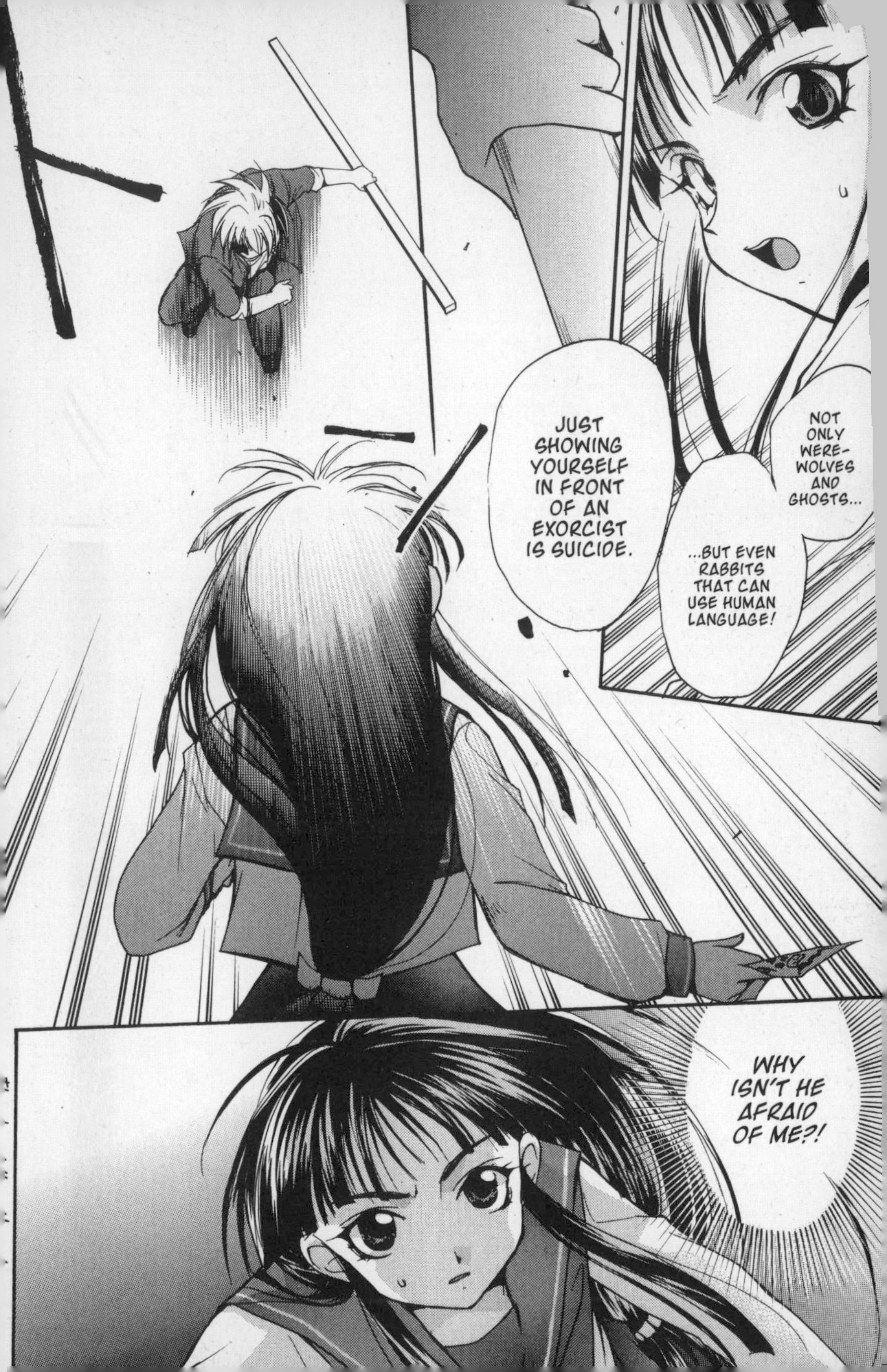
NOT ONLY WERE-WOLVES AND GHOSTS...
...BUT EVEN RABBITS THAT CAN USE HUMAN LANGUAGE!
JUST SHOWING YOURSELF IN FRONT OF AN EXORCIST IS SUICIDE.
WHY ISN'T HE AFRAID OF ME?!

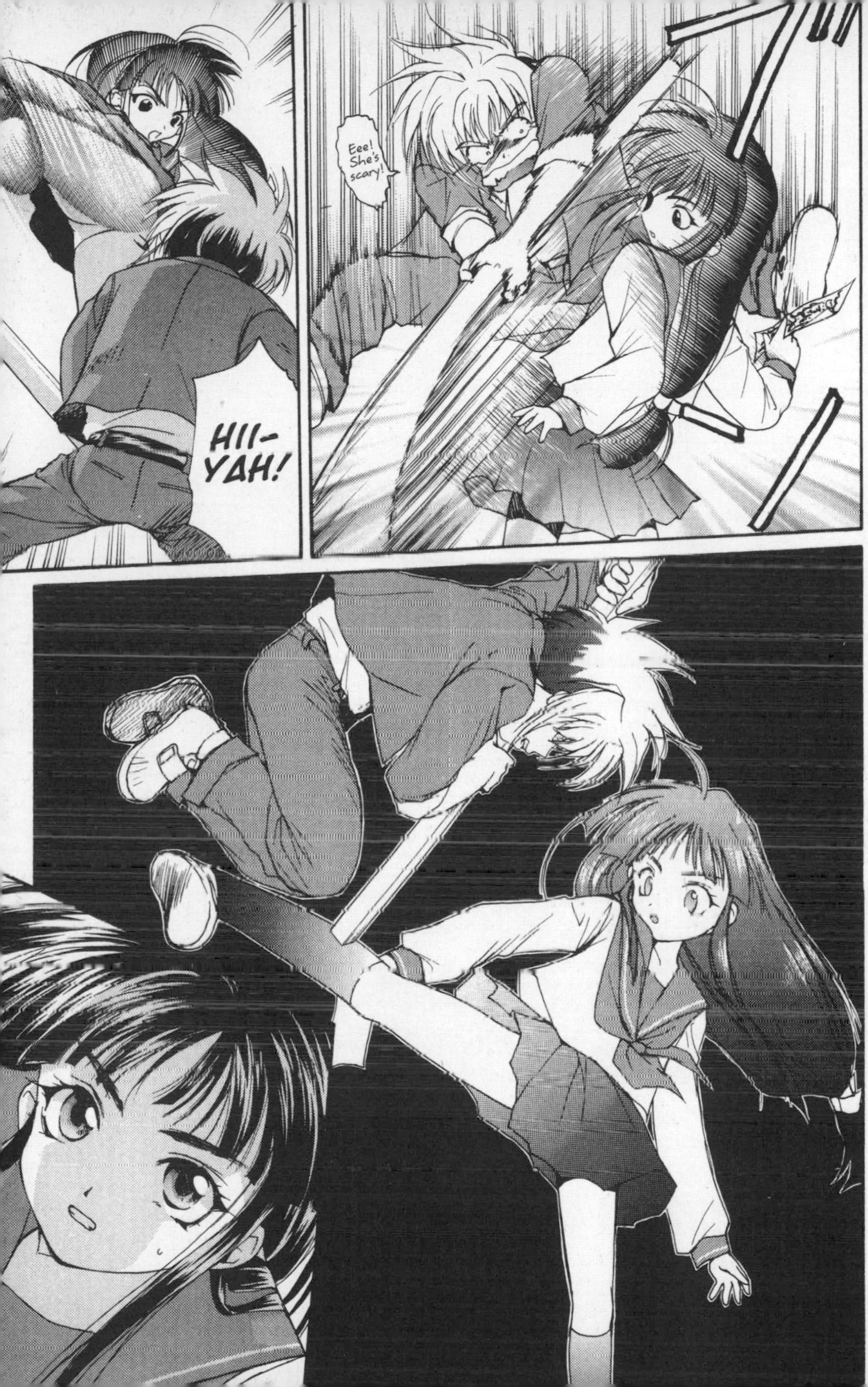
Eee! She's scary!
HII-YAH!

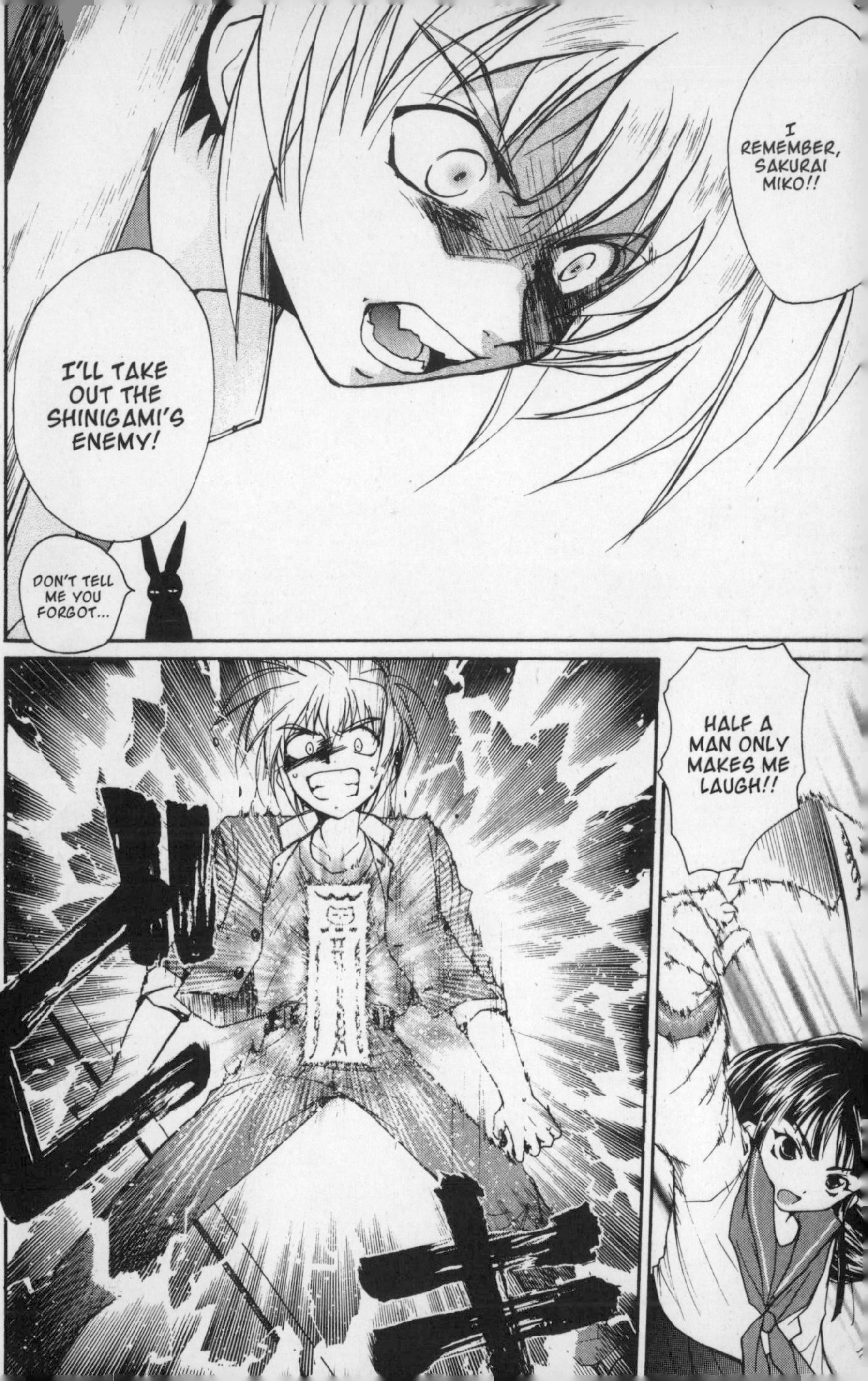
I REMEMBER, SAKURAI MIKO!!
I'LL TAKE OUT THE SHINIGAMI'S ENEMY!
DON'T TELL ME YOU FORGOT...
HALF A MAN ONLY MAKES ME LAUGH!!

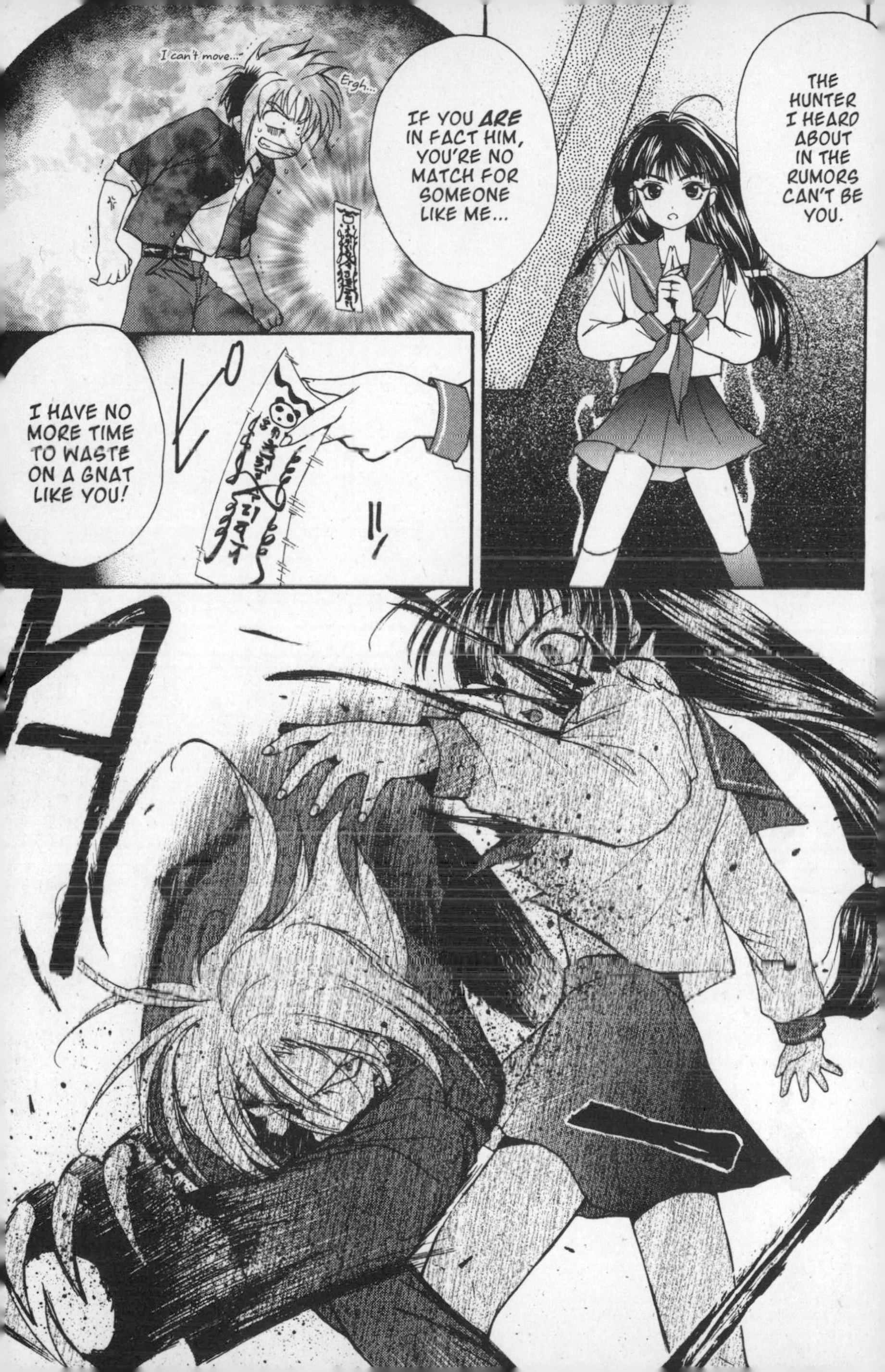
THE HUNTER I HEARD ABOUT IN THE RUMORS CAN'T BE YOU.
IF YOU **ARE** IN FACT HIM, YOU'RE NO MATCH FOR SOMEONE LIKE ME...
Ergh...
I can't move...
I HAVE NO MORE TIME TO WASTE ON A GNAT LIKE YOU!

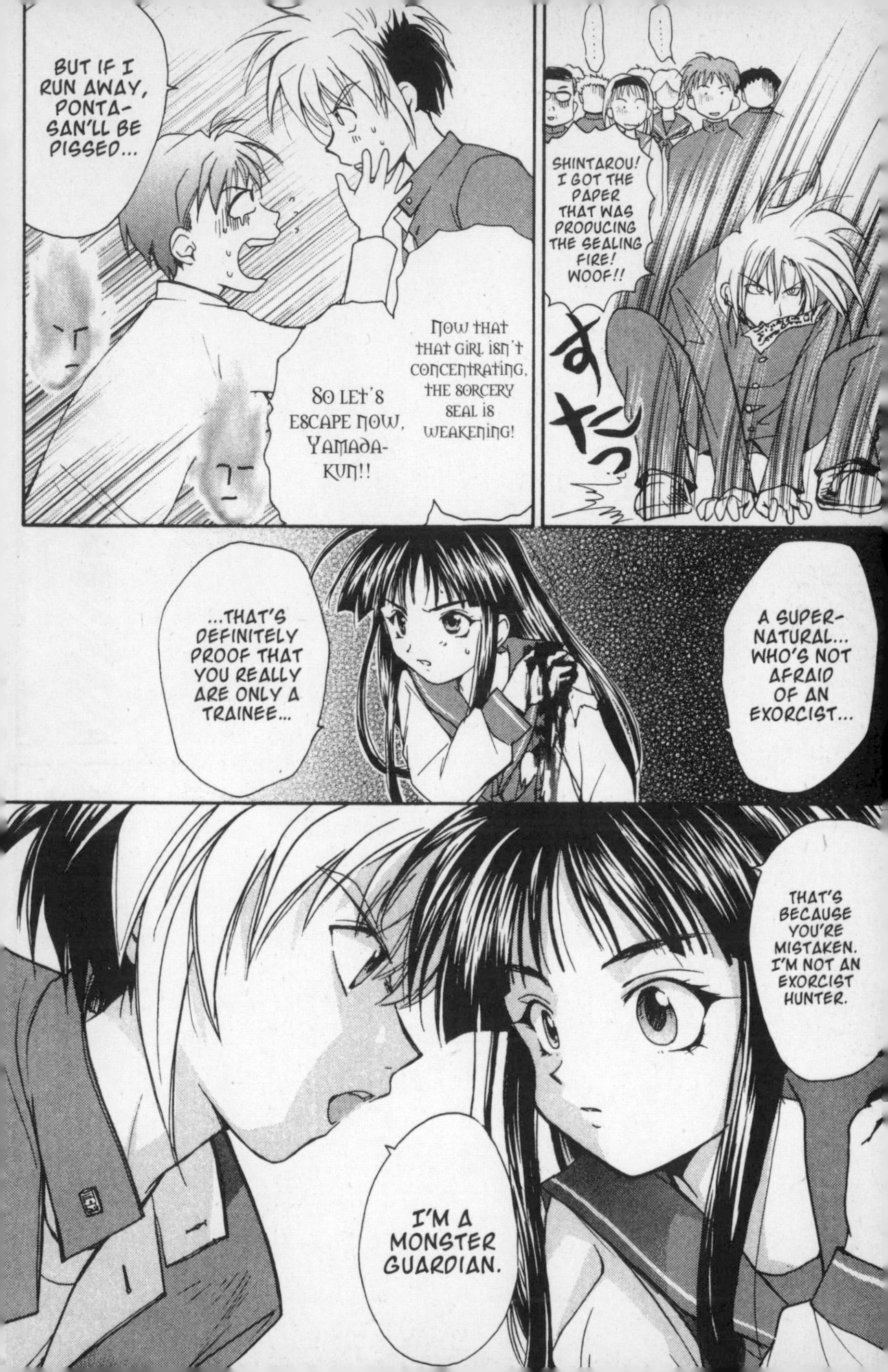

......
......
SHINTAROU! I GOT THE PAPER THAT WAS PRODUCING THE SEALING FIRE! WOOF!!
すたっ
NOW THAT THAT GIRL ISN'T CONCENTRATING, THE SORCERY SEAL IS WEAKENING!
SO LET'S ESCAPE NOW, YAMADA-KUN!!
BUT IF I RUN AWAY, PONTA-SAN'LL BE PISSED...
A SUPER-NATURAL... WHO'S NOT AFRAID OF AN EXORCIST...
...THAT'S DEFINITELY PROOF THAT YOU REALLY ARE ONLY A TRAINEE...
THAT'S BECAUSE YOU'RE MISTAKEN. I'M NOT AN EXORCIST HUNTER.
I'M A MONSTER GUARDIAN.

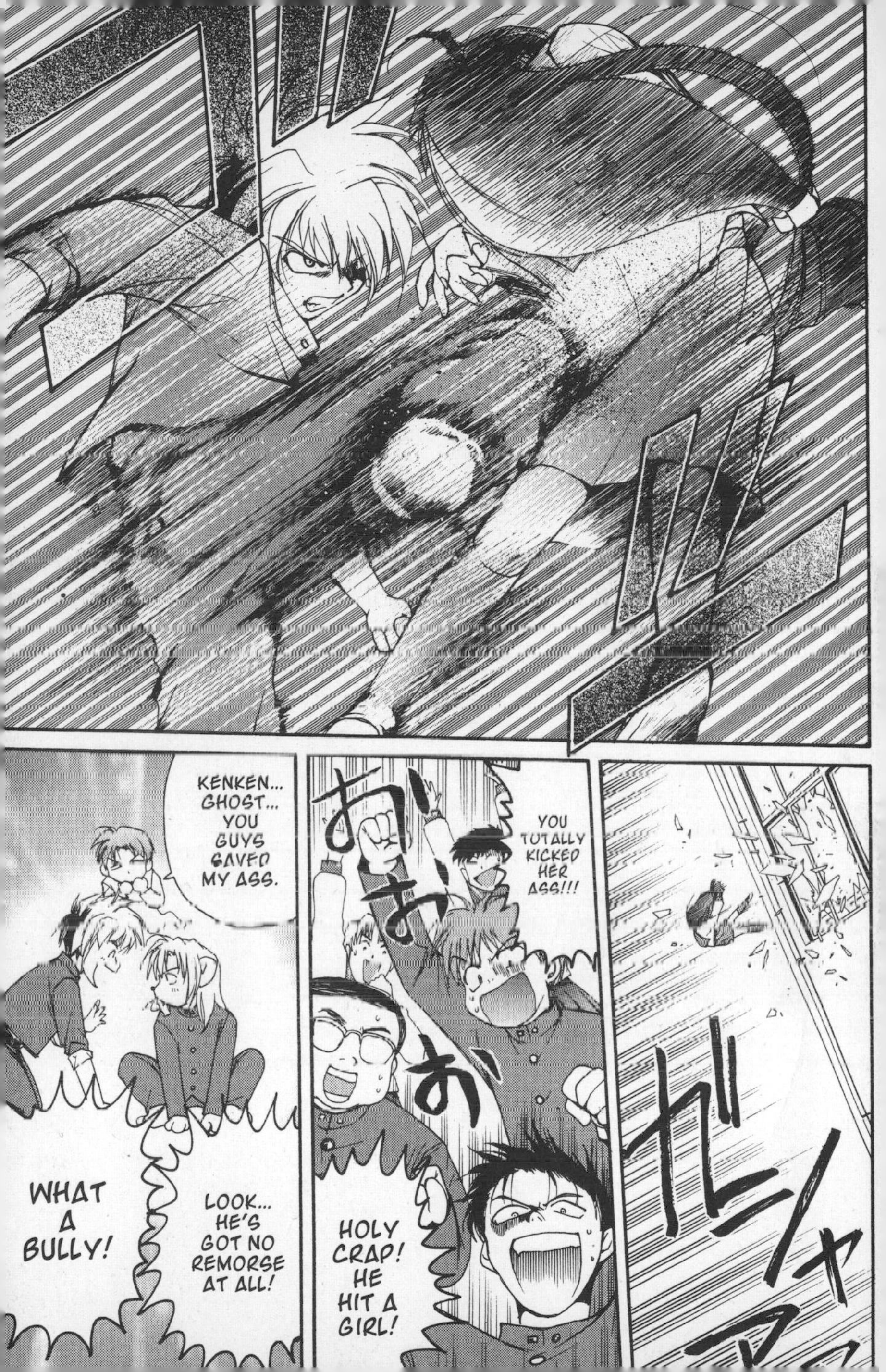
YOU TOTALLY KICKED HER ASS!!!
HOLY CRAP! HE HIT A GIRL!
KENKEN... GHOST... YOU GUYS SAVED MY ASS.
LOOK... HE'S GOT NO REMORSE AT ALL!
WHAT A BULLY!

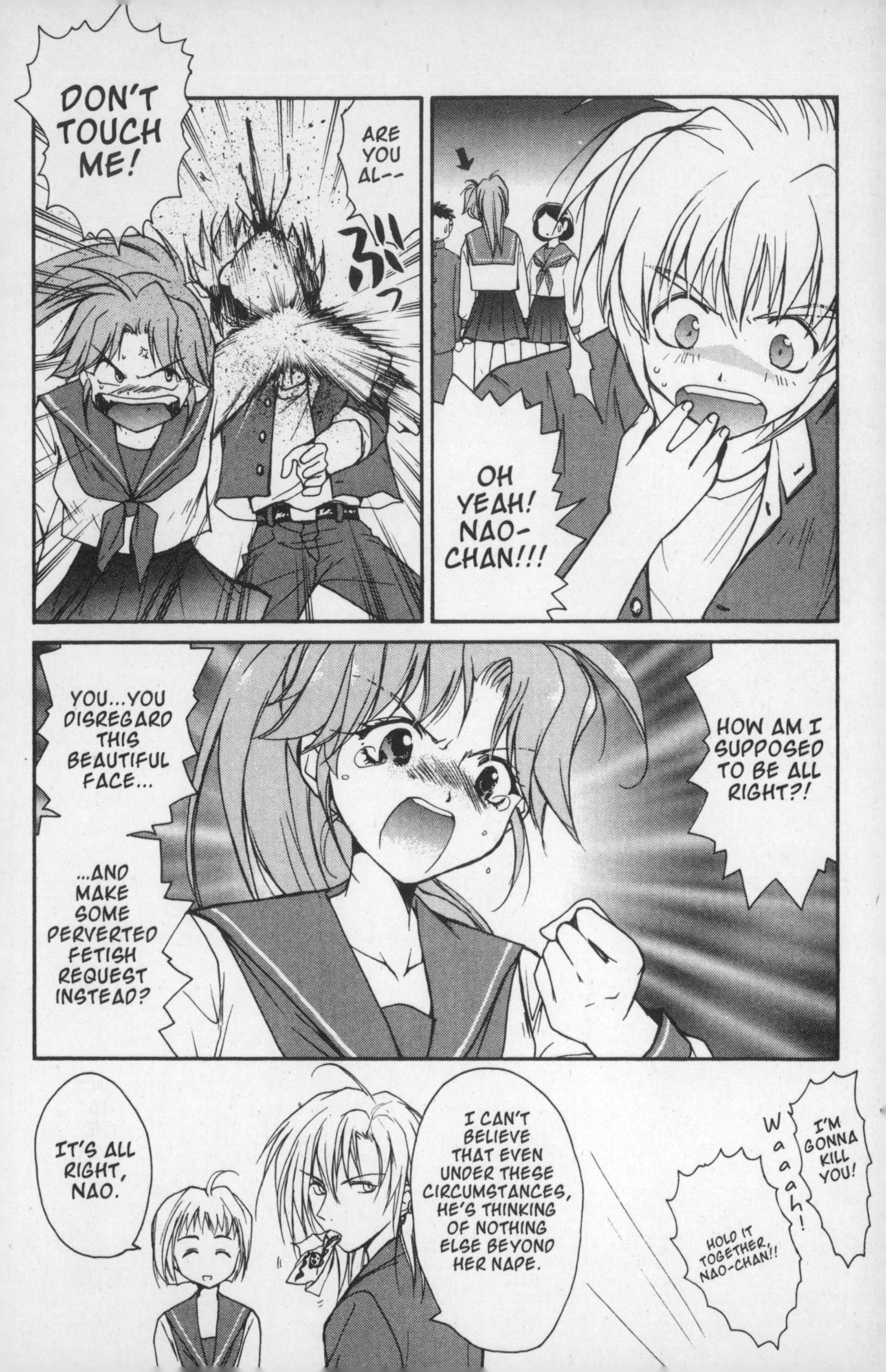
OH YEAH! NAO-CHAN!!!
ARE YOU AL--
DON'T TOUCH ME!
ぶっ
HOW AM I SUPPOSED TO BE ALL RIGHT?!
YOU...YOU DISREGARD THIS BEAUTIFUL FACE...
...AND MAKE SOME PERVERTED FETISH REQUEST INSTEAD?
I'M GONNA KILL YOU!
Waaah!
HOLD IT TOGETHER, NAO-CHAN!!
I CAN'T BELIEVE THAT EVEN UNDER THESE CIRCUMSTANCES, HE'S THINKING OF NOTHING ELSE BEYOND HER NAPE.
IT'S ALL RIGHT, NAO.

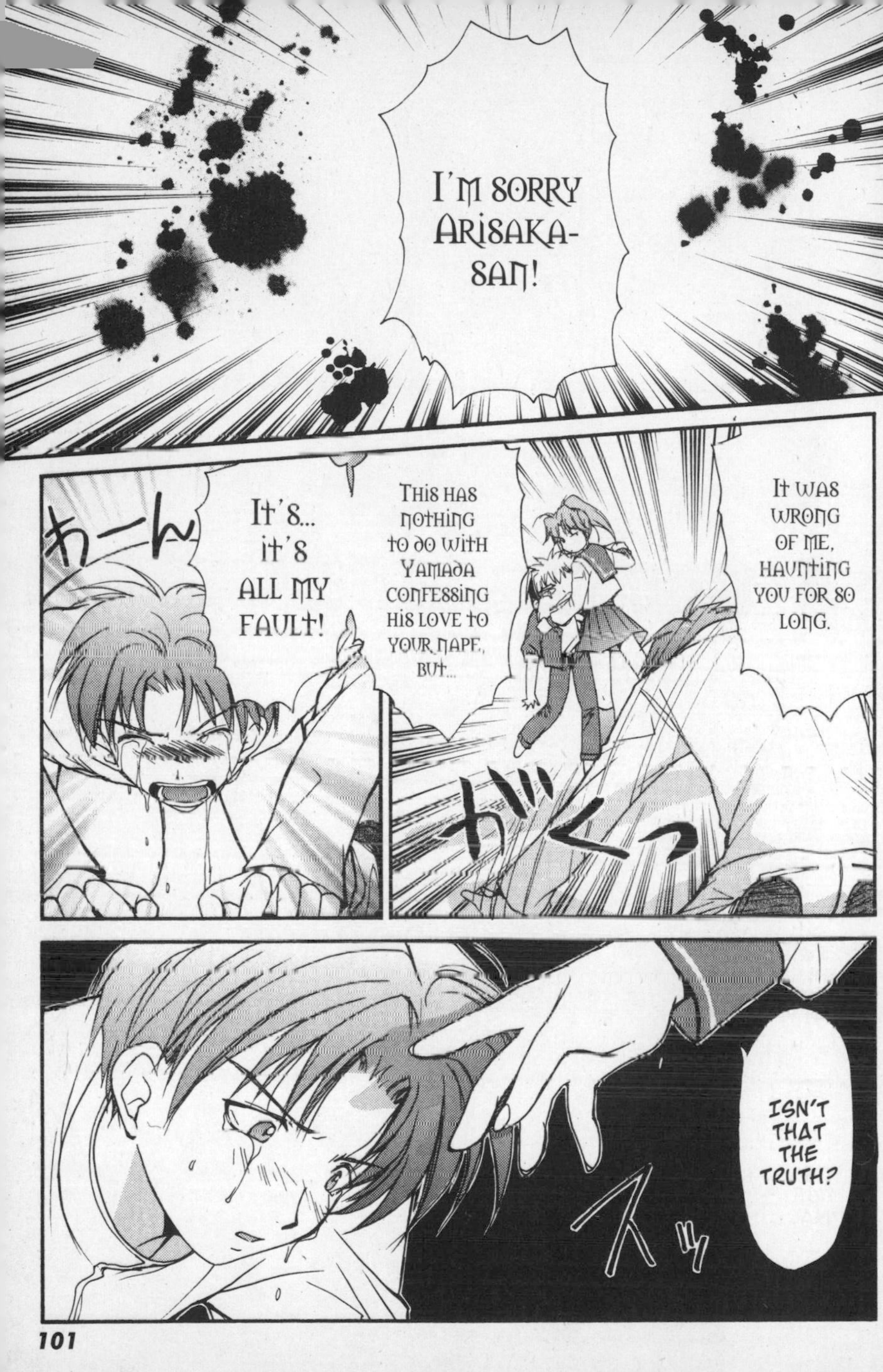
I'M SORRY ARISAKA-SAN!
IT WAS WRONG OF ME, HAUNTING YOU FOR SO LONG.
THIS HAS NOTHING TO DO WITH YAMADA CONFESSING HIS LOVE TO YOUR NAPE, BUT...
がくっ
IT'S... IT'S ALL MY FAULT!
わーん
ISN'T THAT THE TRUTH?
スッ

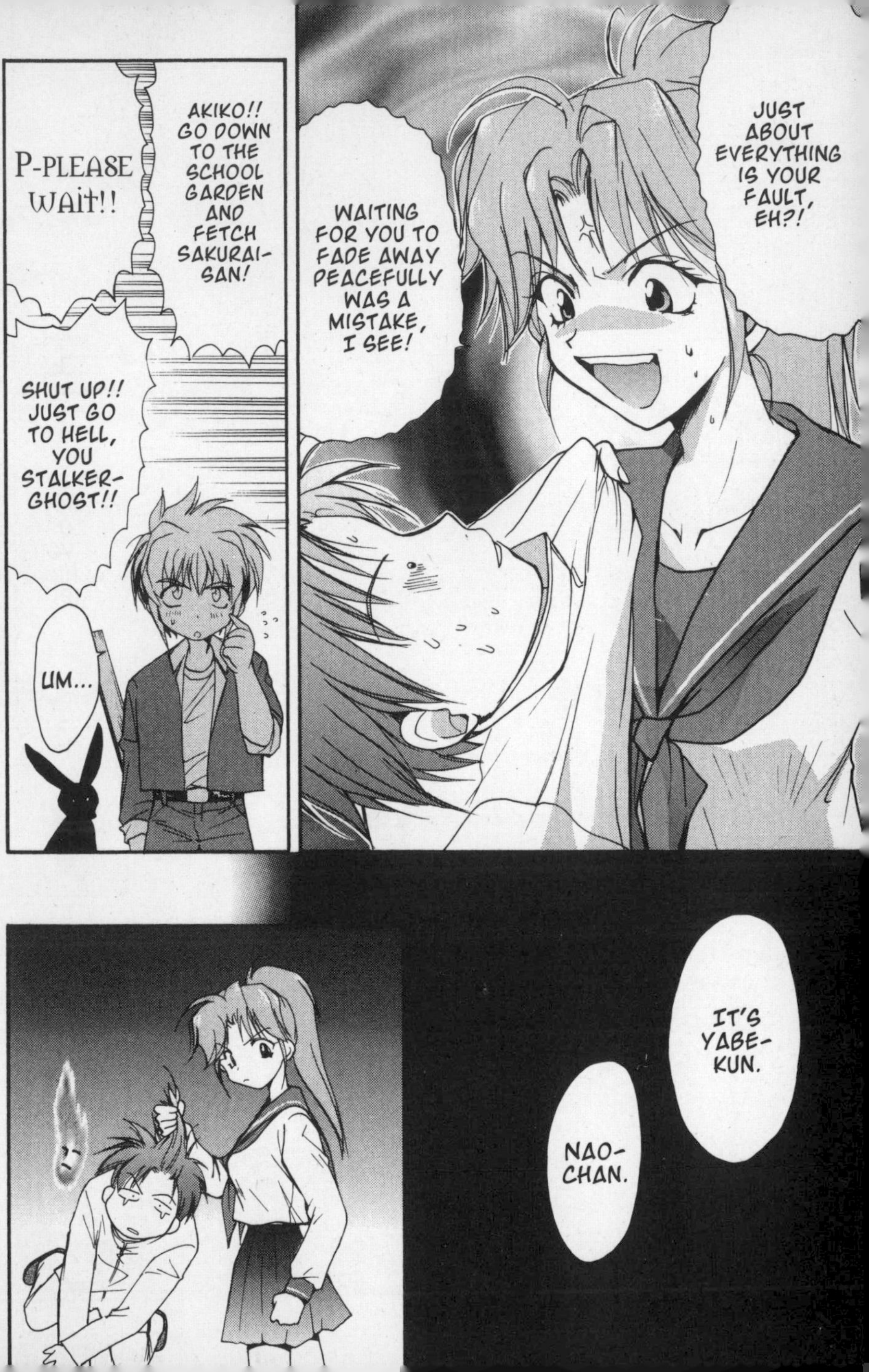
JUST ABOUT EVERYTHING IS YOUR FAULT, EH?!
WAITING FOR YOU TO FADE AWAY PEACEFULLY WAS A MISTAKE, I SEE!
AKIKO!! GO DOWN TO THE SCHOOL GARDEN AND FETCH SAKURAI-SAN!
P-PLEASE WAIT!!
SHUT UP!! JUST GO TO HELL, YOU STALKER-GHOST!!
UM...
IT'S YABE-KUN.
NAO-CHAN.

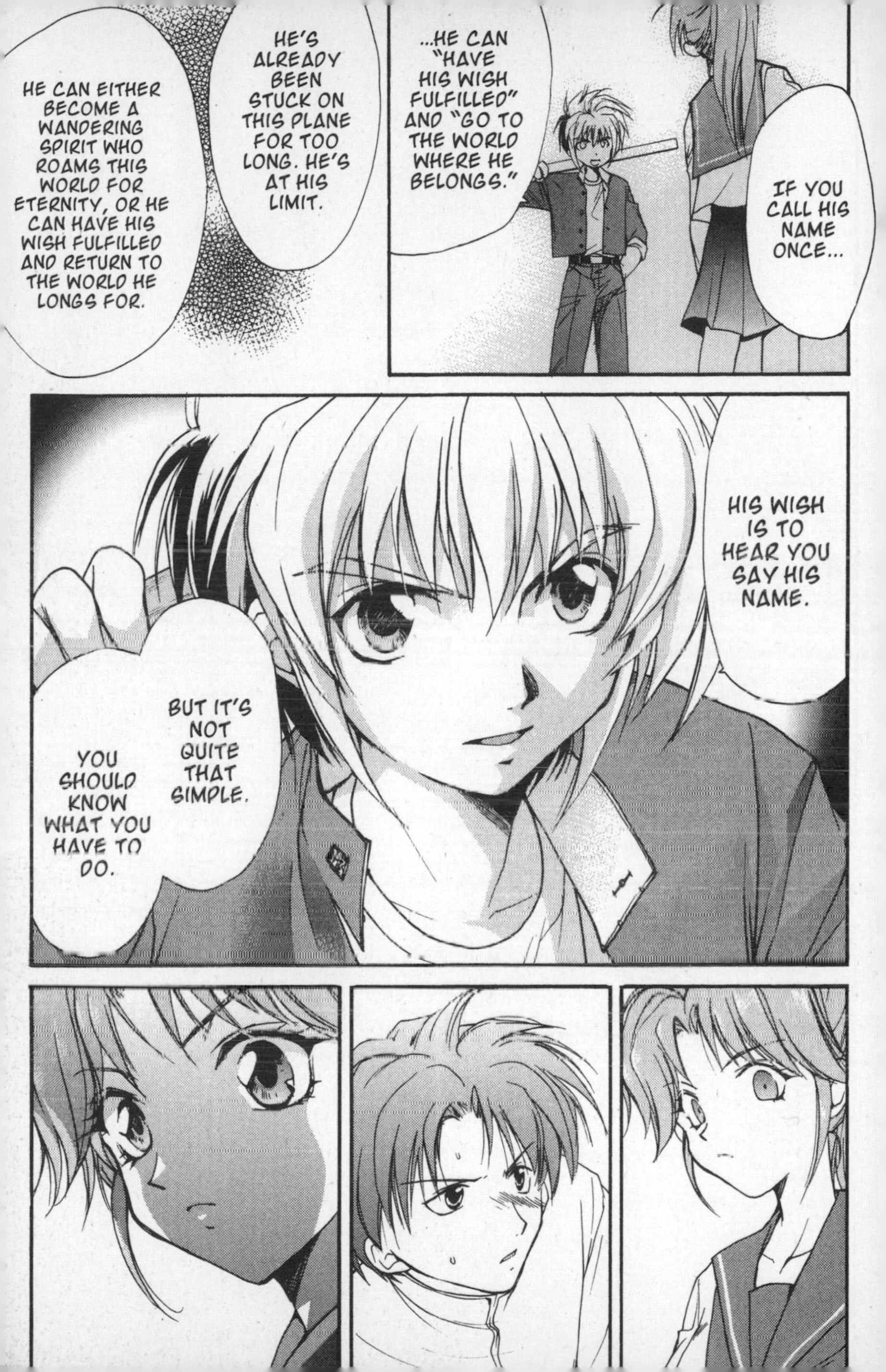
IF YOU CALL HIS NAME ONCE...
...HE CAN "HAVE HIS WISH FULFILLED" AND "GO TO THE WORLD WHERE HE BELONGS."
HE'S ALREADY BEEN STUCK ON THIS PLANE FOR TOO LONG. HE'S AT HIS LIMIT.
HE CAN EITHER BECOME A WANDERING SPIRIT WHO ROAMS THIS WORLD FOR ETERNITY, OR HE CAN HAVE HIS WISH FULFILLED AND RETURN TO THE WORLD HE LONGS FOR.
HIS WISH IS TO HEAR YOU SAY HIS NAME.
BUT IT'S NOT QUITE THAT SIMPLE.
YOU SHOULD KNOW WHAT YOU HAVE TO DO.

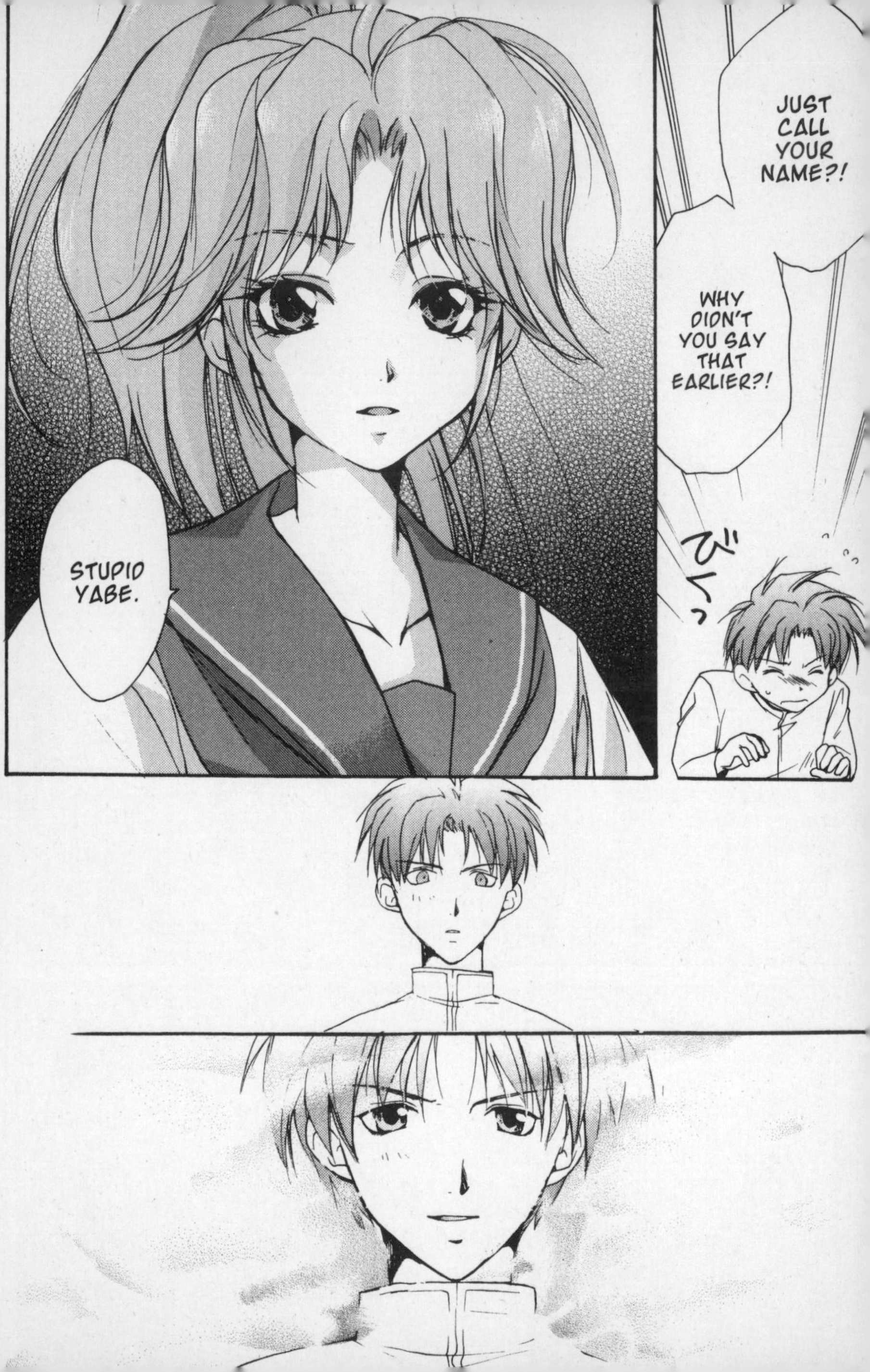
JUST CALL YOUR NAME?!
WHY DIDN'T YOU SAY THAT EARLIER?!
びくっ
STUPID YABE.

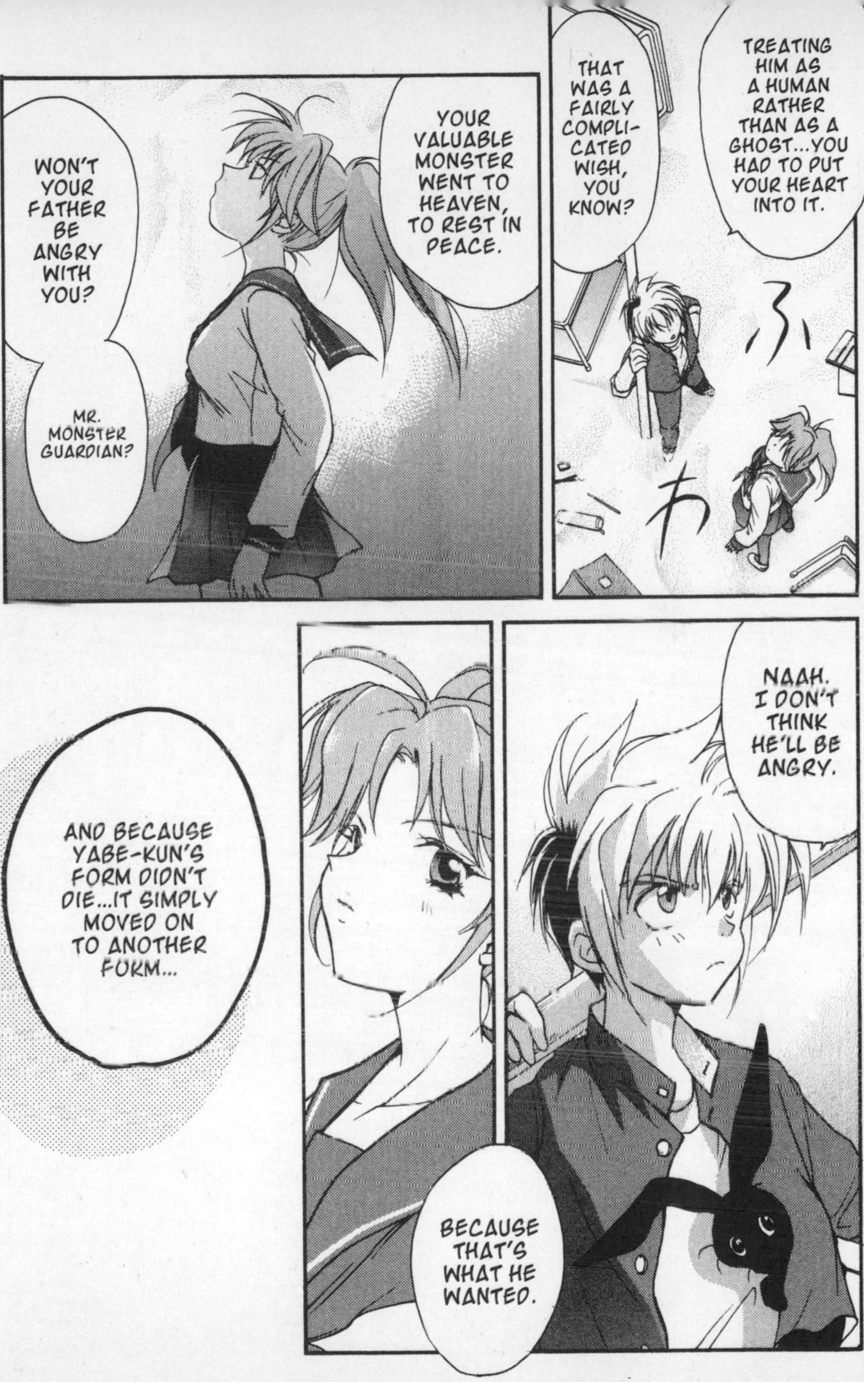
TREATING HIM AS A HUMAN RATHER THAN AS A GHOST...YOU HAD TO PUT YOUR HEART INTO IT.
THAT WAS A FAIRLY COMPLI-CATED WISH, YOU KNOW?
ふ わ
YOUR VALUABLE MONSTER WENT TO HEAVEN, TO REST IN PEACE.
WON'T YOUR FATHER BE ANGRY WITH YOU?
MR. MONSTER GUARDIAN?
NAAH. I DON'T THINK HE'LL BE ANGRY.
BECAUSE THAT'S WHAT HE WANTED.
AND BECAUSE YABE-KUN'S FORM DIDN'T DIE...IT SIMPLY MOVED ON TO ANOTHER FORM...

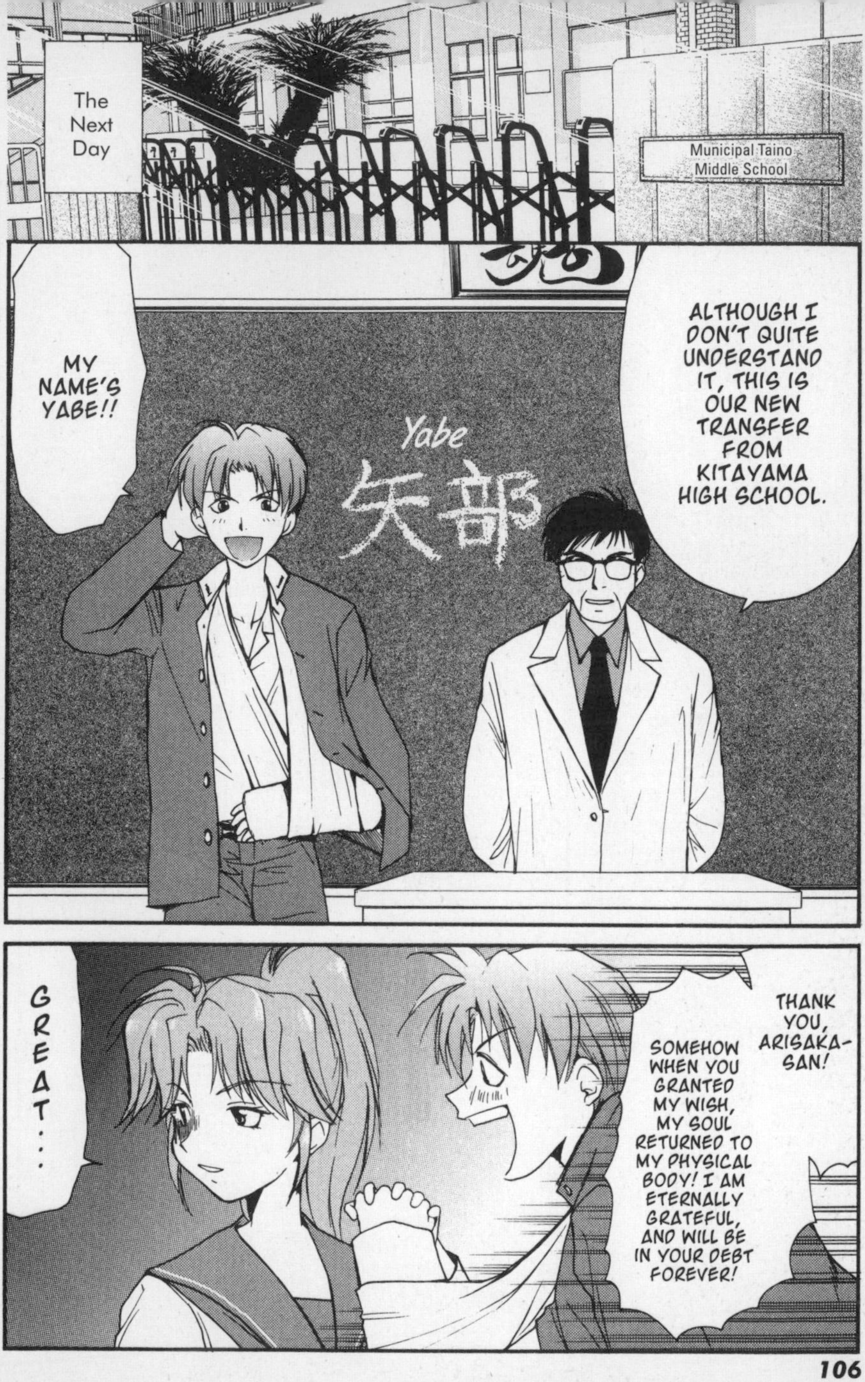
The Next Day
Municipal Taino Middle School
ALTHOUGH I DON'T QUITE UNDERSTAND IT, THIS IS OUR NEW TRANSFER FROM KITAYAMA HIGH SCHOOL.
Yabe
矢部
MY NAME'S YABE!!
THANK YOU, ARISAKA-SAN!
SOMEHOW WHEN YOU GRANTED MY WISH, MY SOUL RETURNED TO MY PHYSICAL BODY! I AM ETERNALLY GRATEFUL, AND WILL BE IN YOUR DEBT FOREVER!
GREAT...

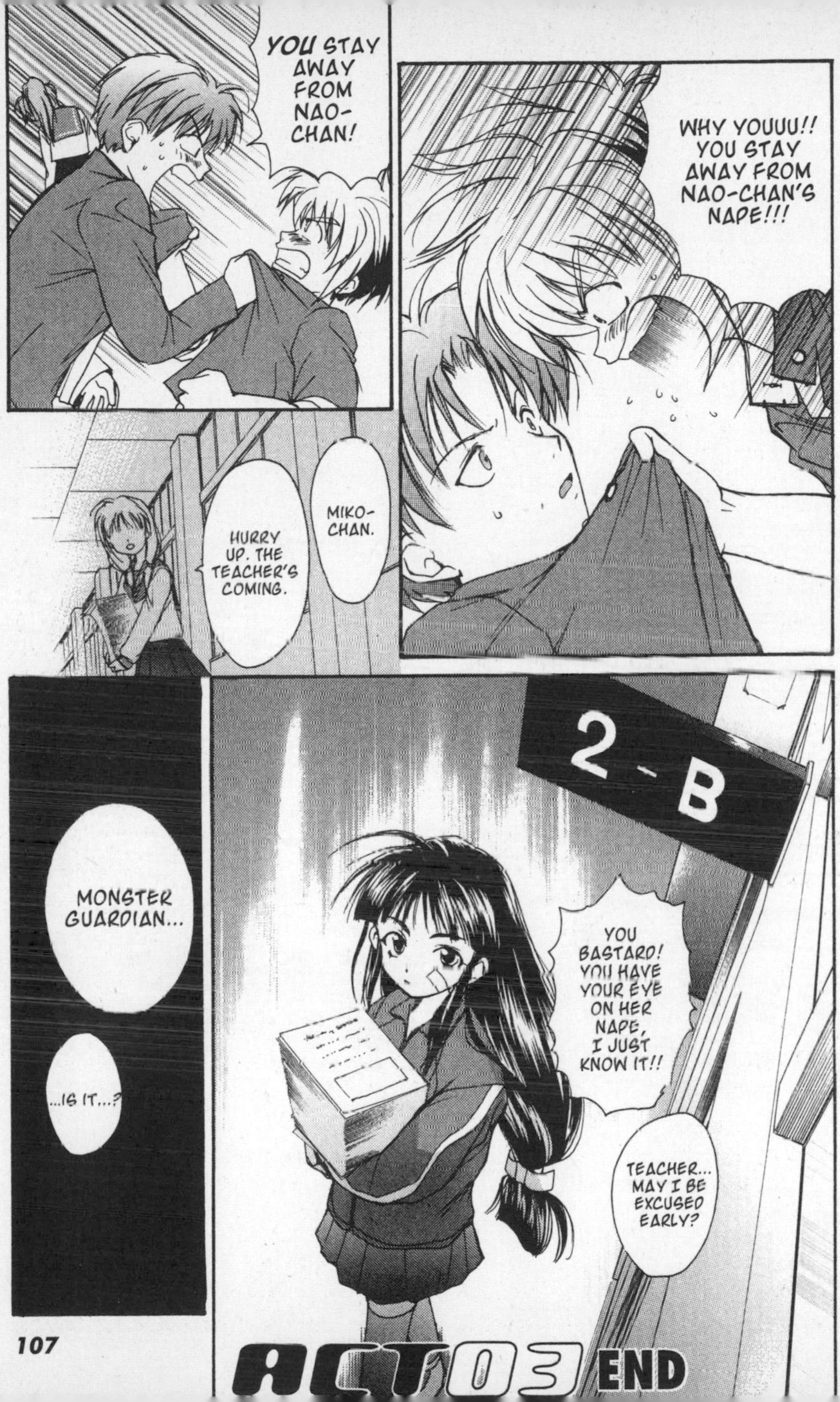
WHY YOUUU!! YOU STAY AWAY FROM NAO-CHAN'S NAPE!!!
YOU STAY AWAY FROM NAO-CHAN!
MIKO-CHAN.
HURRY UP. THE TEACHER'S COMING.
2-B
YOU BASTARD! YOU HAVE YOUR EYE ON HER NAPE, I JUST KNOW IT!!
TEACHER... MAY I BE EXCUSED EARLY?
MONSTER GUARDIAN...
...IS IT...?
ACT 03 END

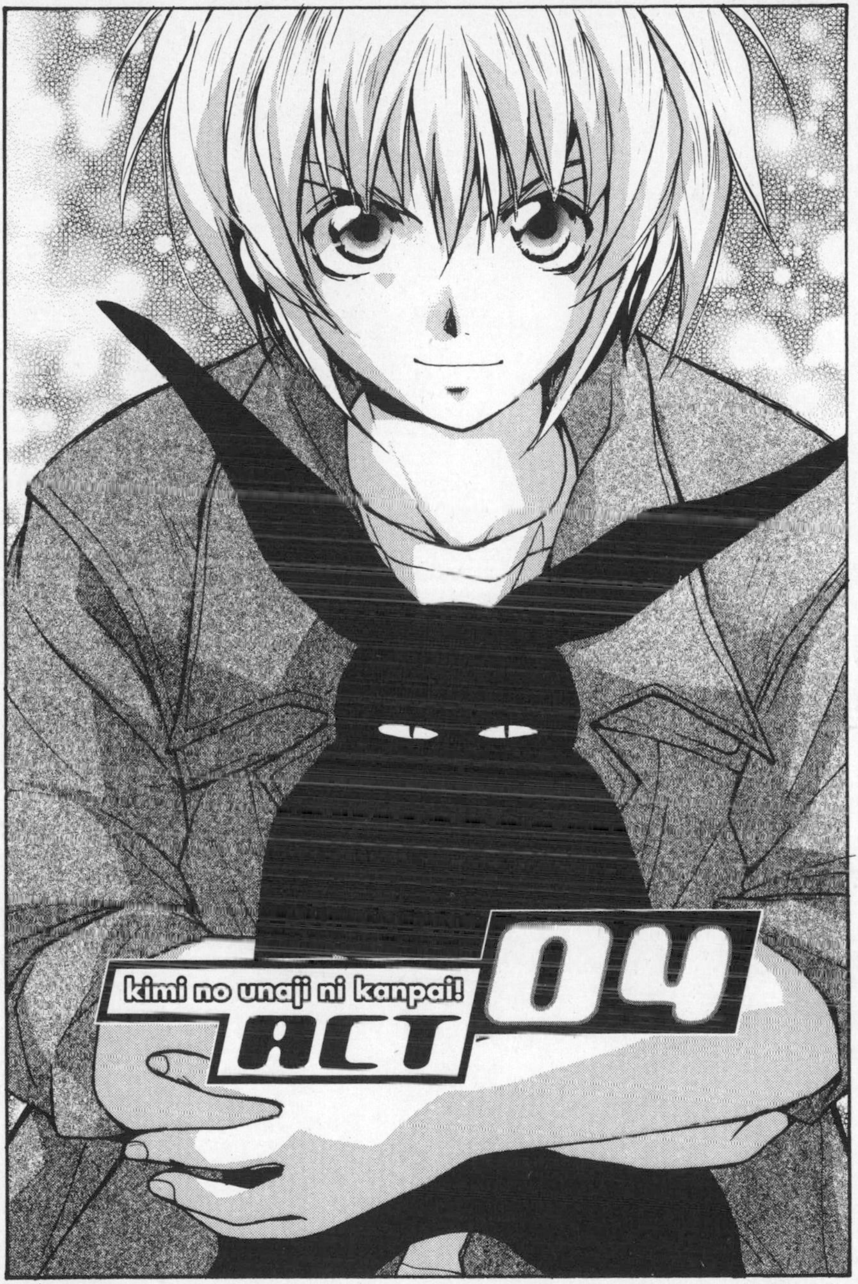

kimi no unaji ni kanpai!
ACT 04

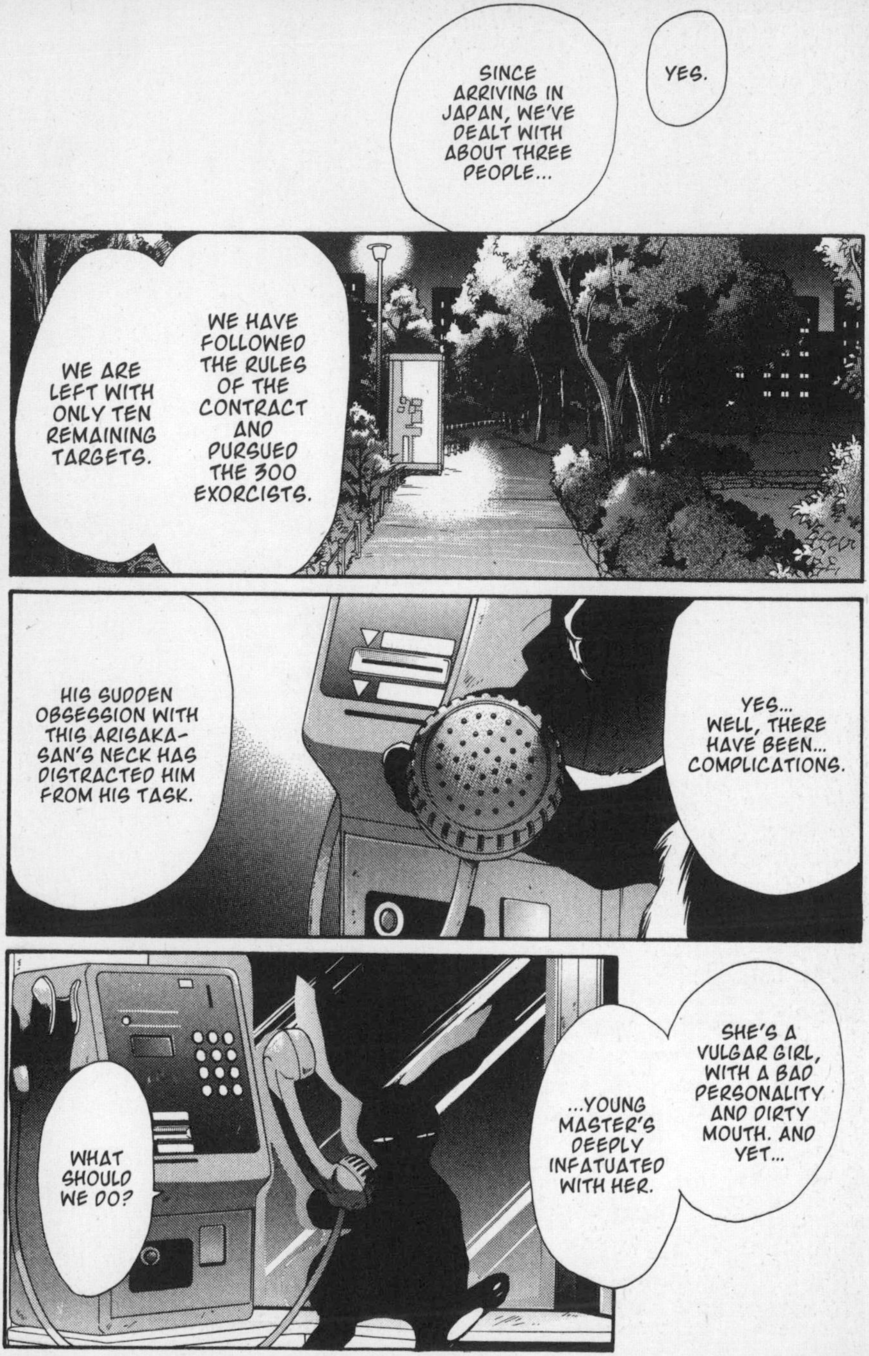
YES.
SINCE ARRIVING IN JAPAN, WE'VE DEALT WITH ABOUT THREE PEOPLE...
WE HAVE FOLLOWED THE RULES OF THE CONTRACT AND PURSUED THE 300 EXORCISTS.
WE ARE LEFT WITH ONLY TEN REMAINING TARGETS.
YES... WELL, THERE HAVE BEEN... COMPLICATIONS.
HIS SUDDEN OBSESSION WITH THIS ARISAKA-SAN'S NECK HAS DISTRACTED HIM FROM HIS TASK.
SHE'S A VULGAR GIRL, WITH A BAD PERSONALITY AND DIRTY MOUTH. AND YET...
...YOUNG MASTER'S DEEPLY INFATUATED WITH HER.
WHAT SHOULD WE DO?

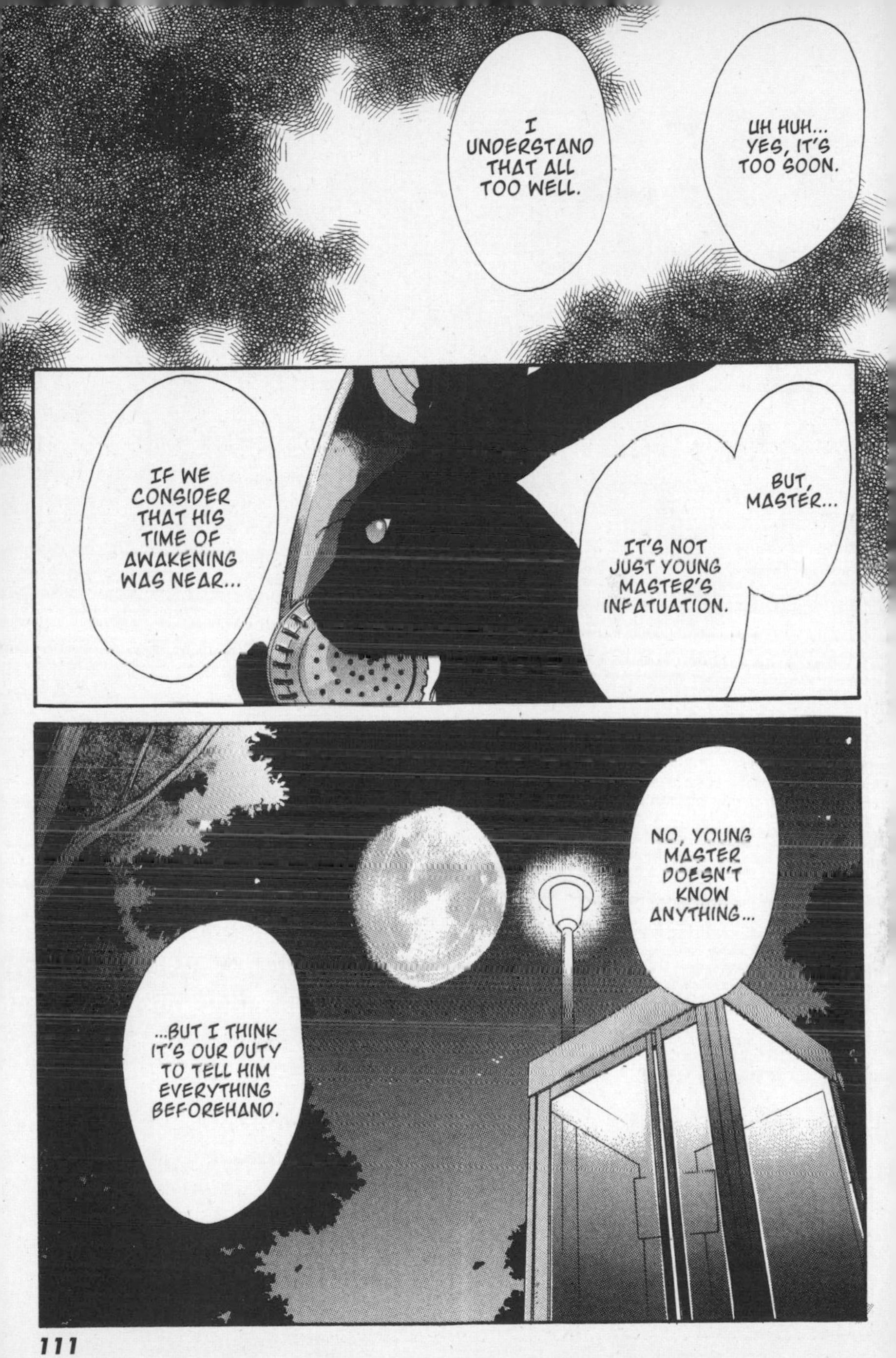
UH HUH... YES, IT'S TOO SOON.
I UNDERSTAND THAT ALL TOO WELL.
BUT, MASTER...
IT'S NOT JUST YOUNG MASTER'S INFATUATION.
IF WE CONSIDER THAT HIS TIME OF AWAKENING WAS NEAR...
NO, YOUNG MASTER DOESN'T KNOW ANYTHING...
...BUT I THINK IT'S OUR DUTY TO TELL HIM EVERYTHING BEFOREHAND.

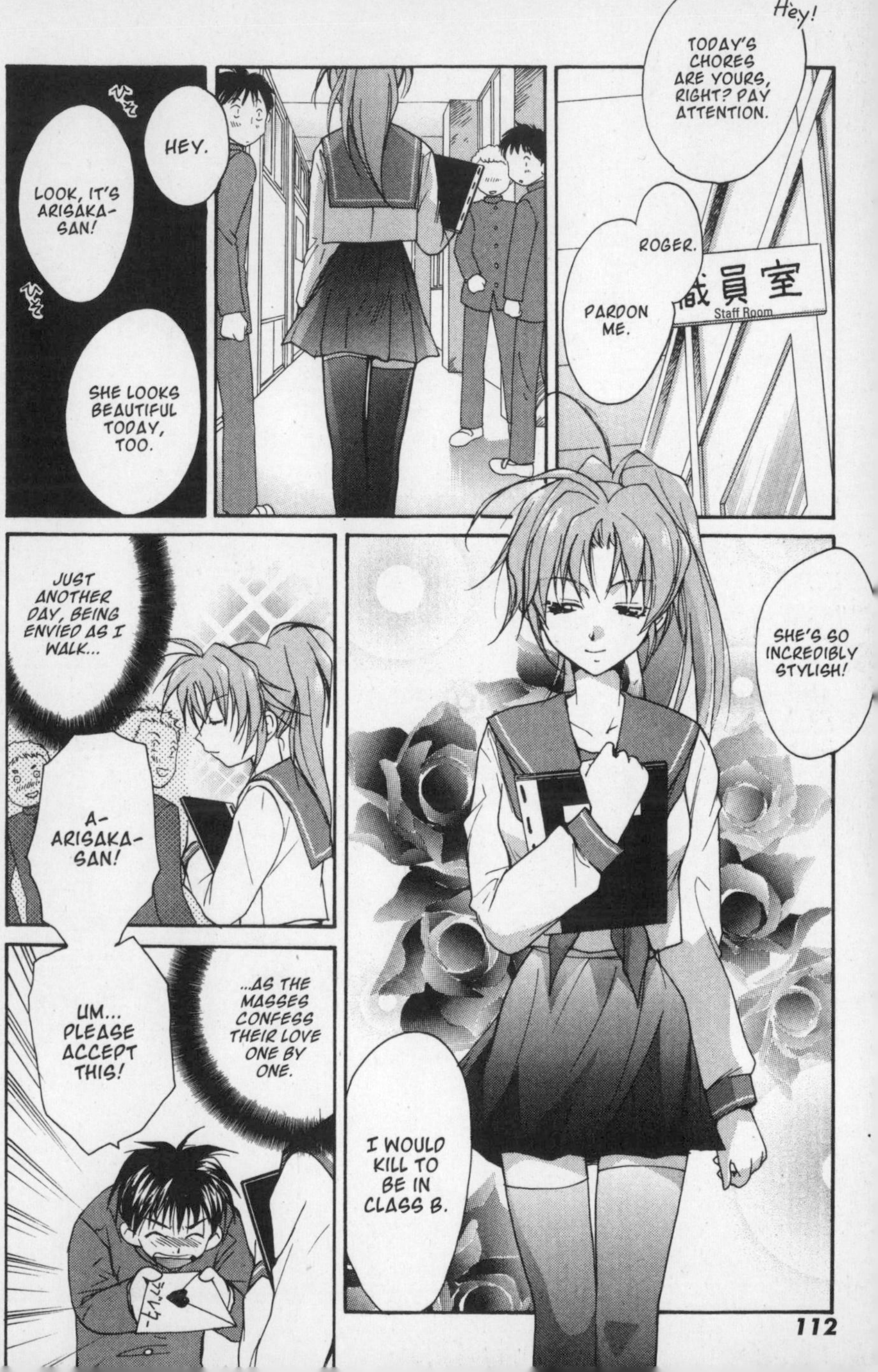
Hey!
TODAY'S CHORES ARE YOURS, RIGHT? PAY ATTENTION.
ROGER.
職員室
Staff Room
PARDON ME.
HEY.
LOOK, IT'S ARISAKA-SAN!
SHE LOOKS BEAUTIFUL TODAY, TOO.
SHE'S SO INCREDIBLY STYLISH!
I WOULD KILL TO BE IN CLASS B.
JUST ANOTHER DAY, BEING ENVIED AS I WALK...
A-ARISAKA-SAN!
...AS THE MASSES CONFESS THEIR LOVE ONE BY ONE.
UM... PLEASE ACCEPT THIS!

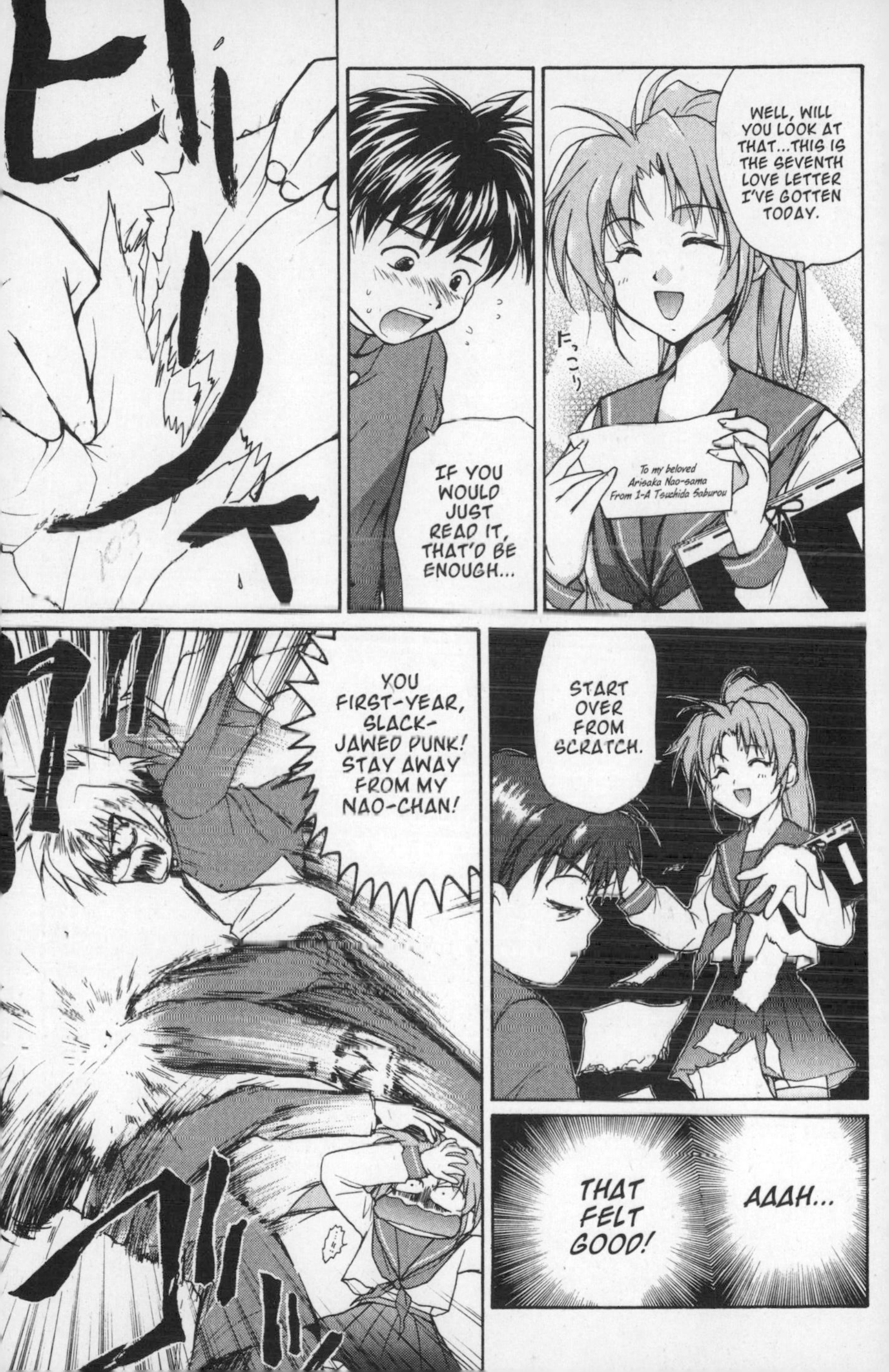
WELL, WILL YOU LOOK AT THAT...THIS IS THE SEVENTH LOVE LETTER I'VE GOTTEN TODAY.
To my beloved Arisaka Nao-sama From 1-A Tsuchida Saburou
IF YOU WOULD JUST READ IT, THAT'D BE ENOUGH...
START OVER FROM SCRATCH.
AAAH...
THAT FELT GOOD!
YOU FIRST-YEAR, SLACK-JAWED PUNK! STAY AWAY FROM MY NAO-CHAN!

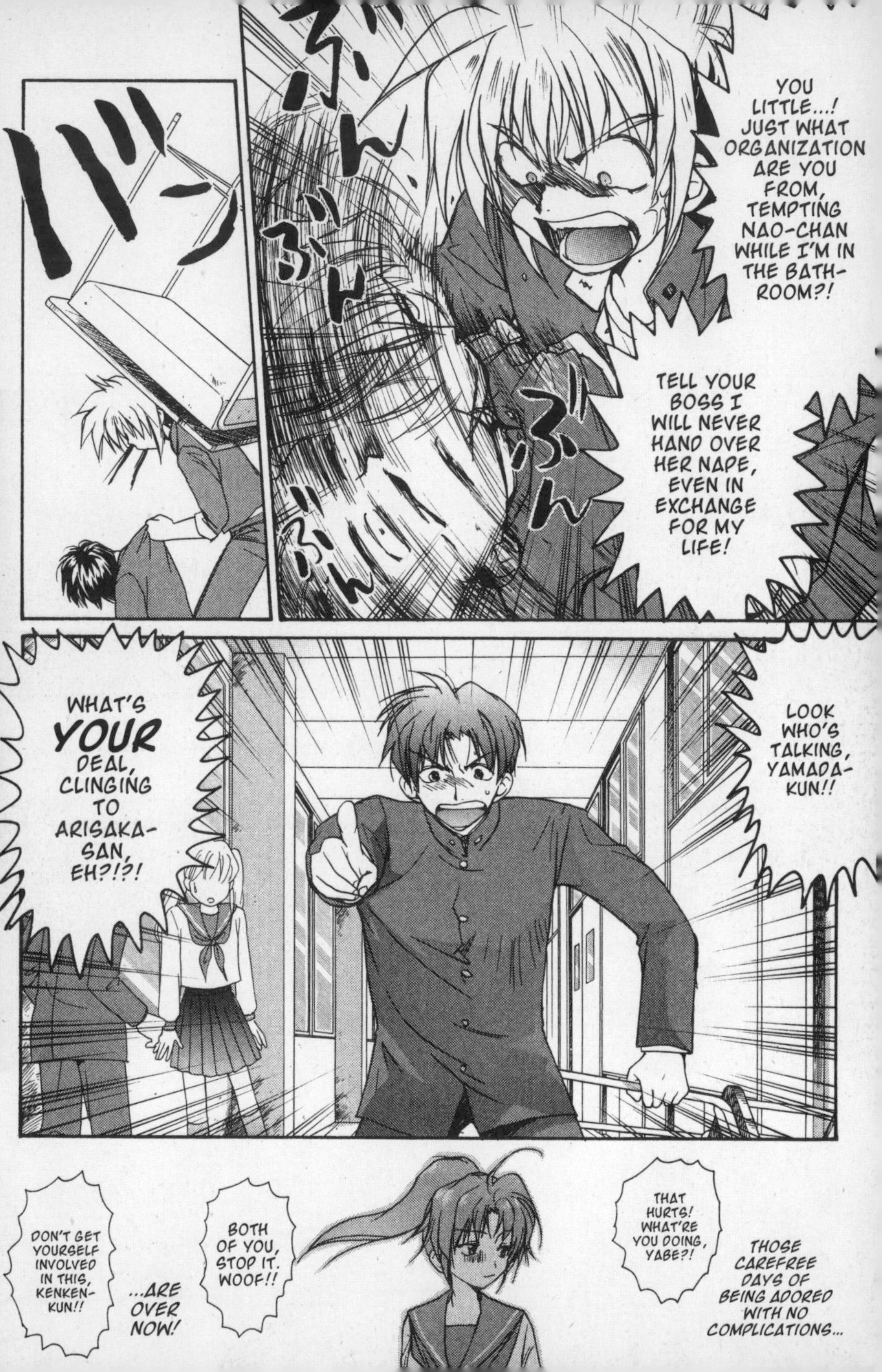
YOU LITTLE...! JUST WHAT ORGANIZATION ARE YOU FROM, TEMPTING NAO-CHAN WHILE I'M IN THE BATH-ROOM?!
TELL YOUR BOSS I WILL NEVER HAND OVER HER NAPE, EVEN IN EXCHANGE FOR MY LIFE!
LOOK WHO'S TALKING, YAMADA-KUN!!
WHAT'S *YOUR* DEAL, CLINGING TO ARISAKA-SAN, EH?!?!
THOSE CAREFREE DAYS OF BEING ADORED WITH NO COMPLICATIONS...
THAT HURTS! WHAT'RE YOU DOING, YABE?!
BOTH OF YOU, STOP IT. WOOF!!
...ARE OVER NOW!
DON'T GET YOURSELF INVOLVED IN THIS, KENKEN-KUN!!

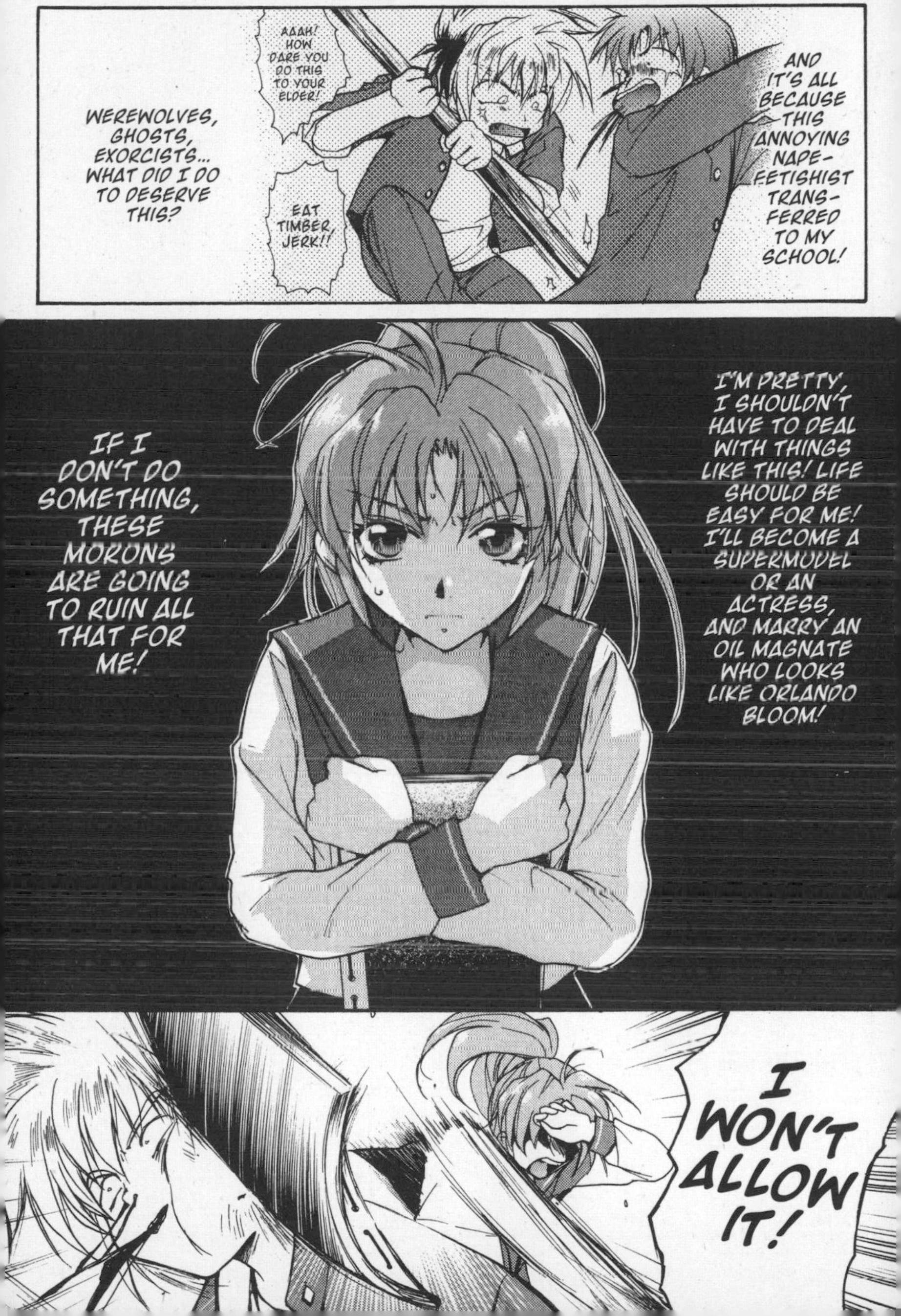
AND IT'S ALL BECAUSE THIS ANNOYING NAPE-FETISHIST TRANSFERRED TO MY SCHOOL!
AAAH! HOW DARE YOU DO THIS TO YOUR ELDER!
EAT TIMBER, JERK!!
WEREWOLVES, GHOSTS, EXORCISTS... WHAT DID I DO TO DESERVE THIS?
I'M PRETTY, I SHOULDN'T HAVE TO DEAL WITH THINGS LIKE THIS! LIFE SHOULD BE EASY FOR ME! I'LL BECOME A SUPERMODEL OR AN ACTRESS, AND MARRY AN OIL MAGNATE WHO LOOKS LIKE ORLANDO BLOOM!
IF I DON'T DO SOMETHING, THESE MORONS ARE GOING TO RUIN ALL THAT FOR ME!
I WON'T ALLOW IT!

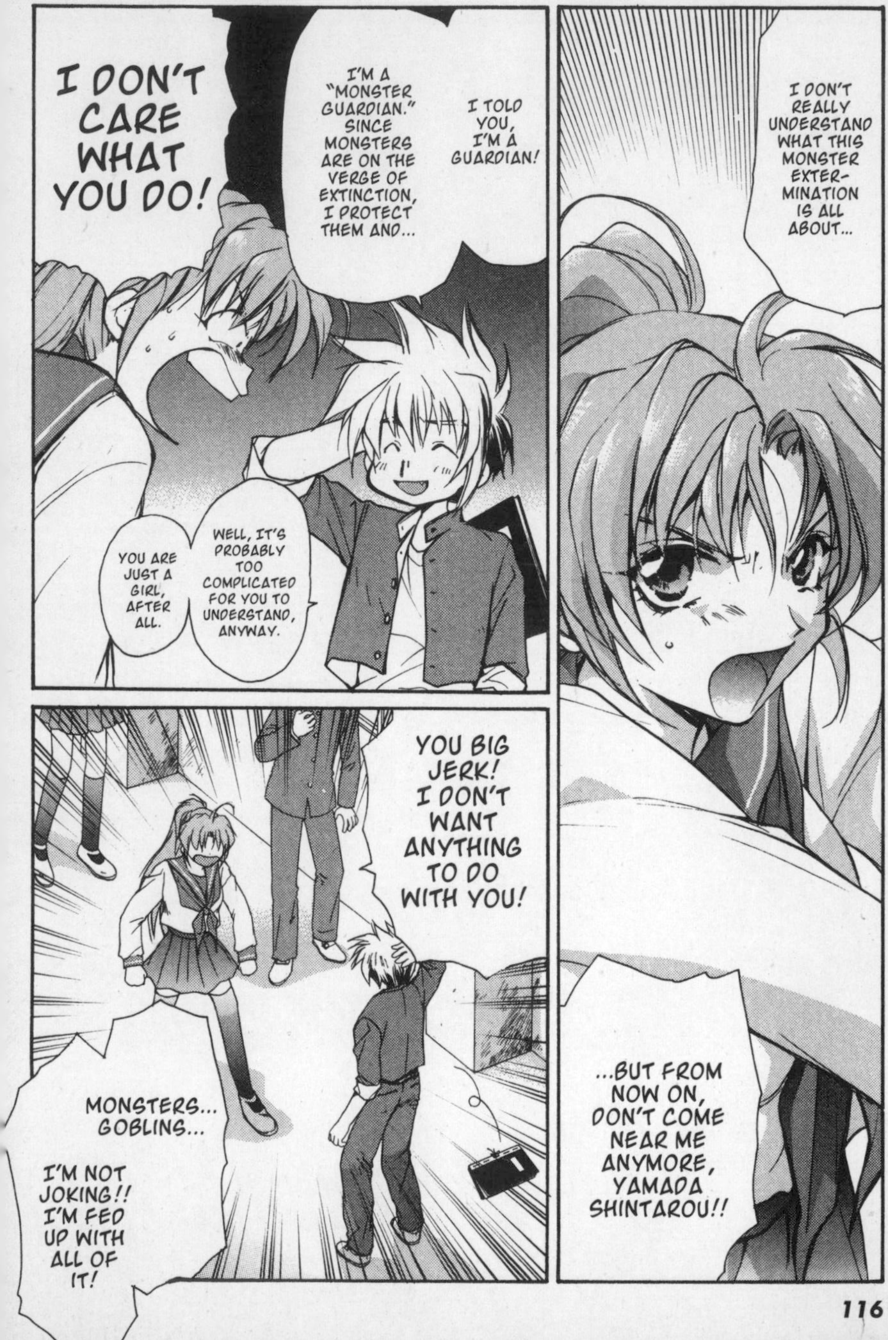
I DON'T REALLY UNDERSTAND WHAT THIS MONSTER EXTER-MINATION IS ALL ABOUT...
...BUT FROM NOW ON, DON'T COME NEAR ME ANYMORE, YAMADA SHINTAROU!!
I TOLD YOU, I'M A GUARDIAN!
I'M A "MONSTER GUARDIAN." SINCE MONSTERS ARE ON THE VERGE OF EXTINCTION, I PROTECT THEM AND...
I DON'T CARE WHAT YOU DO!
WELL, IT'S PROBABLY TOO COMPLICATED FOR YOU TO UNDERSTAND, ANYWAY.
YOU ARE JUST A GIRL, AFTER ALL.
YOU BIG JERK! I DON'T WANT ANYTHING TO DO WITH YOU!
MONSTERS... GOBLINS...
I'M NOT JOKING!! I'M FED UP WITH ALL OF IT!

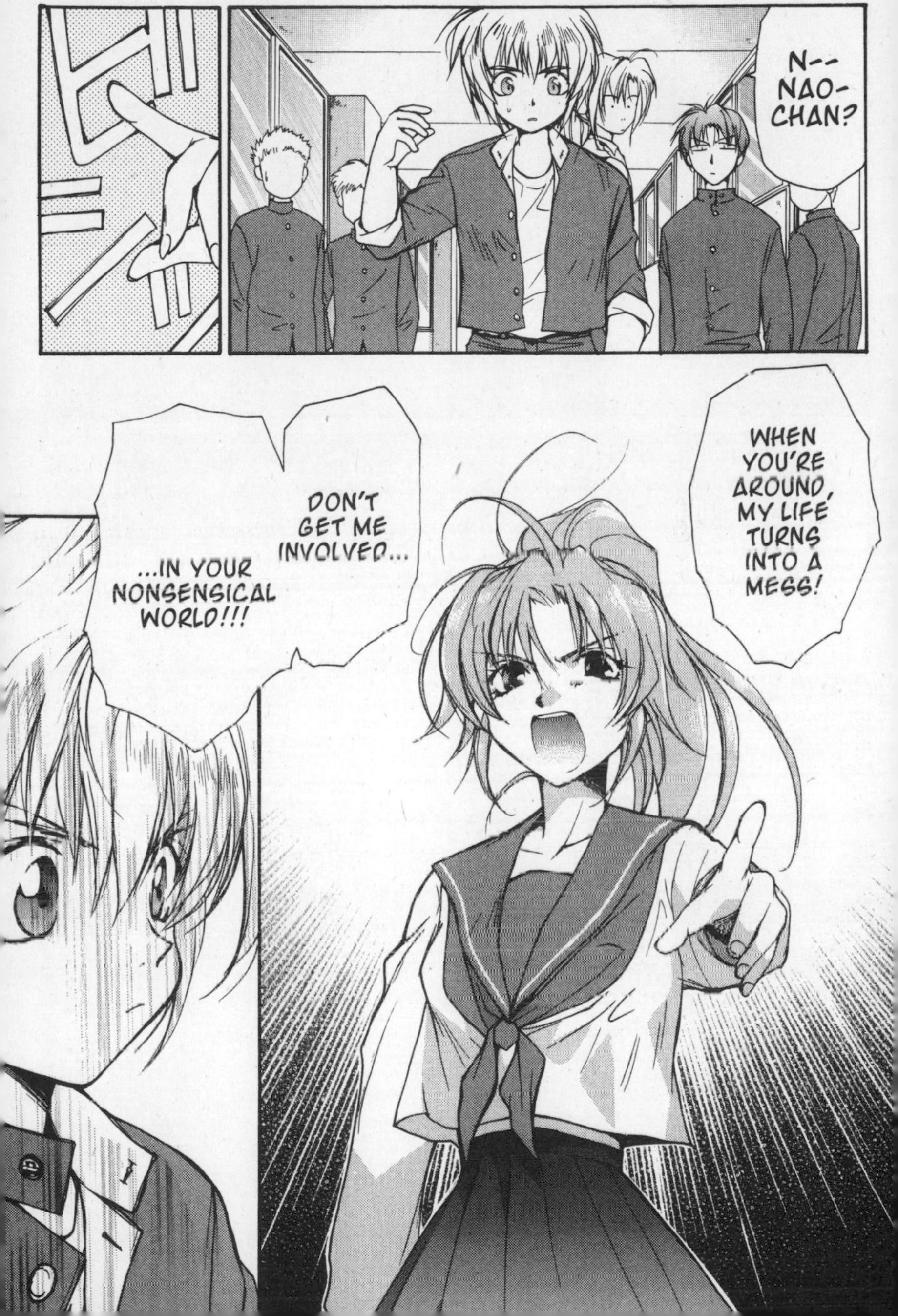
N-- NAO-CHAN?
WHEN YOU'RE AROUND, MY LIFE TURNS INTO A MESS!
DON'T GET ME INVOLVED...
...IN YOUR NONSENSICAL WORLD!!!

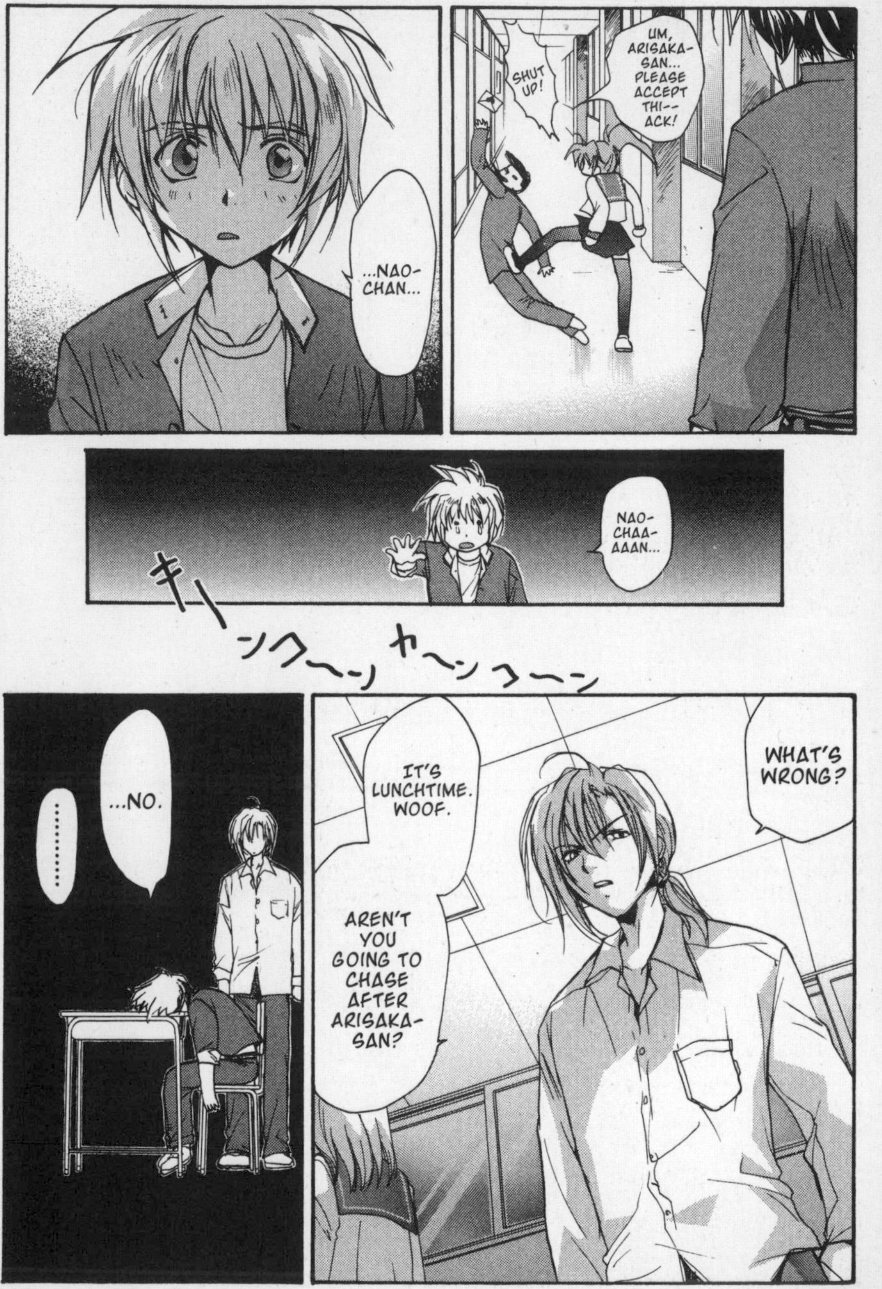
UM, ARISAKA-SAN... PLEASE ACCEPT THI--ACK!
SHUT UP!
...NAO-CHAN...
NAO-CHAAAAAN...
キーンコーン カーンコーン
WHAT'S WRONG?
IT'S LUNCHTIME. WOOF.
AREN'T YOU GOING TO CHASE AFTER ARISAKA-SAN?
...NO.
......

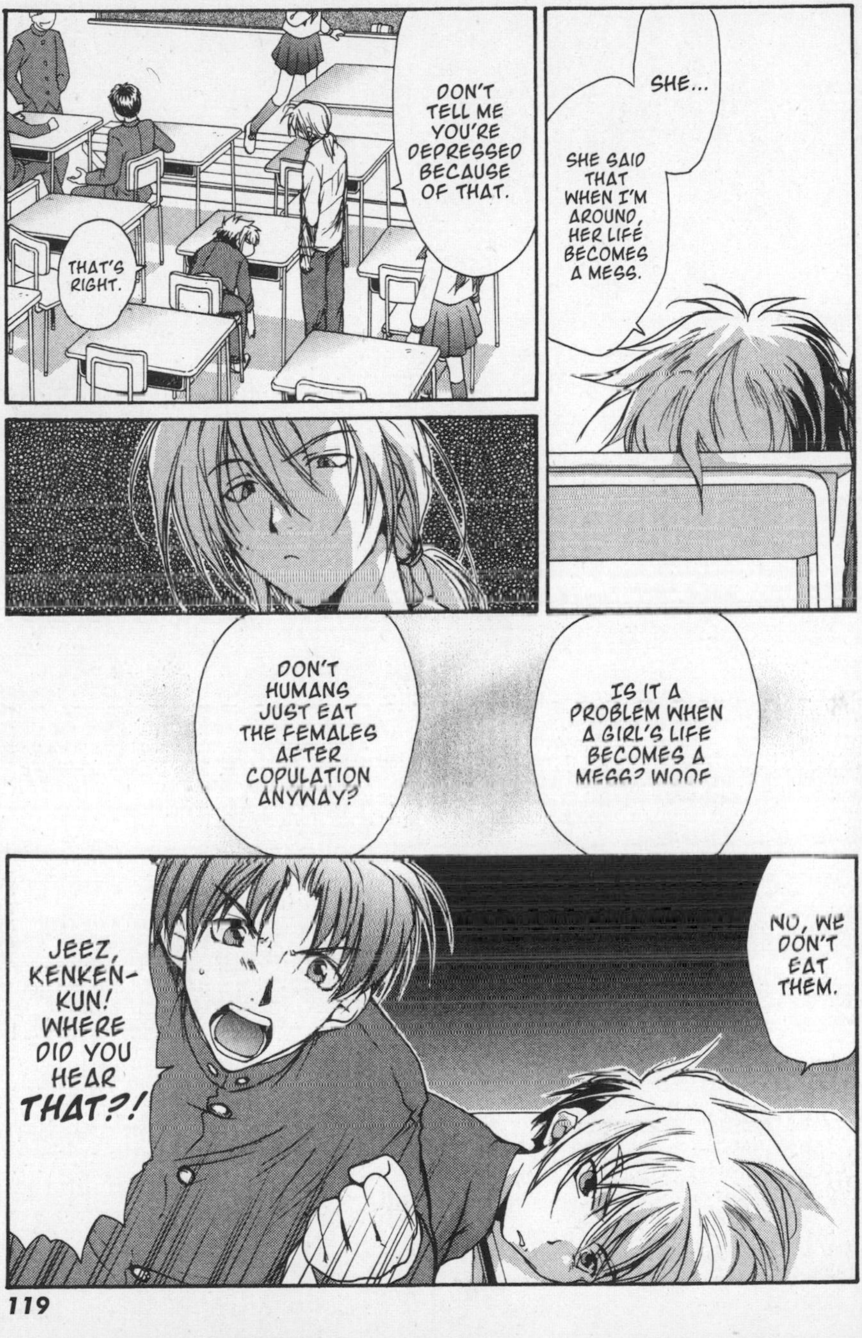
SHE...
SHE SAID THAT WHEN I'M AROUND, HER LIFE BECOMES A MESS.
DON'T TELL ME YOU'RE DEPRESSED BECAUSE OF THAT.
THAT'S RIGHT.
IS IT A PROBLEM WHEN A GIRL'S LIFE BECOMES A MESS? WOOF
DON'T HUMANS JUST EAT THE FEMALES AFTER COPULATION ANYWAY?
NO, WE DON'T EAT THEM.
JEEZ, KENKEN-KUN! WHERE DID YOU HEAR THAT?!

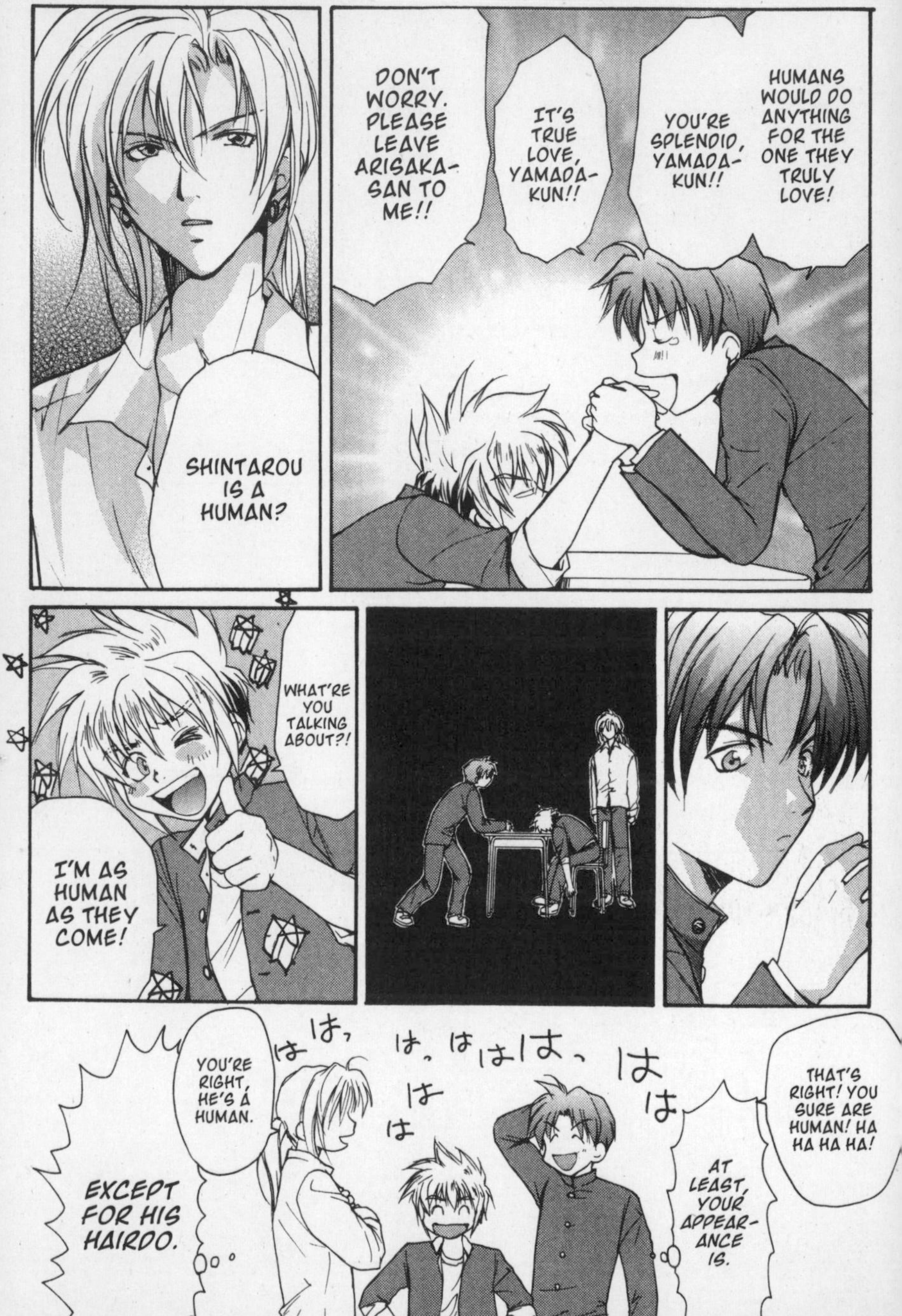
HUMANS WOULD DO ANYTHING FOR THE ONE THEY TRULY LOVE!
YOU'RE SPLENDID, YAMADA-KUN!!
IT'S TRUE LOVE, YAMADA-KUN!!
DON'T WORRY. PLEASE LEAVE ARISAKA-SAN TO ME!!
SHINTAROU IS A HUMAN?
WHAT'RE YOU TALKING ABOUT?!
I'M AS HUMAN AS THEY COME!
THAT'S RIGHT! YOU SURE ARE HUMAN! HA HA HA HA!
AT LEAST, YOUR APPEARANCE IS.
はは
は、ははは、
はは
ははっ
YOU'RE RIGHT, HE'S A HUMAN.
EXCEPT FOR HIS HAIRDO.

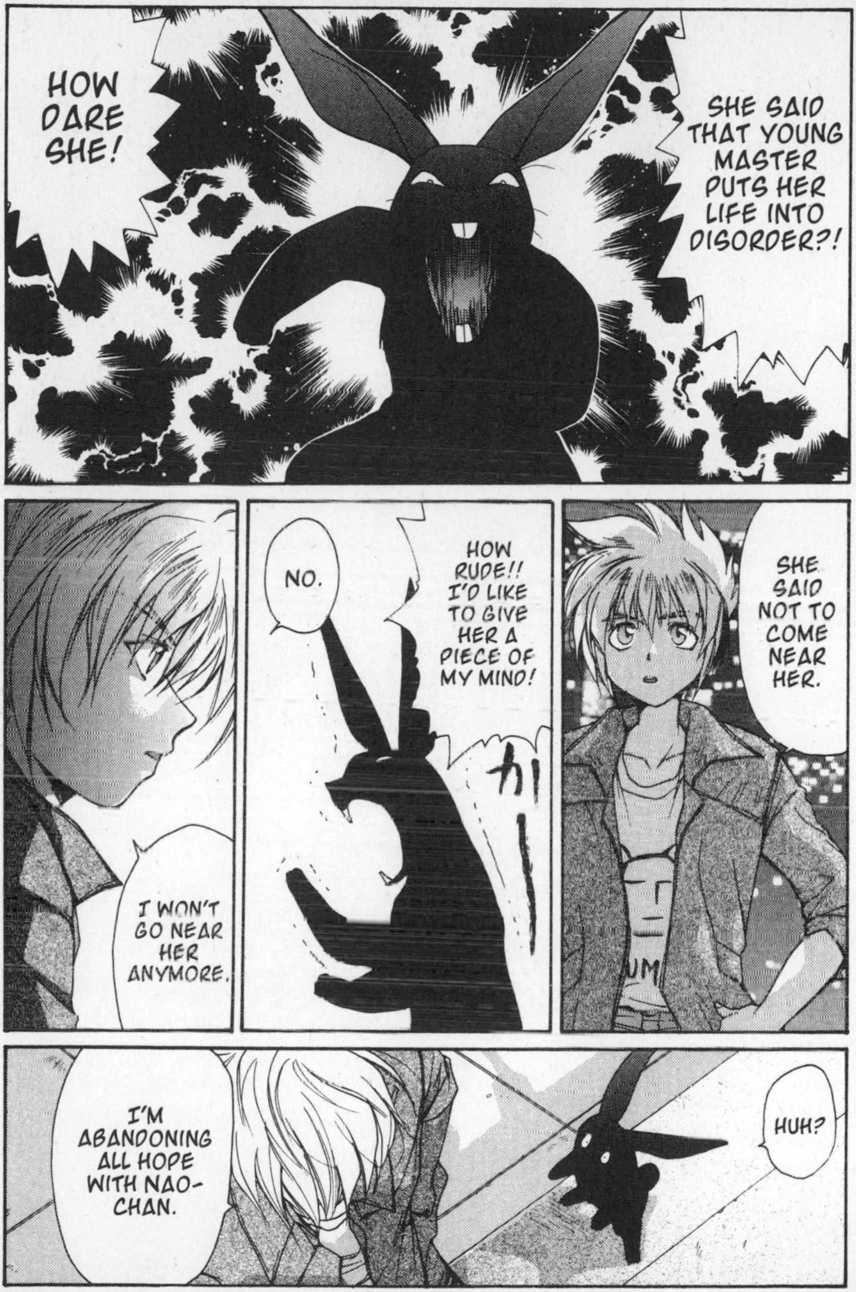
SHE SAID THAT YOUNG MASTER PUTS HER LIFE INTO DISORDER?!
HOW DARE SHE!
SHE SAID NOT TO COME NEAR HER.
HOW RUDE!! I'D LIKE TO GIVE HER A PIECE OF MY MIND!
カー
NO.
I WON'T GO NEAR HER ANYMORE.
HUH?
I'M ABANDONING ALL HOPE WITH NAO-CHAN.

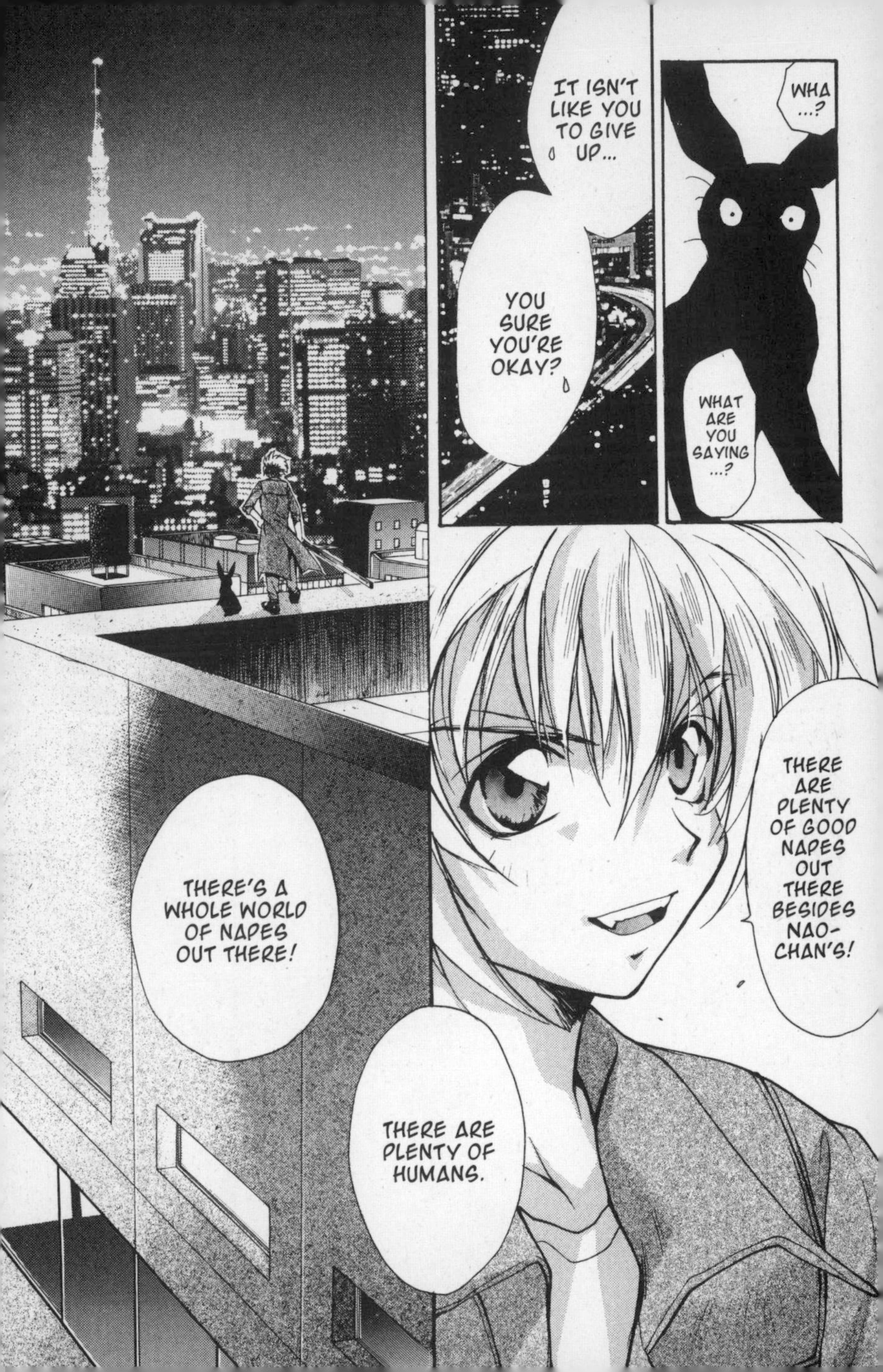
WHA ...?
WHAT ARE YOU SAYING ...?
IT ISN'T LIKE YOU TO GIVE UP...
YOU SURE YOU'RE OKAY?
THERE ARE PLENTY OF GOOD NAPES OUT THERE BESIDES NAO-CHAN'S!
THERE ARE PLENTY OF HUMANS.
THERE'S A WHOLE WORLD OF NAPES OUT THERE!

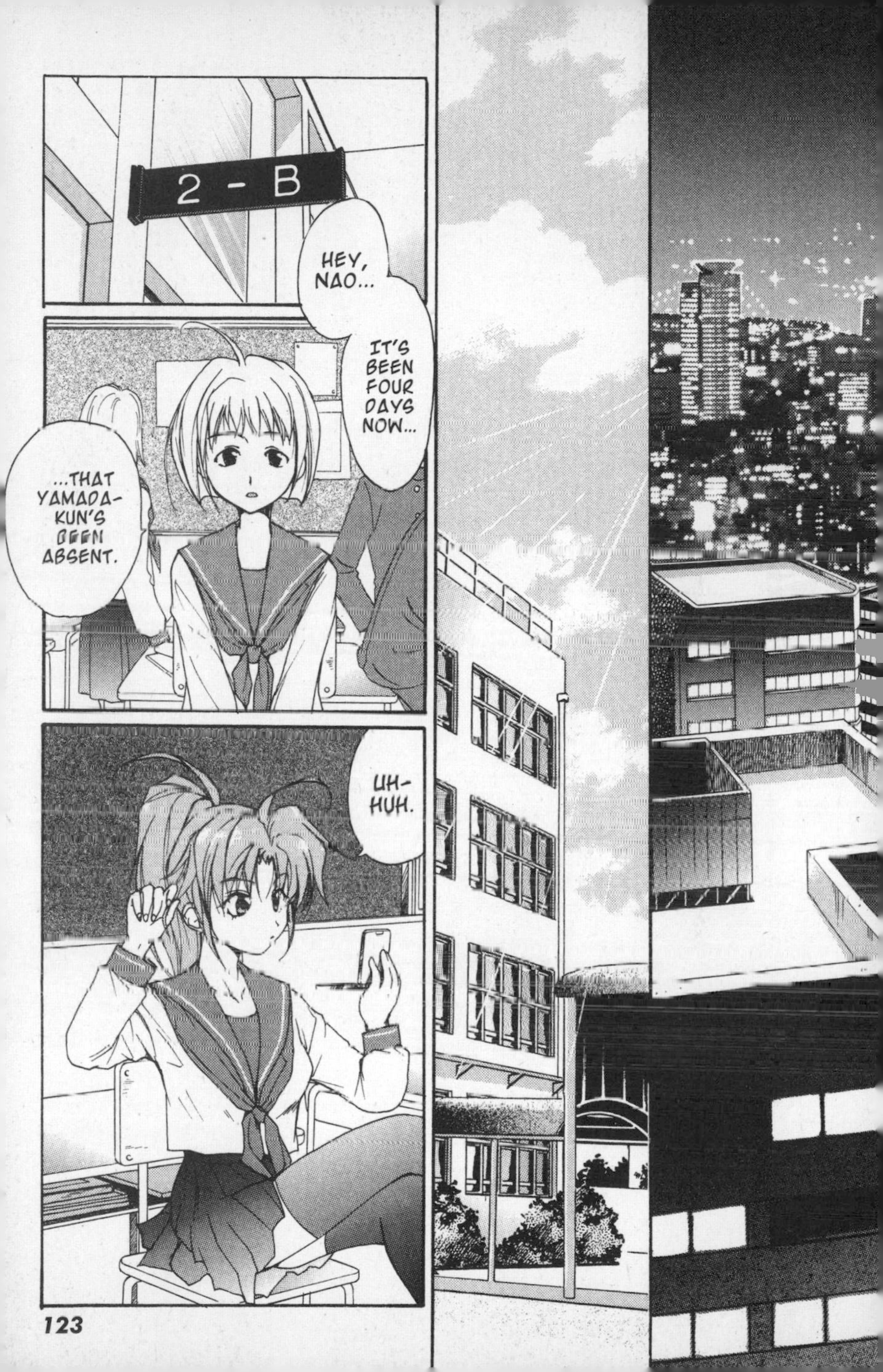
2 - B
HEY, NAO...
IT'S BEEN FOUR DAYS NOW...
...THAT YAMADA-KUN'S BEEN ABSENT.
UH-HUH.

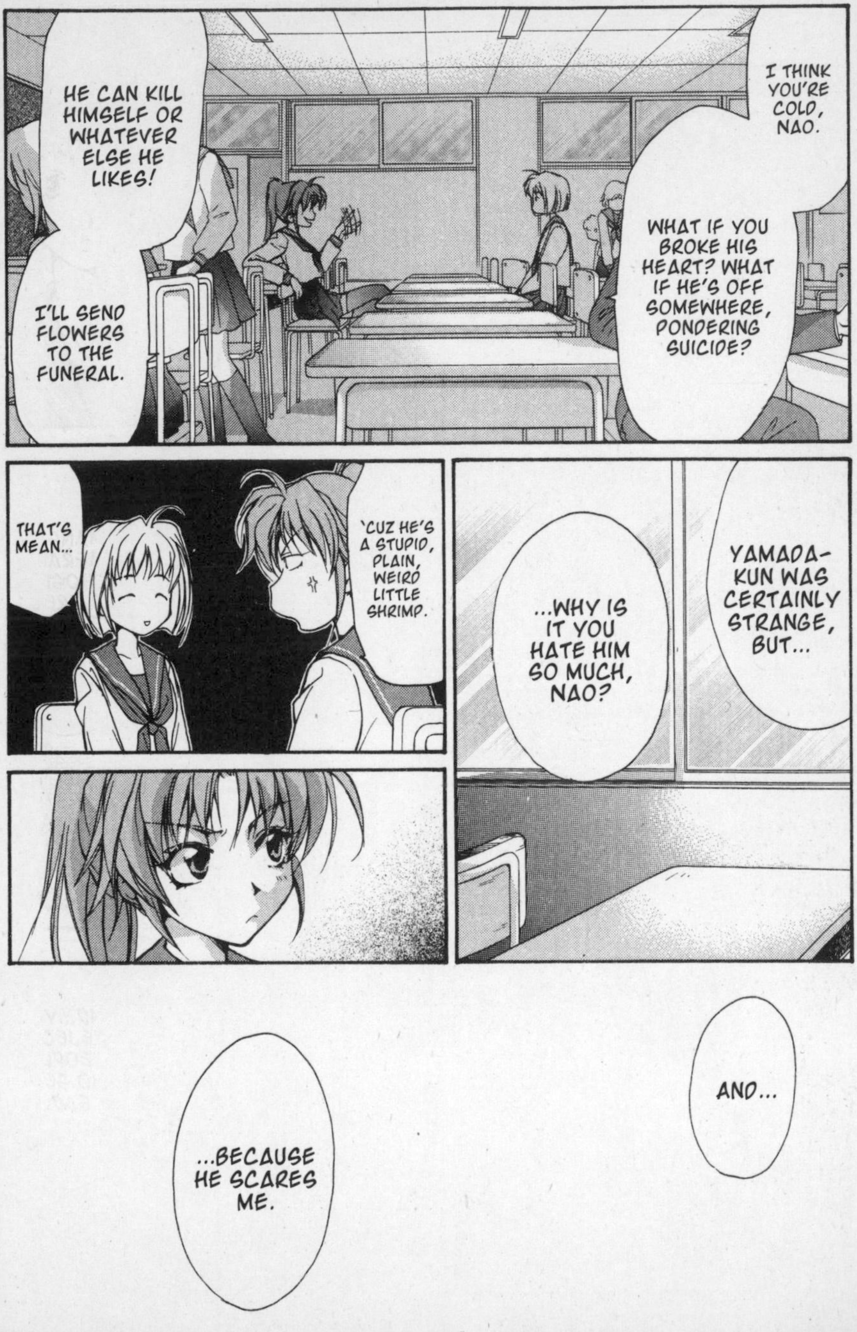
I THINK YOU'RE COLD, NAO.
WHAT IF YOU BROKE HIS HEART? WHAT IF HE'S OFF SOMEWHERE, PONDERING SUICIDE?
HE CAN KILL HIMSELF OR WHATEVER ELSE HE LIKES!
I'LL SEND FLOWERS TO THE FUNERAL.
YAMADA-KUN WAS CERTAINLY STRANGE, BUT...
...WHY IS IT YOU HATE HIM SO MUCH, NAO?
'CUZ HE'S A STUPID, PLAIN, WEIRD LITTLE SHRIMP.
THAT'S MEAN...
AND...
...BECAUSE HE SCARES ME.

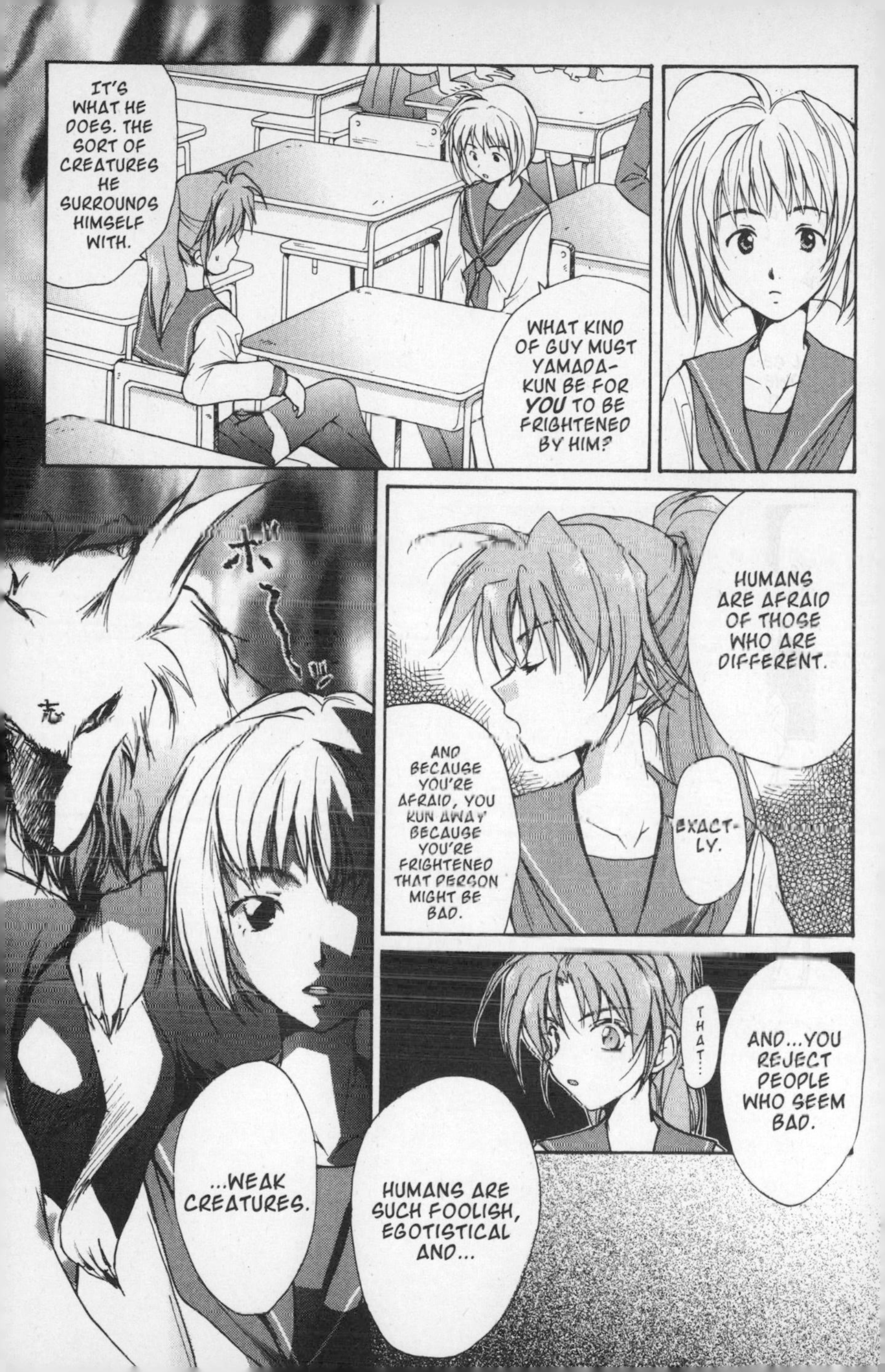
WHAT KIND OF GUY MUST YAMADA-KUN BE FOR *YOU* TO BE FRIGHTENED BY HIM?
IT'S WHAT HE DOES. THE SORT OF CREATURES HE SURROUNDS HIMSELF WITH.
HUMANS ARE AFRAID OF THOSE WHO ARE DIFFERENT.
EXACT-LY.
AND BECAUSE YOU'RE AFRAID, YOU RUN AWAY BECAUSE YOU'RE FRIGHTENED THAT PERSON MIGHT BE BAD.
AND...YOU REJECT PEOPLE WHO SEEM BAD.
THAT...
HUMANS ARE SUCH FOOLISH, EGOTISTICAL AND...
...WEAK CREATURES.

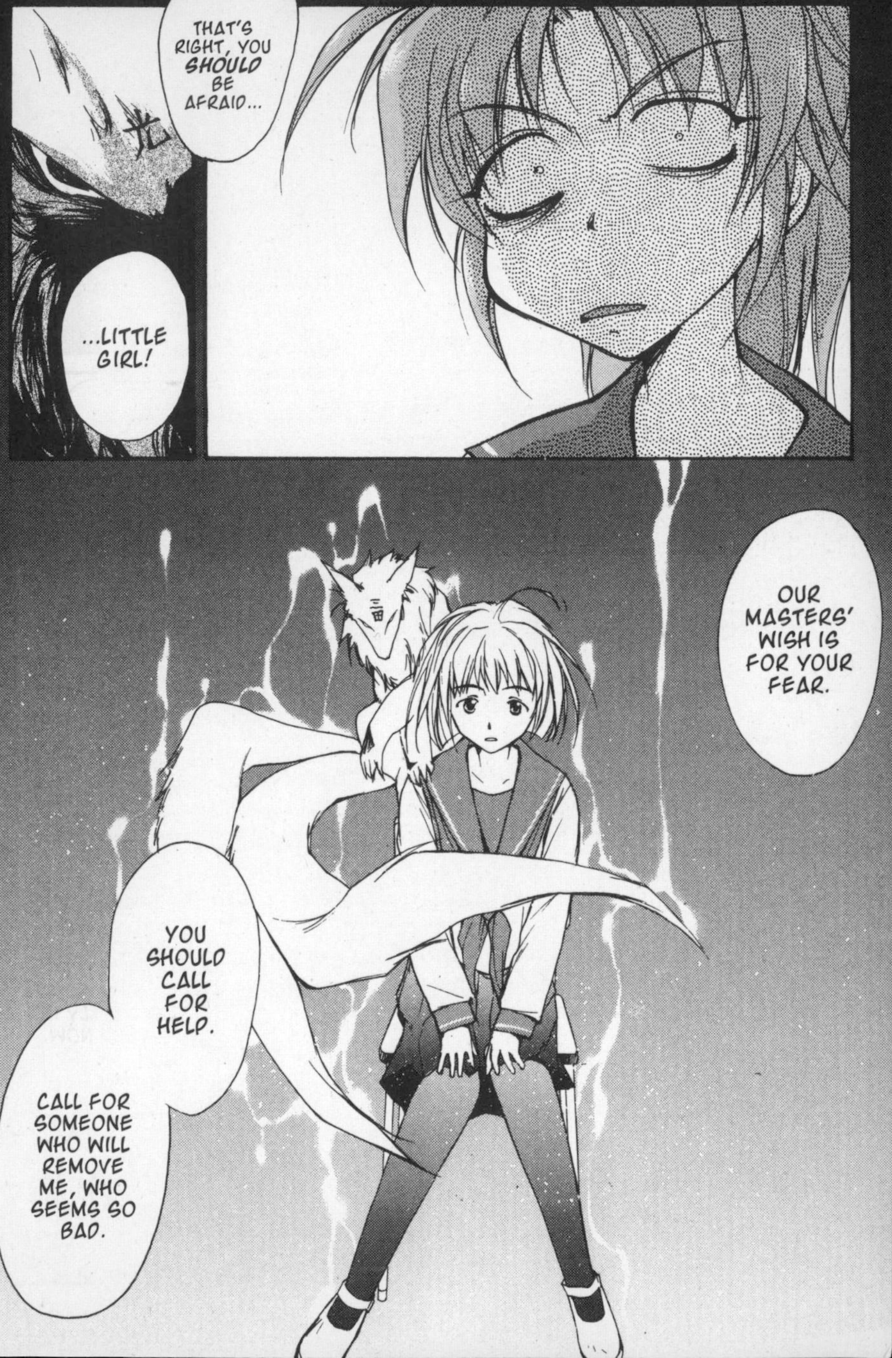
THAT'S RIGHT, YOU *SHOULD* BE AFRAID...
...LITTLE GIRL!
OUR MASTERS' WISH IS FOR YOUR FEAR.
YOU SHOULD CALL FOR HELP.
CALL FOR SOMEONE WHO WILL REMOVE ME, WHO SEEMS SO BAD.

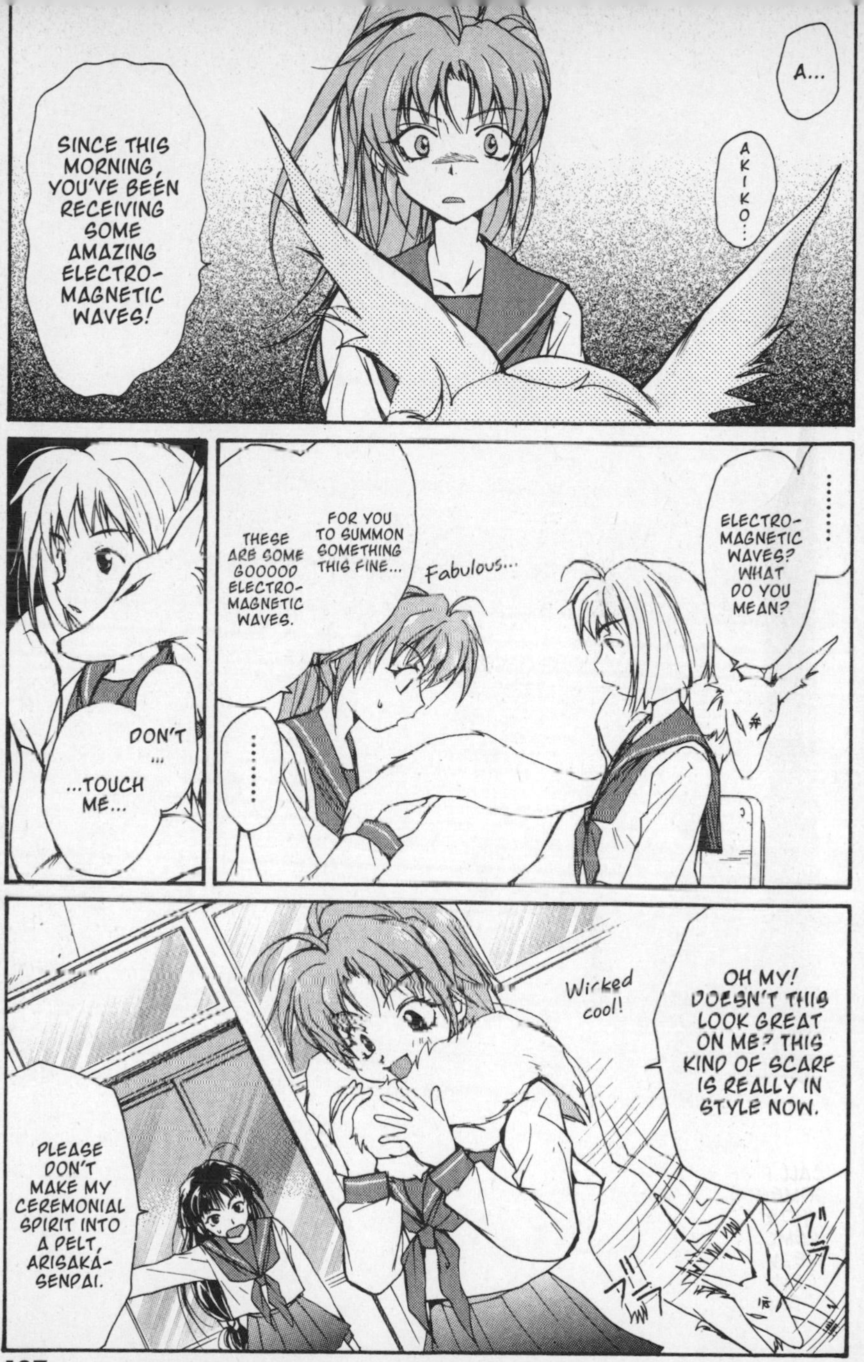
A...
AKIKO...
SINCE THIS MORNING, YOU'VE BEEN RECEIVING SOME AMAZING ELECTRO-MAGNETIC WAVES!
......
ELECTRO-MAGNETIC WAVES? WHAT DO YOU MEAN?
Fabulous...
FOR YOU TO SUMMON SOMETHING THIS FINE...
THESE ARE SOME GOOOOD ELECTRO-MAGNETIC WAVES.
......
DON'T ...
...TOUCH ME...
OH MY! DOESN'T THIS LOOK GREAT ON ME? THIS KIND OF SCARF IS REALLY IN STYLE NOW.
Wicked cool!
PLEASE DON'T MAKE MY CEREMONIAL SPIRIT INTO A PELT, ARISAKA-SENPAI.

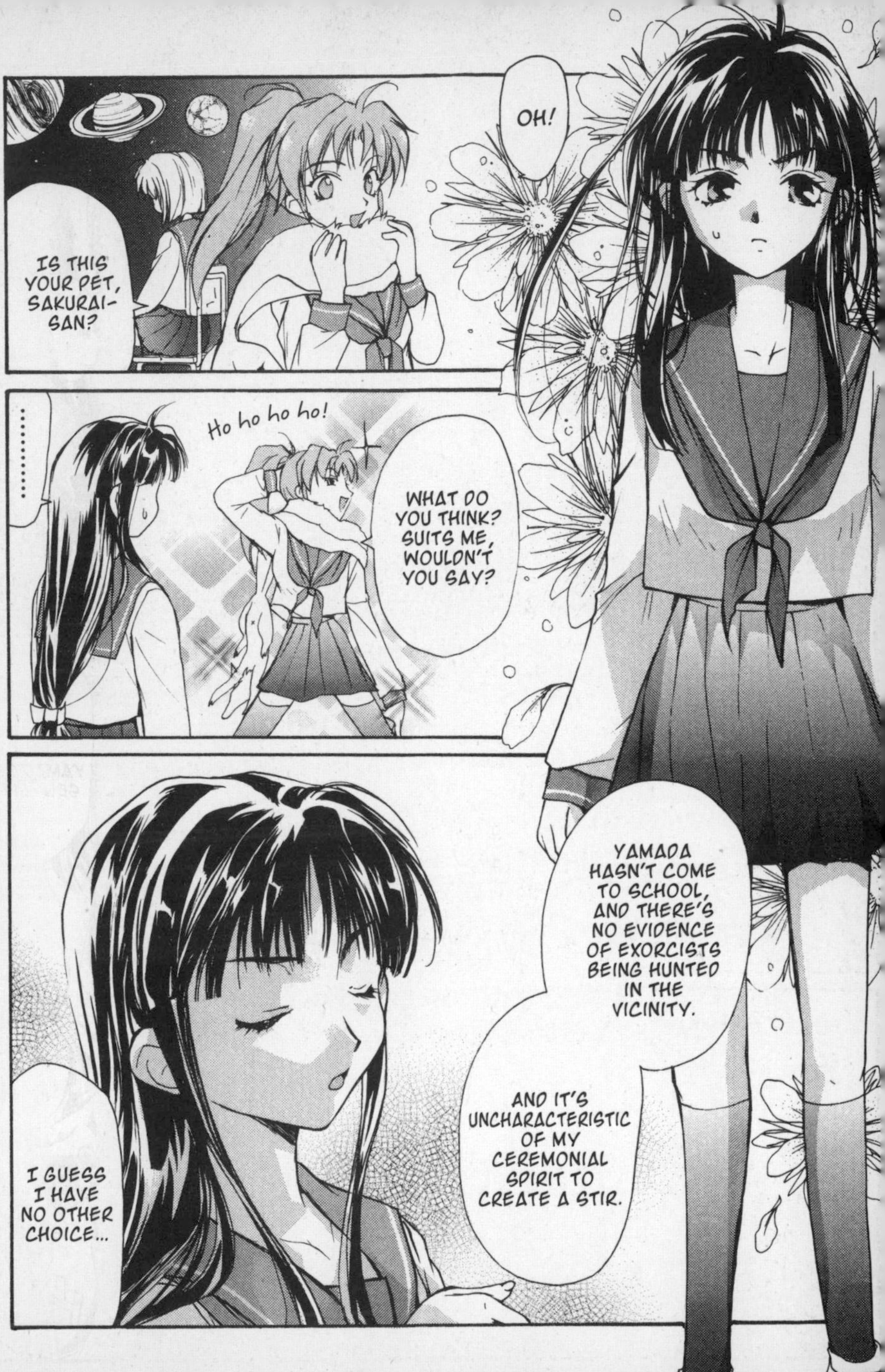

OH!
IS THIS YOUR PET, SAKURAI-SAN?
......
Ho ho ho ho!
WHAT DO YOU THINK? SUITS ME, WOULDN'T YOU SAY?
YAMADA HASN'T COME TO SCHOOL, AND THERE'S NO EVIDENCE OF EXORCISTS BEING HUNTED IN THE VICINITY.
AND IT'S UNCHARACTERISTIC OF MY CEREMONIAL SPIRIT TO CREATE A STIR.
I GUESS I HAVE NO OTHER CHOICE...

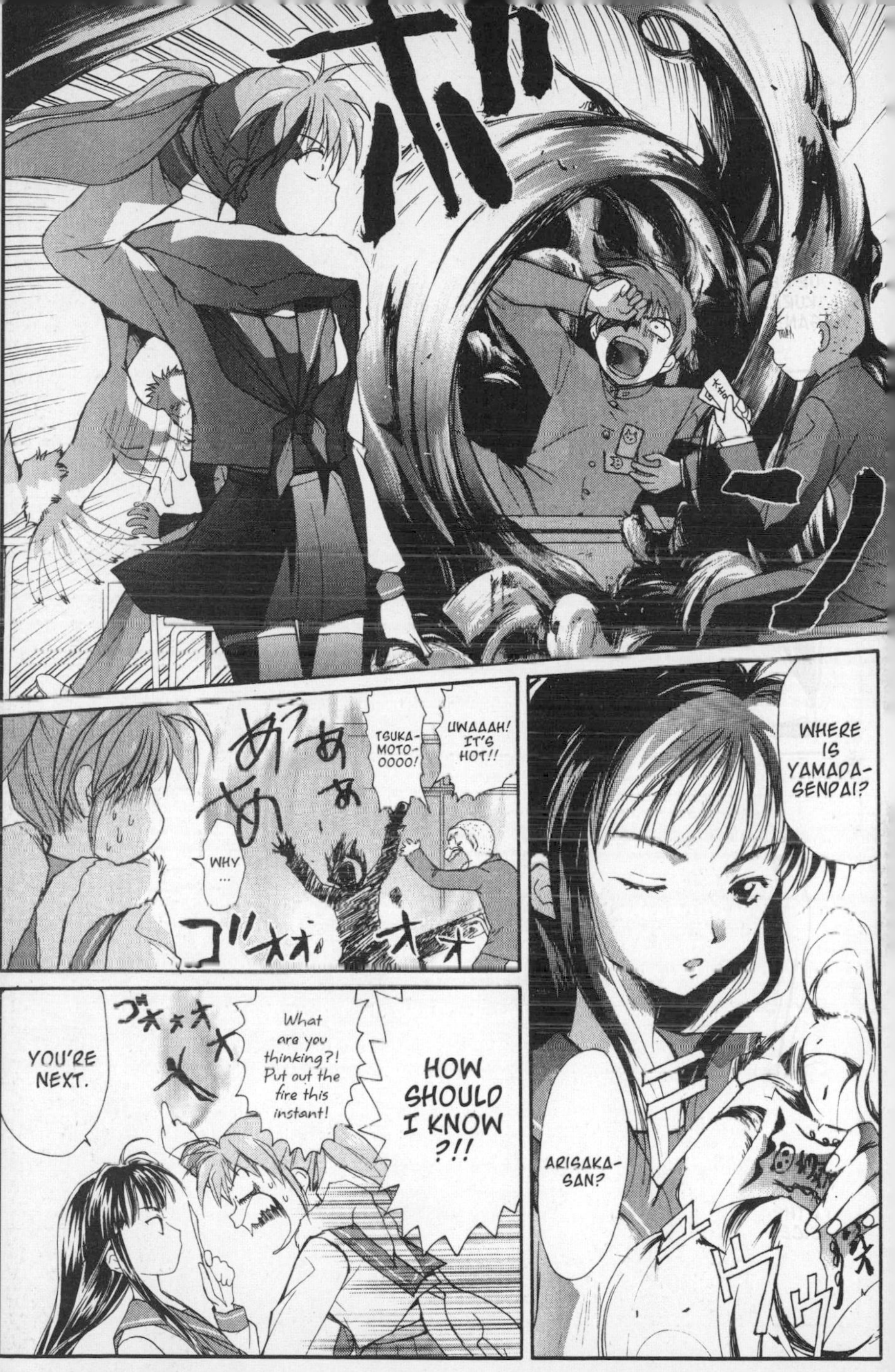
WHERE IS YAMADA-SENPAI?
ARISAKA-SAN?
UWAAAH! IT'S HOT!!
TSUKA-MOTO-OOOO!
WHY ...
HOW SHOULD I KNOW ?!!
What are you thinking?! Put out the fire this instant!
YOU'RE NEXT.

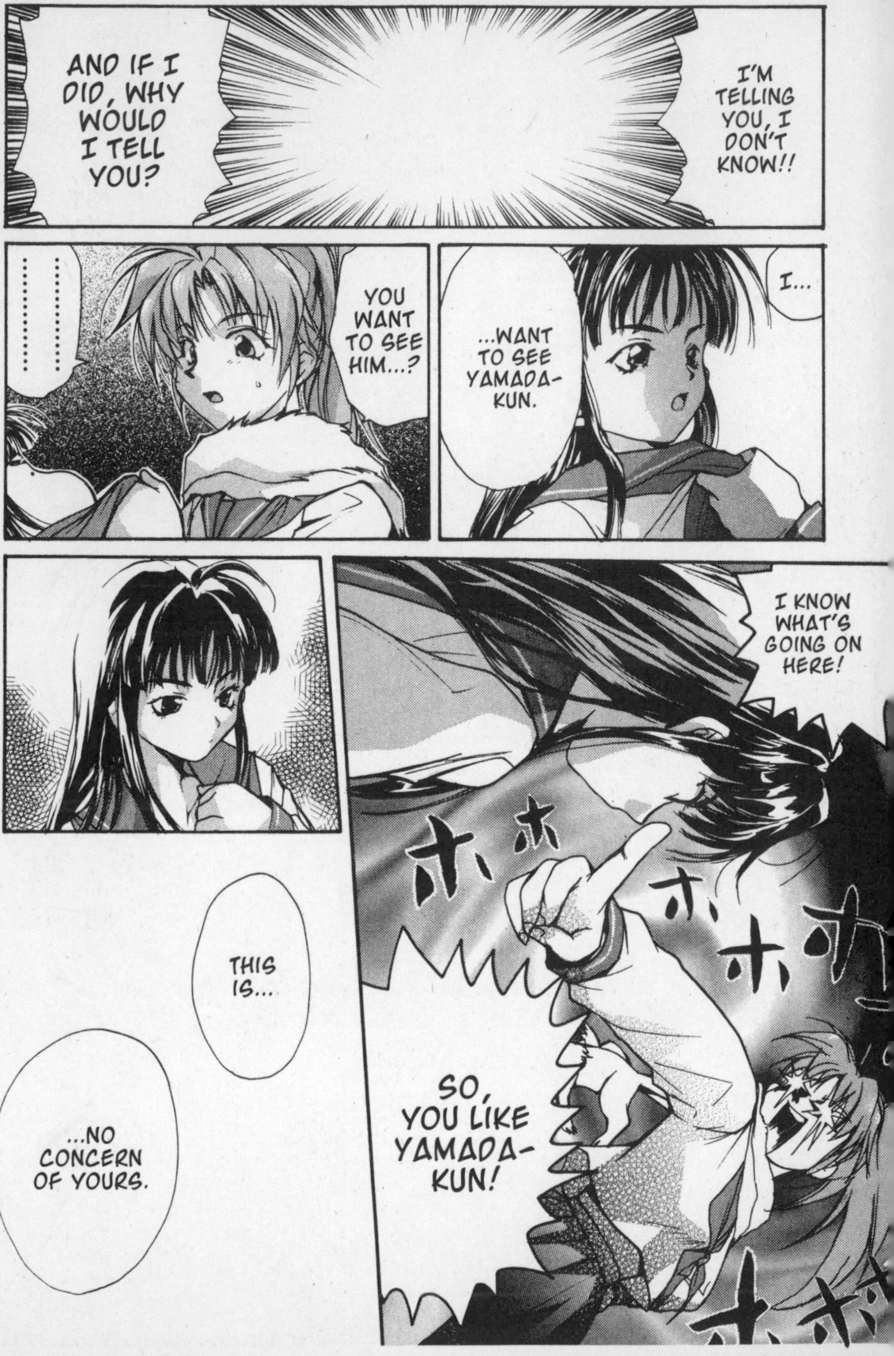
I'M TELLING YOU, I DON'T KNOW!!
AND IF I DID, WHY WOULD I TELL YOU?
I...
...WANT TO SEE YAMADA-KUN.
YOU WANT TO SEE HIM...?
......
I KNOW WHAT'S GOING ON HERE!
SO, YOU LIKE YAMADA-KUN!
ホホホ
THIS IS...
...NO CONCERN OF YOURS.

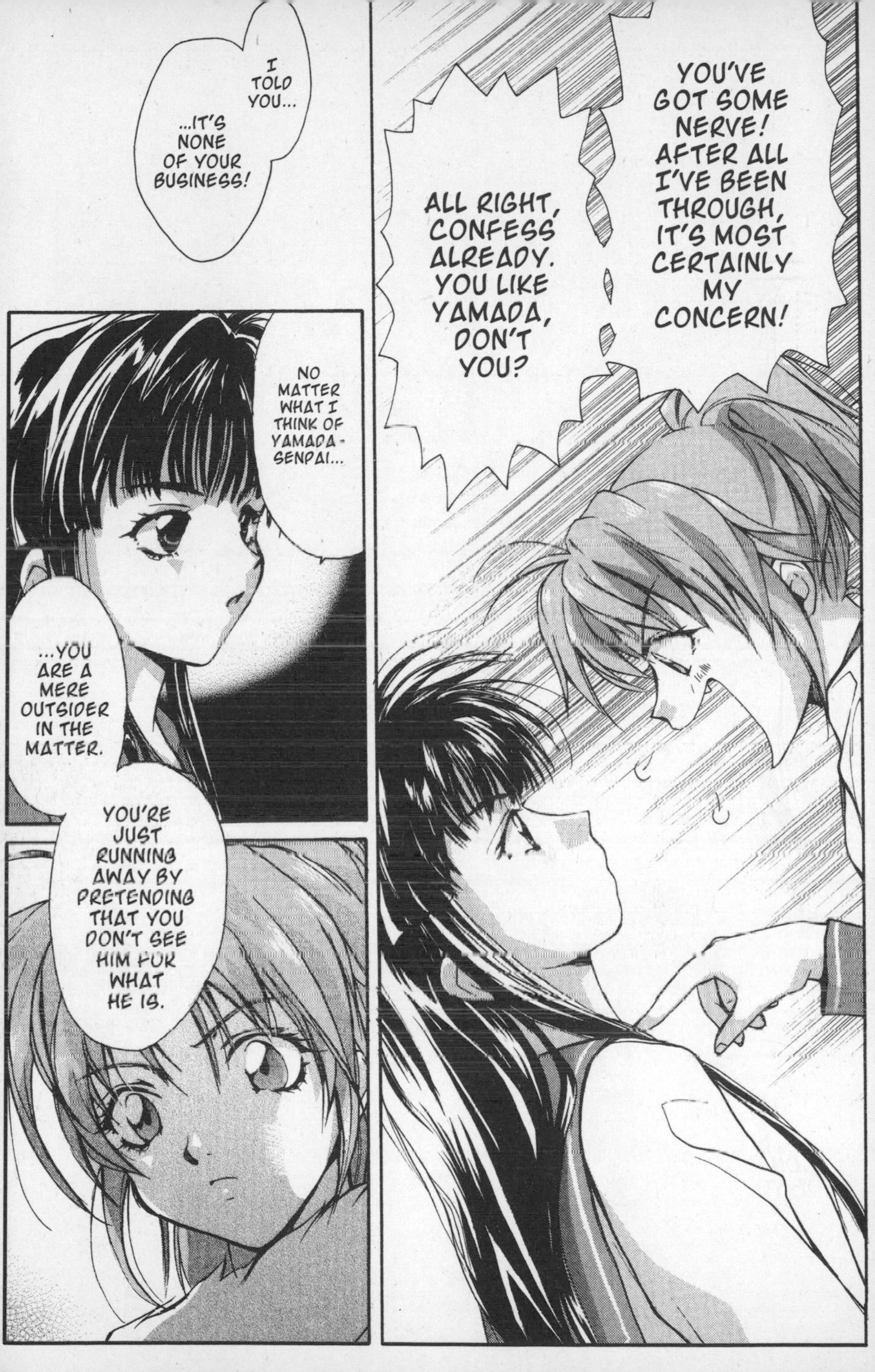
YOU'VE GOT SOME NERVE! AFTER ALL I'VE BEEN THROUGH, IT'S MOST CERTAINLY MY CONCERN!
ALL RIGHT, CONFESS ALREADY. YOU LIKE YAMADA, DON'T YOU?
I TOLD YOU... ...IT'S NONE OF YOUR BUSINESS!
NO MATTER WHAT I THINK OF YAMADA-SENPAI...
...YOU ARE A MERE OUTSIDER IN THE MATTER.
YOU'RE JUST RUNNING AWAY BY PRETENDING THAT YOU DON'T SEE HIM FOR WHAT HE IS.

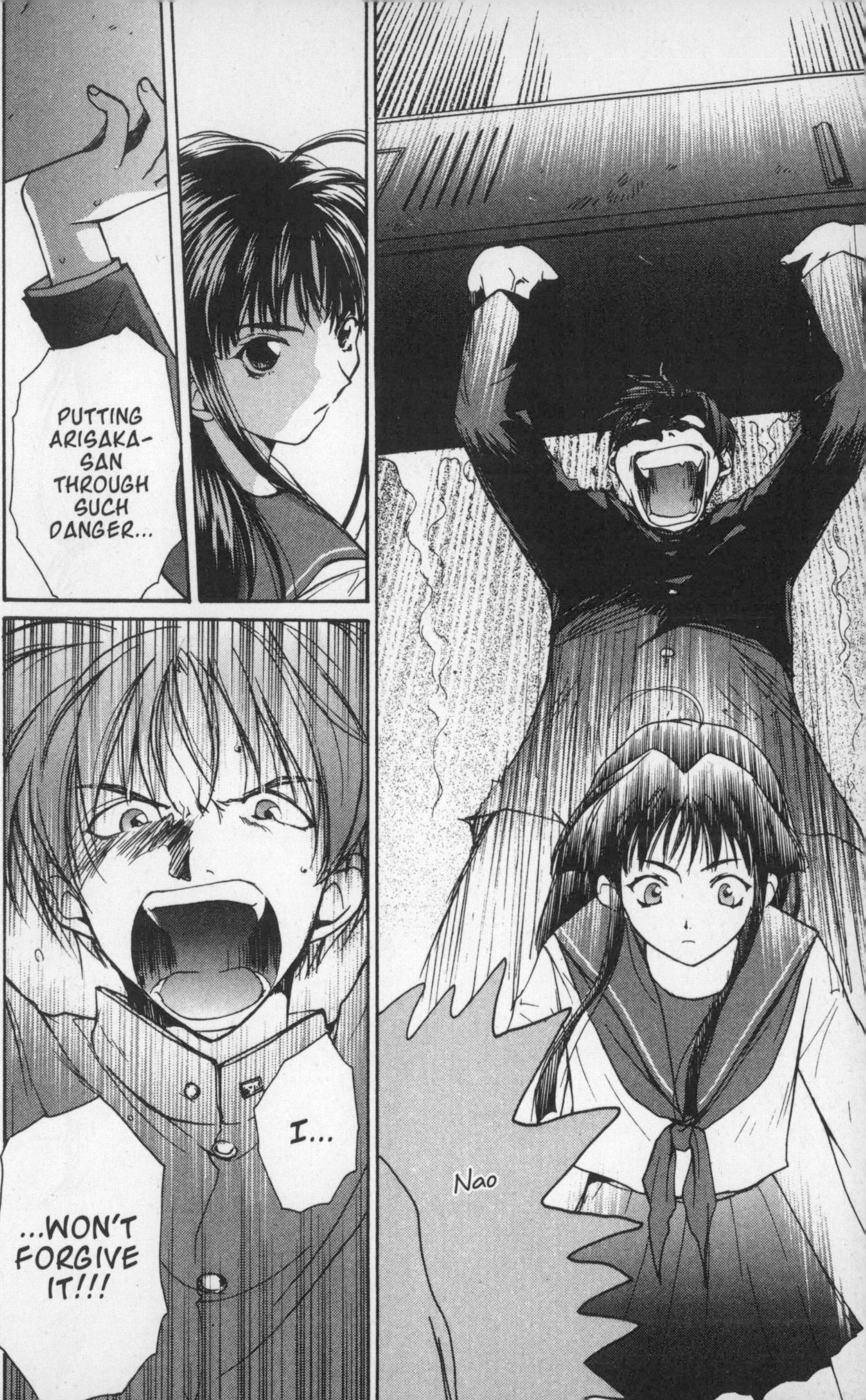
Nao
PUTTING ARISAKA-SAN THROUGH SUCH DANGER...
I...
...WON'T FORGIVE IT!!!

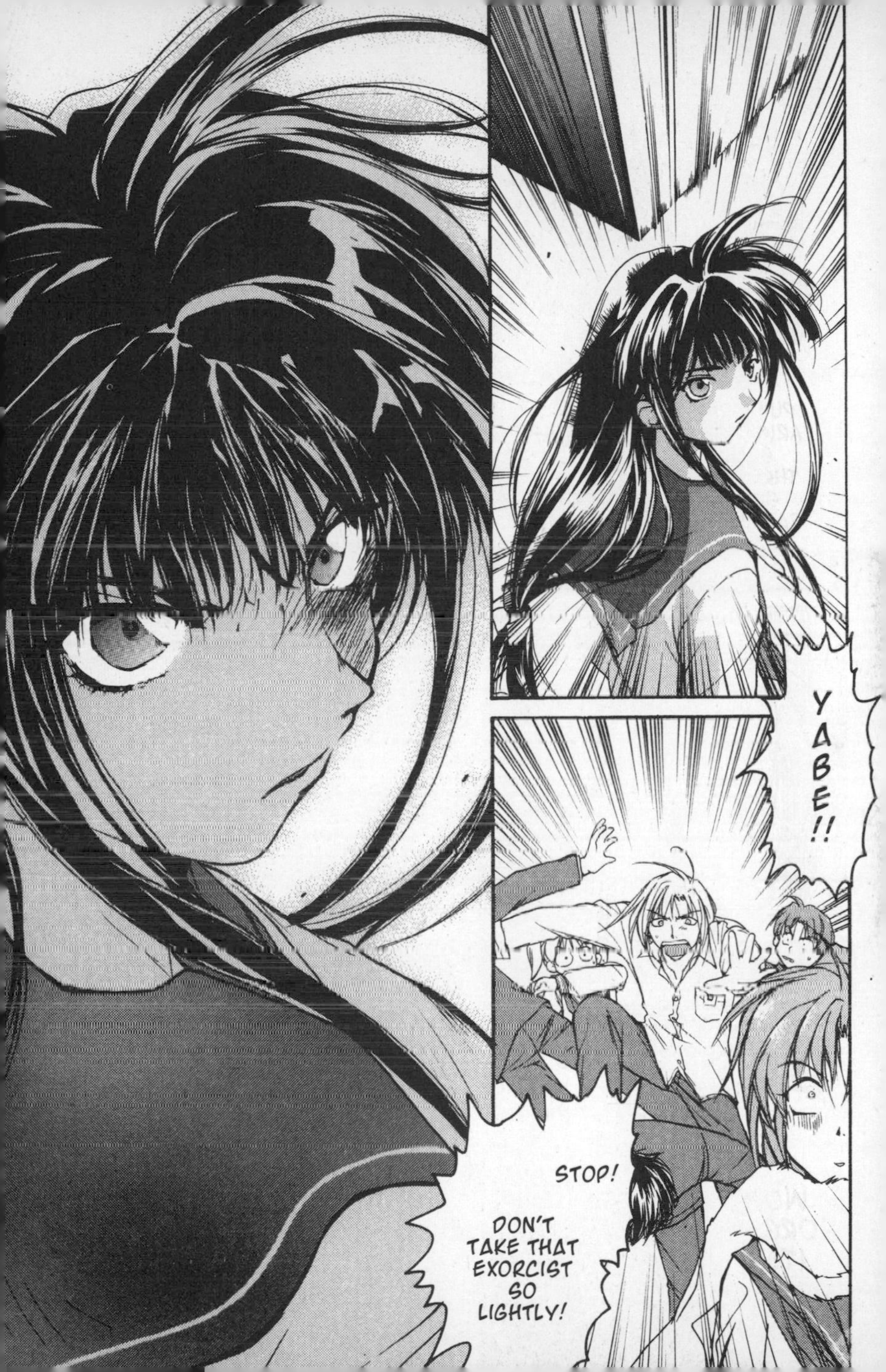
YABE!!
STOP!
DON'T TAKE THAT EXORCIST SO LIGHTLY!

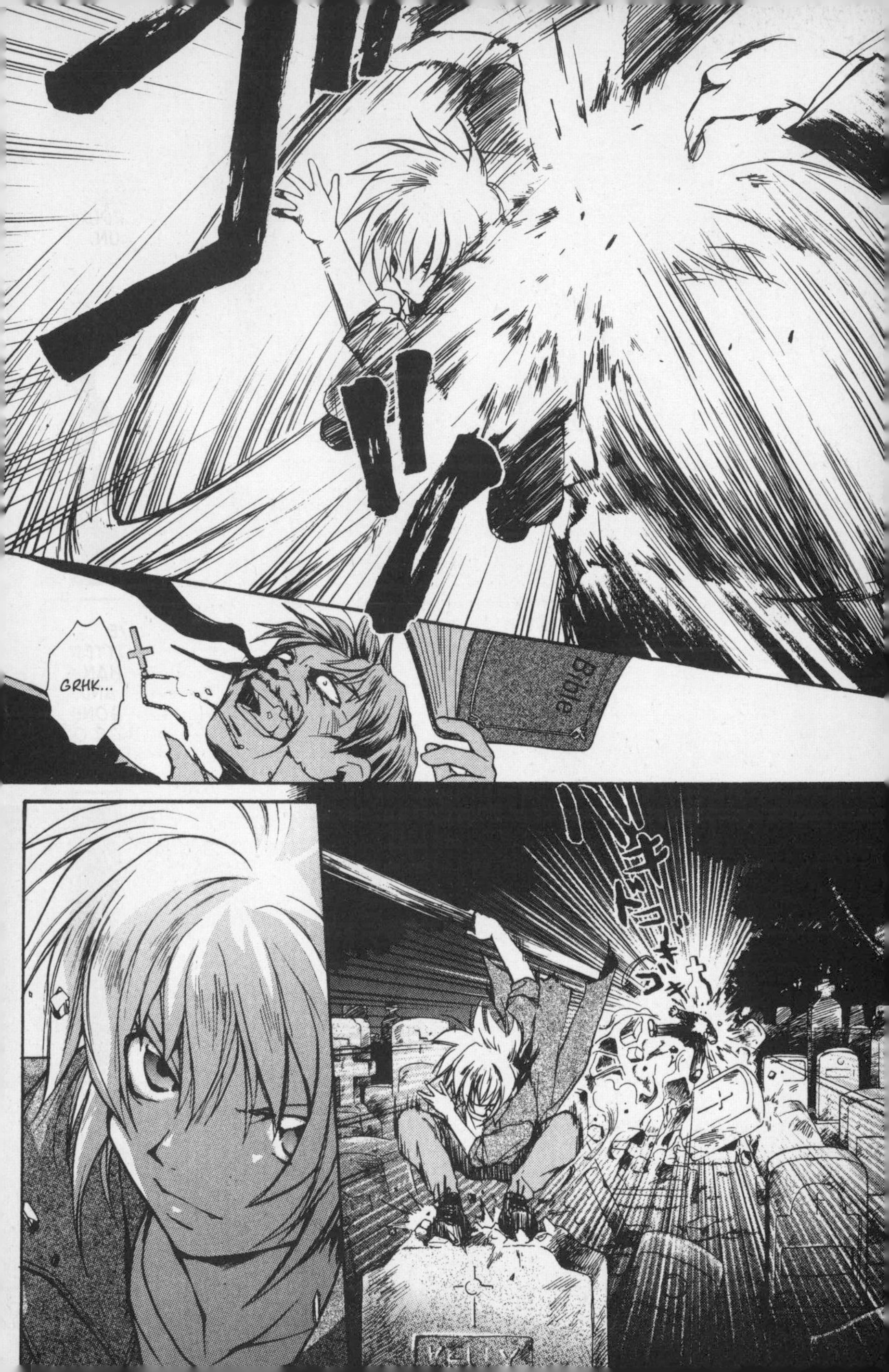
GRHK...
Bible

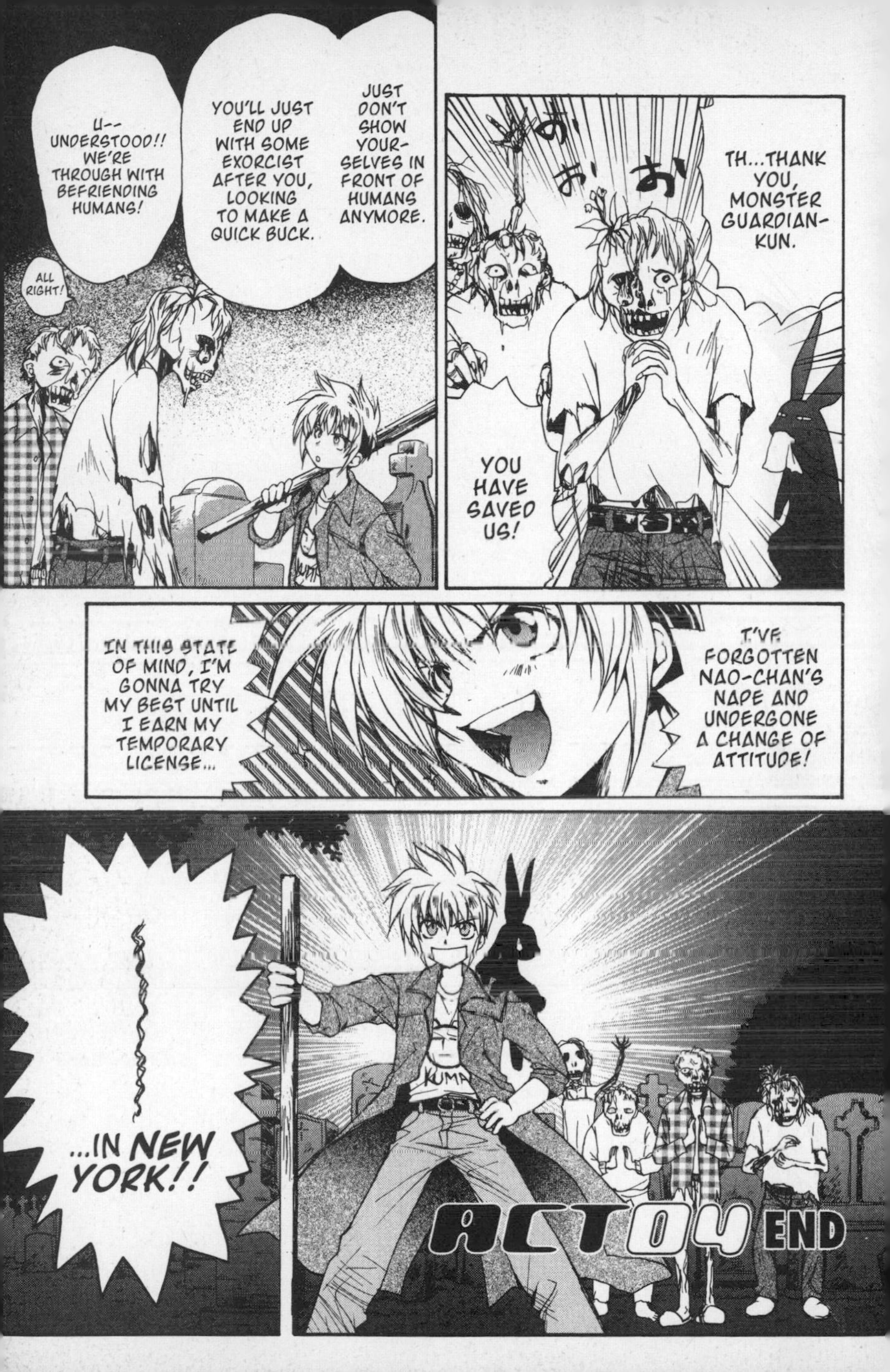
TH...THANK YOU, MONSTER GUARDIAN-KUN.
YOU HAVE SAVED US!
JUST DON'T SHOW YOURSELVES IN FRONT OF HUMANS ANYMORE.
YOU'LL JUST END UP WITH SOME EXORCIST AFTER YOU, LOOKING TO MAKE A QUICK BUCK.
U--UNDERSTOOD!! WE'RE THROUGH WITH BEFRIENDING HUMANS!
ALL RIGHT!
I'VE FORGOTTEN NAO-CHAN'S NAPE AND UNDERGONE A CHANGE OF ATTITUDE!
IN THIS STATE OF MIND, I'M GONNA TRY MY BEST UNTIL I EARN MY TEMPORARY LICENSE...
...IN NEW YORK!!
ACT 04 END

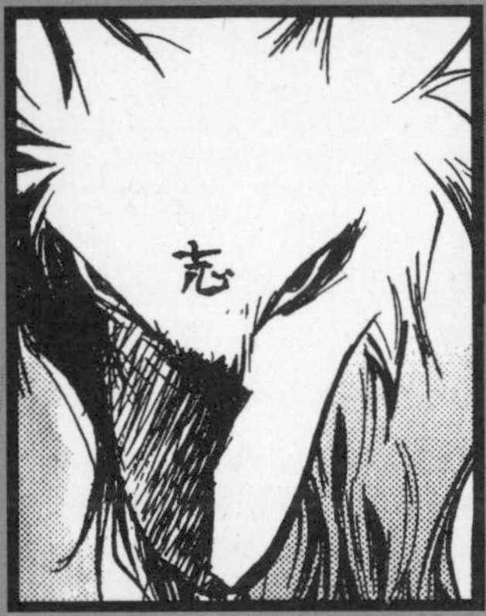
志

kimi no unaji ni kanpai! ACT 05

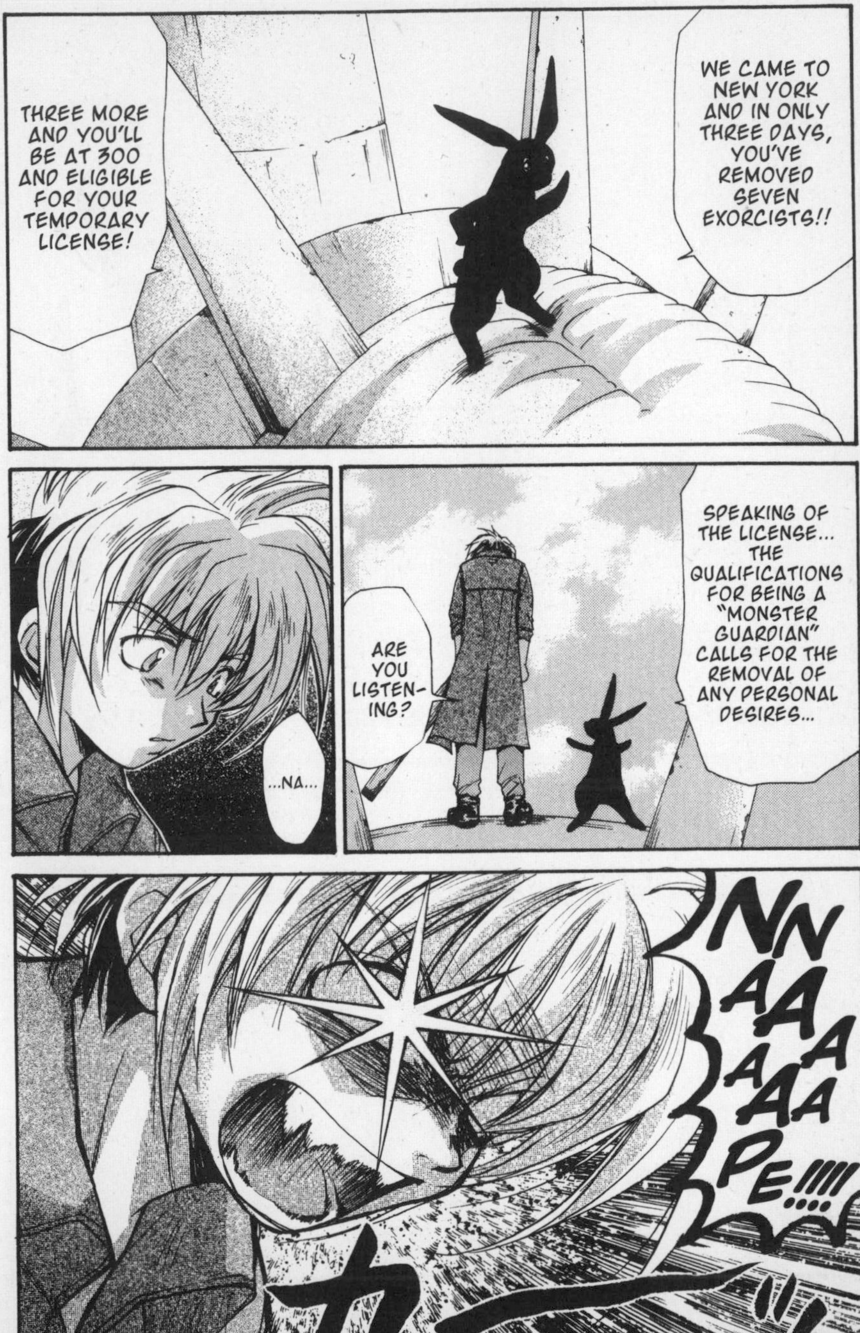
WE CAME TO NEW YORK AND IN ONLY THREE DAYS, YOU'VE REMOVED SEVEN EXORCISTS!!
THREE MORE AND YOU'LL BE AT 300 AND ELIGIBLE FOR YOUR TEMPORARY LICENSE!
SPEAKING OF THE LICENSE... THE QUALIFICATIONS FOR BEING A "MONSTER GUARDIAN" CALLS FOR THE REMOVAL OF ANY PERSONAL DESIRES...
ARE YOU LISTENING?
...NA...
NNAAAAAAAPE!!!!
カー!!

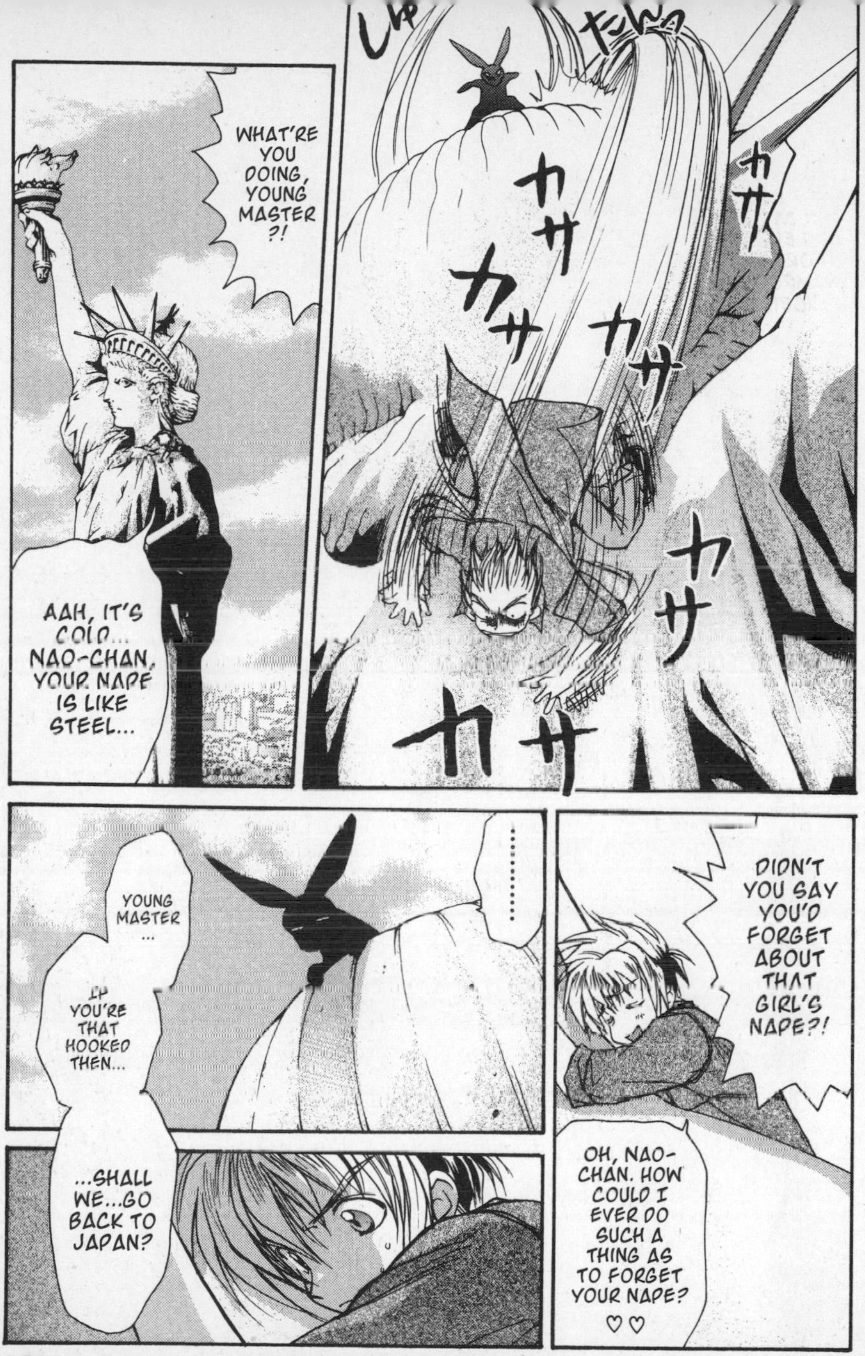
カサ
カサ
カサ
カサ
カサ
カサ
WHAT'RE YOU DOING, YOUNG MASTER?!
AAH, IT'S COLD... NAO-CHAN, YOUR NAPE IS LIKE STEEL...
DIDN'T YOU SAY YOU'D FORGET ABOUT THAT GIRL'S NAPE?!
OH, NAO-CHAN. HOW COULD I EVER DO SUCH A THING AS TO FORGET YOUR NAPE? ♡♡
......
YOUNG MASTER...
IF YOU'RE THAT HOOKED THEN...
...SHALL WE...GO BACK TO JAPAN?

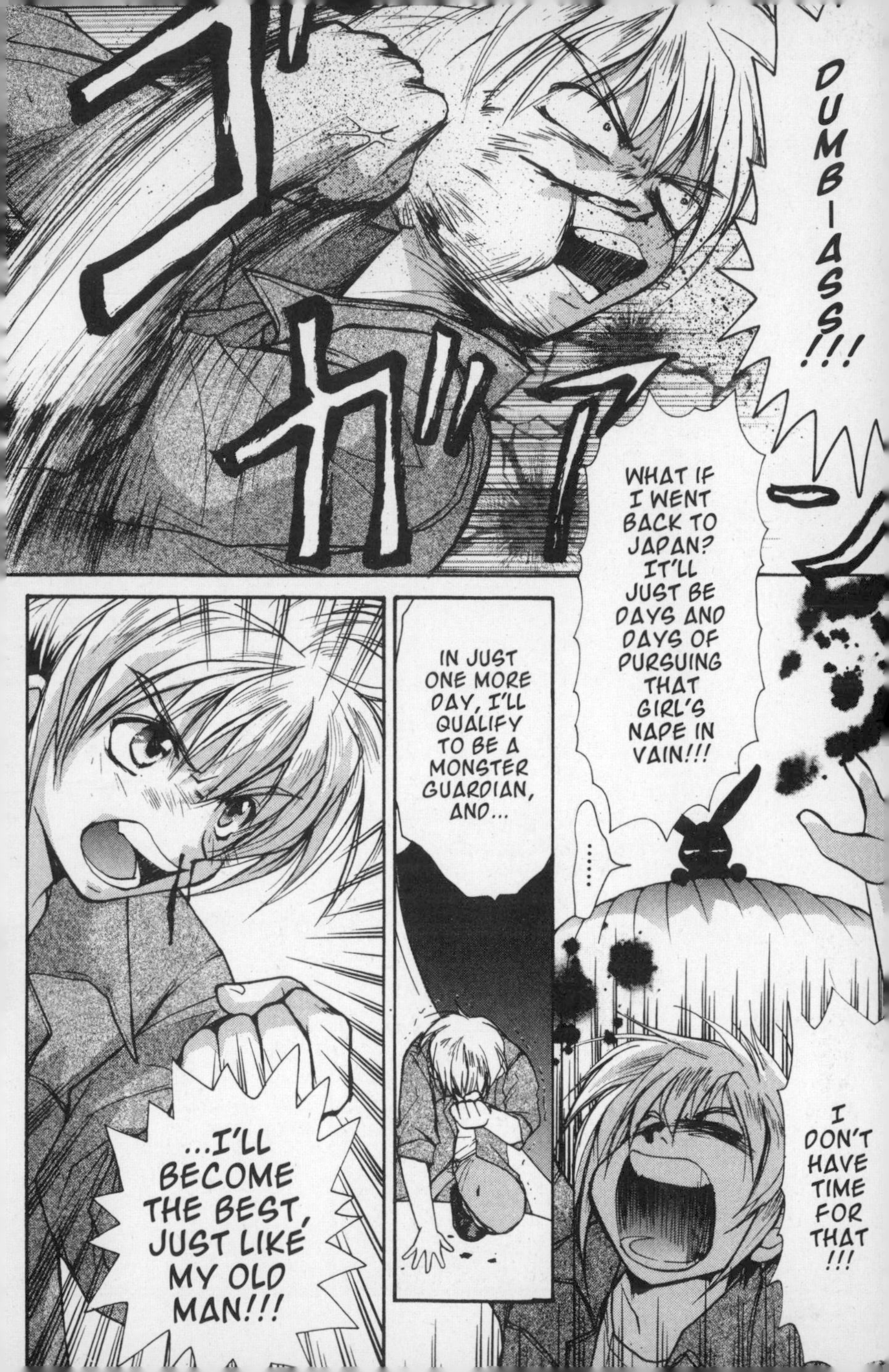
DUMBIASS!!!
WHAT IF I WENT BACK TO JAPAN? IT'LL JUST BE DAYS AND DAYS OF PURSUING THAT GIRL'S NAPE IN VAIN!!!
......
I DON'T HAVE TIME FOR THAT!!!
IN JUST ONE MORE DAY, I'LL QUALIFY TO BE A MONSTER GUARDIAN, AND...
...I'LL BECOME THE BEST, JUST LIKE MY OLD MAN!!!

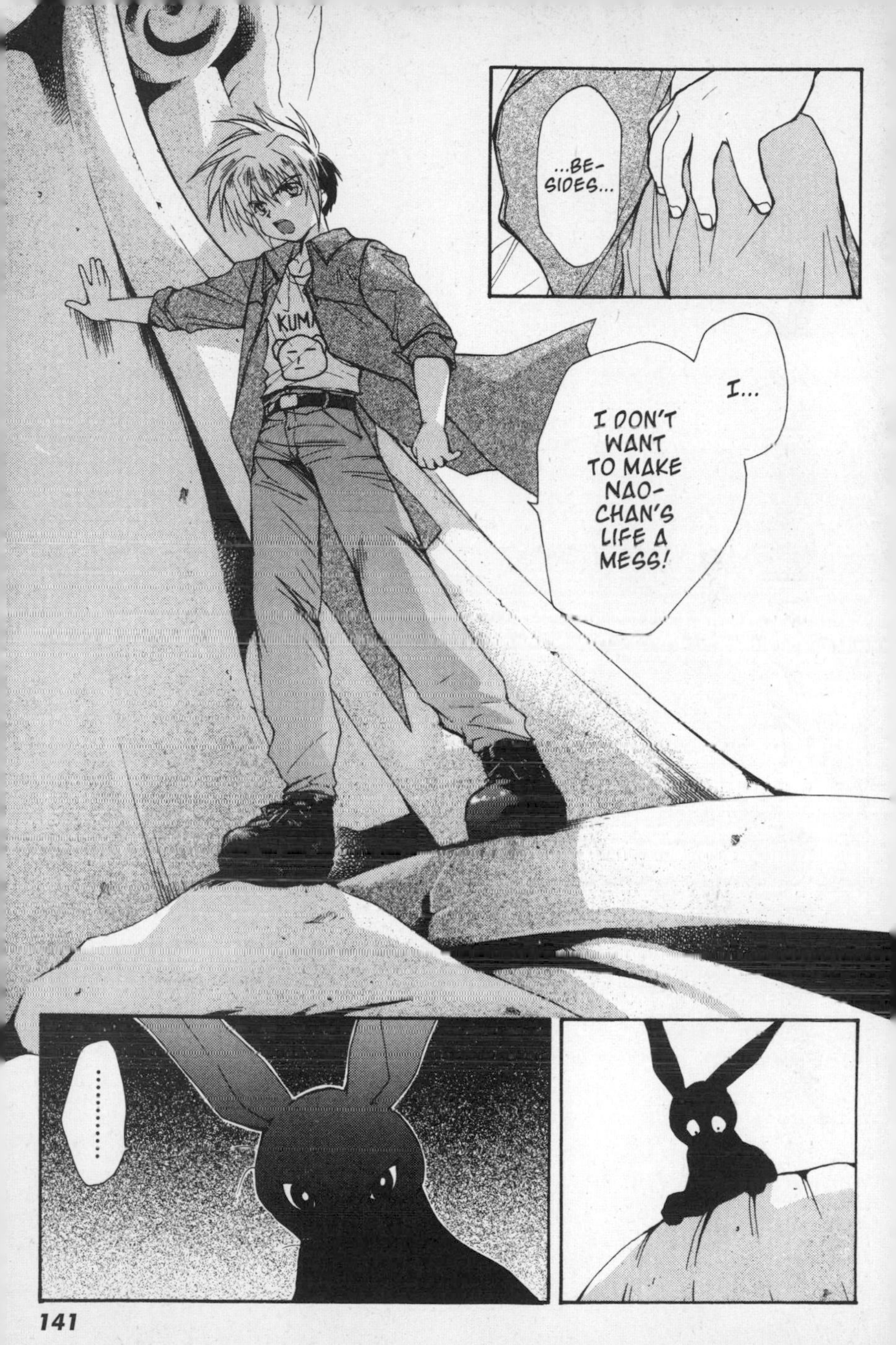
...BE-SIDES...
I...
I DON'T WANT TO MAKE NAO-CHAN'S LIFE A MESS!
....

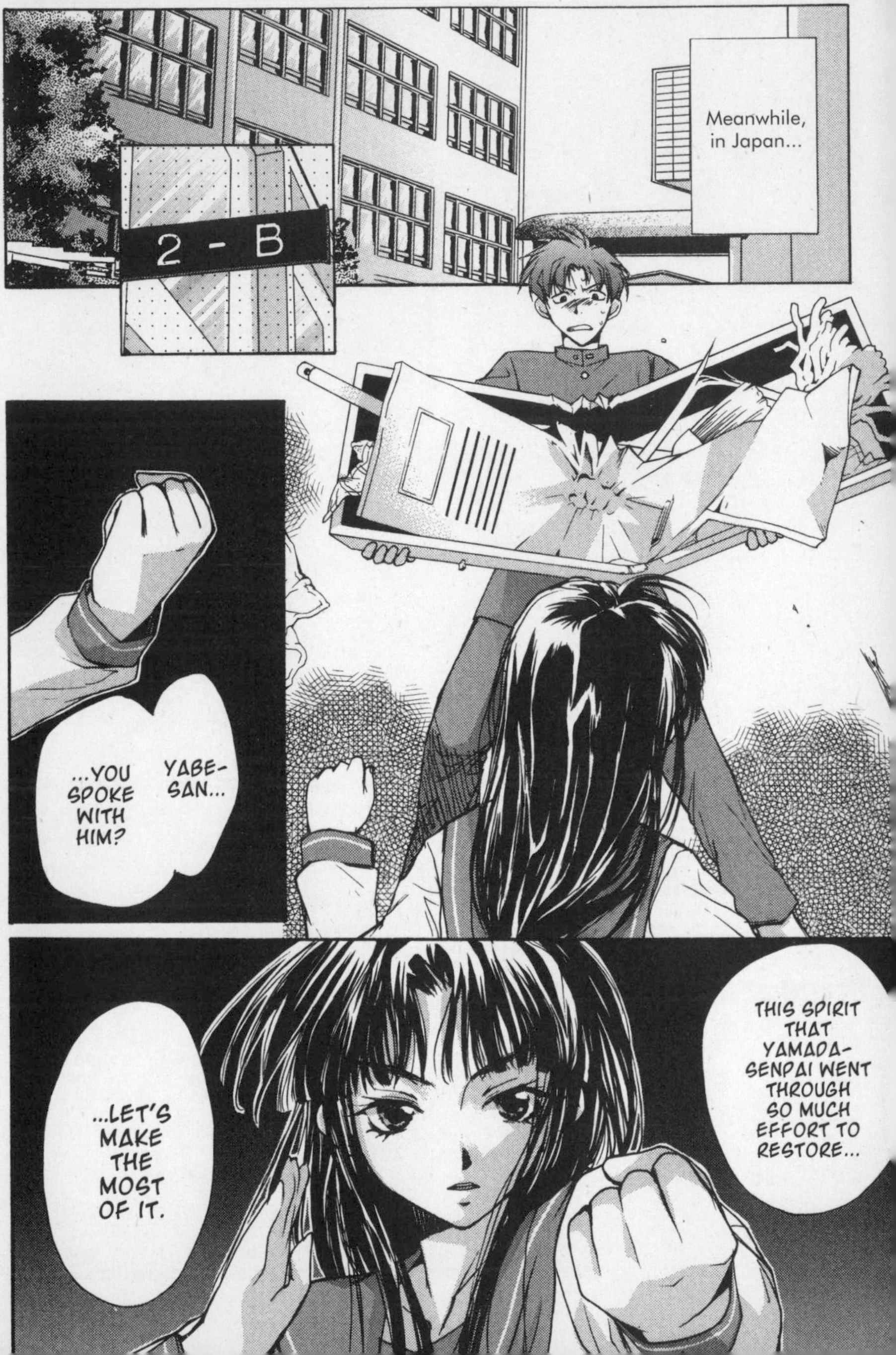
Meanwhile, in Japan...
2-B
YABE-SAN...
...YOU SPOKE WITH HIM?
THIS SPIRIT THAT YAMADA-SENPAI WENT THROUGH SO MUCH EFFORT TO RESTORE...
...LET'S MAKE THE MOST OF IT.

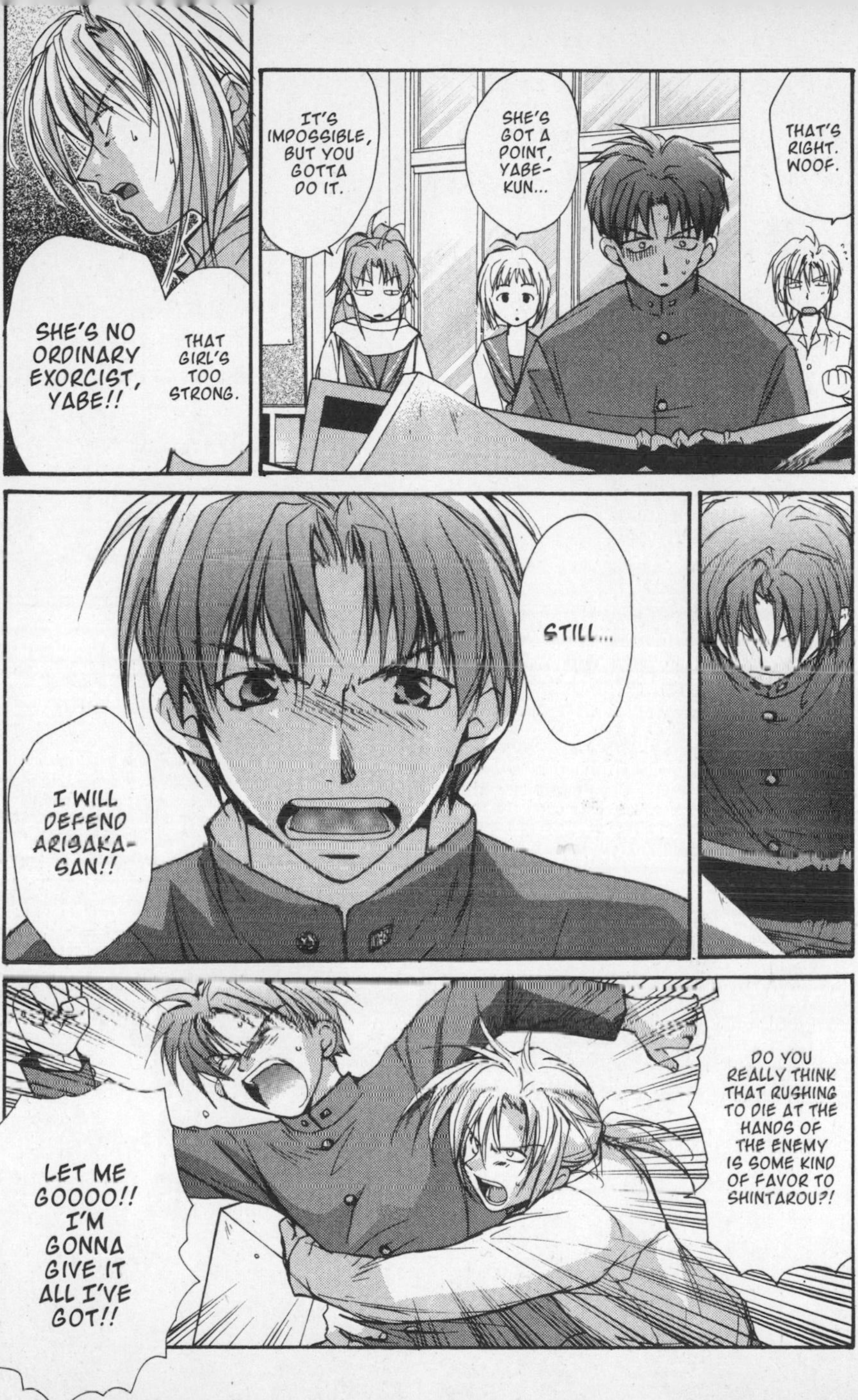
THAT'S RIGHT. WOOF.
SHE'S GOT A POINT, YABE-KUN...
IT'S IMPOSSIBLE, BUT YOU GOTTA DO IT.
THAT GIRL'S TOO STRONG.
SHE'S NO ORDINARY EXORCIST, YABE!!
STILL...
I WILL DEFEND ARISAKA-SAN!!
DO YOU REALLY THINK THAT RUSHING TO DIE AT THE HANDS OF THE ENEMY IS SOME KIND OF FAVOR TO SHINTAROU?!
LET ME GOOOO!! I'M GONNA GIVE IT ALL I'VE GOT!!

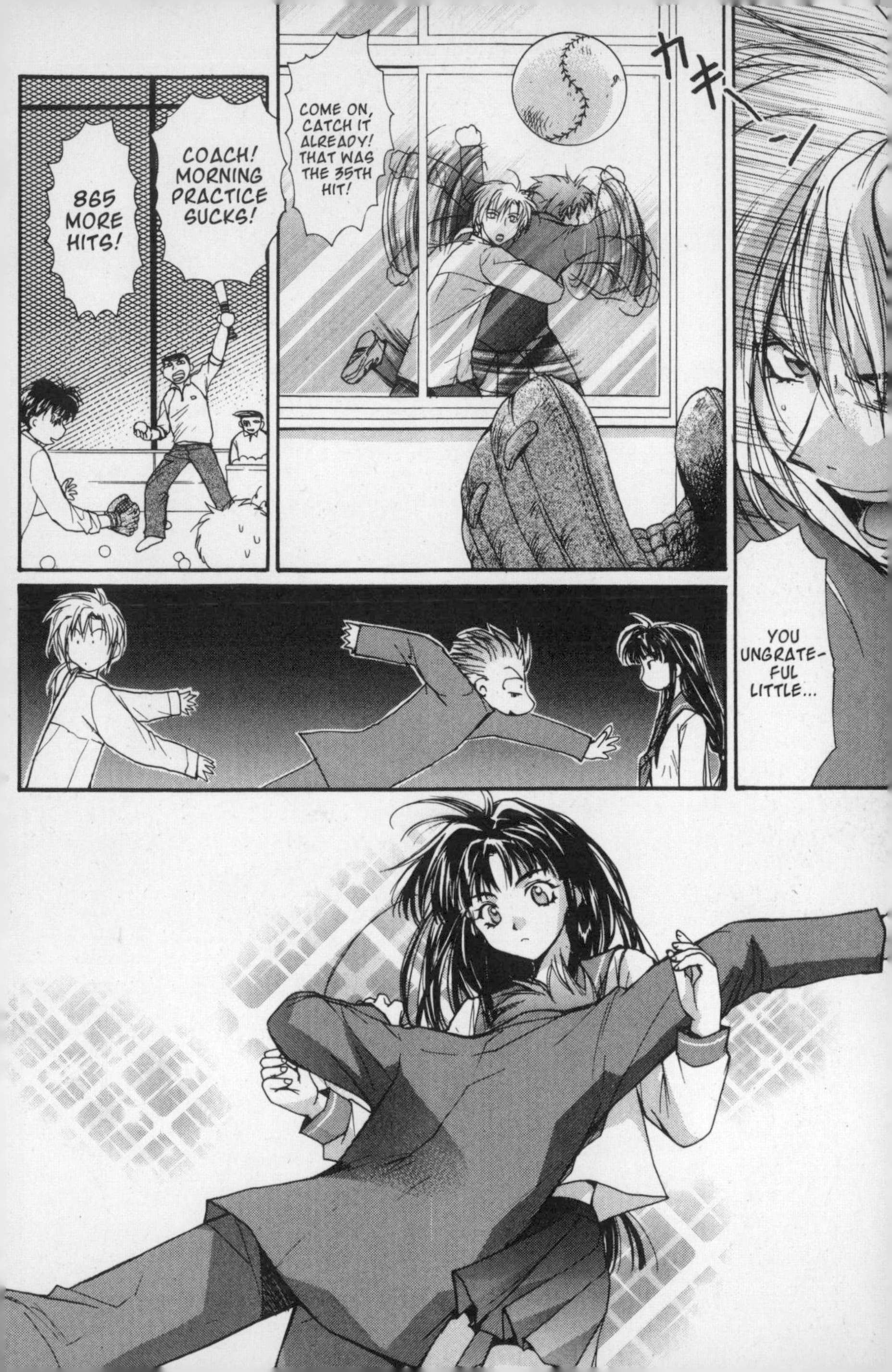
カキー
YOU UNGRATEFUL LITTLE...
COME ON, CATCH IT ALREADY! THAT WAS THE 35TH HIT!
COACH! MORNING PRACTICE SUCKS!
865 MORE HITS!

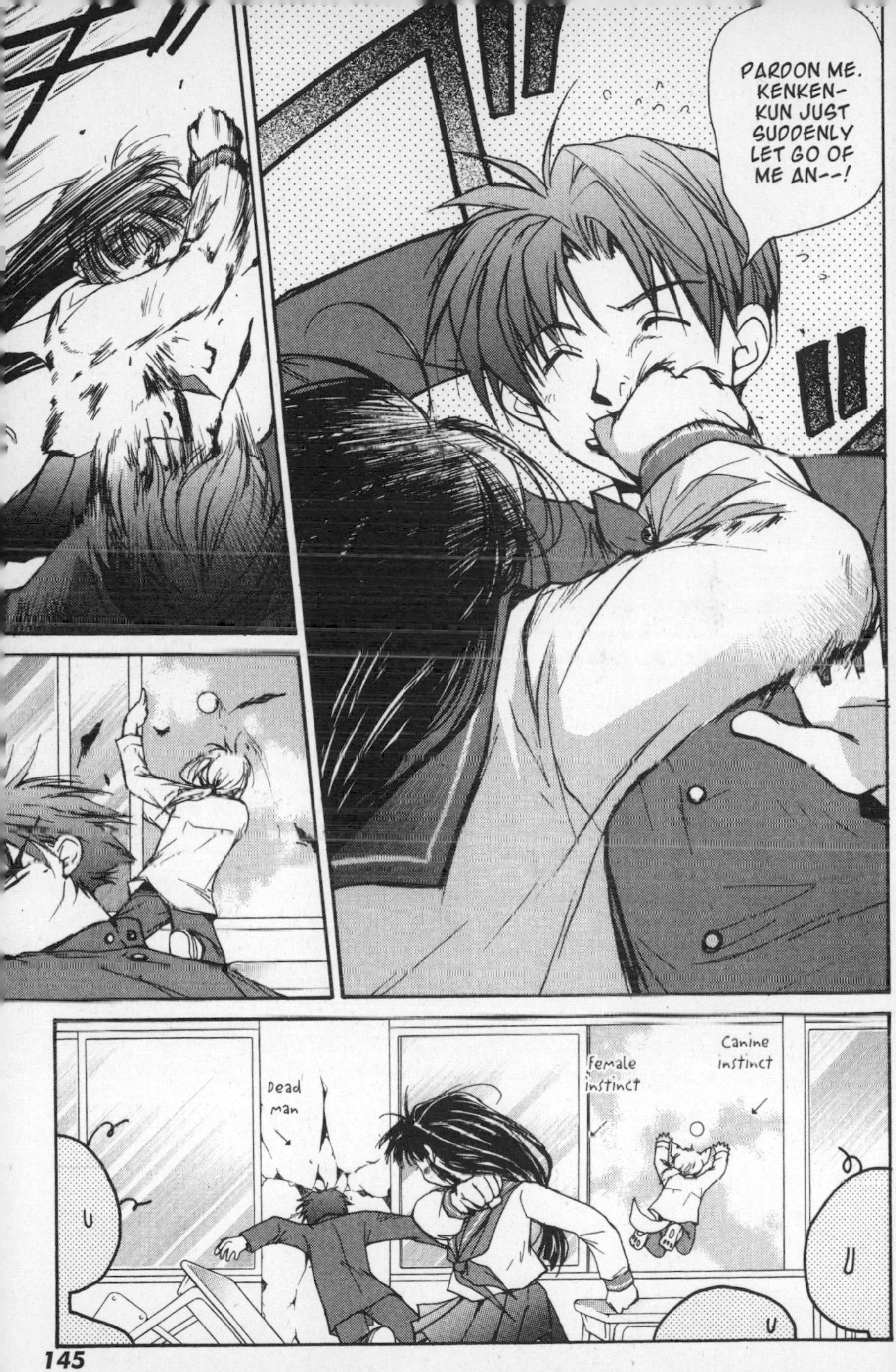
PARDON ME. KENKEN-KUN JUST SUDDENLY LET GO OF ME AN--!
Canine instinct
Female instinct
Dead man

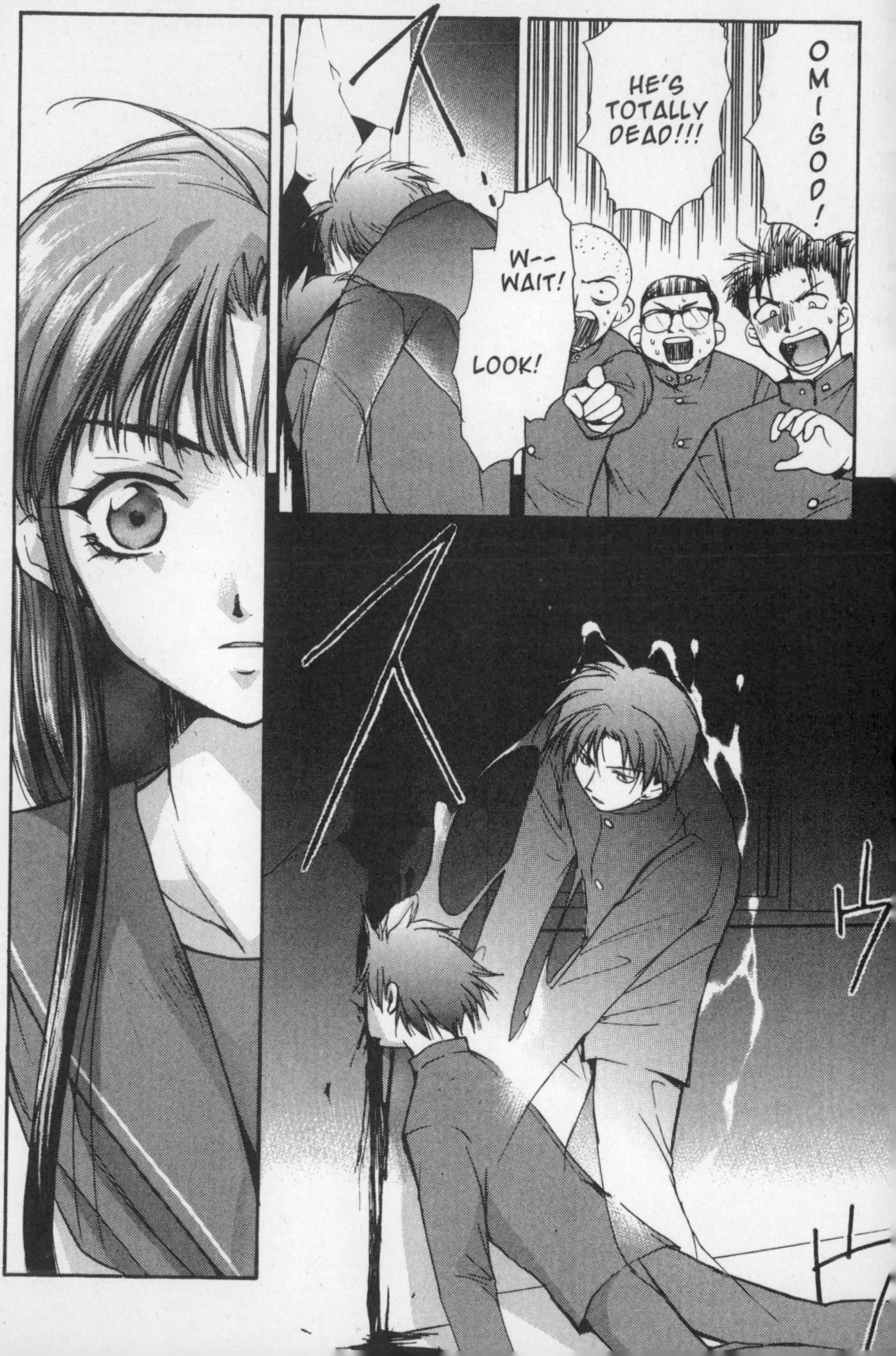
OMIGOD!
HE'S TOTALLY DEAD!!!
W--WAIT!
LOOK!

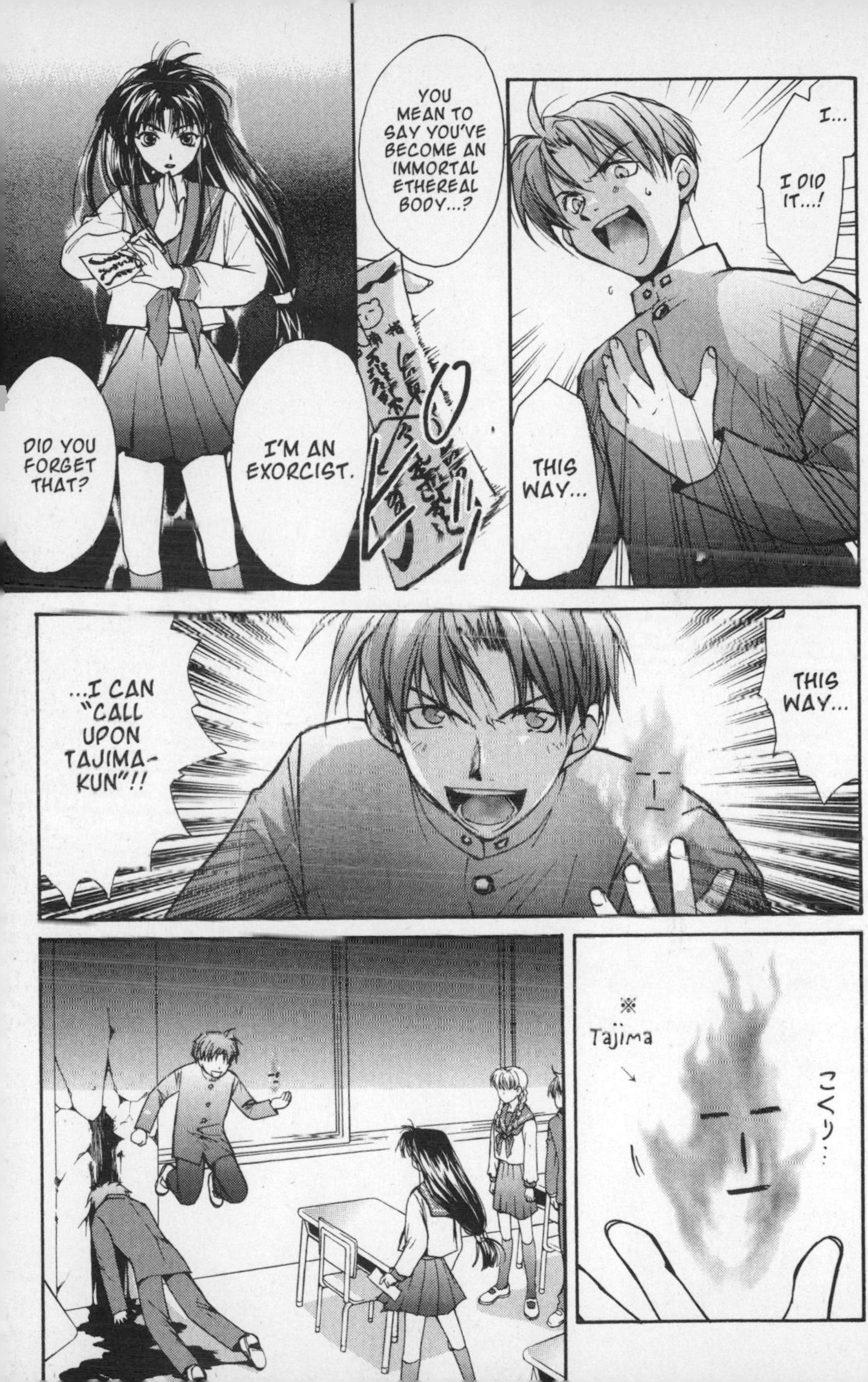
I...
I DID IT...!
THIS WAY...
YOU MEAN TO SAY YOU'VE BECOME AN IMMORTAL ETHEREAL BODY...?
I'M AN EXORCIST.
DID YOU FORGET THAT?
THIS WAY...
...I CAN "CALL UPON TAJIMA-KUN"!!
※ Tajima
こくり…

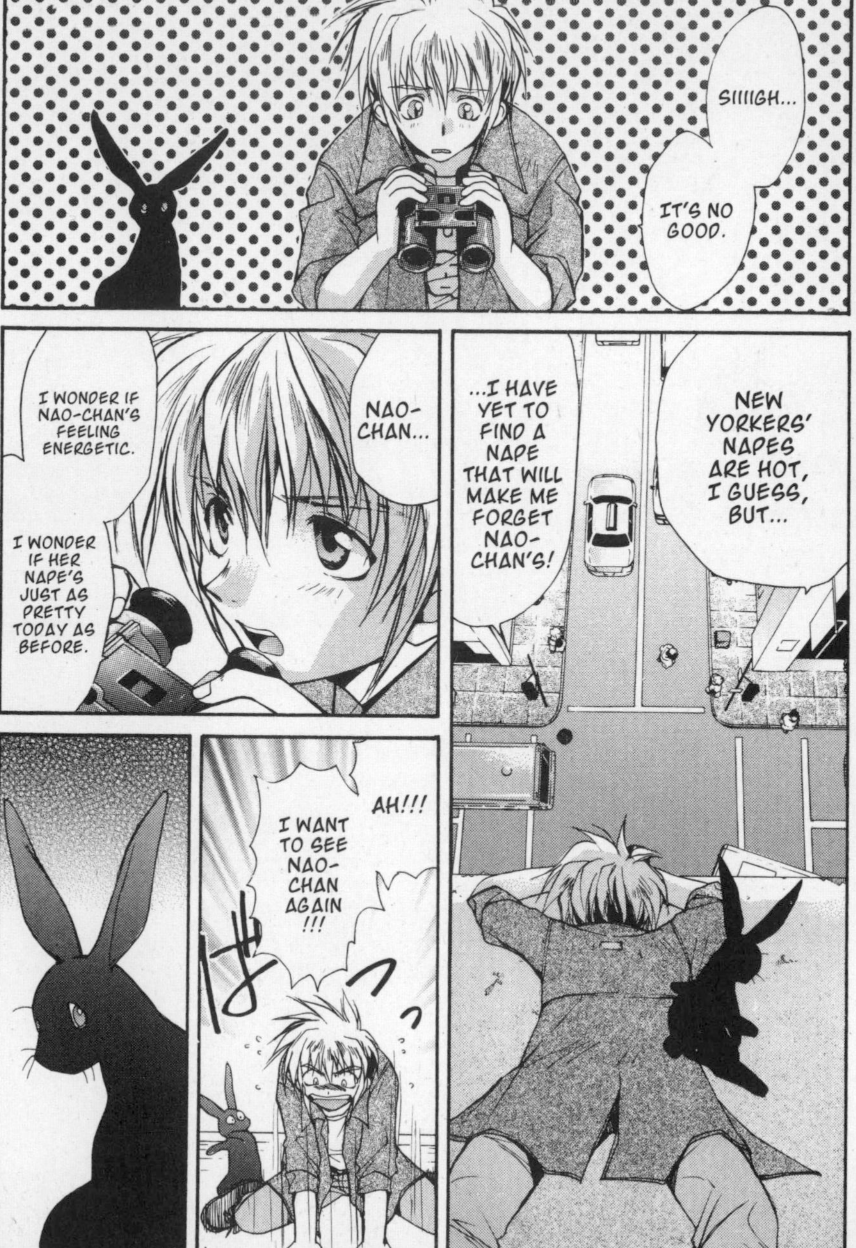
SIIIIGH...
IT'S NO GOOD.
NEW YORKERS' NAPES ARE HOT, I GUESS, BUT...
...I HAVE YET TO FIND A NAPE THAT WILL MAKE ME FORGET NAO-CHAN'S!
NAO-CHAN...
I WONDER IF NAO-CHAN'S FEELING ENERGETIC.
I WONDER IF HER NAPE'S JUST AS PRETTY TODAY AS BEFORE.
AH!!!
I WANT TO SEE NAO-CHAN AGAIN!!!

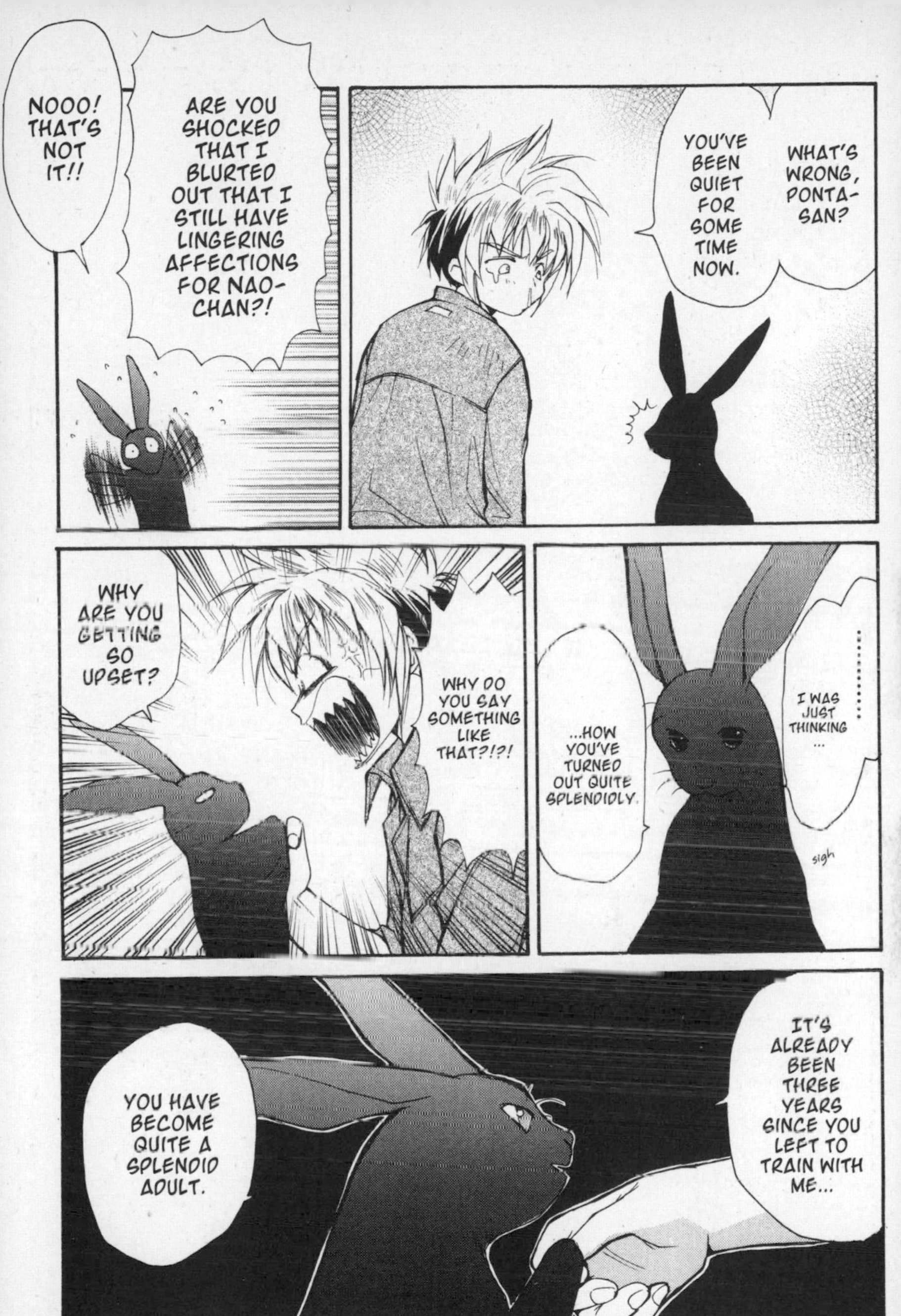
WHAT'S WRONG, PONTA-SAN?
YOU'VE BEEN QUIET FOR SOME TIME NOW.
ARE YOU SHOCKED THAT I BLURTED OUT THAT I STILL HAVE LINGERING AFFECTIONS FOR NAO-CHAN?!
NOOO! THAT'S NOT IT!!
....
I WAS JUST THINKING...
...HOW YOU'VE TURNED OUT QUITE SPLENDIDLY.
sigh
WHY DO YOU SAY SOMETHING LIKE THAT?!?!
WHY ARE YOU GETTING SO UPSET?
IT'S ALREADY BEEN THREE YEARS SINCE YOU LEFT TO TRAIN WITH ME...
YOU HAVE BECOME QUITE A SPLENDID ADULT.

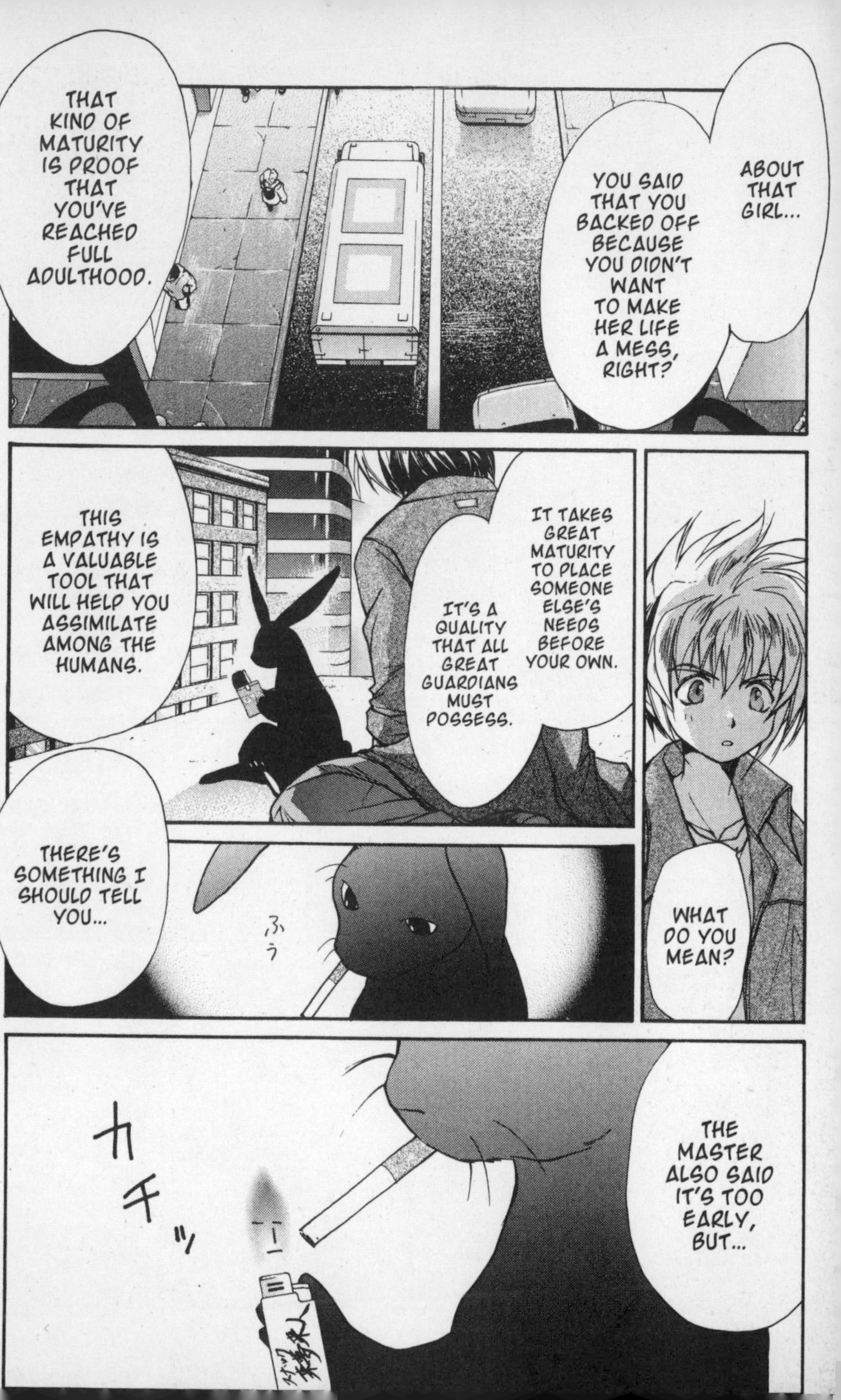
ABOUT THAT GIRL...
YOU SAID THAT YOU BACKED OFF BECAUSE YOU DIDN'T WANT TO MAKE HER LIFE A MESS, RIGHT?
THAT KIND OF MATURITY IS PROOF THAT YOU'VE REACHED FULL ADULTHOOD.
WHAT DO YOU MEAN?
IT TAKES GREAT MATURITY TO PLACE SOMEONE ELSE'S NEEDS BEFORE YOUR OWN.
IT'S A QUALITY THAT ALL GREAT GUARDIANS MUST POSSESS.
THIS EMPATHY IS A VALUABLE TOOL THAT WILL HELP YOU ASSIMILATE AMONG THE HUMANS.
ふう
THERE'S SOMETHING I SHOULD TELL YOU...
THE MASTER ALSO SAID IT'S TOO EARLY, BUT...
カチッ

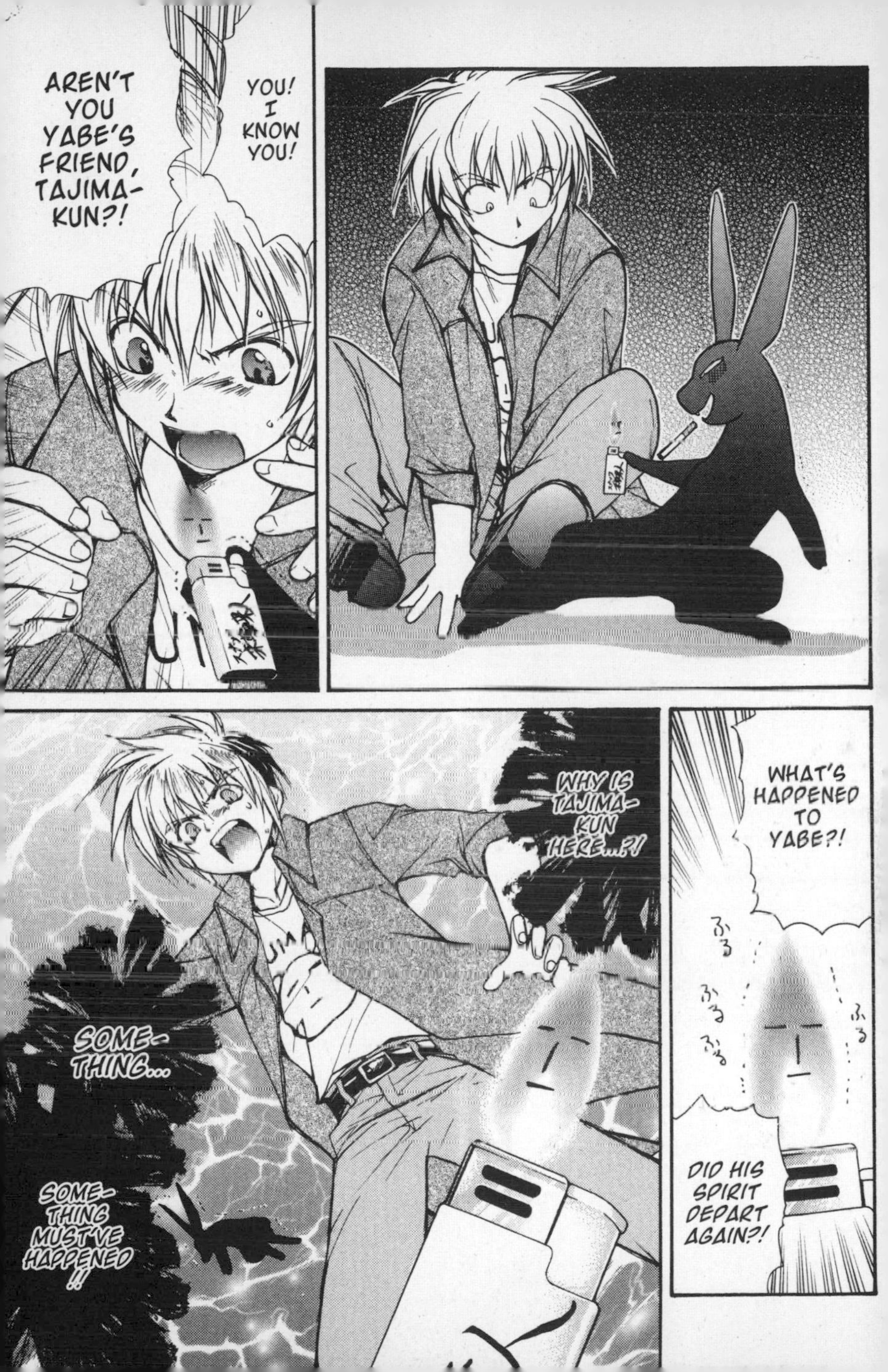
YOU! I KNOW YOU!
AREN'T YOU YABE'S FRIEND, TAJIMA-KUN?!
WHAT'S HAPPENED TO YABE?!
ふる
ふる
ふる
ふる
DID HIS SPIRIT DEPART AGAIN?!
WHY IS TAJIMA-KUN HERE...?!
SOME-THING...
SOME-THING MUST'VE HAPPENED!!

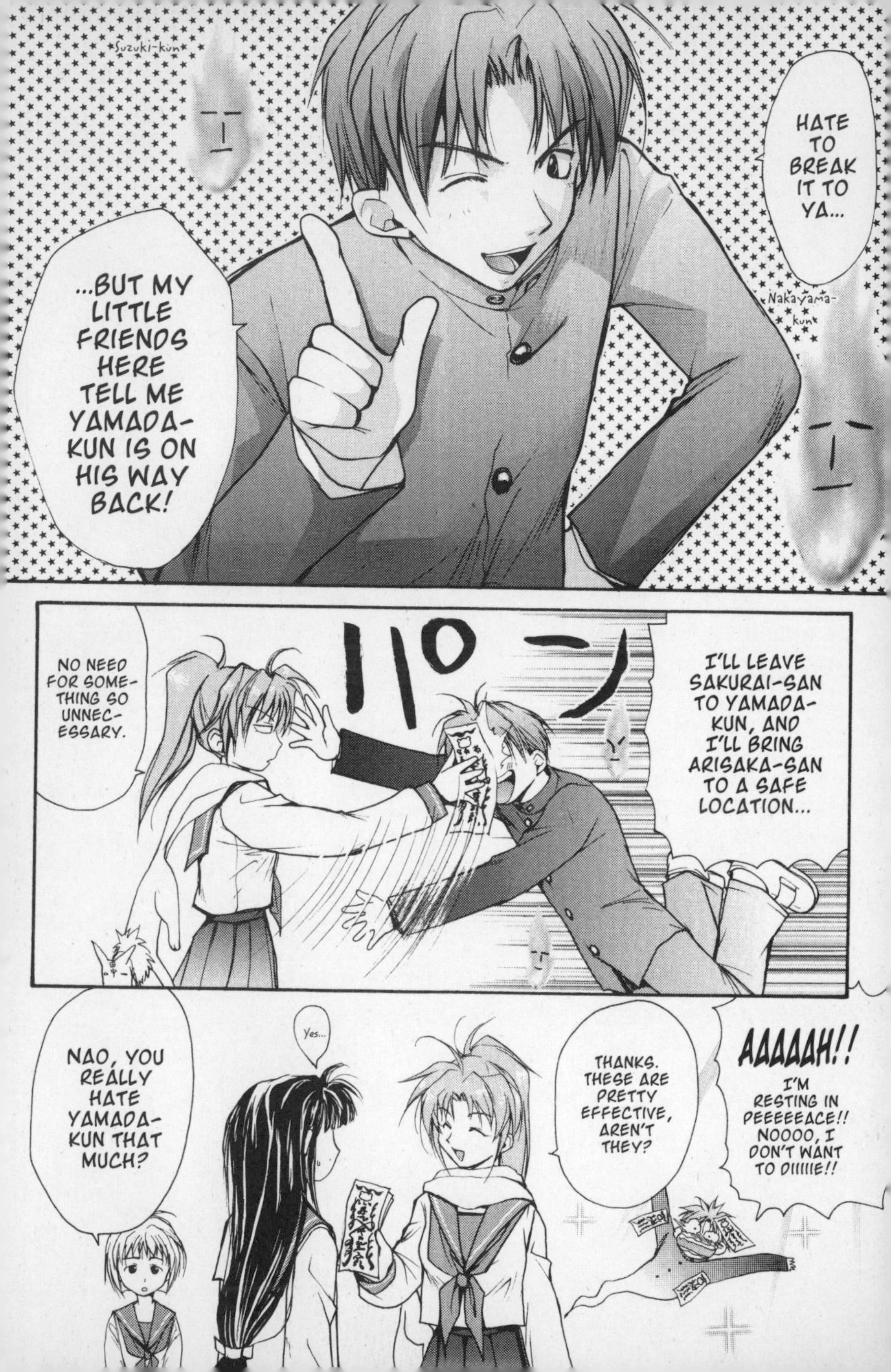
HATE TO BREAK IT TO YA...
Nakayama-kun
...BUT MY LITTLE FRIENDS HERE TELL ME YAMADA-KUN IS ON HIS WAY BACK!
Suzuki-kun
I'LL LEAVE SAKURAI-SAN TO YAMADA-KUN, AND I'LL BRING ARISAKA-SAN TO A SAFE LOCATION...
NO NEED FOR SOME-THING SO UNNEC-ESSARY.
AAAAAH!!
I'M RESTING IN PEEEEEACE!! NOOOO, I DON'T WANT TO DIIIIIE!!
THANKS. THESE ARE PRETTY EFFECTIVE, AREN'T THEY?
Yes...
NAO, YOU REALLY HATE YAMADA-KUN THAT MUCH?

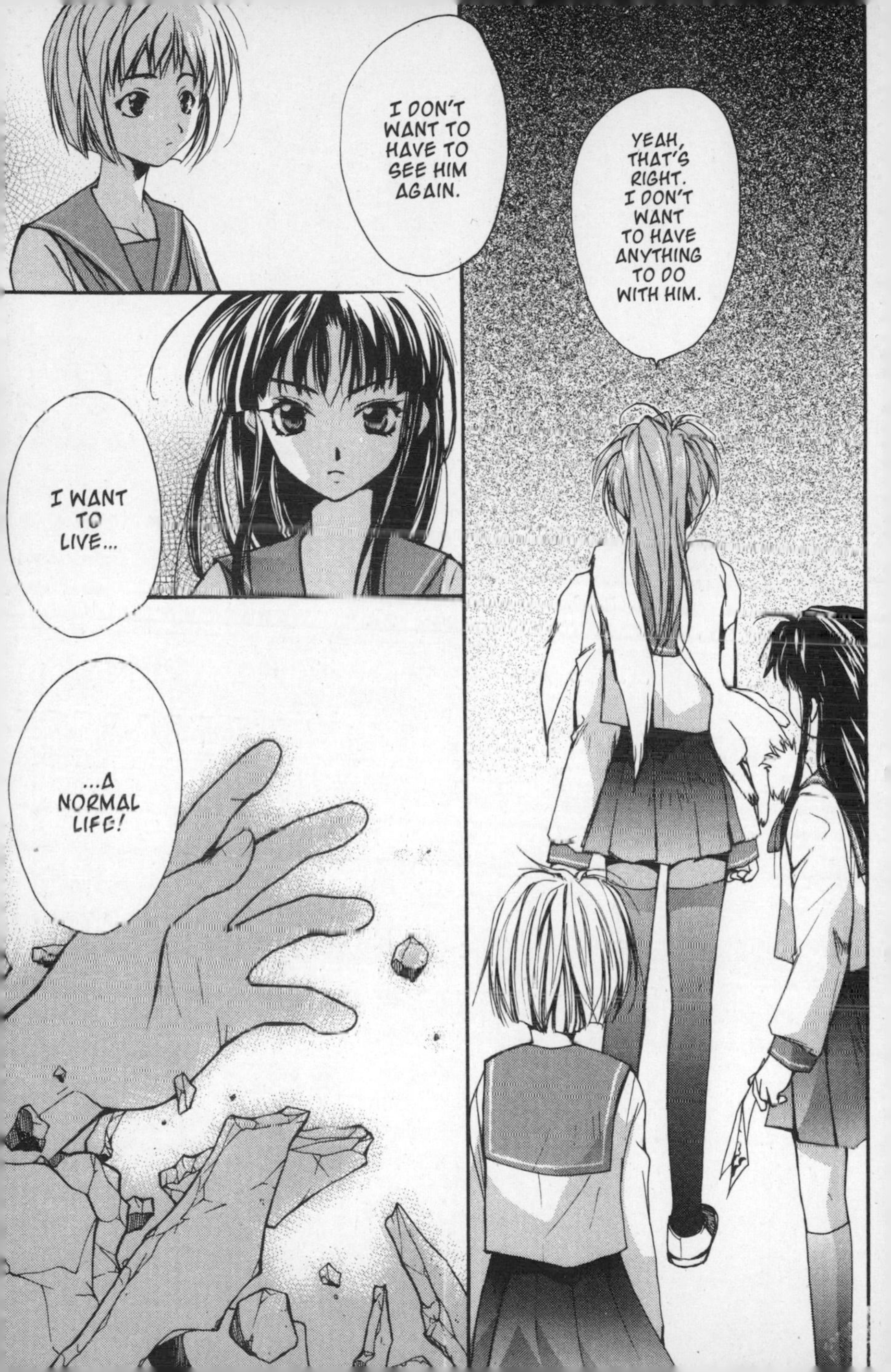
YEAH, THAT'S RIGHT. I DON'T WANT TO HAVE ANYTHING TO DO WITH HIM.
I DON'T WANT TO HAVE TO SEE HIM AGAIN.
I WANT TO LIVE...
...A NORMAL LIFE!

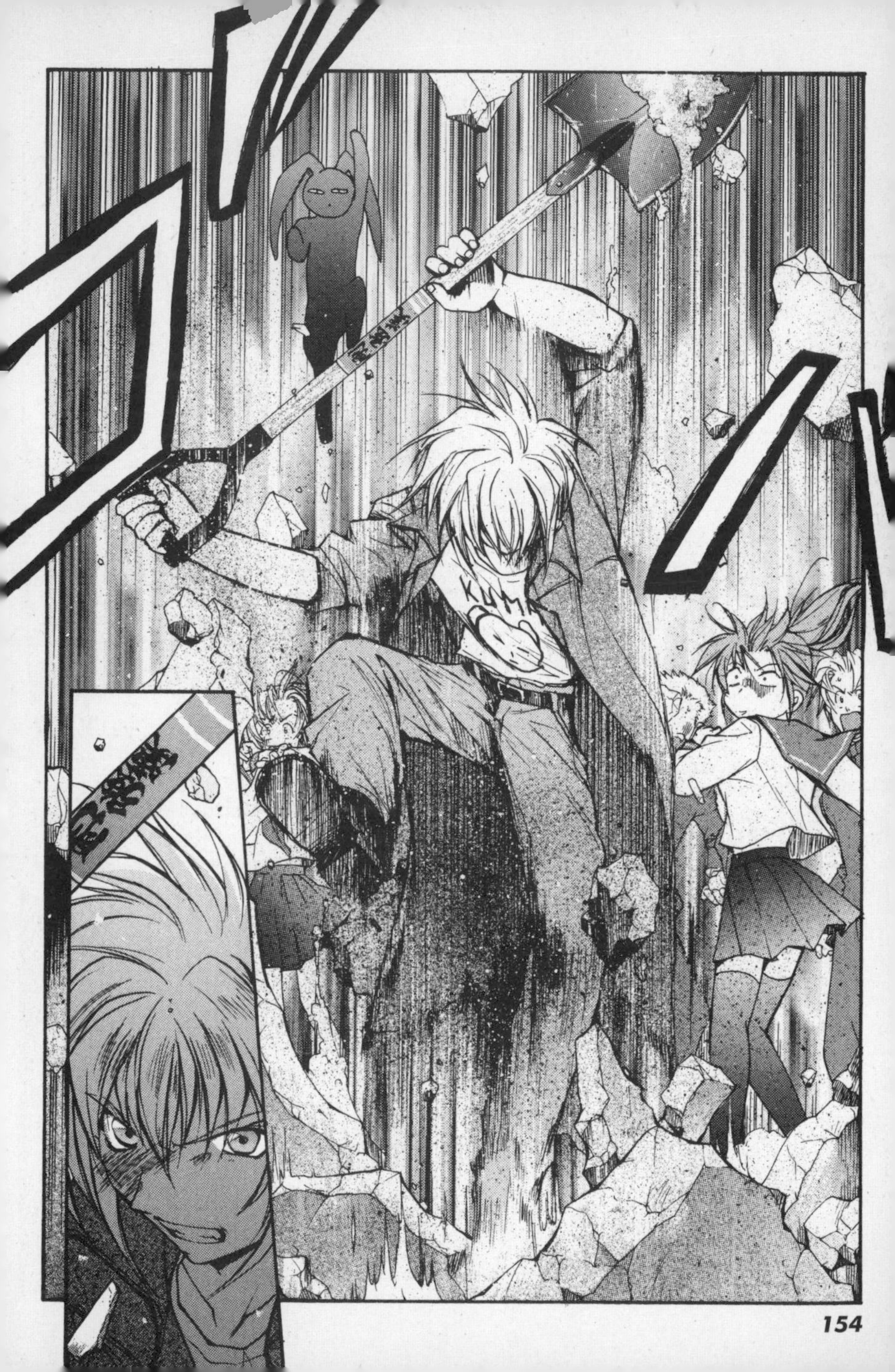

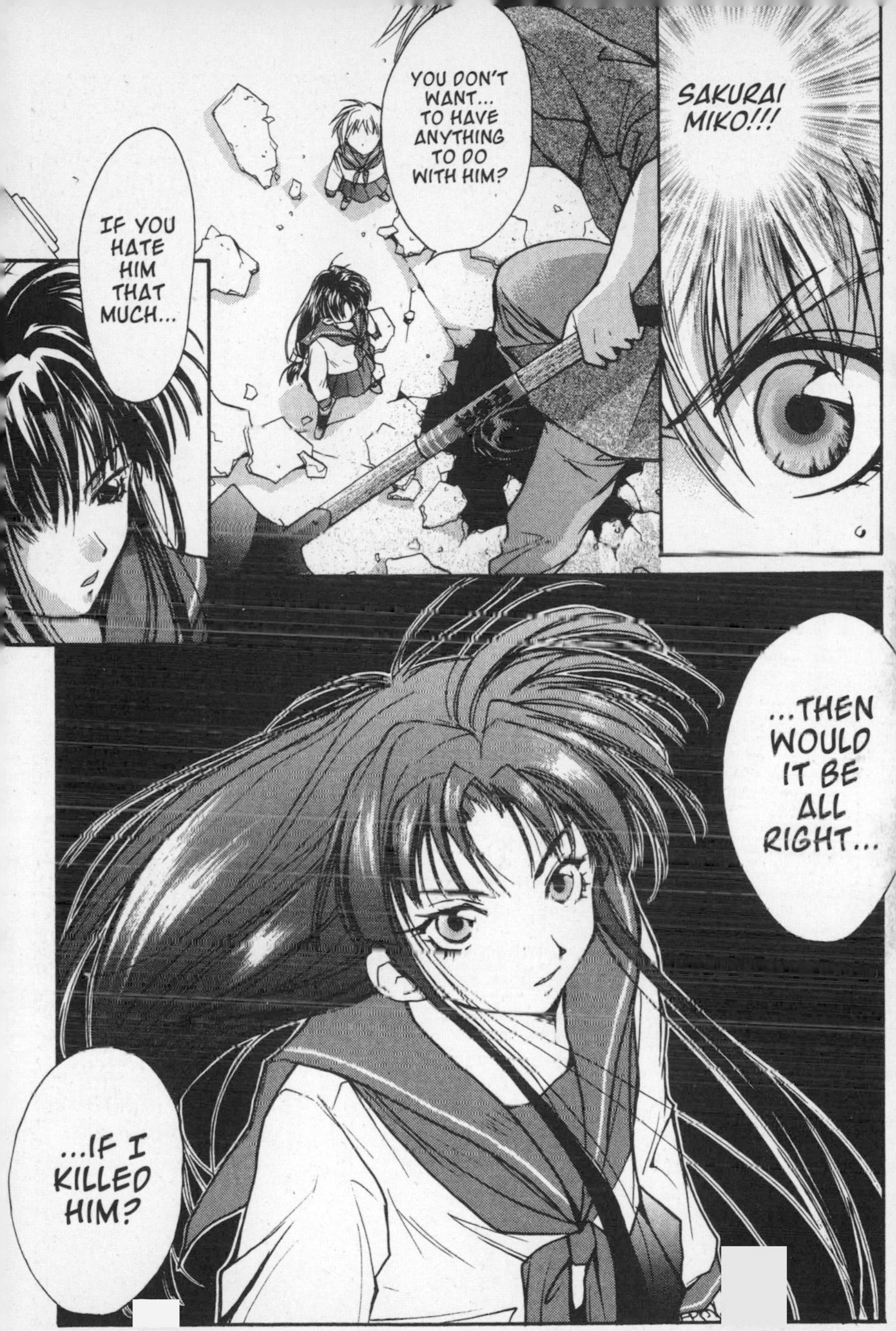
SAKURAI MIKO!!!
YOU DON'T WANT... TO HAVE ANYTHING TO DO WITH HIM?
IF YOU HATE HIM THAT MUCH...
...THEN WOULD IT BE ALL RIGHT...
...IF I KILLED HIM?

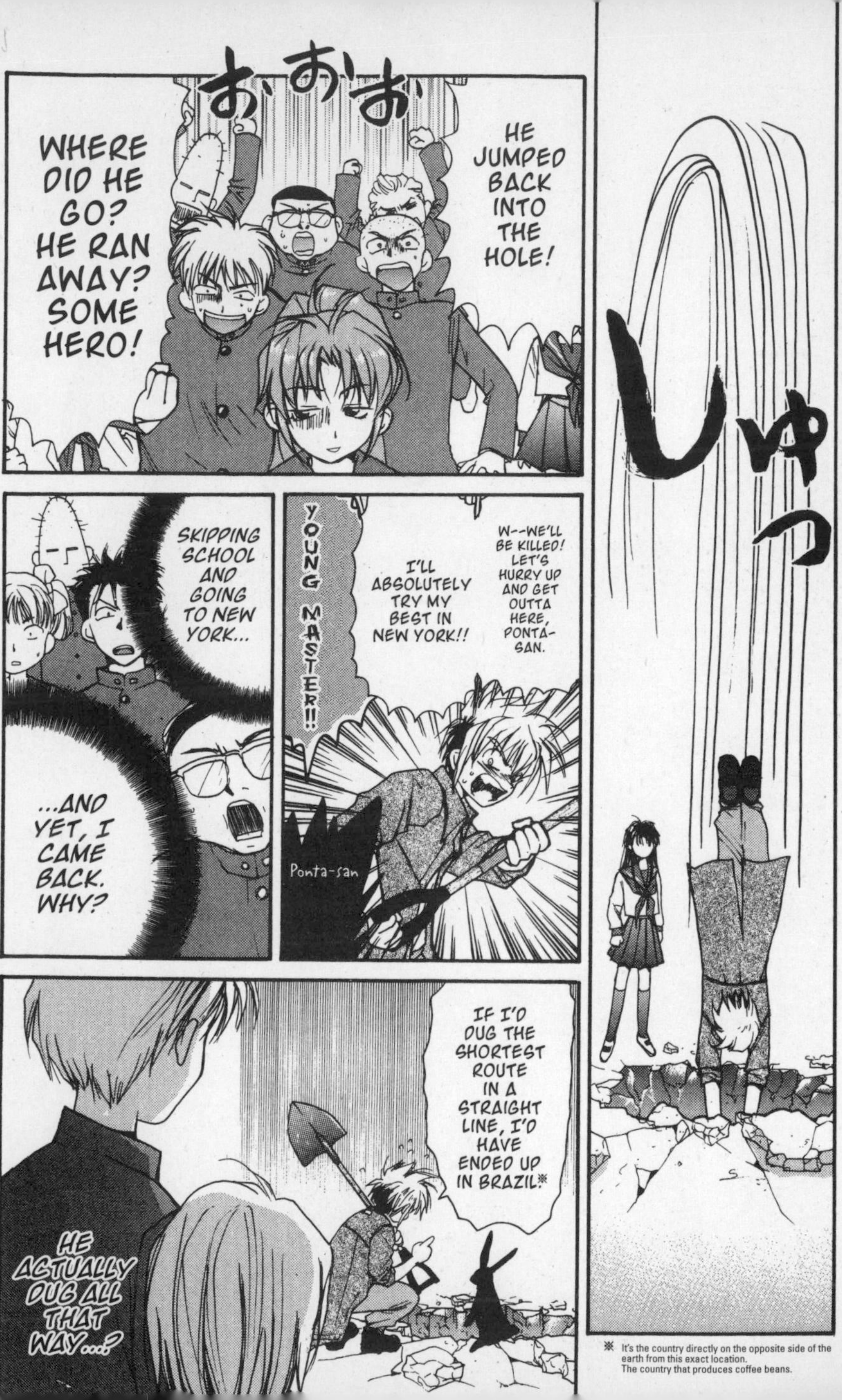
しゅっ
おおお
HE JUMPED BACK INTO THE HOLE!
WHERE DID HE GO? HE RAN AWAY? SOME HERO!
W--WE'LL BE KILLED! LET'S HURRY UP AND GET OUTTA HERE, PONTA-SAN.
I'LL ABSOLUTELY TRY MY BEST IN NEW YORK!!
YOUNG MASTER!!
Ponta-san
SKIPPING SCHOOL AND GOING TO NEW YORK...
...AND YET, I CAME BACK. WHY?
IF I'D DUG THE SHORTEST ROUTE IN A STRAIGHT LINE, I'D HAVE ENDED UP IN BRAZIL!※
HE ACTUALLY DUG ALL THAT WAY...?

※ It's the country directly on the opposite side of the earth from this exact location. The country that produces coffee beans.

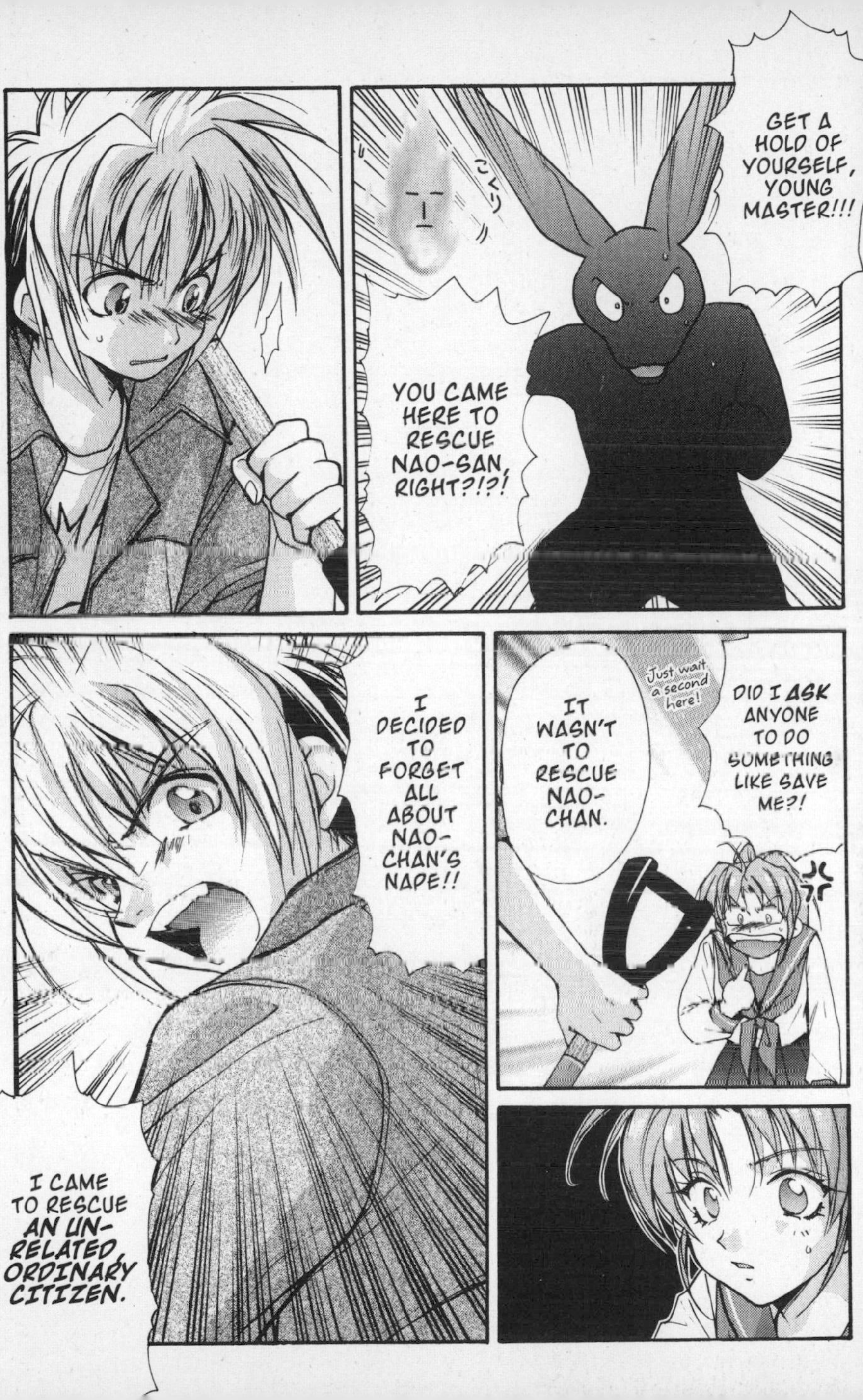
GET A HOLD OF YOURSELF, YOUNG MASTER!!!
こくり
YOU CAME HERE TO RESCUE NAO-SAN, RIGHT?!?!
DID I ASK ANYONE TO DO SOMETHING LIKE SAVE ME?!
Just wait a second here!
IT WASN'T TO RESCUE NAO-CHAN.
I DECIDED TO FORGET ALL ABOUT NAO-CHAN'S NAPE!!
I CAME TO RESCUE AN UN-RELATED, ORDINARY CITIZEN.

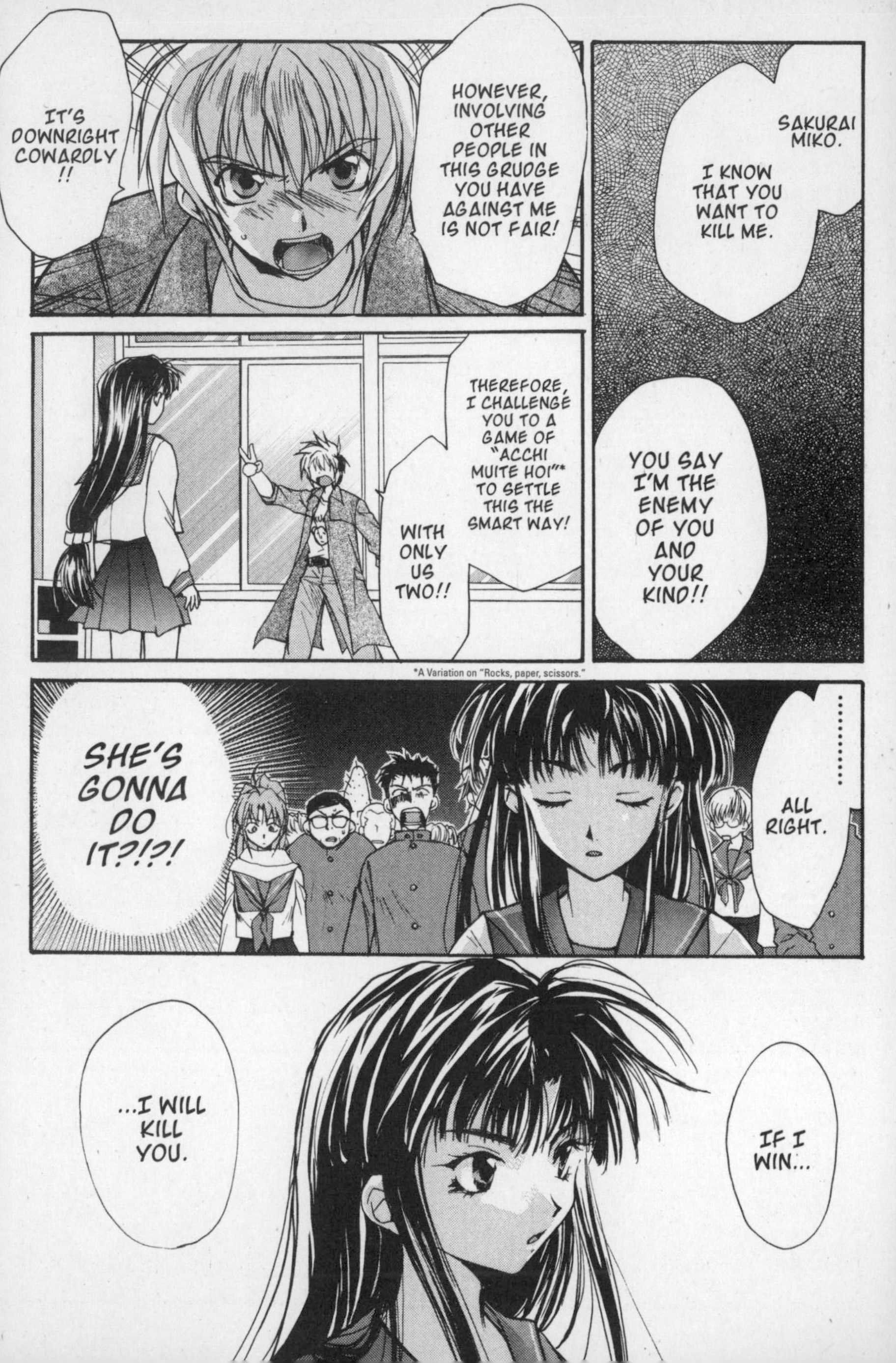
SAKURAI MIKO.
I KNOW THAT YOU WANT TO KILL ME.
YOU SAY I'M THE ENEMY OF YOU AND YOUR KIND!!
HOWEVER, INVOLVING OTHER PEOPLE IN THIS GRUDGE YOU HAVE AGAINST ME IS NOT FAIR!
IT'S DOWNRIGHT COWARDLY!!
THEREFORE, I CHALLENGE YOU TO A GAME OF "ACCHI MUITE HOI"* TO SETTLE THIS THE SMART WAY!
WITH ONLY US TWO!!
......
ALL RIGHT.
SHE'S GONNA DO IT?!?!
IF I WIN...
...I WILL KILL YOU.
*A Variation on "Rocks, paper, scissors."

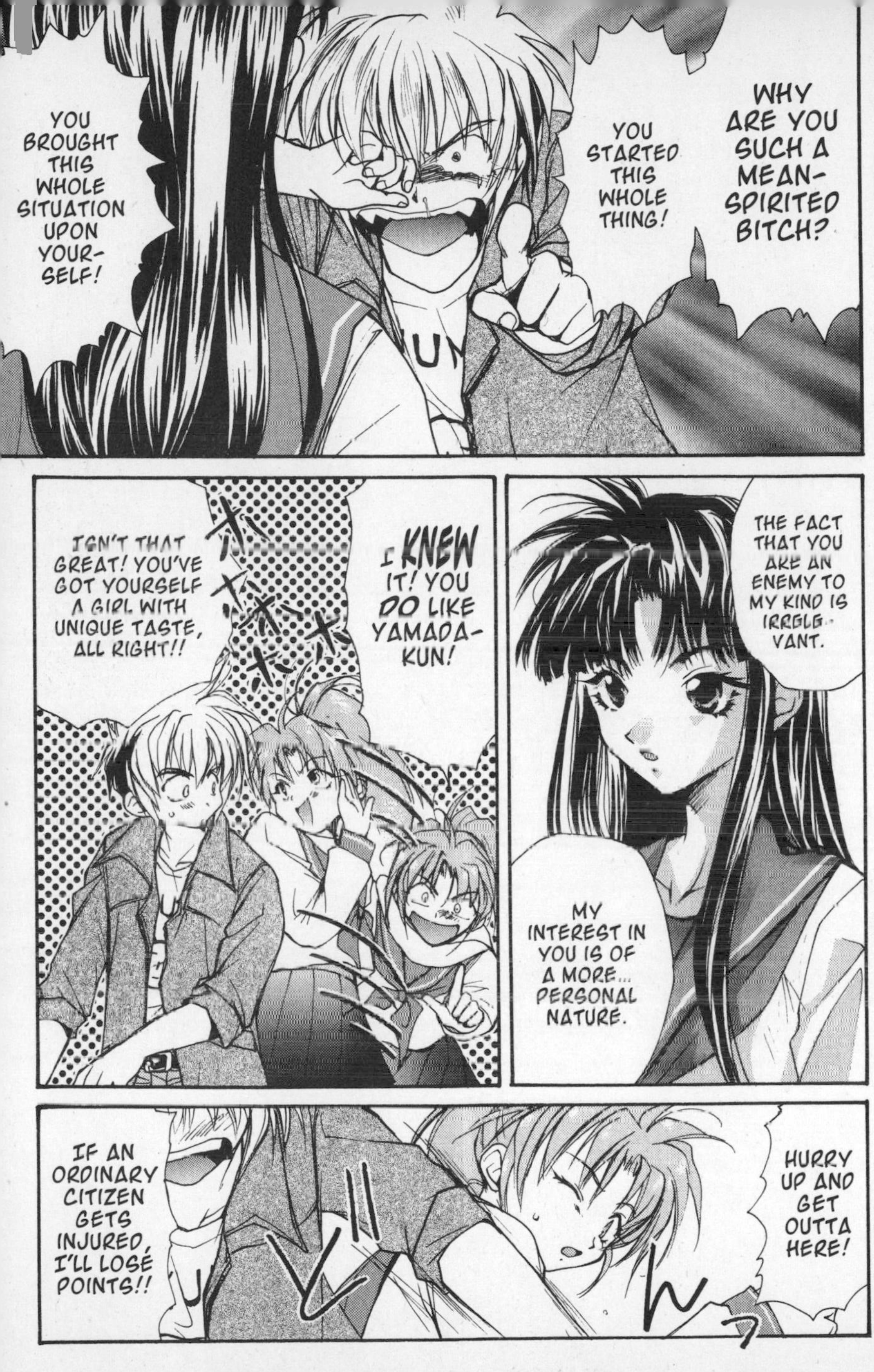
WHY ARE YOU SUCH A MEAN-SPIRITED BITCH?
YOU STARTED THIS WHOLE THING!
YOU BROUGHT THIS WHOLE SITUATION UPON YOURSELF!
THE FACT THAT YOU ARE AN ENEMY TO MY KIND IS IRRELEVANT.
MY INTEREST IN YOU IS OF A MORE... PERSONAL NATURE.
I KNEW IT! YOU DO LIKE YAMADA-KUN!
ISN'T THAT GREAT! YOU'VE GOT YOURSELF A GIRL WITH UNIQUE TASTE, ALL RIGHT!!
HURRY UP AND GET OUTTA HERE!
IF AN ORDINARY CITIZEN GETS INJURED, I'LL LOSE POINTS!!

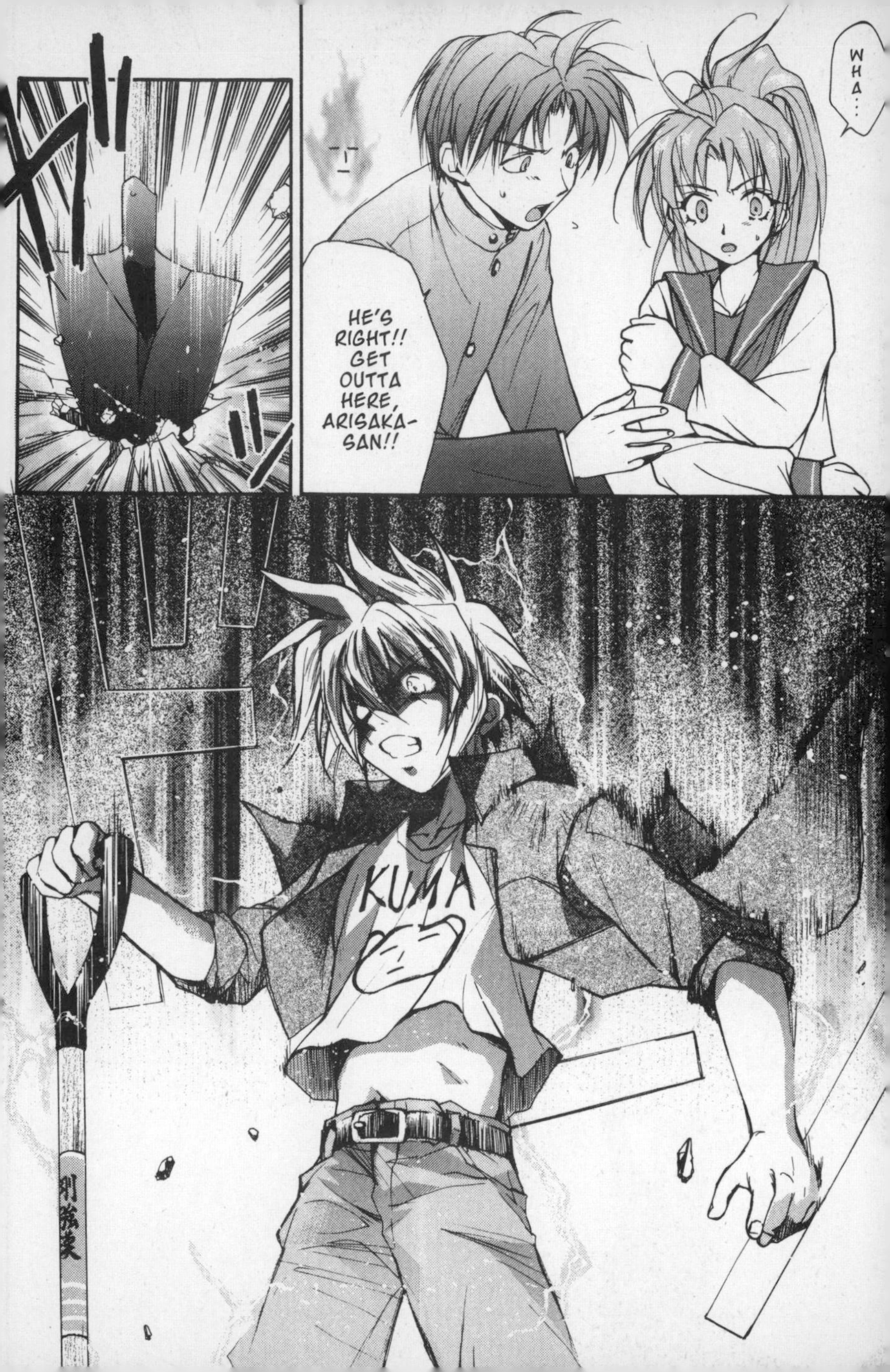
WHA...
HE'S RIGHT!! GET OUTTA HERE, ARISAKA-SAN!!
KUMA

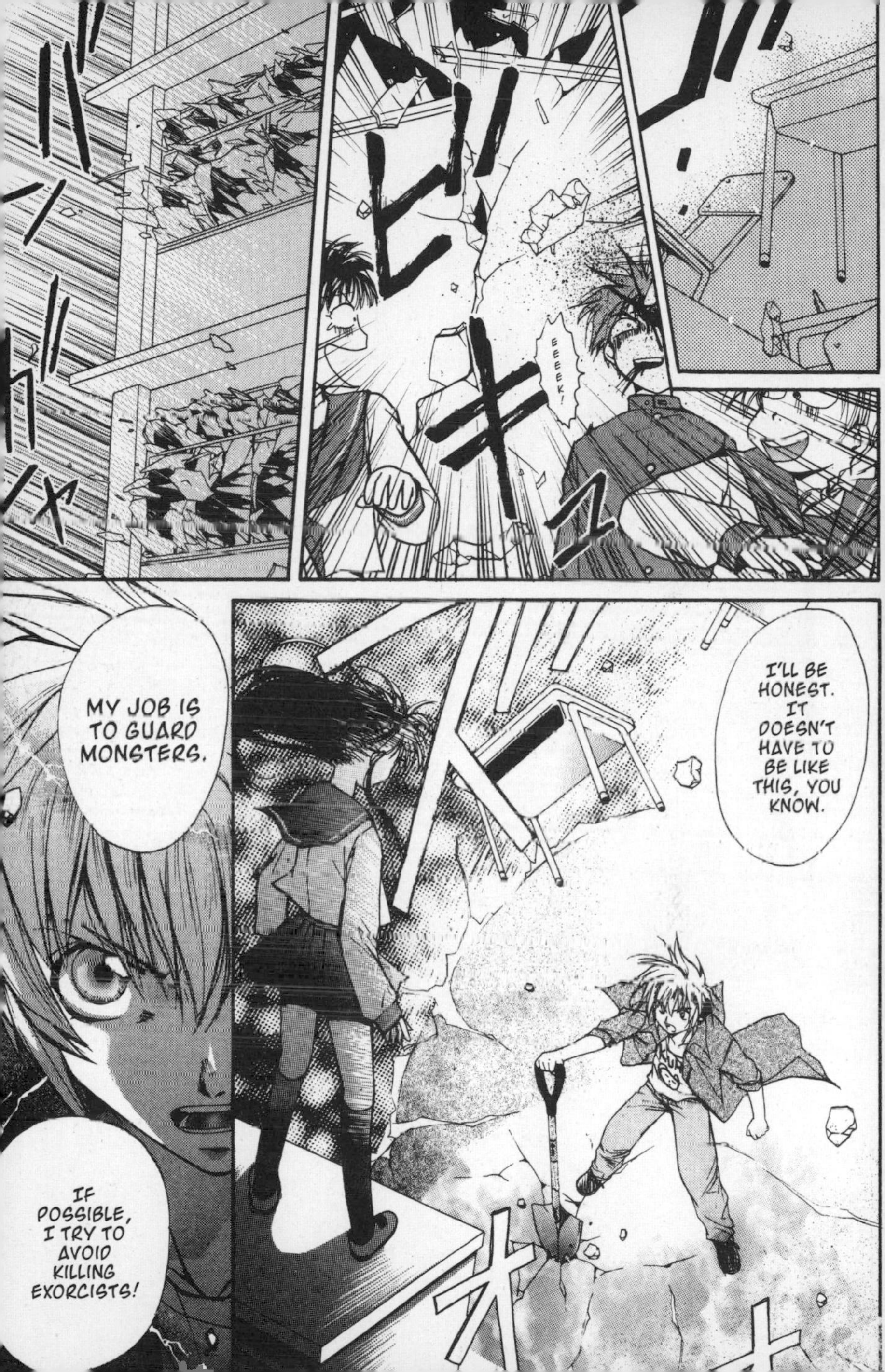
EEEEK!
I'LL BE HONEST. IT DOESN'T HAVE TO BE LIKE THIS, YOU KNOW.
MY JOB IS TO GUARD MONSTERS.
IF POSSIBLE, I TRY TO AVOID KILLING EXORCISTS!

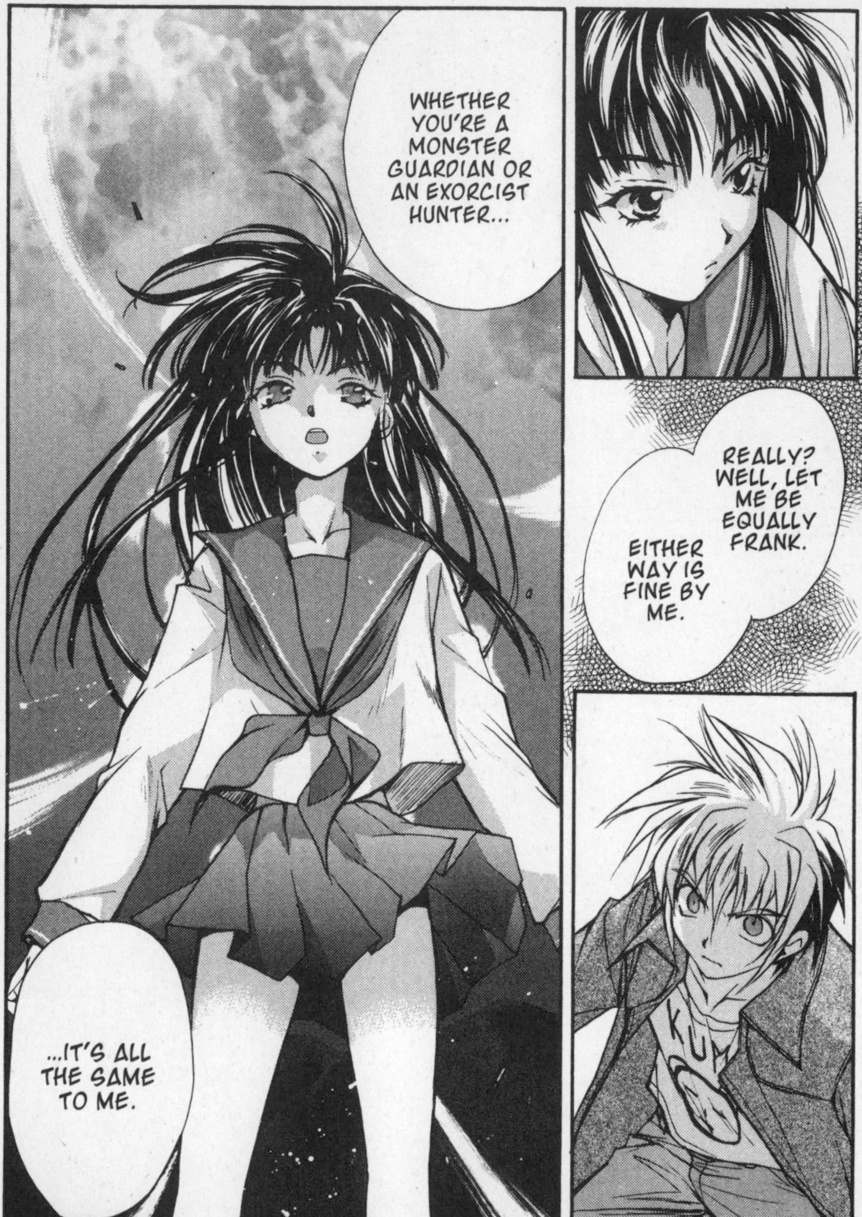
WHETHER YOU'RE A MONSTER GUARDIAN OR AN EXORCIST HUNTER...
...IT'S ALL THE SAME TO ME.
REALLY? WELL, LET ME BE EQUALLY FRANK.
EITHER WAY IS FINE BY ME.
KUM

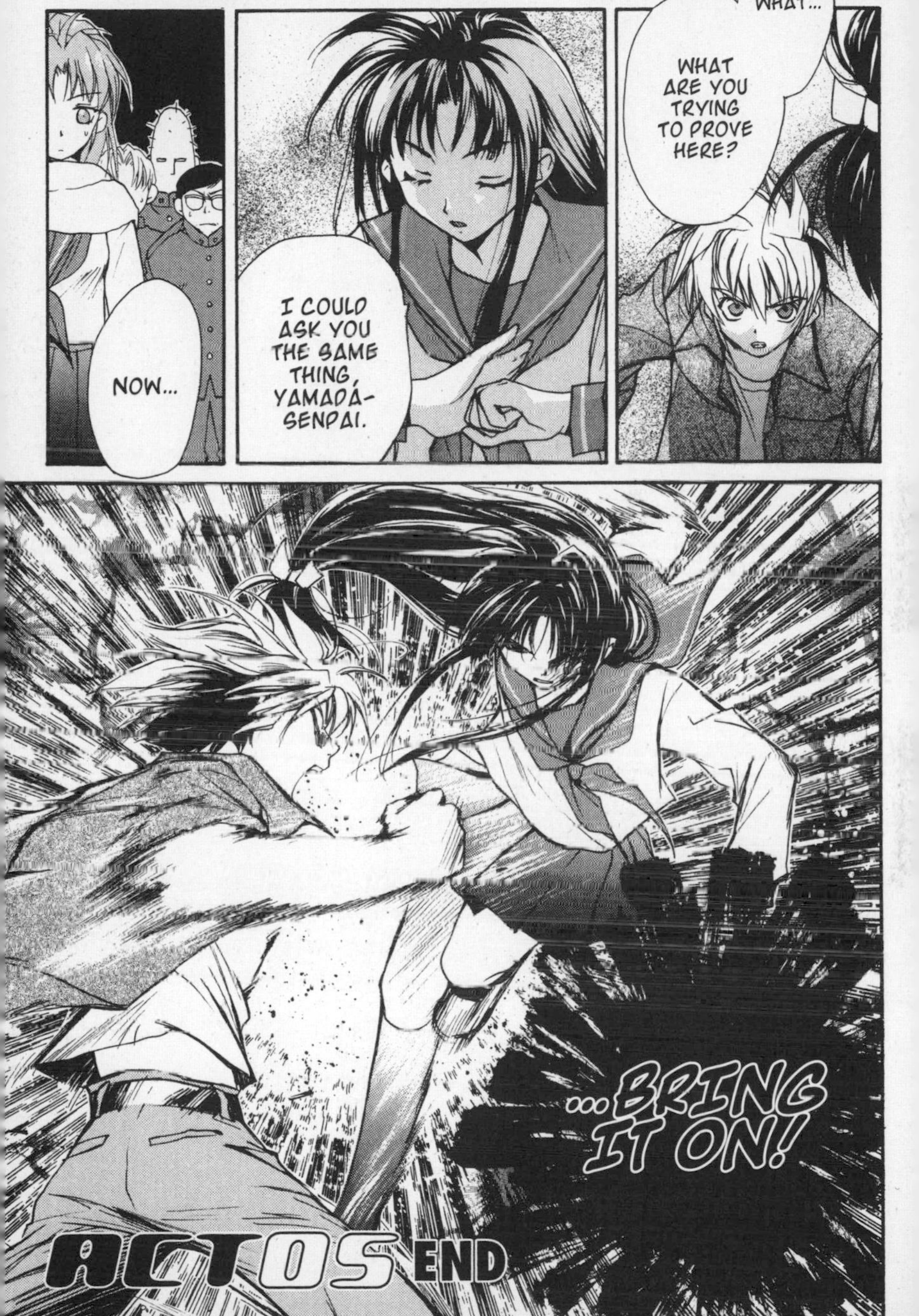
WHAT...
WHAT ARE YOU TRYING TO PROVE HERE?
I COULD ASK YOU THE SAME THING, YAMADA-SENPAI.
NOW...
...BRING IT ON!
ACT 05 END

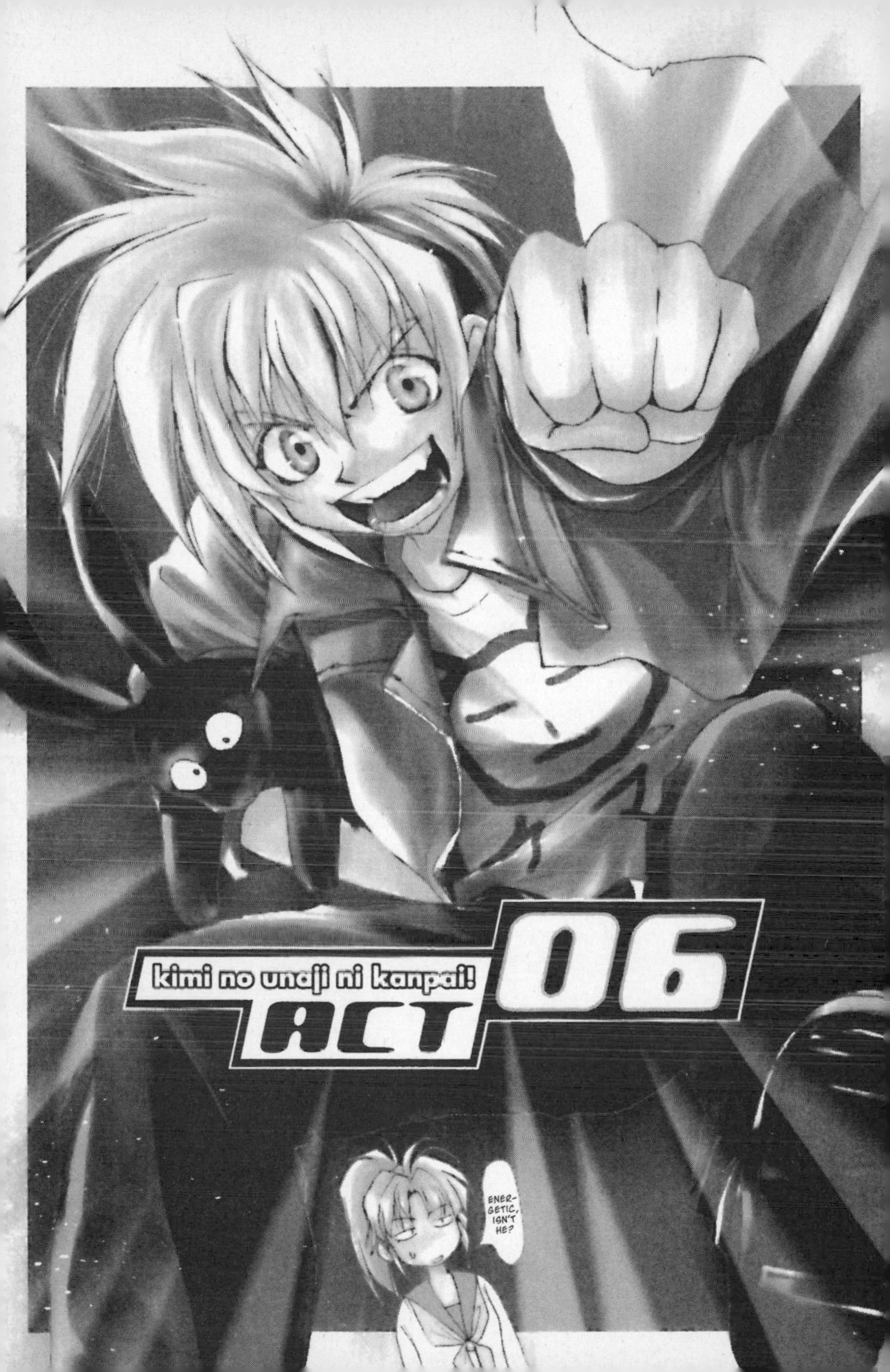
kimi no unaji ni kanpai!
ACT 06
...
ENER-
GETIC,
ISN'T
HE?

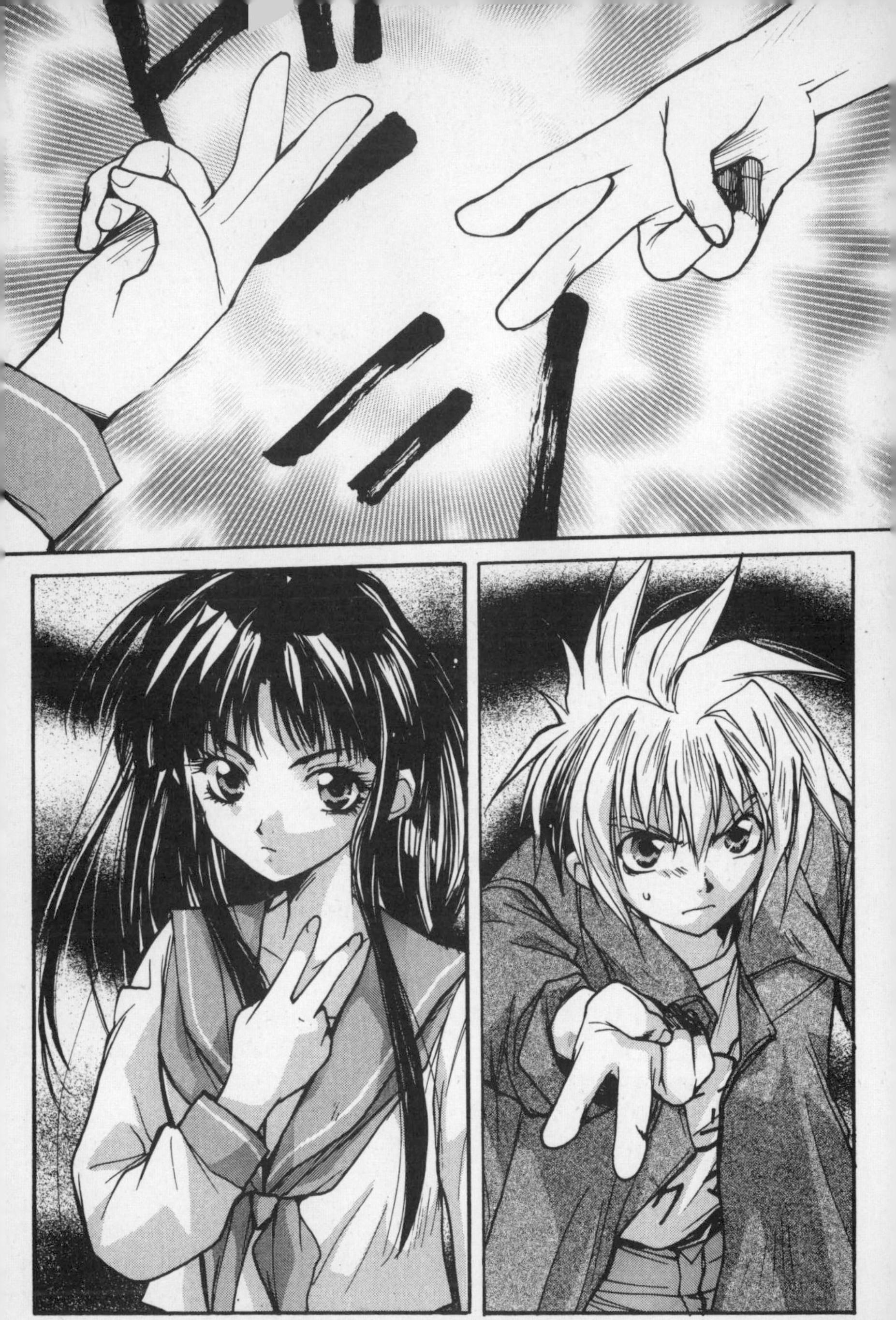

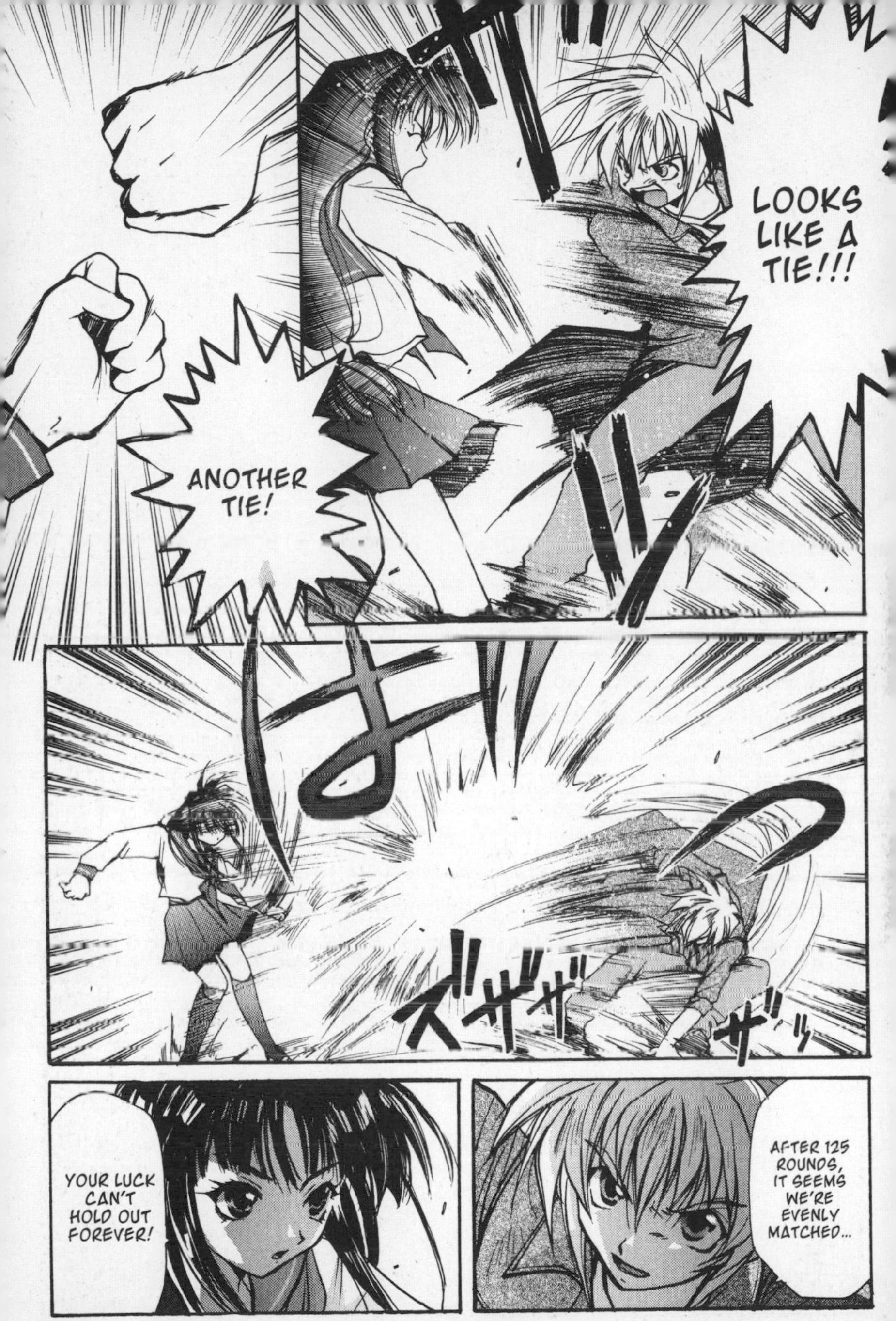
LOOKS LIKE A TIE!!!
ANOTHER TIE!
AFTER 125 ROUNDS, IT SEEMS WE'RE EVENLY MATCHED...
YOUR LUCK CAN'T HOLD OUT FOREVER!

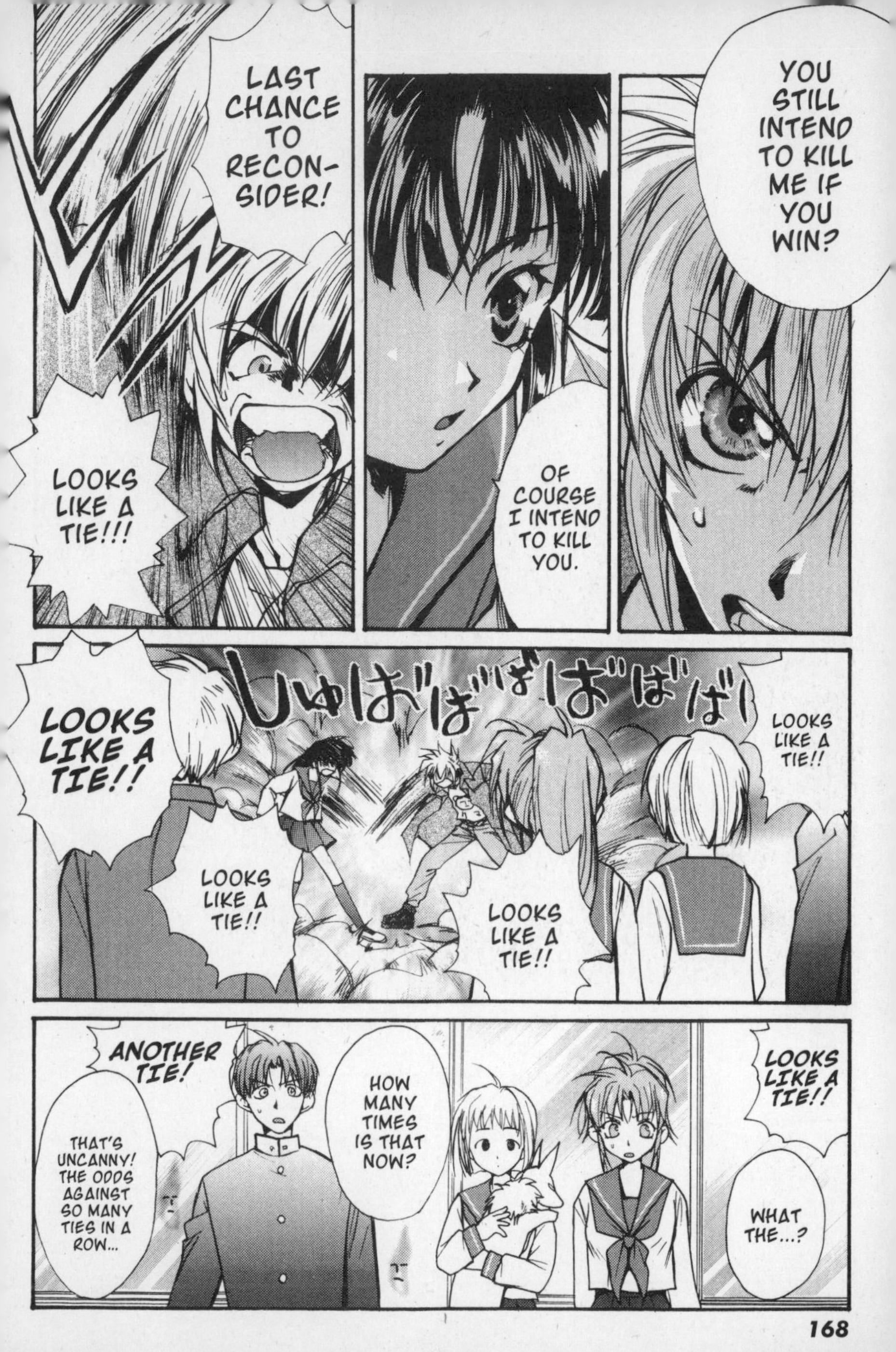
YOU STILL INTEND TO KILL ME IF YOU WIN?
OF COURSE I INTEND TO KILL YOU.
LAST CHANCE TO RECONSIDER!
LOOKS LIKE A TIE!!!
しゅばばばばば
LOOKS LIKE A TIE!!
LOOKS LIKE A TIE!!
LOOKS LIKE A TIE!!
LOOKS LIKE A TIE!!
LOOKS LIKE A TIE!!
WHAT THE...?
HOW MANY TIMES IS THAT NOW?
ANOTHER TIE!
THAT'S UNCANNY! THE ODDS AGAINST SO MANY TIES IN A ROW...

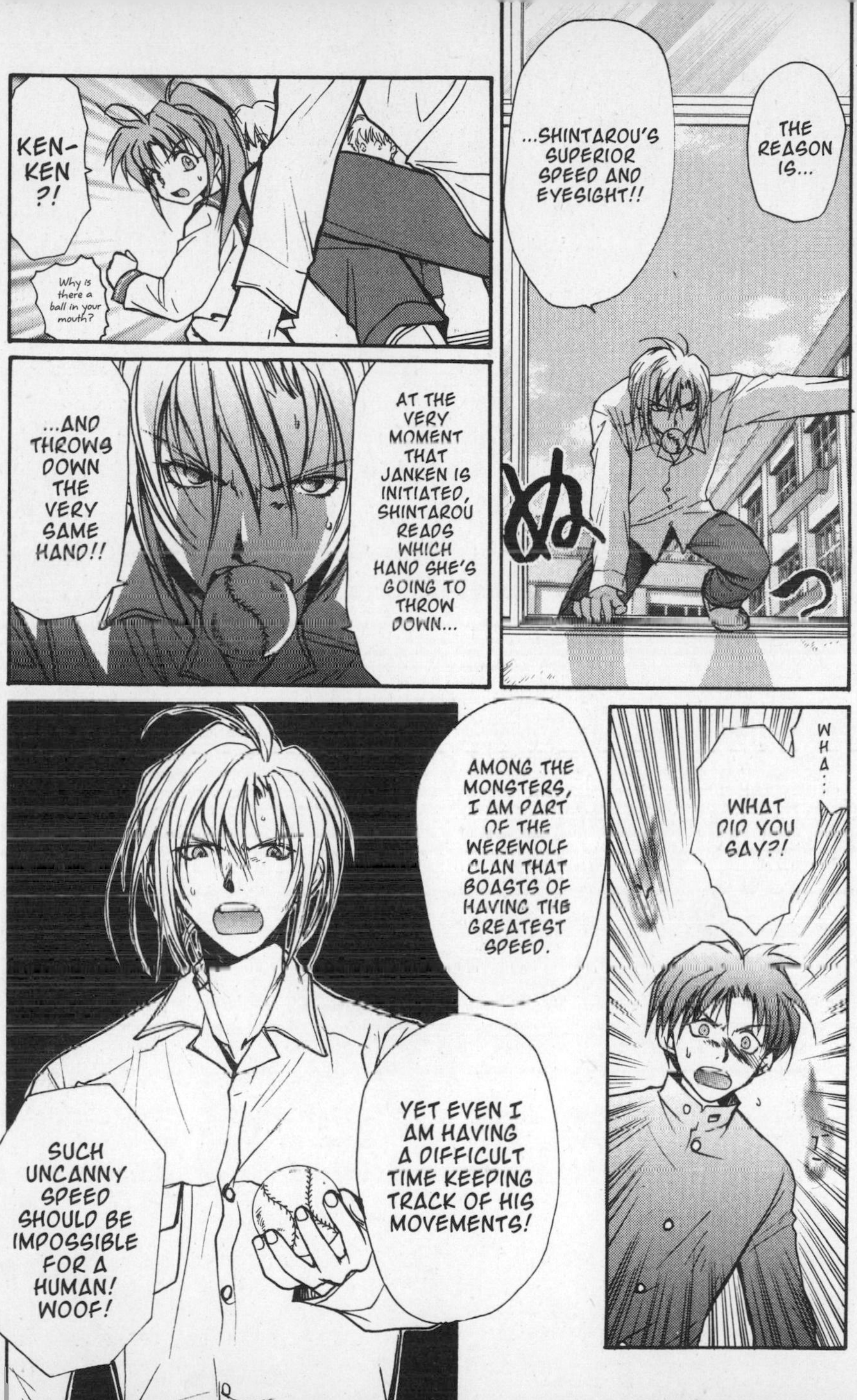
THE REASON IS...
...SHINTAROU'S SUPERIOR SPEED AND EYESIGHT!!
ぬ
KEN-KEN ?!
Why is there a ball in your mouth?
AT THE VERY MOMENT THAT JANKEN IS INITIATED, SHINTAROU READS WHICH HAND SHE'S GOING TO THROW DOWN...
...AND THROWS DOWN THE VERY SAME HAND!!
WHA...
WHAT DID YOU SAY?!
AMONG THE MONSTERS, I AM PART OF THE WEREWOLF CLAN THAT BOASTS OF HAVING THE GREATEST SPEED.
YET EVEN I AM HAVING A DIFFICULT TIME KEEPING TRACK OF HIS MOVEMENTS!
SUCH UNCANNY SPEED SHOULD BE IMPOSSIBLE FOR A HUMAN! WOOF!

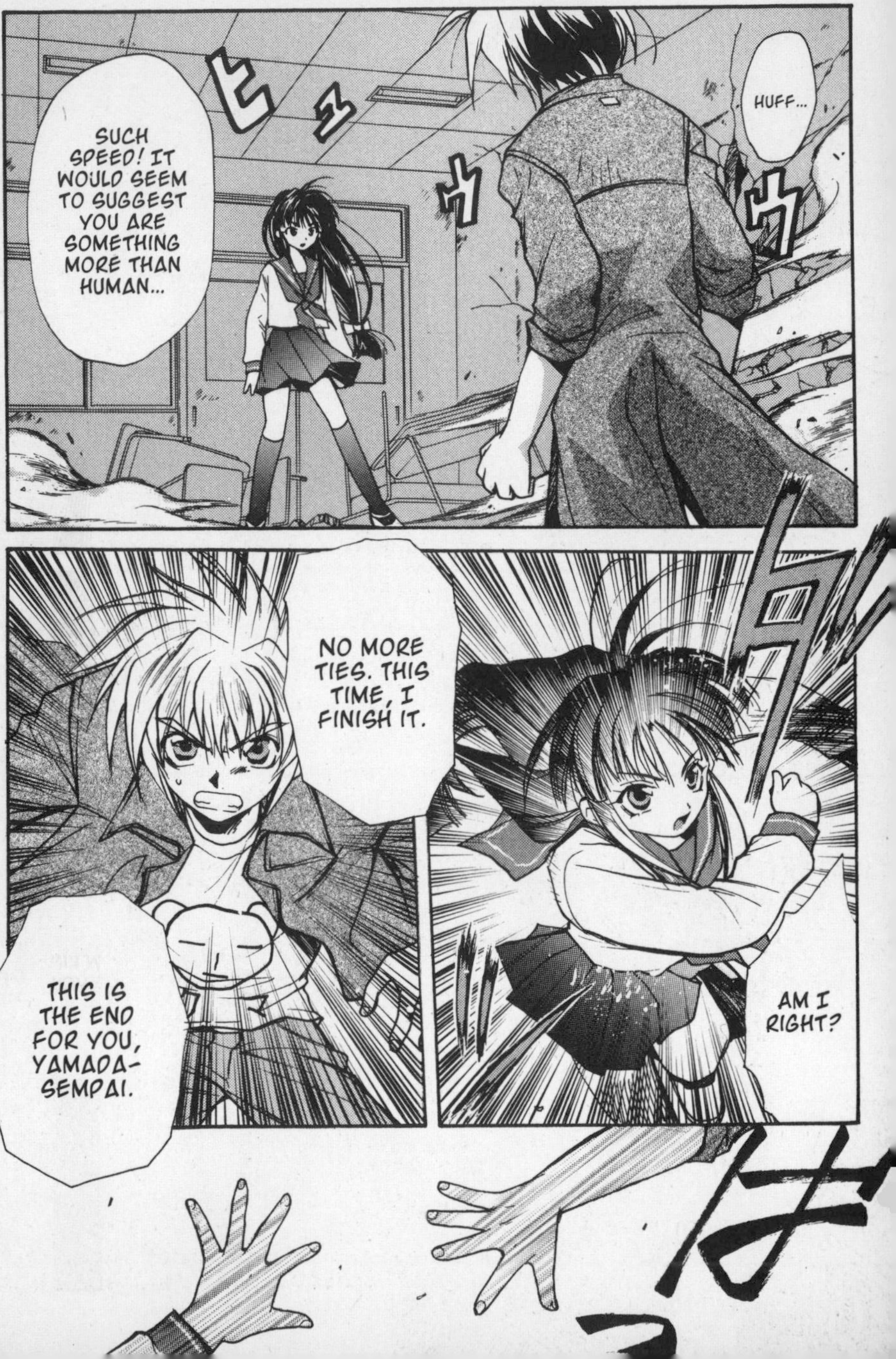
HUFF...
SUCH SPEED! IT WOULD SEEM TO SUGGEST YOU ARE SOMETHING MORE THAN HUMAN...
AM I RIGHT?
NO MORE TIES. THIS TIME, I FINISH IT.
THIS IS THE END FOR YOU, YAMADA-SEMPAI.

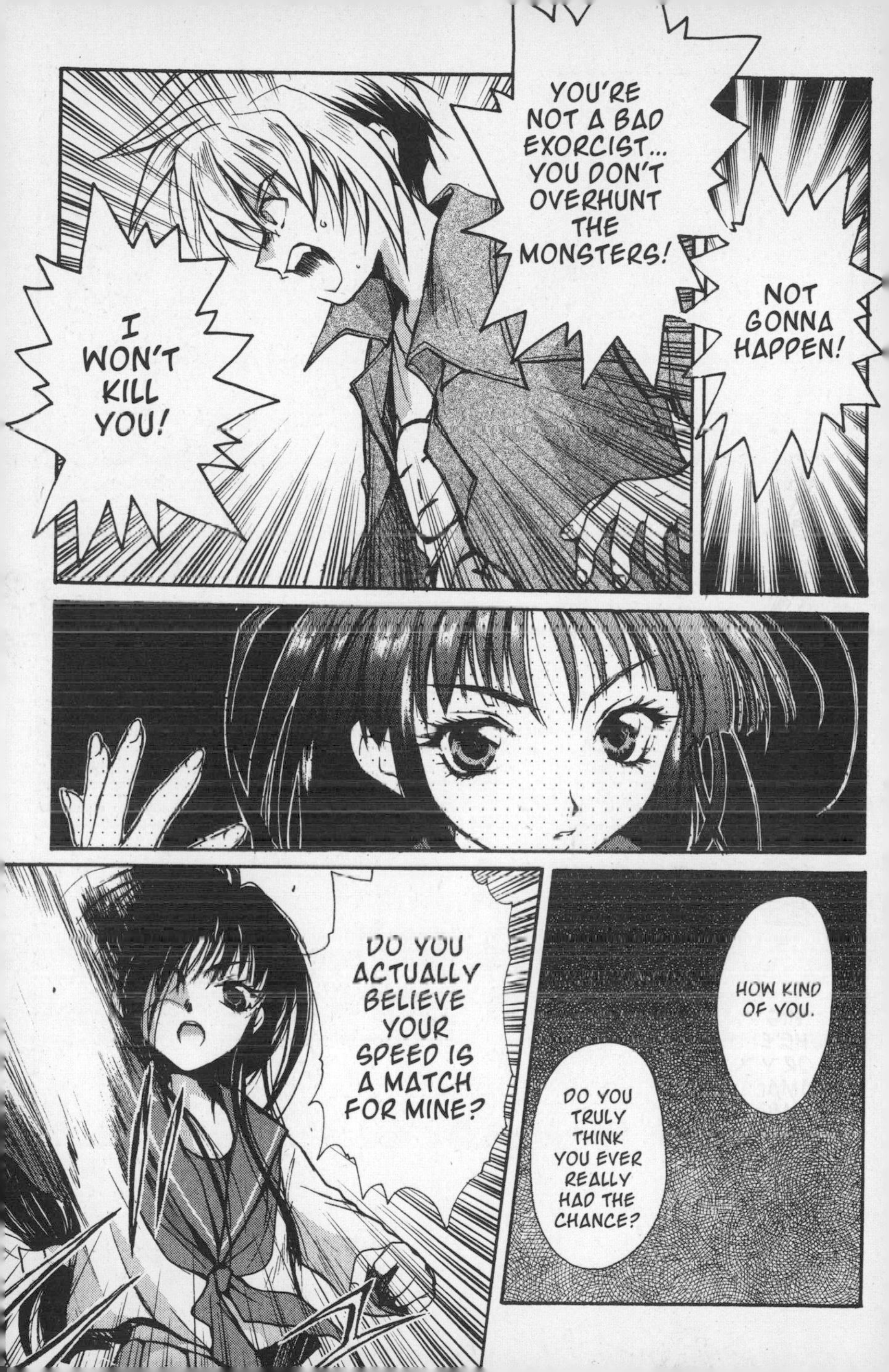
YOU'RE NOT A BAD EXORCIST... YOU DON'T OVERHUNT THE MONSTERS!
NOT GONNA HAPPEN!
I WON'T KILL YOU!
HOW KIND OF YOU.
DO YOU TRULY THINK YOU EVER REALLY HAD THE CHANCE?
DO YOU ACTUALLY BELIEVE YOUR SPEED IS A MATCH FOR MINE?

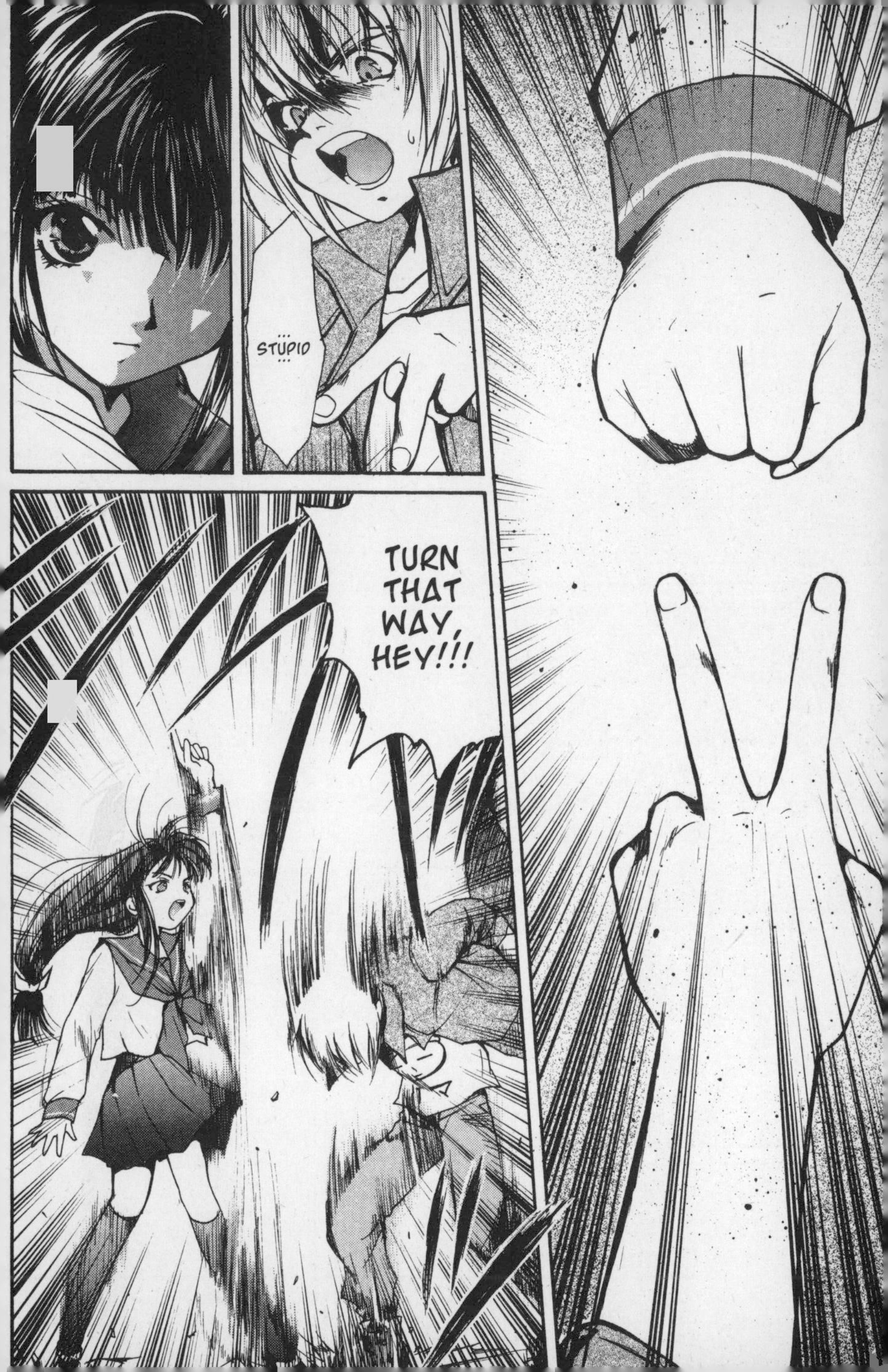

...
STUPID
...
TURN THAT WAY, HEY!!!

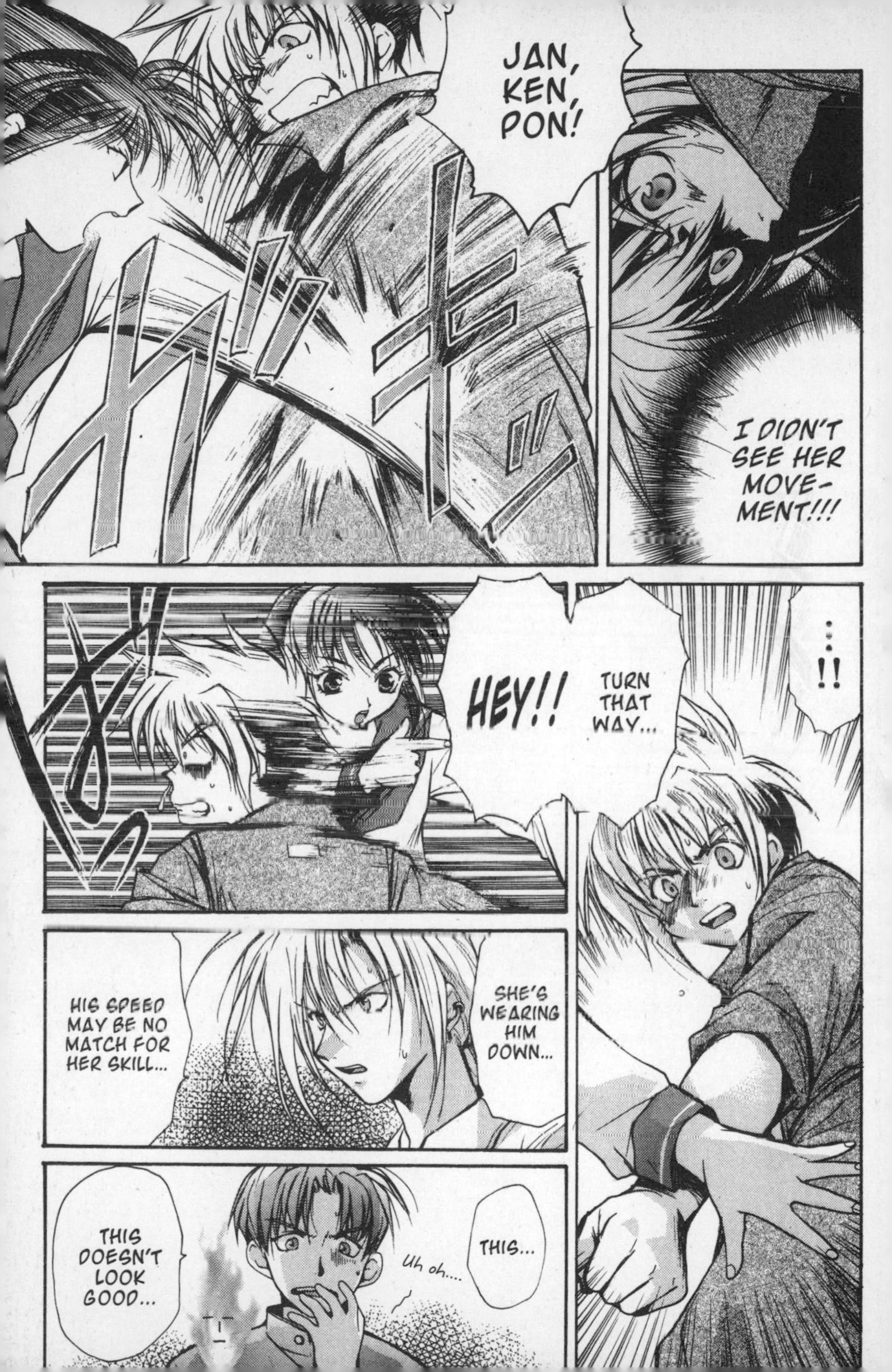
JAN, KEN, PON!
I DIDN'T SEE HER MOVEMENT!!!
..!!
TURN THAT WAY...
HEY!!
SHE'S WEARING HIM DOWN...
HIS SPEED MAY BE NO MATCH FOR HER SKILL...
THIS...
Uh oh....
THIS DOESN'T LOOK GOOD...

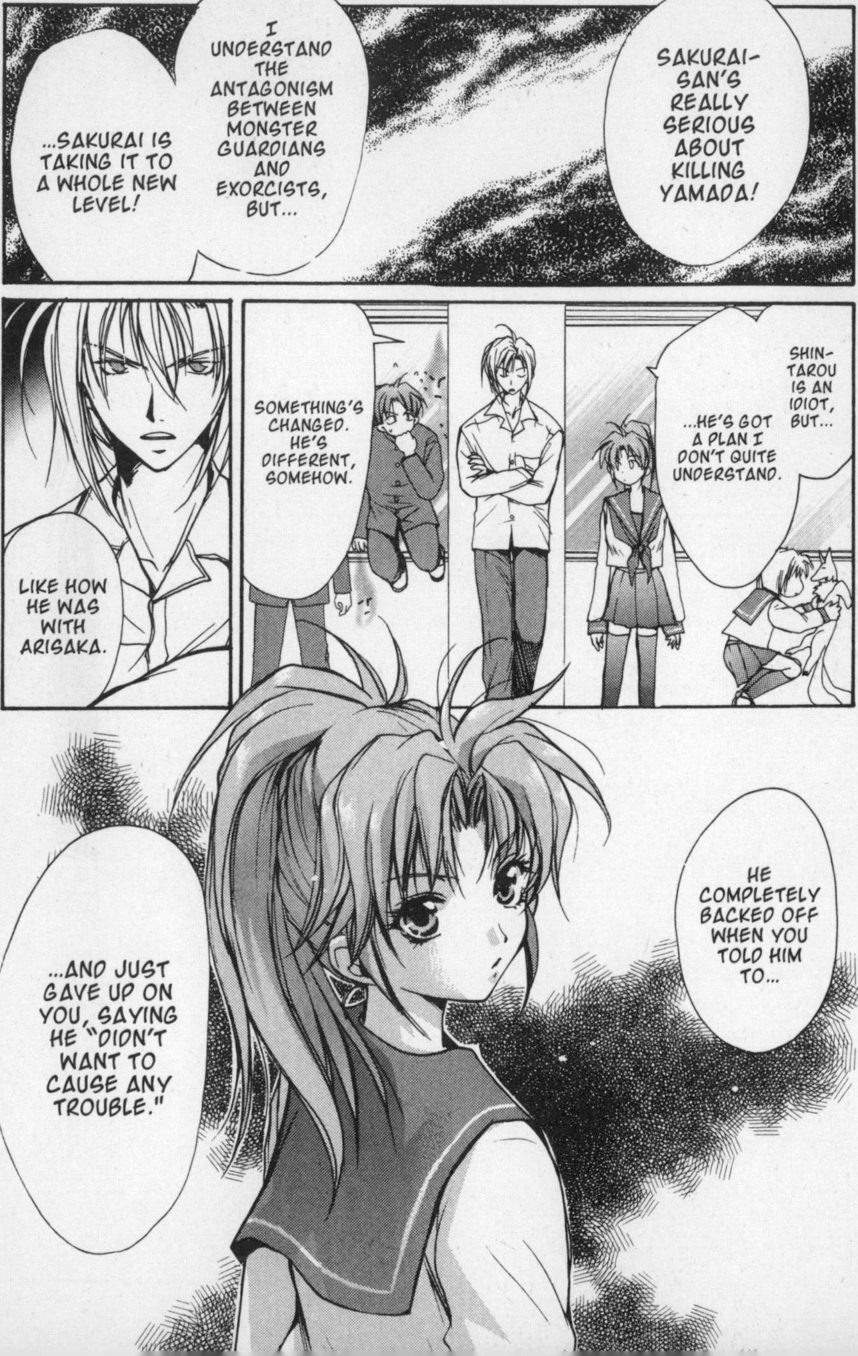
SAKURAI-SAN'S REALLY SERIOUS ABOUT KILLING YAMADA!
I UNDERSTAND THE ANTAGONISM BETWEEN MONSTER GUARDIANS AND EXORCISTS, BUT...
...SAKURAI IS TAKING IT TO A WHOLE NEW LEVEL!
SHIN-TAROU IS AN IDIOT, BUT...
...HE'S GOT A PLAN I DON'T QUITE UNDERSTAND.
SOMETHING'S CHANGED. HE'S DIFFERENT, SOMEHOW.
LIKE HOW HE WAS WITH ARISAKA.
HE COMPLETELY BACKED OFF WHEN YOU TOLD HIM TO...
...AND JUST GAVE UP ON YOU, SAYING HE "DIDN'T WANT TO CAUSE ANY TROUBLE."

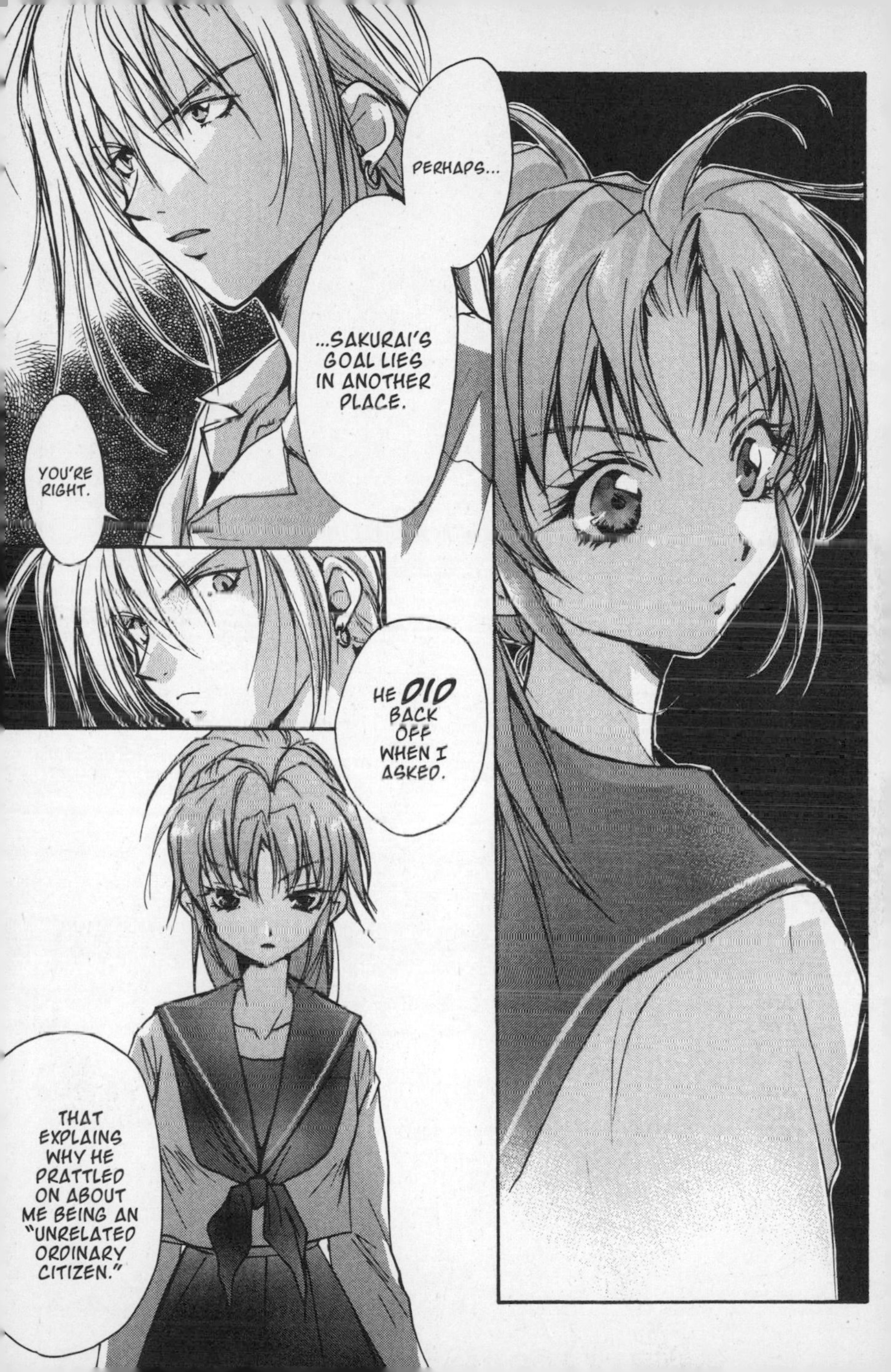
PERHAPS...
...SAKURAI'S GOAL LIES IN ANOTHER PLACE.
YOU'RE RIGHT.
HE DID BACK OFF WHEN I ASKED.
THAT EXPLAINING WHY HE PRATTLED ON ABOUT ME BEING AN "UNRELATED ORDINARY CITIZEN."

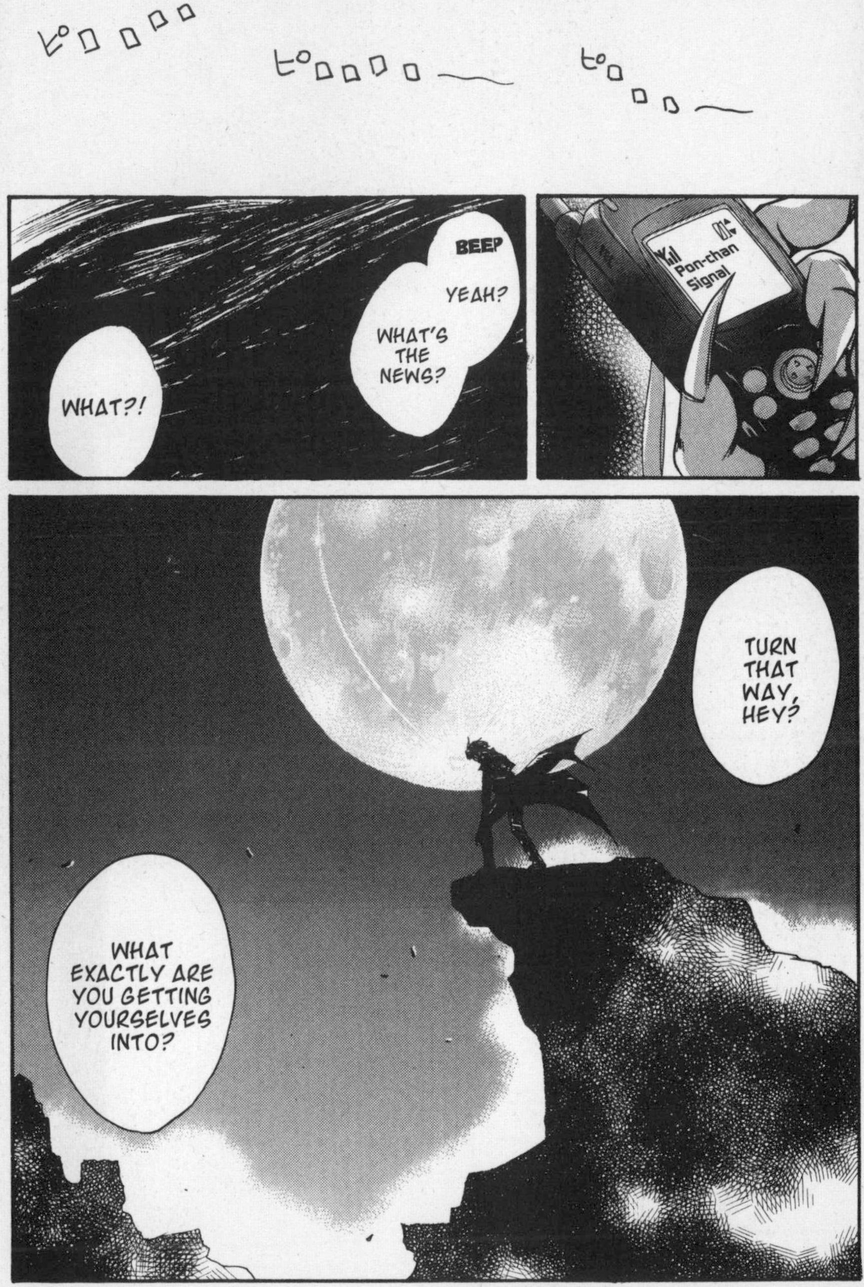
ピロ ロロロ
ピロロロロロ—
ピロロロ—
Pon-chan Signal
BEEP
YEAH?
WHAT'S THE NEWS?
WHAT?!
TURN THAT WAY, HEY?
WHAT EXACTLY ARE YOU GETTING YOURSELVES INTO?

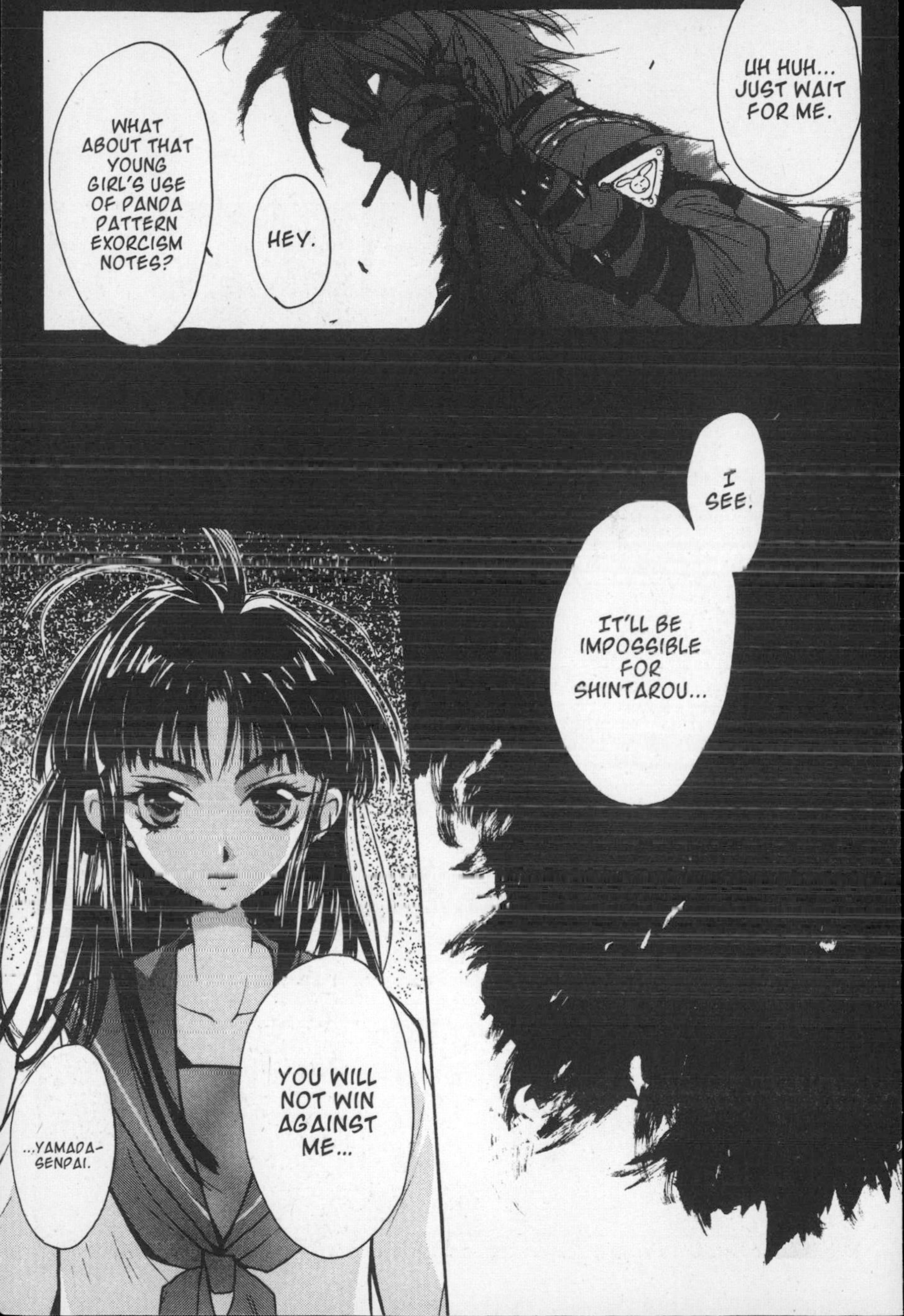
UH HUH... JUST WAIT FOR ME.
HEY.
WHAT ABOUT THAT YOUNG GIRL'S USE OF PANDA PATTERN EXORCISM NOTES?
I SEE.
IT'LL BE IMPOSSIBLE FOR SHINTAROU...
YOU WILL NOT WIN AGAINST ME...
...YAMADA-SENPAI.

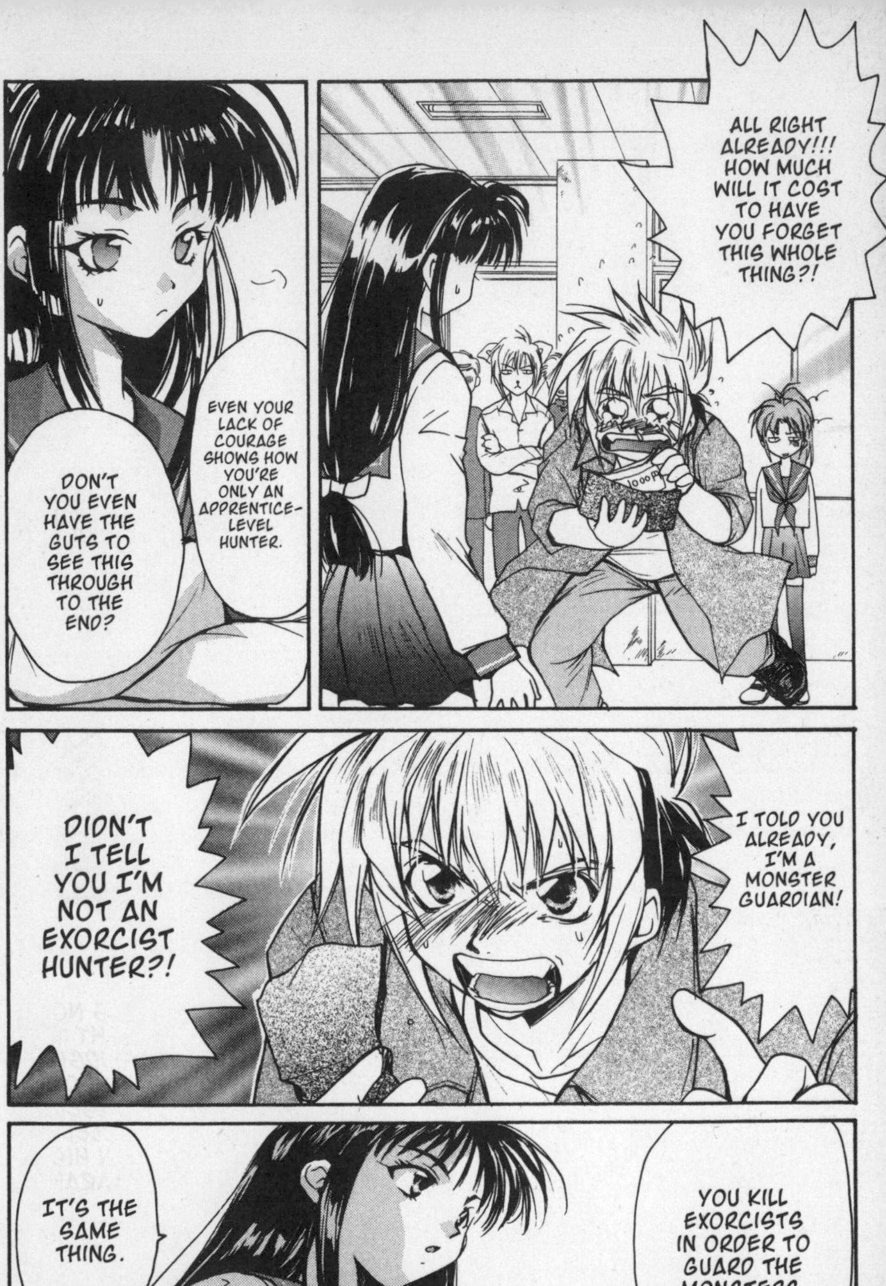
ALL RIGHT ALREADY!!! HOW MUCH WILL IT COST TO HAVE YOU FORGET THIS WHOLE THING?!
EVEN YOUR LACK OF COURAGE SHOWS HOW YOU'RE ONLY AN APPRENTICE-LEVEL HUNTER.
DON'T YOU EVEN HAVE THE GUTS TO SEE THIS THROUGH TO THE END?
I TOLD YOU ALREADY, I'M A MONSTER GUARDIAN!
DIDN'T I TELL YOU I'M NOT AN EXORCIST HUNTER?!
YOU KILL EXORCISTS IN ORDER TO GUARD THE MONSTERS.
IT'S THE SAME THING.

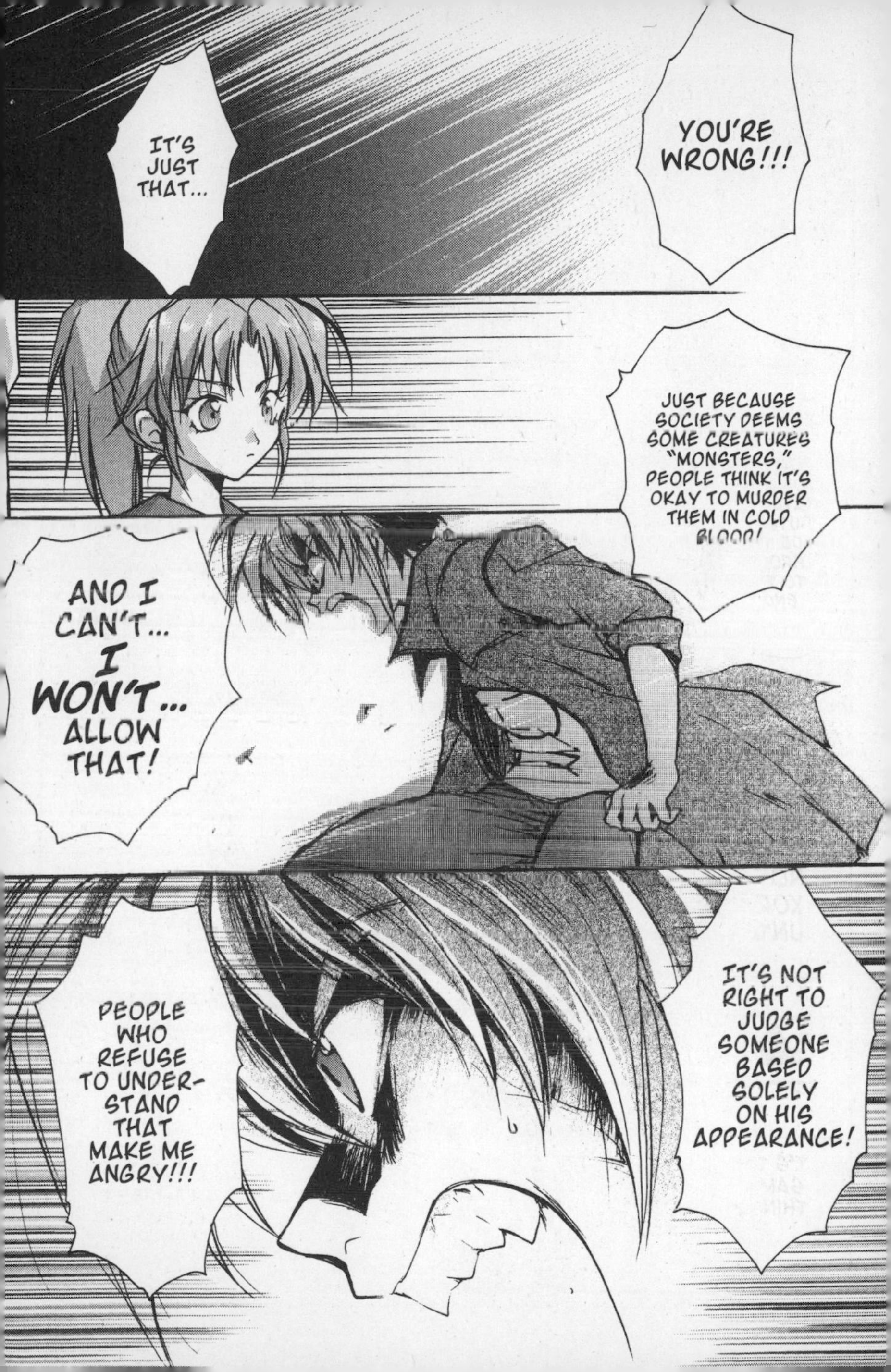
YOU'RE WRONG!!!
IT'S JUST THAT...
JUST BECAUSE SOCIETY DEEMS SOME CREATURES "MONSTERS," PEOPLE THINK IT'S OKAY TO MURDER THEM IN COLD BLOOD!
AND I CAN'T... I WON'T... ALLOW THAT!
IT'S NOT RIGHT TO JUDGE SOMEONE BASED SOLELY ON HIS APPEARANCE!
PEOPLE WHO REFUSE TO UNDER-STAND THAT MAKE ME ANGRY!!!

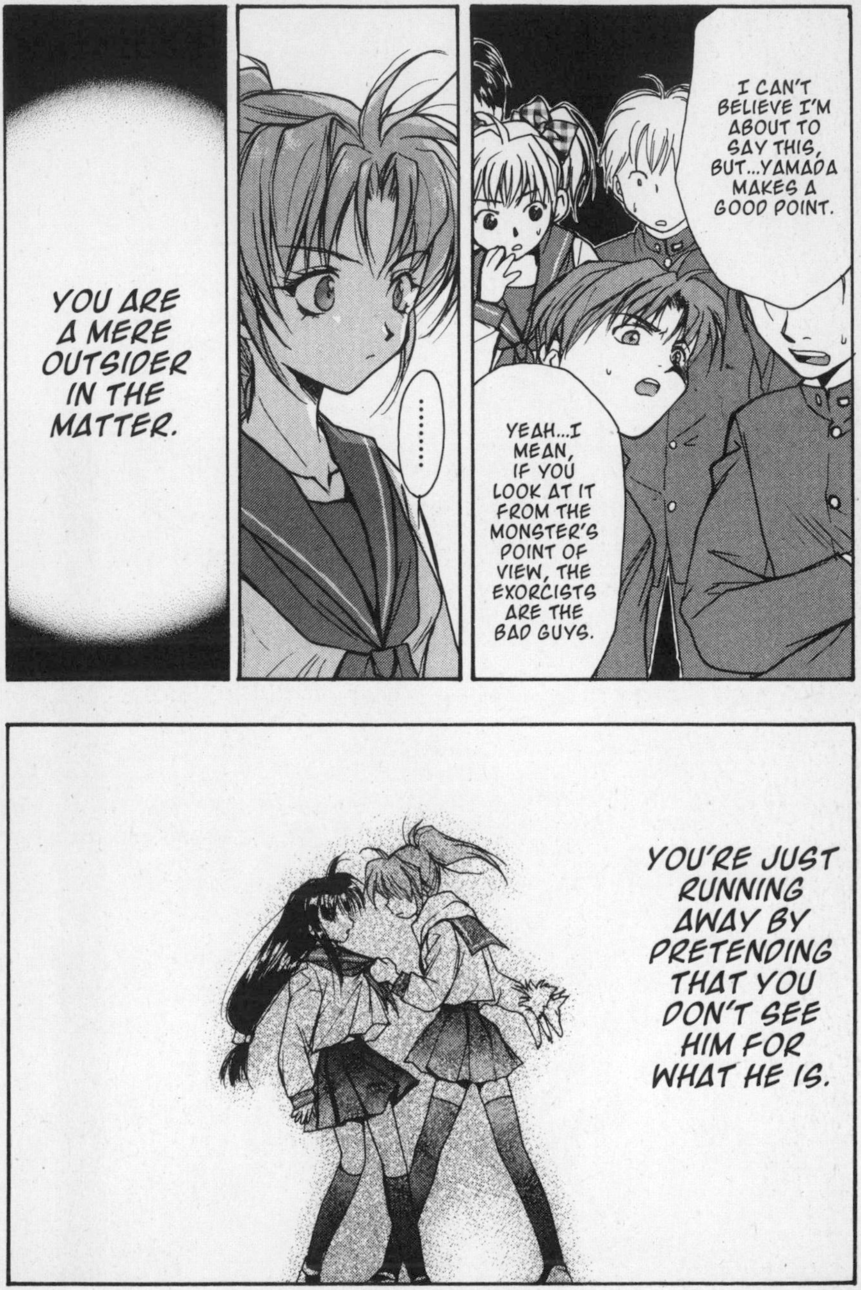
I CAN'T BELIEVE I'M ABOUT TO SAY THIS, BUT...YAMADA MAKES A GOOD POINT.
YEAH...I MEAN, IF YOU LOOK AT IT FROM THE MONSTER'S POINT OF VIEW, THE EXORCISTS ARE THE BAD GUYS.
....
YOU ARE A MERE OUTSIDER IN THE MATTER.
YOU'RE JUST RUNNING AWAY BY PRETENDING THAT YOU DON'T SEE HIM FOR WHAT HE IS.

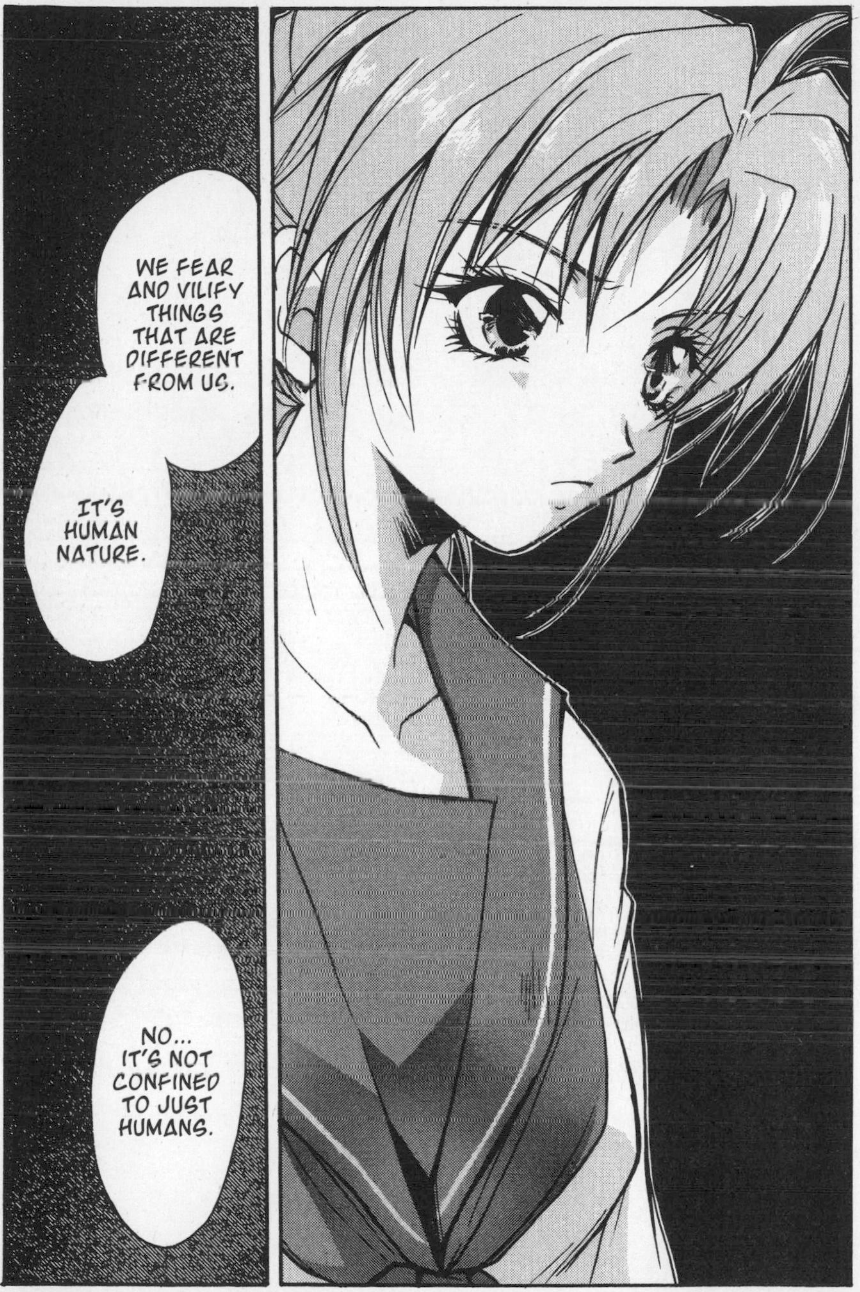
WE FEAR AND VILIFY THINGS THAT ARE DIFFERENT FROM US.
IT'S HUMAN NATURE.
NO... IT'S NOT CONFINED TO JUST HUMANS.

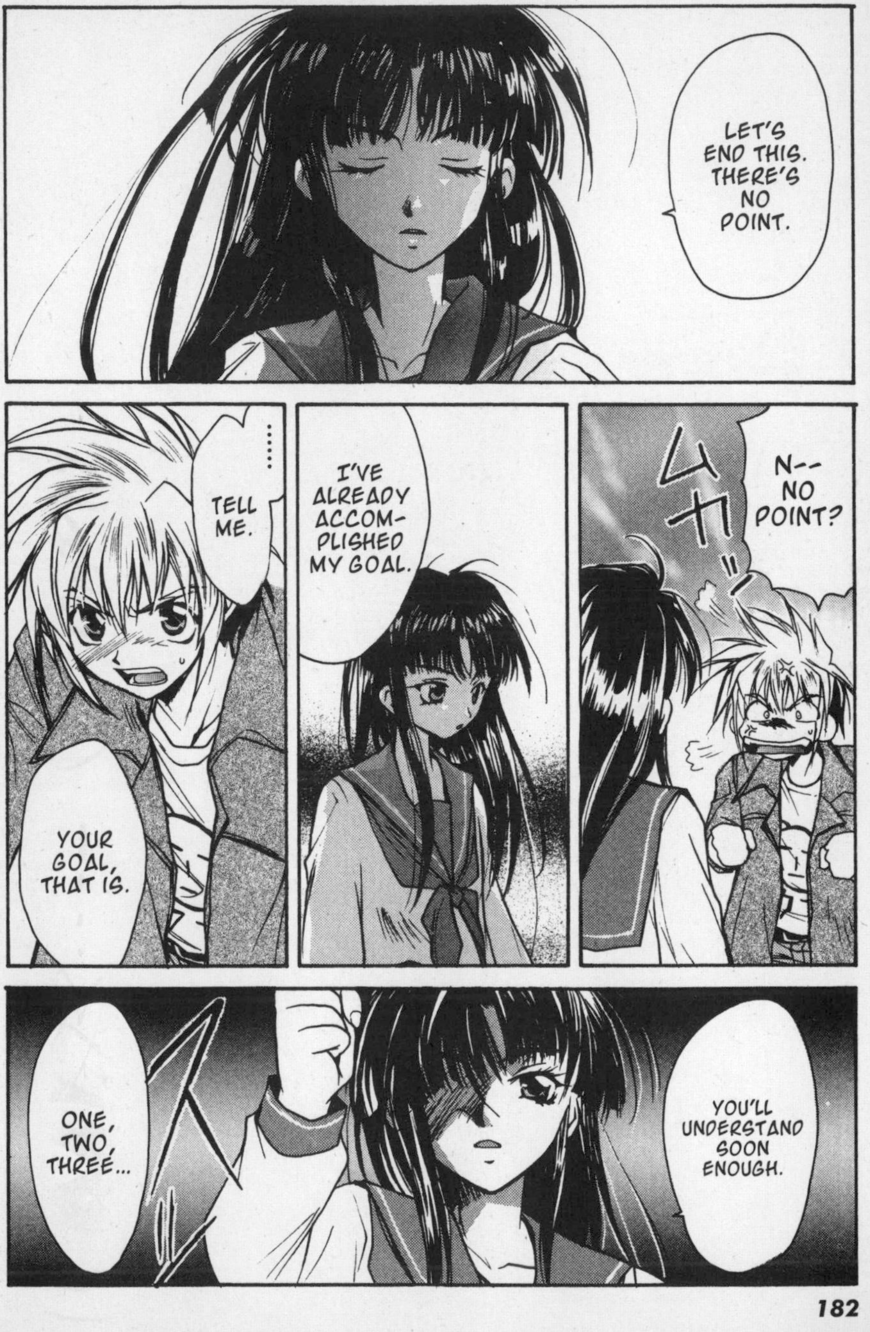
LET'S END THIS. THERE'S NO POINT.
ムカッ
N-- NO POINT?
I'VE ALREADY ACCOMPLISHED MY GOAL.
......
TELL ME.
YOUR GOAL, THAT IS.
YOU'LL UNDERSTAND SOON ENOUGH.
ONE, TWO, THREE...

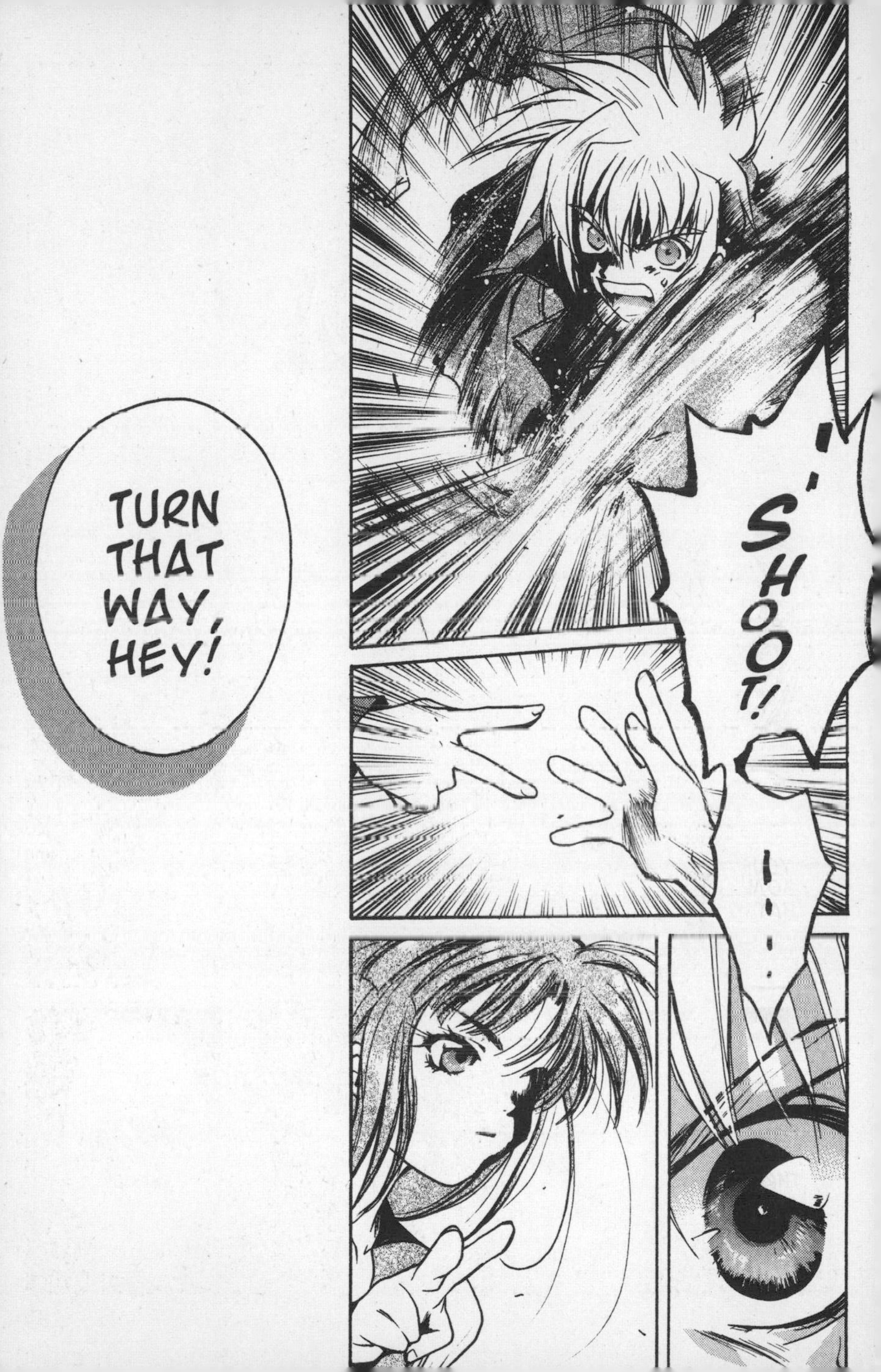
SHOOT!!
TURN THAT WAY HEY!

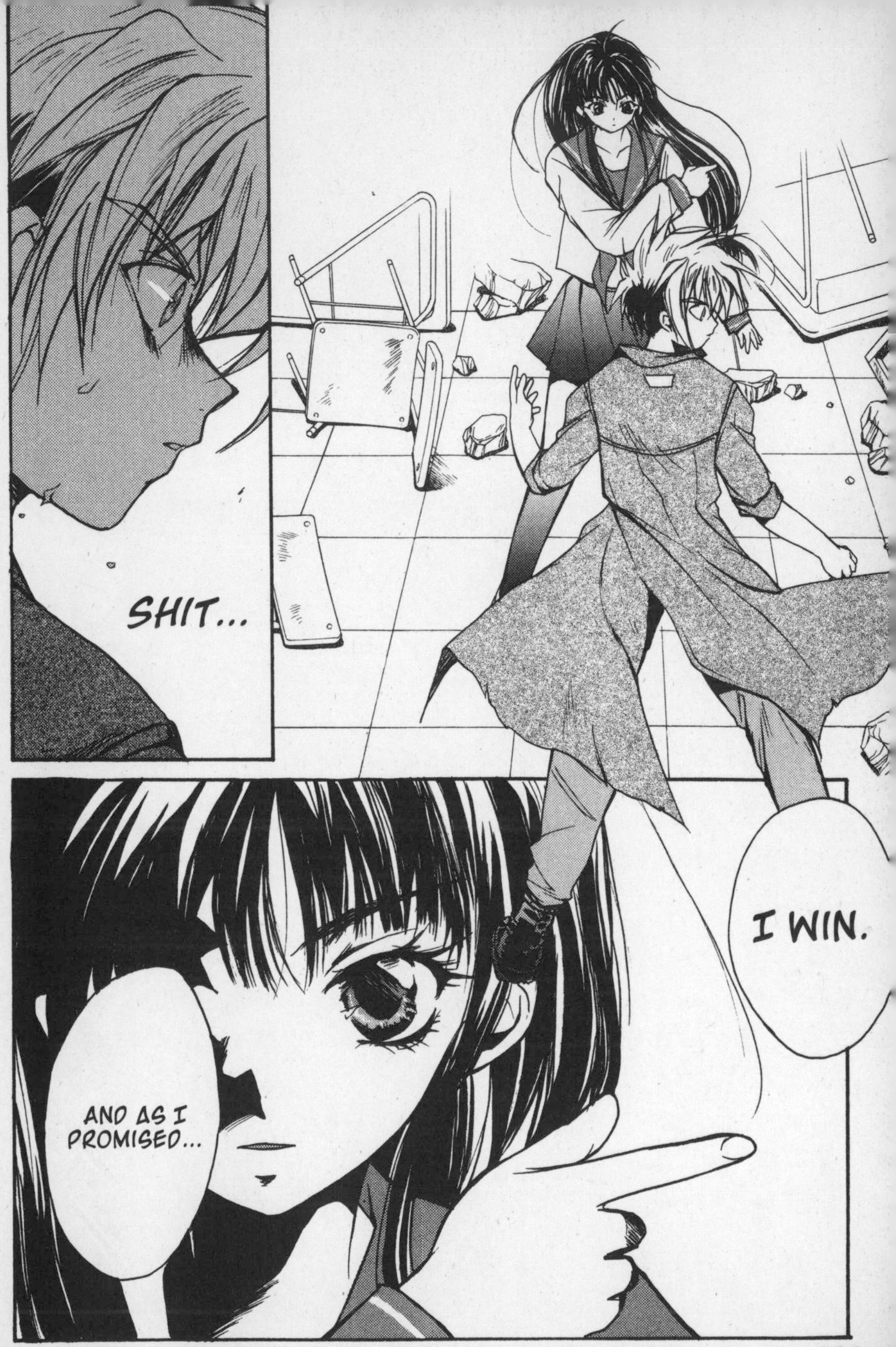
SHIT...
I WIN.
AND AS I PROMISED...

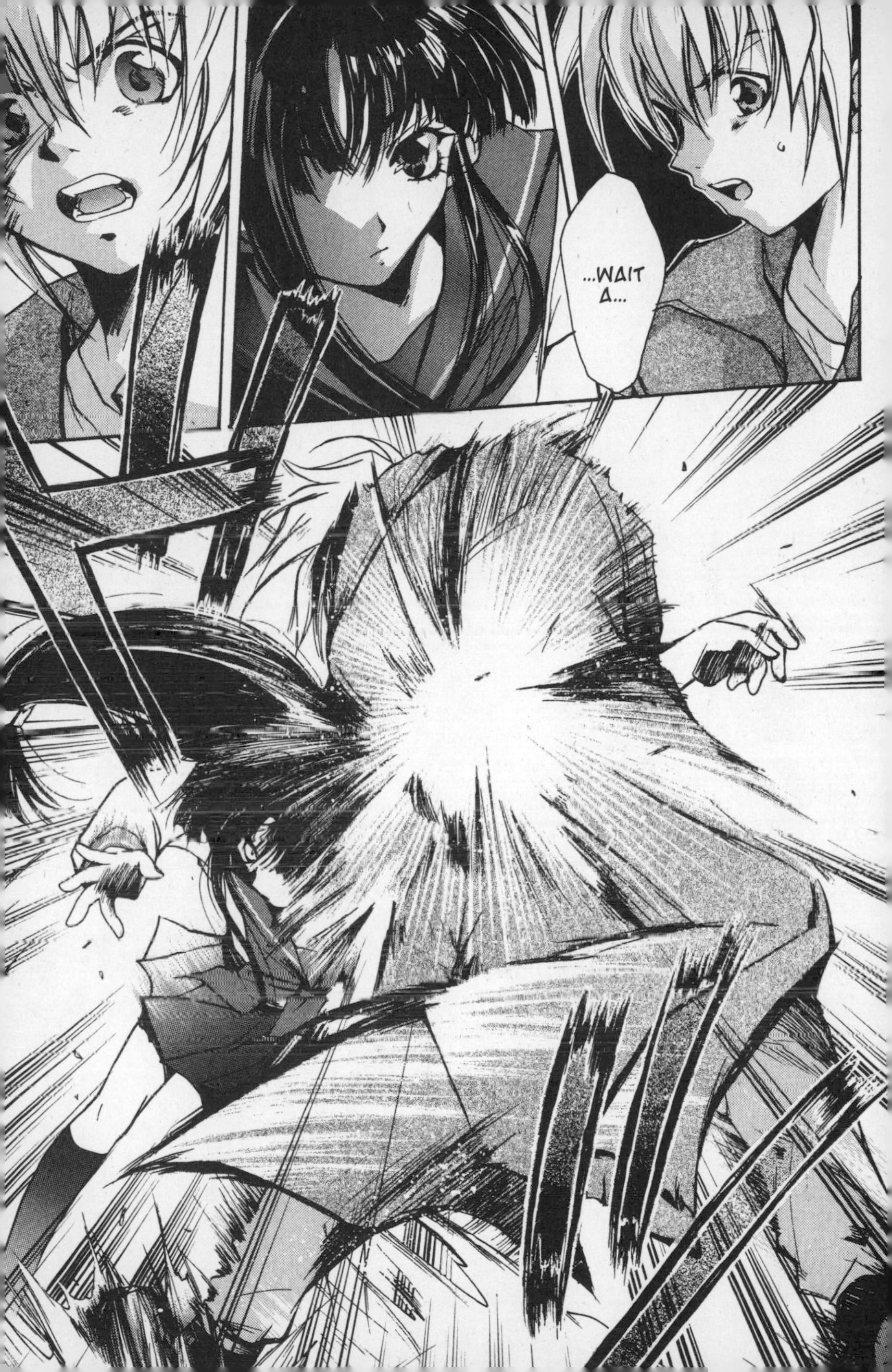
...WAIT A...

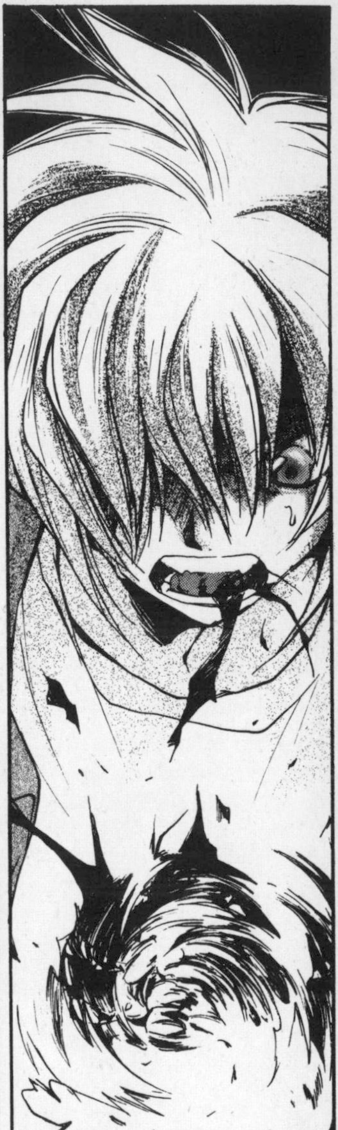

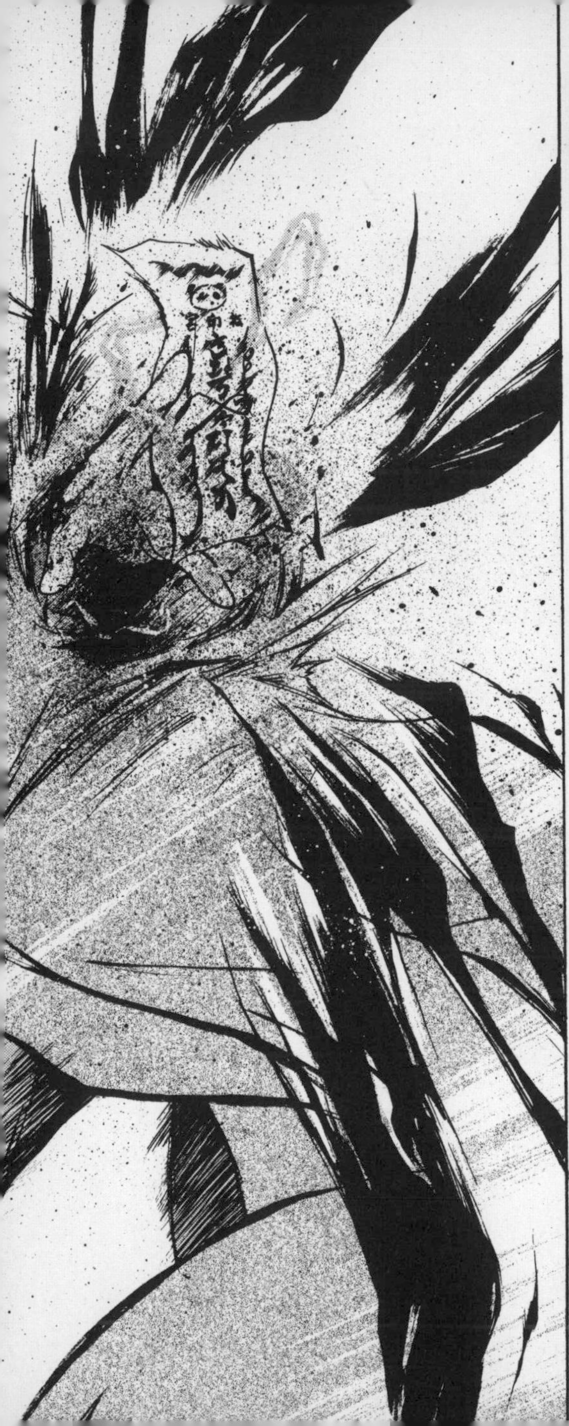

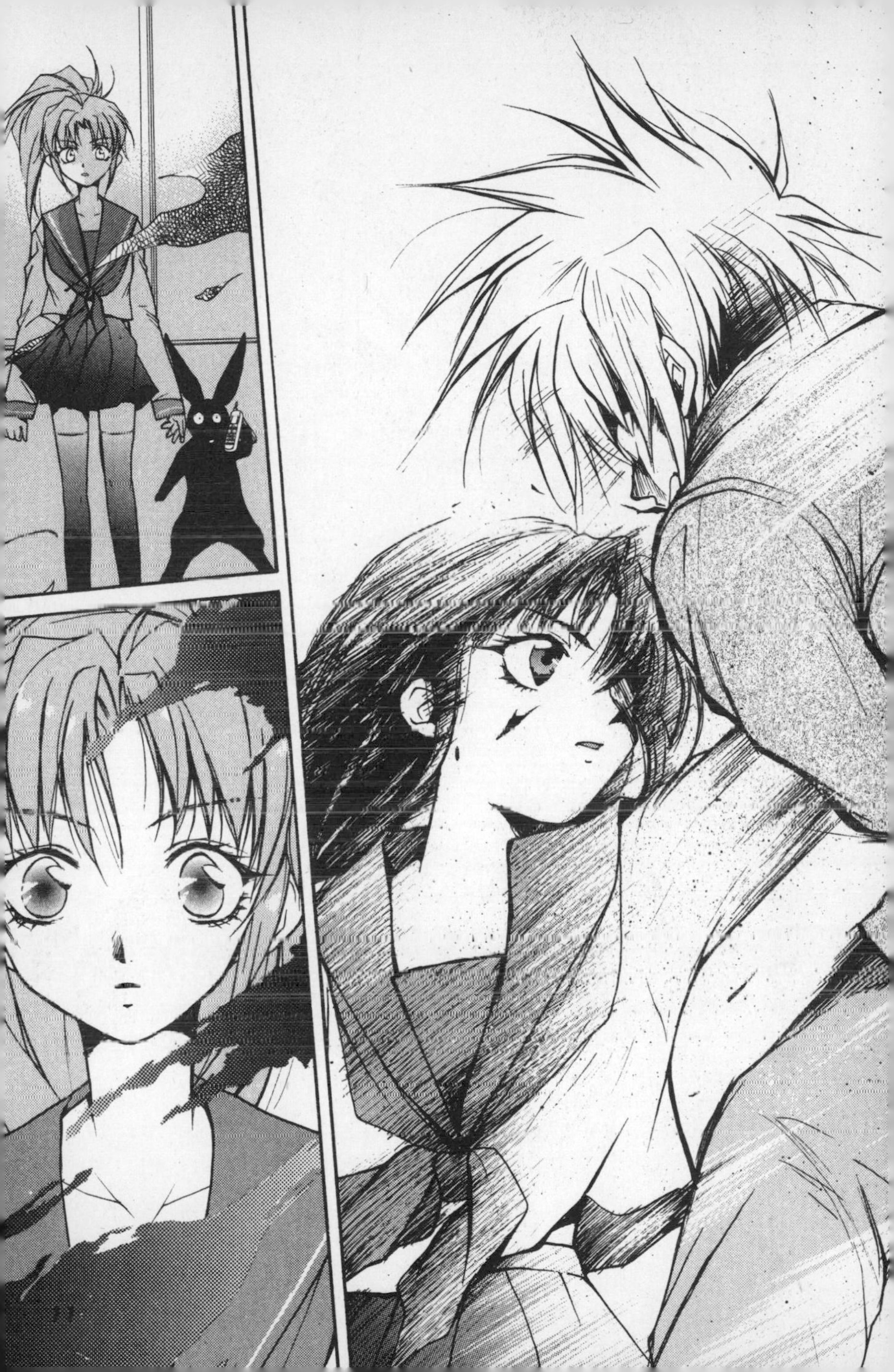

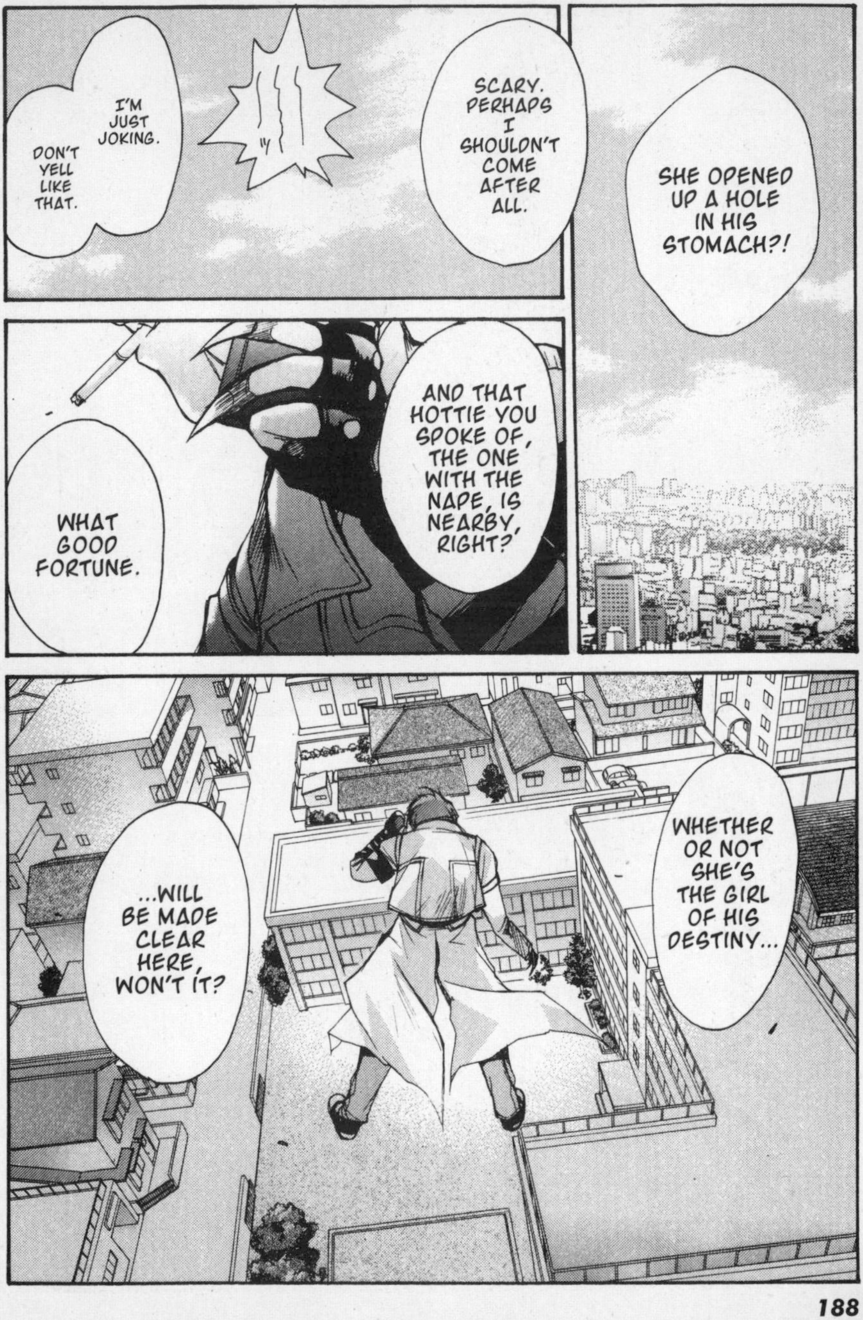
SHE OPENED UP A HOLE IN HIS STOMACH?!
SCARY. PERHAPS I SHOULDN'T COME AFTER ALL.
I'M JUST JOKING.
DON'T YELL LIKE THAT.
AND THAT HOTTIE YOU SPOKE OF, THE ONE WITH THE NAPE, IS NEARBY, RIGHT?
WHAT GOOD FORTUNE.
WHETHER OR NOT SHE'S THE GIRL OF HIS DESTINY...
...WILL BE MADE CLEAR HERE, WON'T IT?

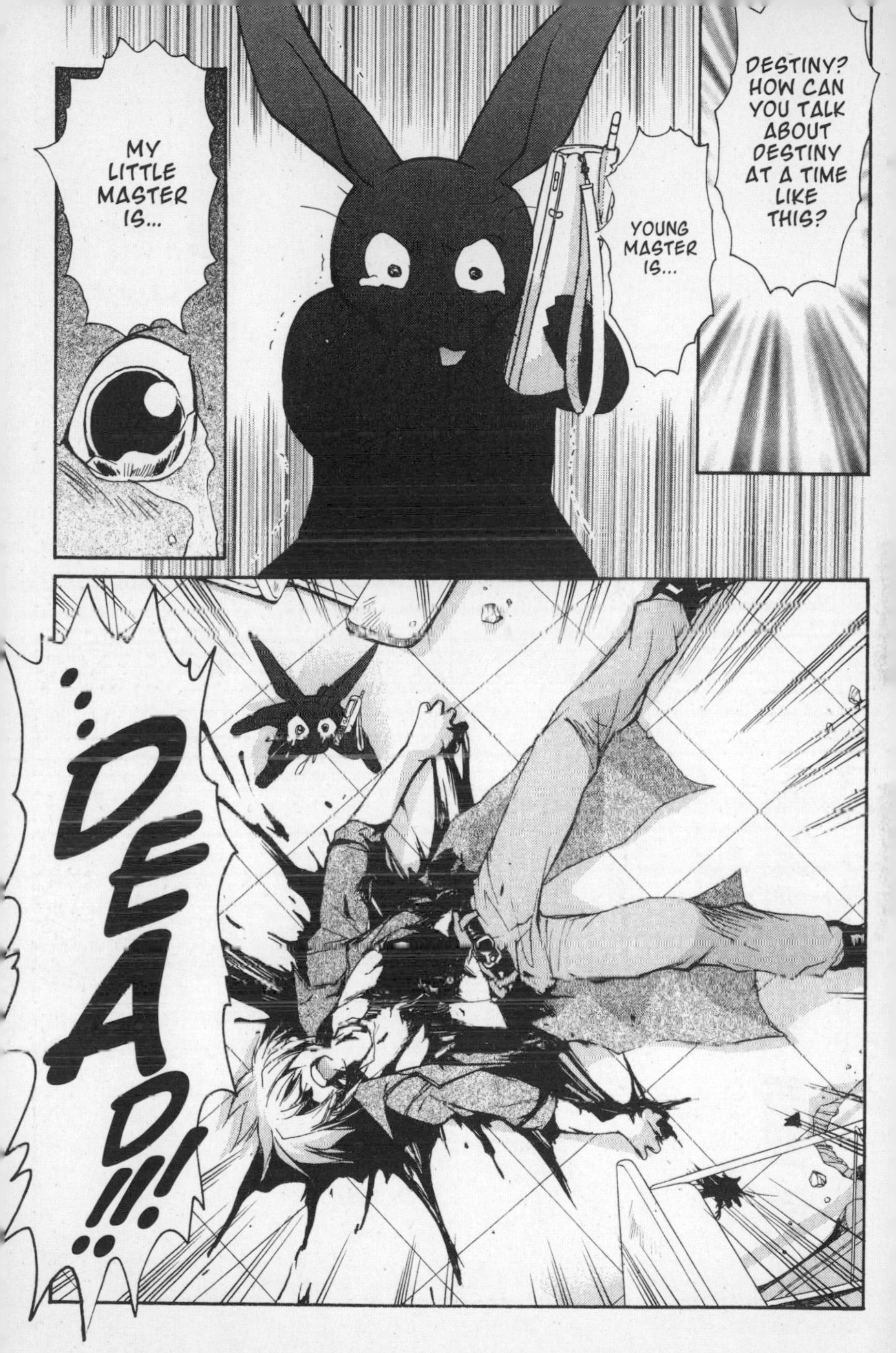
DESTINY? HOW CAN YOU TALK ABOUT DESTINY AT A TIME LIKE THIS?
YOUNG MASTER IS...
MY LITTLE MASTER IS...
...DEAD!!...

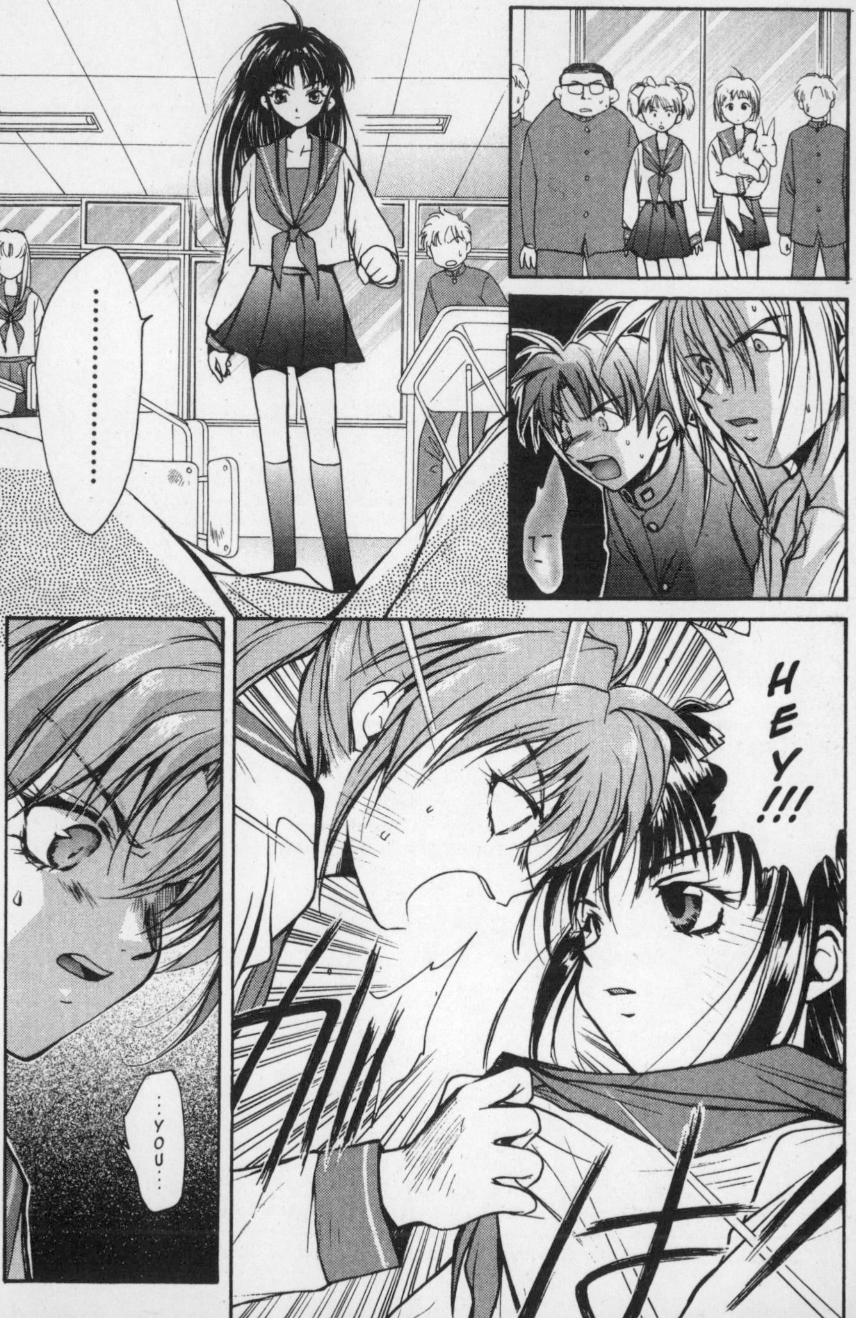

....
HEY!!!
...YOU...

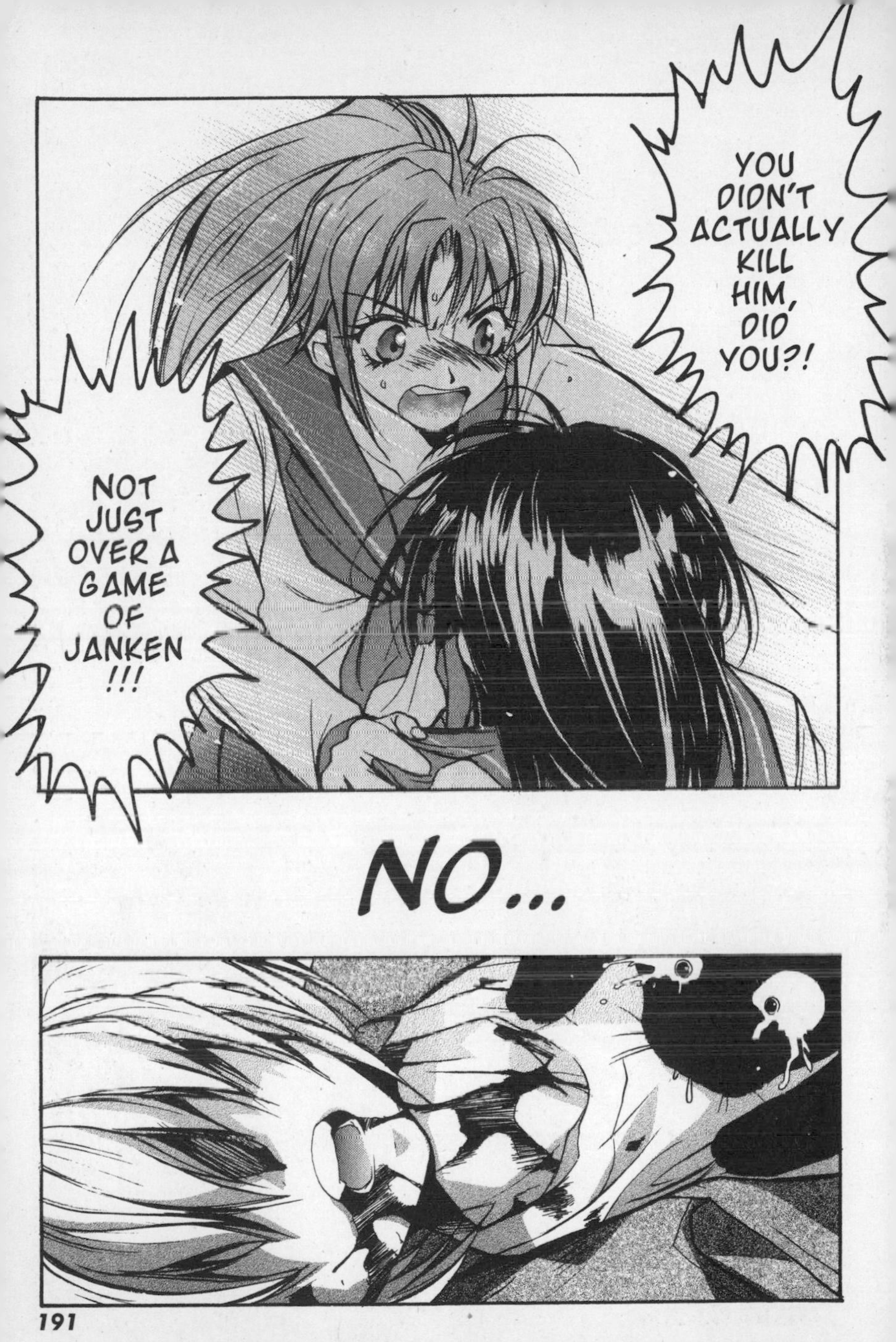
YOU DIDN'T ACTUALLY KILL HIM, DID YOU?!
NOT JUST OVER A GAME OF JANKEN !!!
NO...

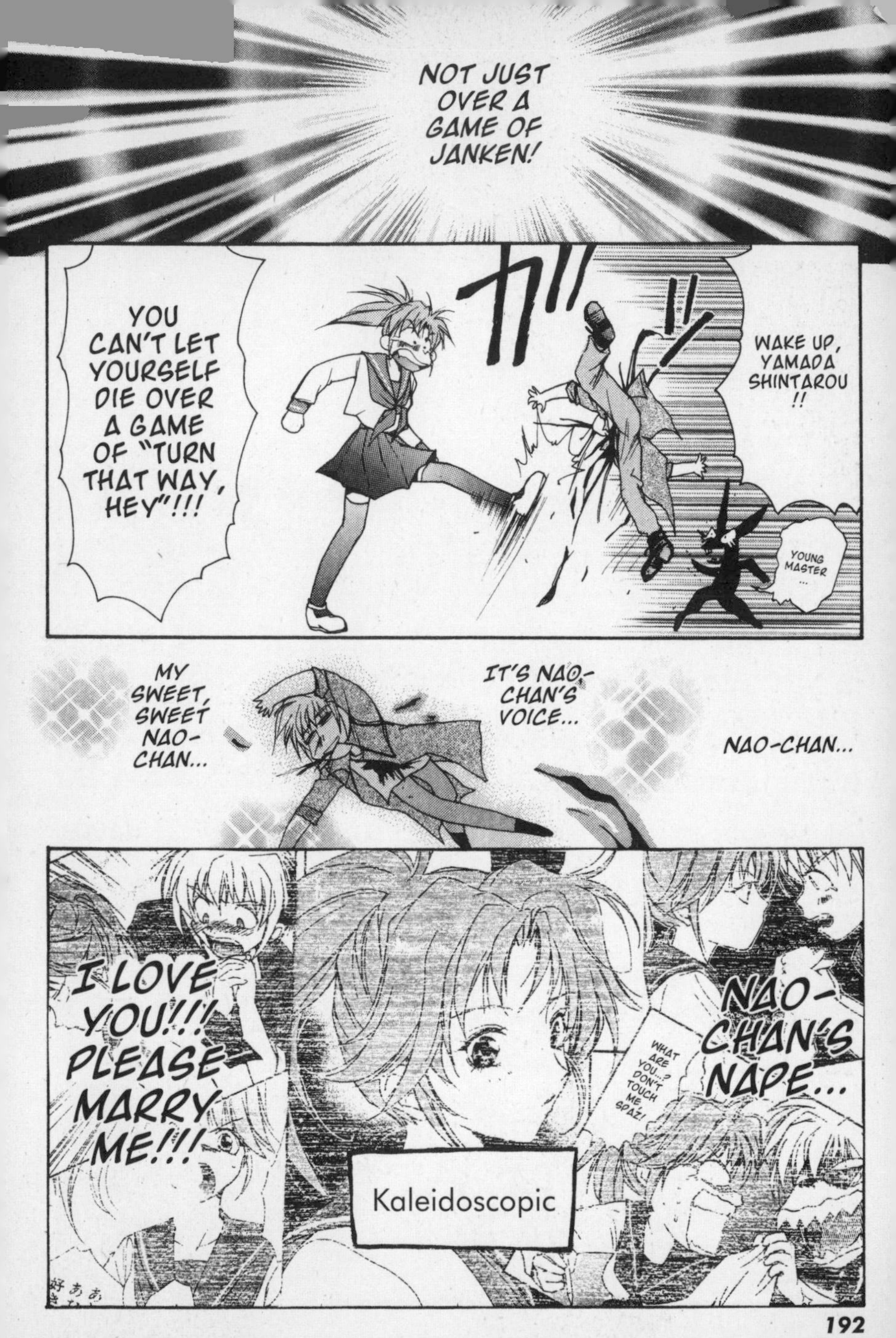
NOT JUST OVER A GAME OF JANKEN!
WAKE UP, YAMADA SHINTAROU!!
YOUNG MASTER...
YOU CAN'T LET YOURSELF DIE OVER A GAME OF "TURN THAT WAY, HEY"!!!
NAO-CHAN...
IT'S NAO-CHAN'S VOICE...
MY SWEET, SWEET NAO-CHAN...
NAO-CHAN'S NAPE...
WHAT ARE YOU...? DON'T TOUCH ME, SPAZ!
I LOVE YOU!!! PLEASE MARRY ME!!!
Kaleidoscopic

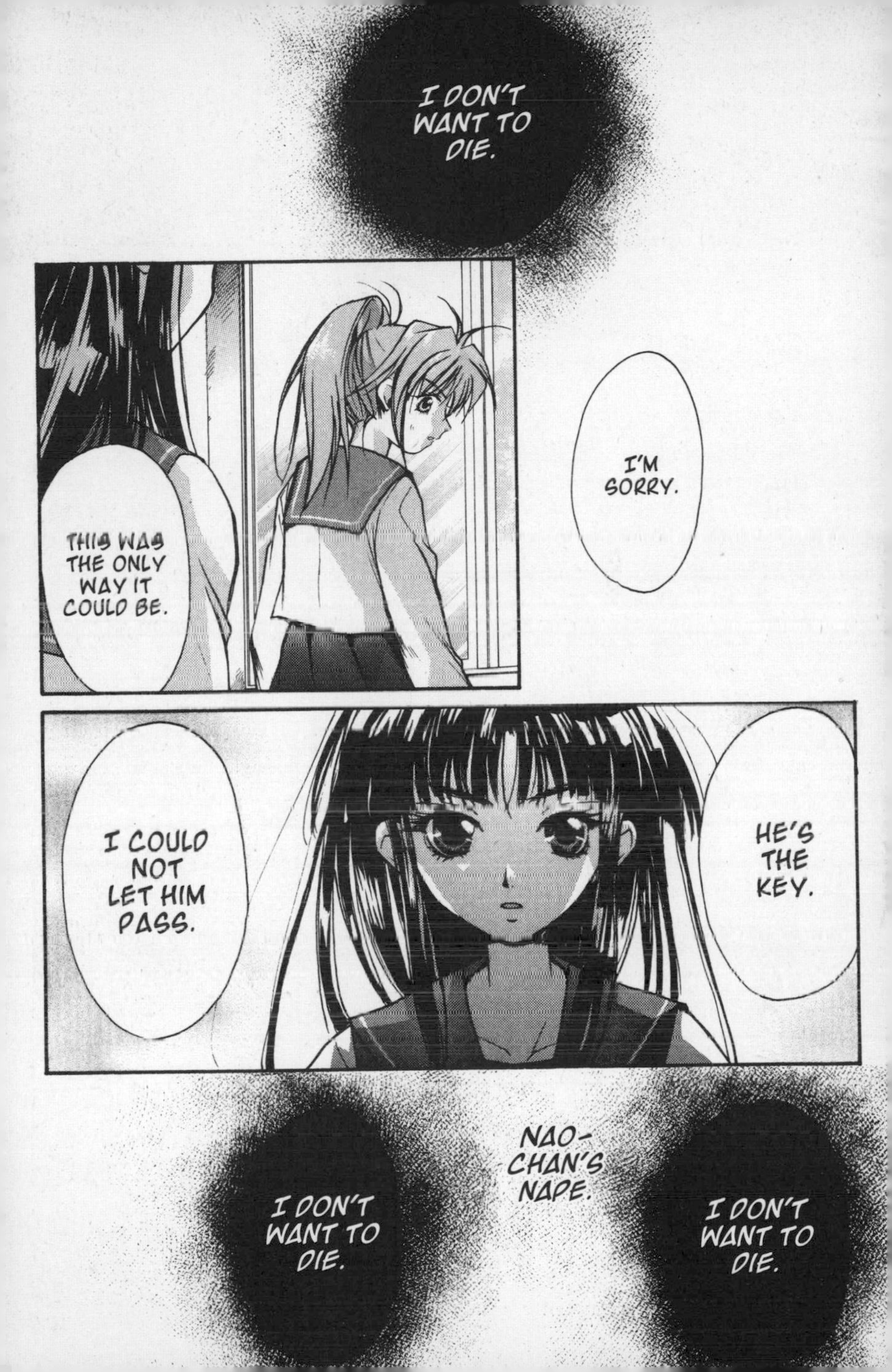
I DON'T WANT TO DIE.
I'M SORRY.
THIS WAS THE ONLY WAY IT COULD BE.
HE'S THE KEY.
I COULD NOT LET HIM PASS.
I DON'T WANT TO DIE.
NAO-CHAN'S NAPE.
I DON'T WANT TO DIE.

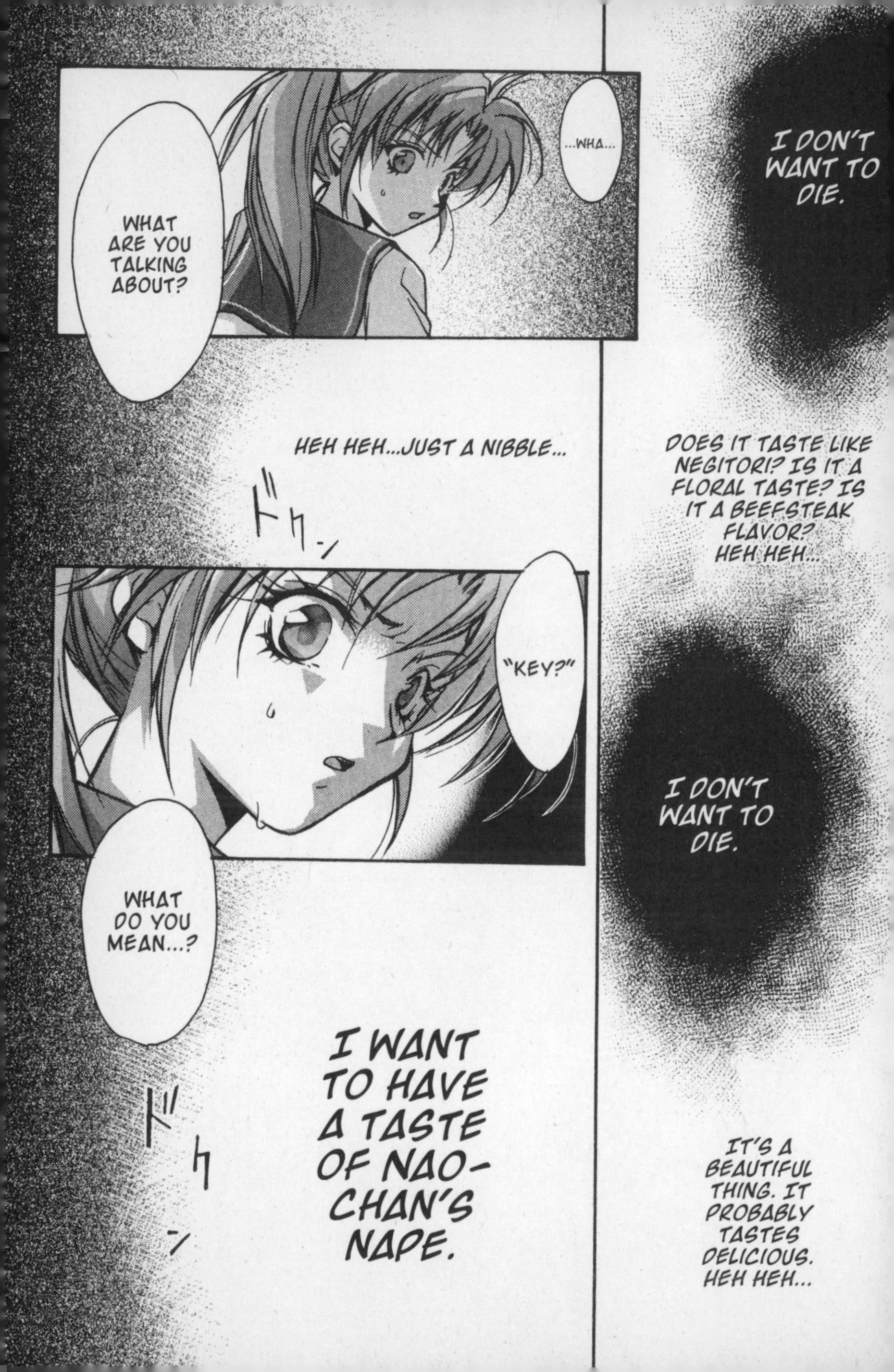
I DON'T WANT TO DIE.
DOES IT TASTE LIKE NEGITORI? IS IT A FLORAL TASTE? IS IT A BEEFSTEAK FLAVOR? HEH HEH...
I DON'T WANT TO DIE.
IT'S A BEAUTIFUL THING. IT PROBABLY TASTES DELICIOUS. HEH HEH...
...WHA...
WHAT ARE YOU TALKING ABOUT?
HEH HEH...JUST A NIBBLE...
"KEY?"
WHAT DO YOU MEAN...?
I WANT TO HAVE A TASTE OF NAO-CHAN'S NAPE.

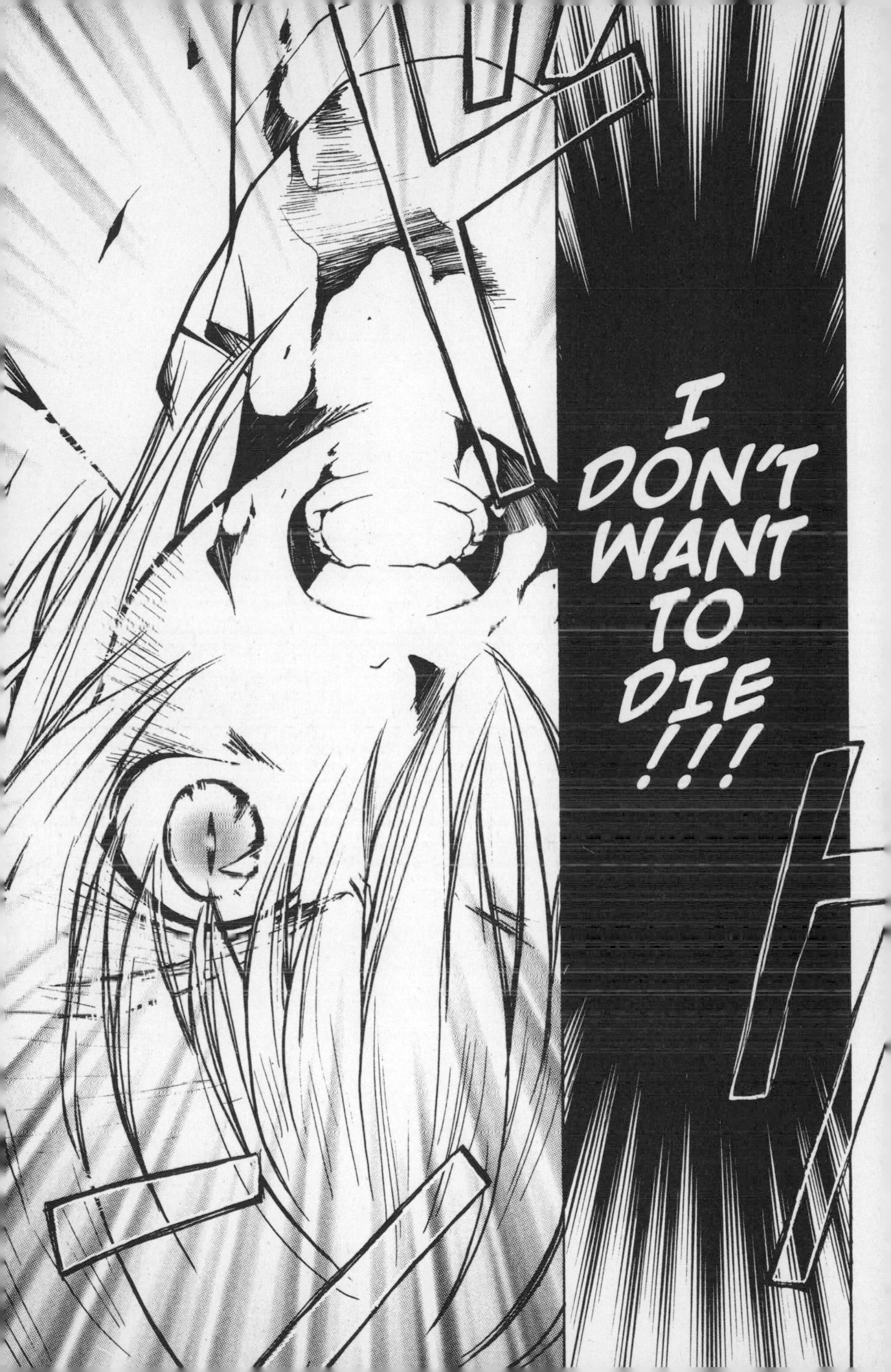
I DON'T WANT TO DIE!!!

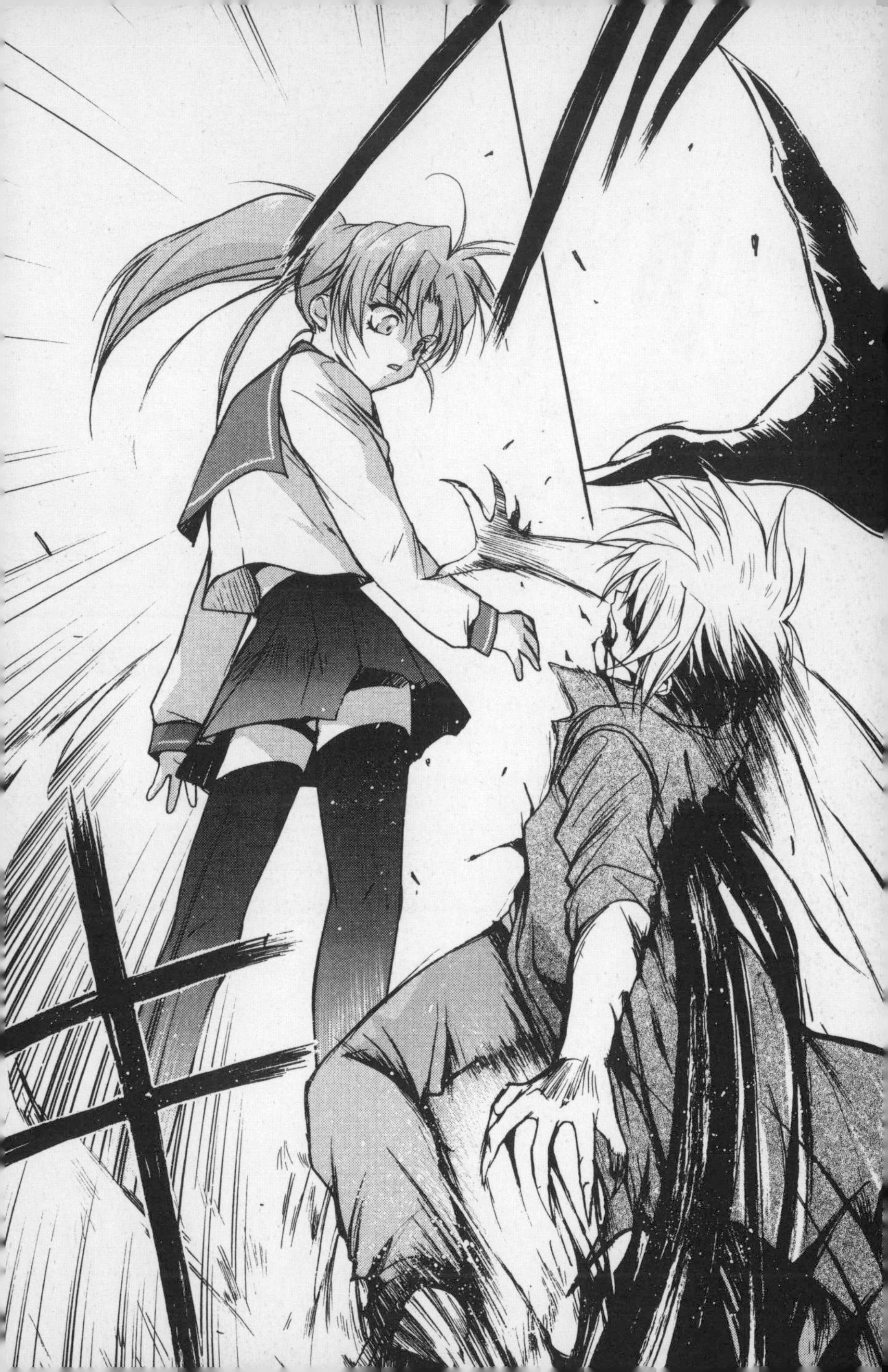

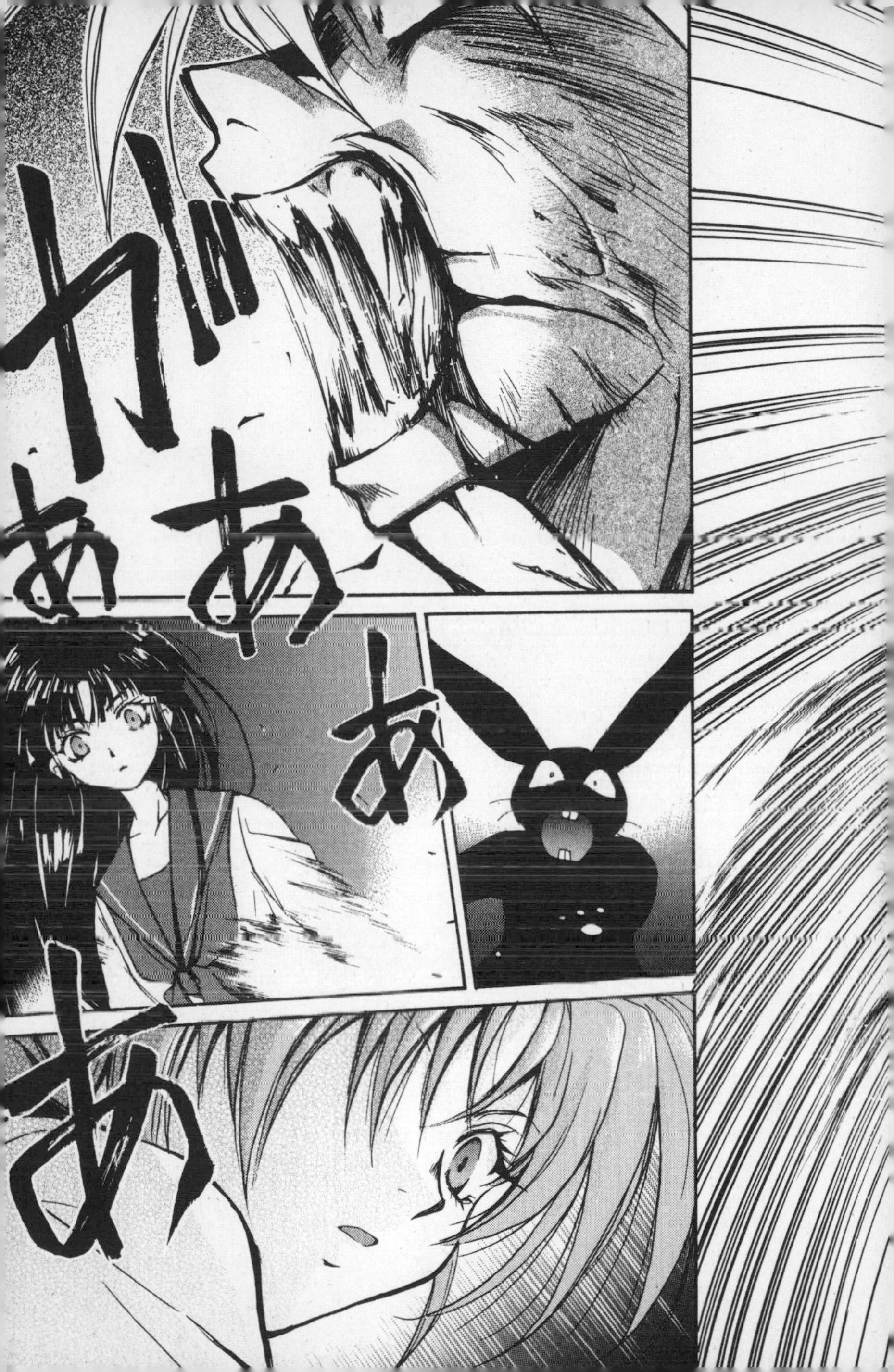
カッ
ああああ

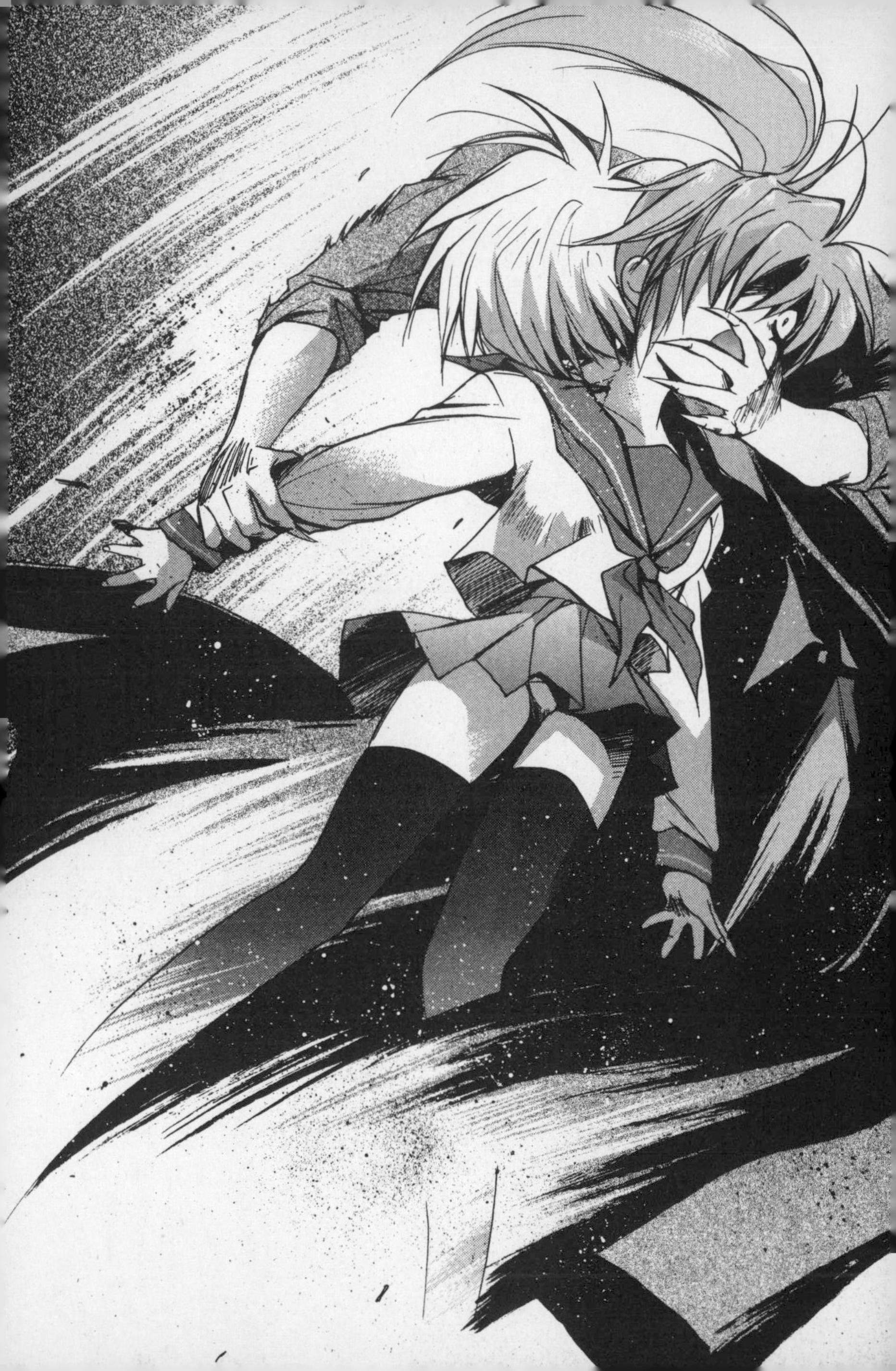

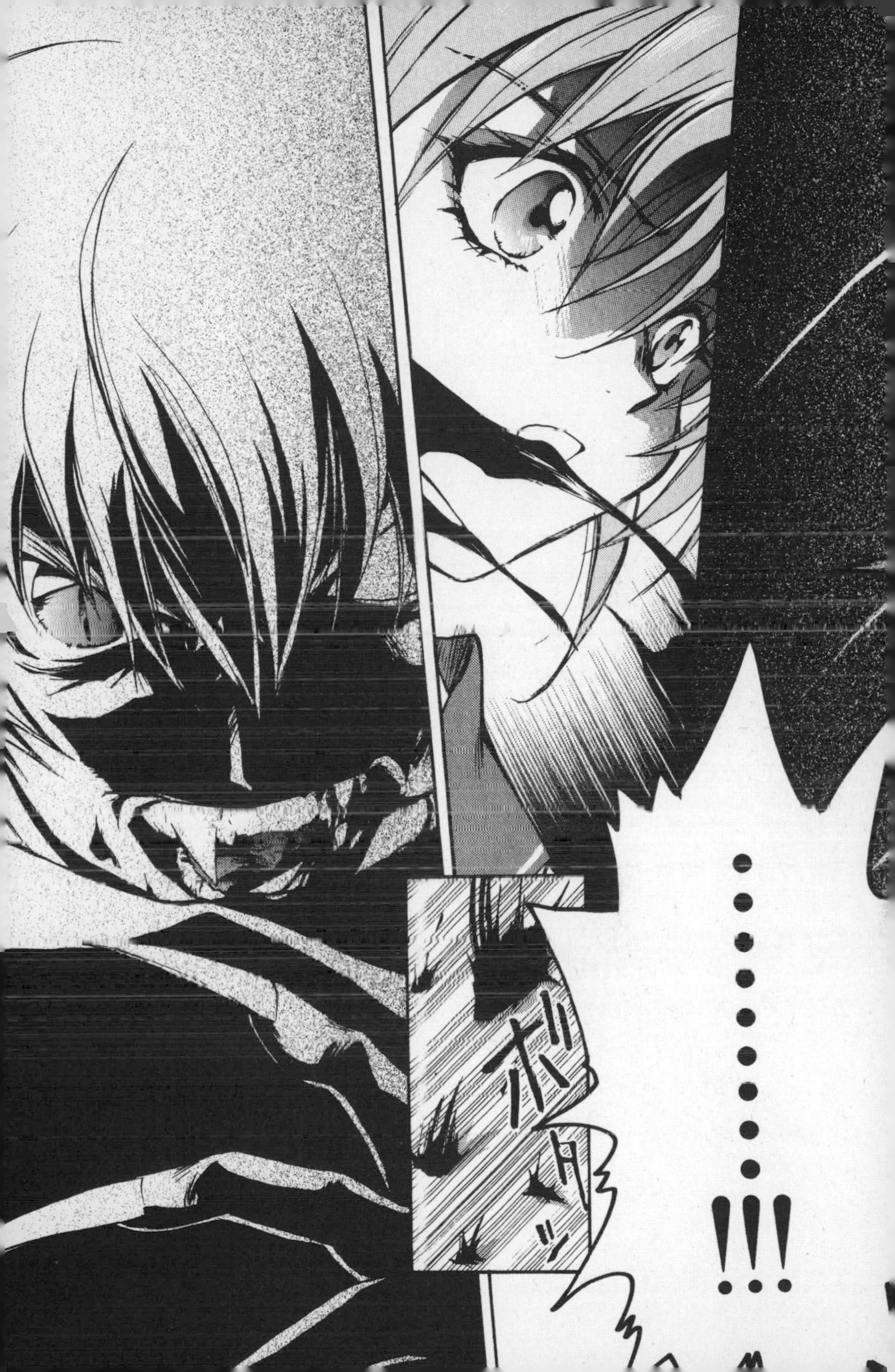

……!!!
ボタッ

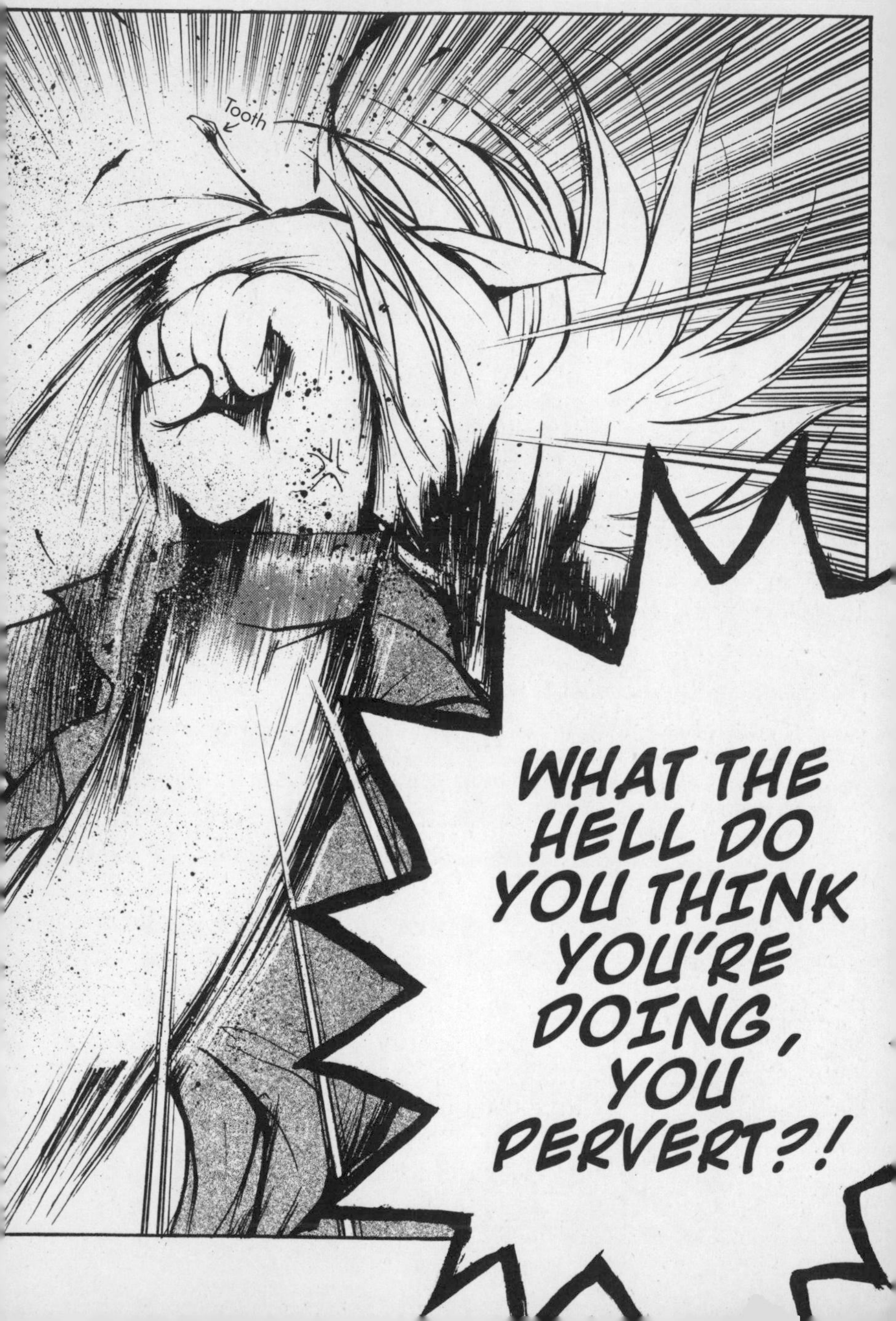
Tooth
WHAT THE HELL DO YOU THINK YOU'RE DOING, YOU PERVERT?!

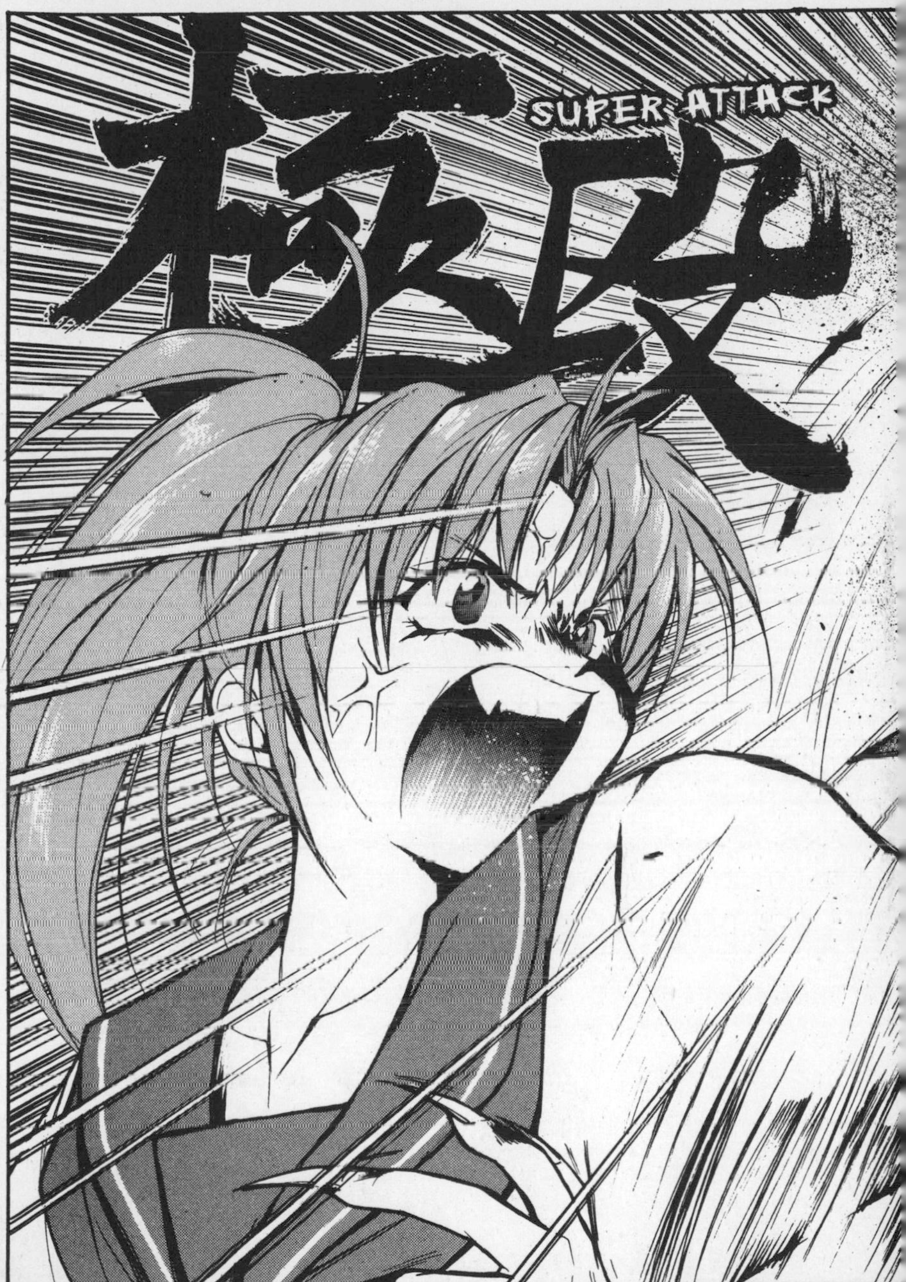
極攻
SUPER ATTACK

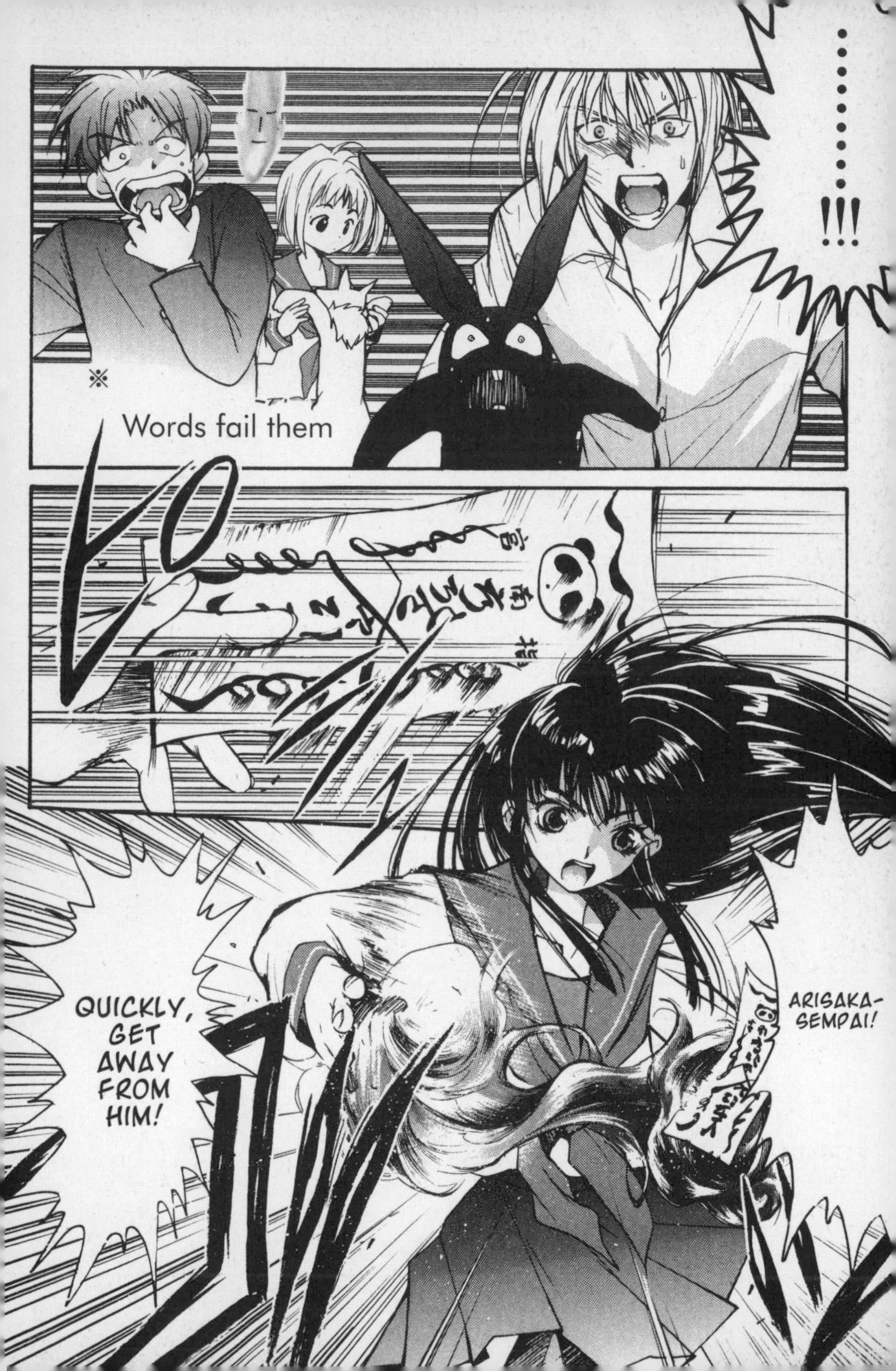

......!!!
※ Words fail them
ARISAKA-SEMPAI!
QUICKLY, GET AWAY FROM HIM!

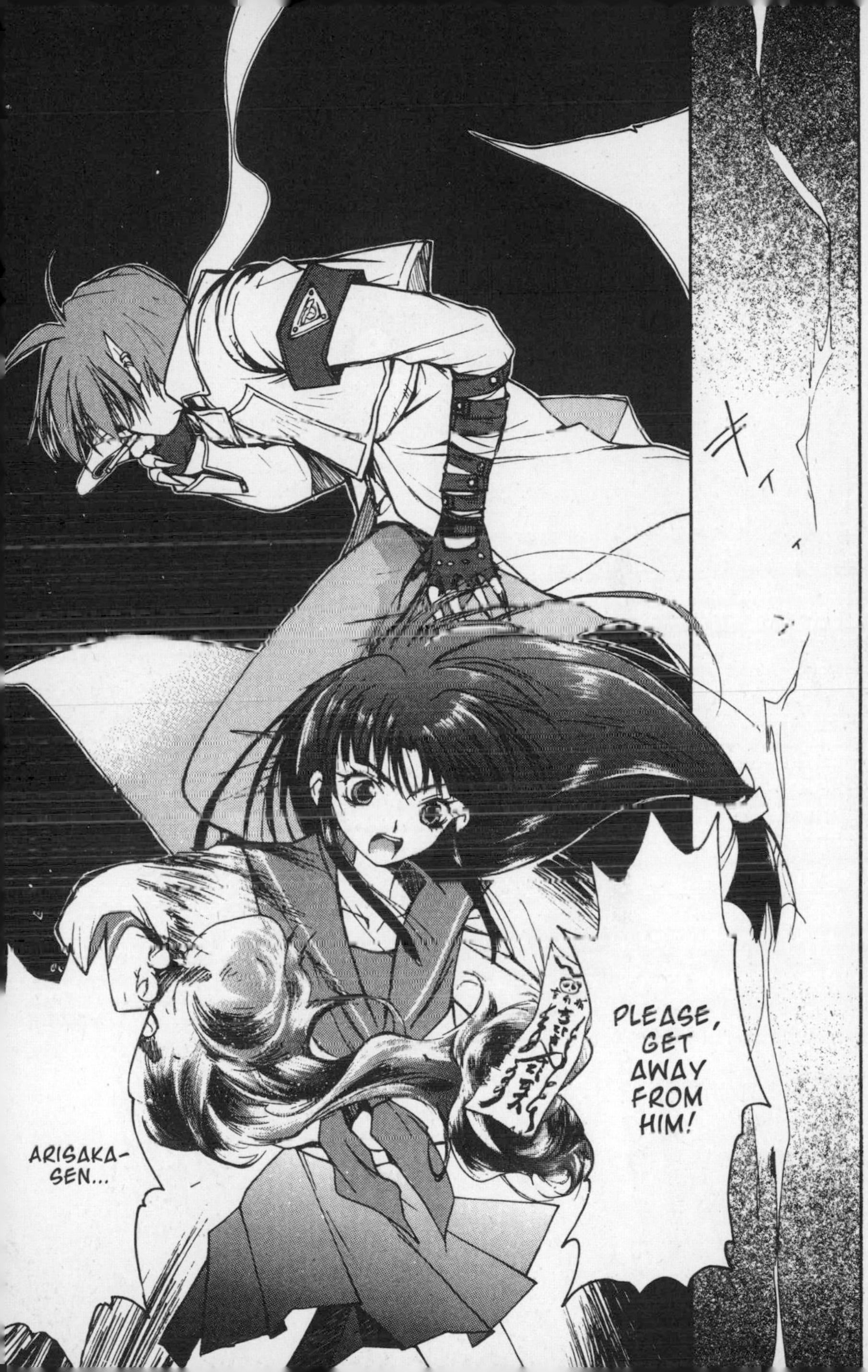
PLEASE, GET AWAY FROM HIM!
ARISAKA-SEN...

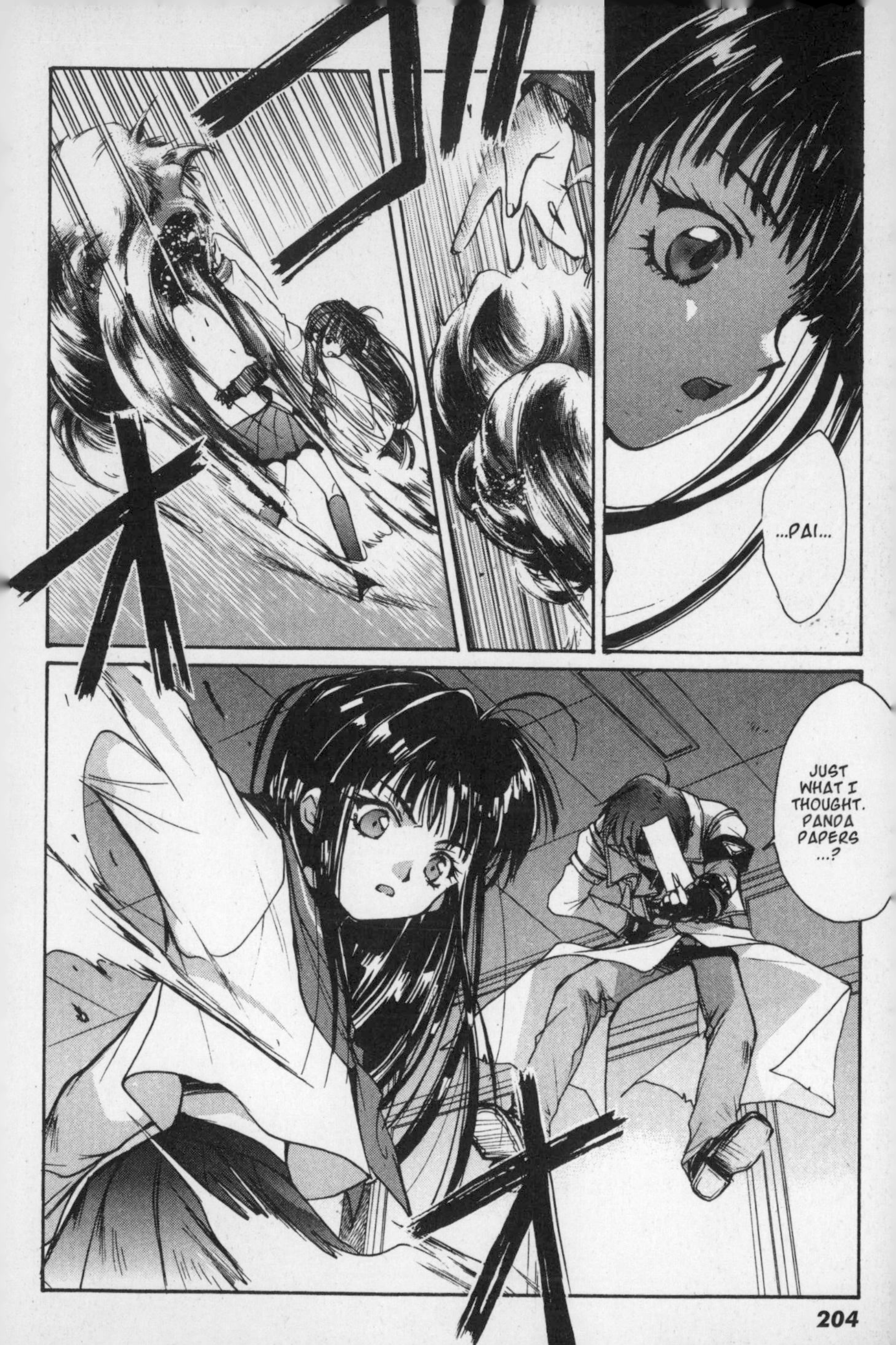
...PAI...
JUST WHAT I THOUGHT. PANDA PAPERS ...?

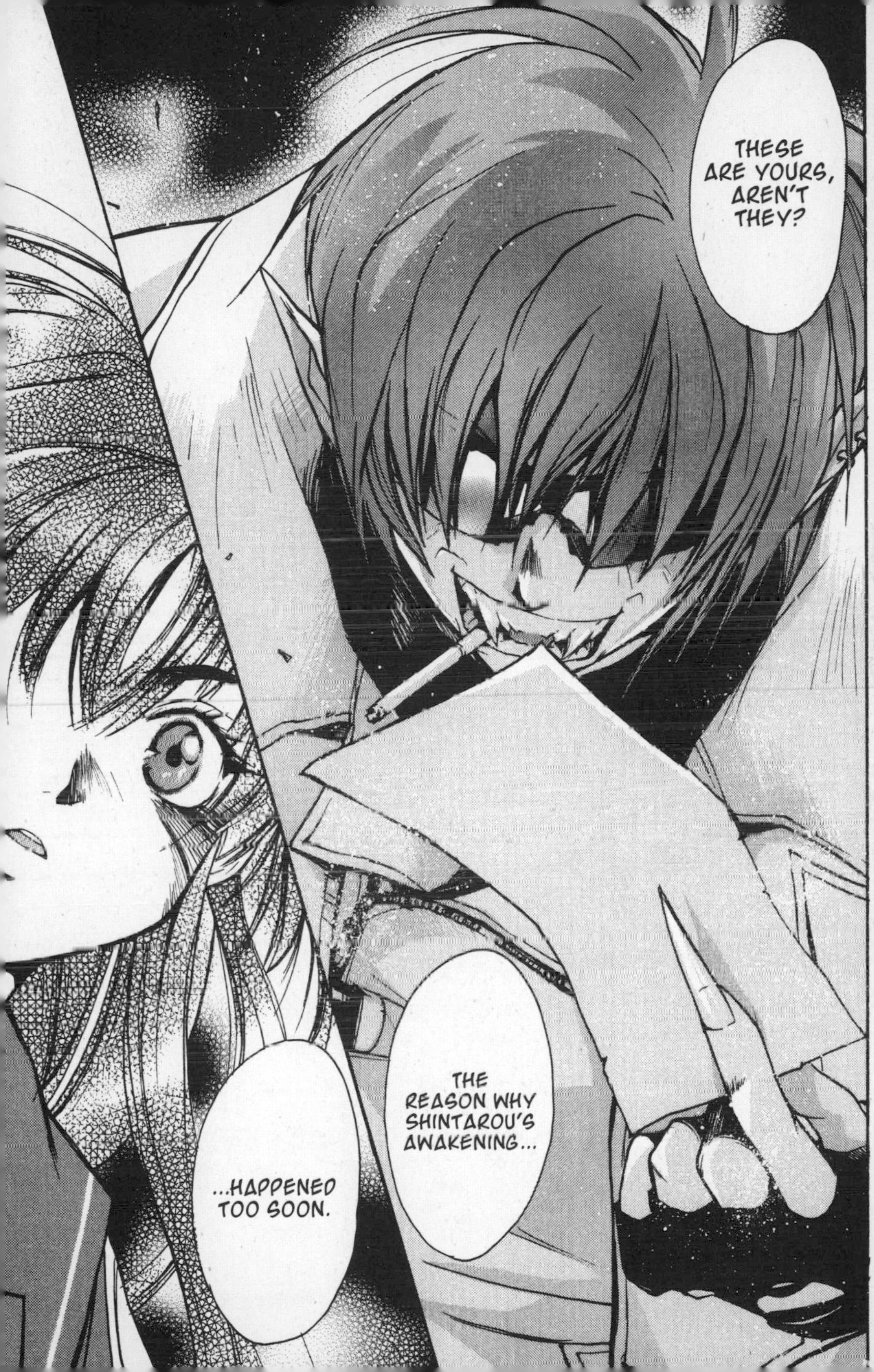
THESE ARE YOURS, AREN'T THEY?
THE REASON WHY SHINTAROU'S AWAKENING...
...HAPPENED TOO SOON.

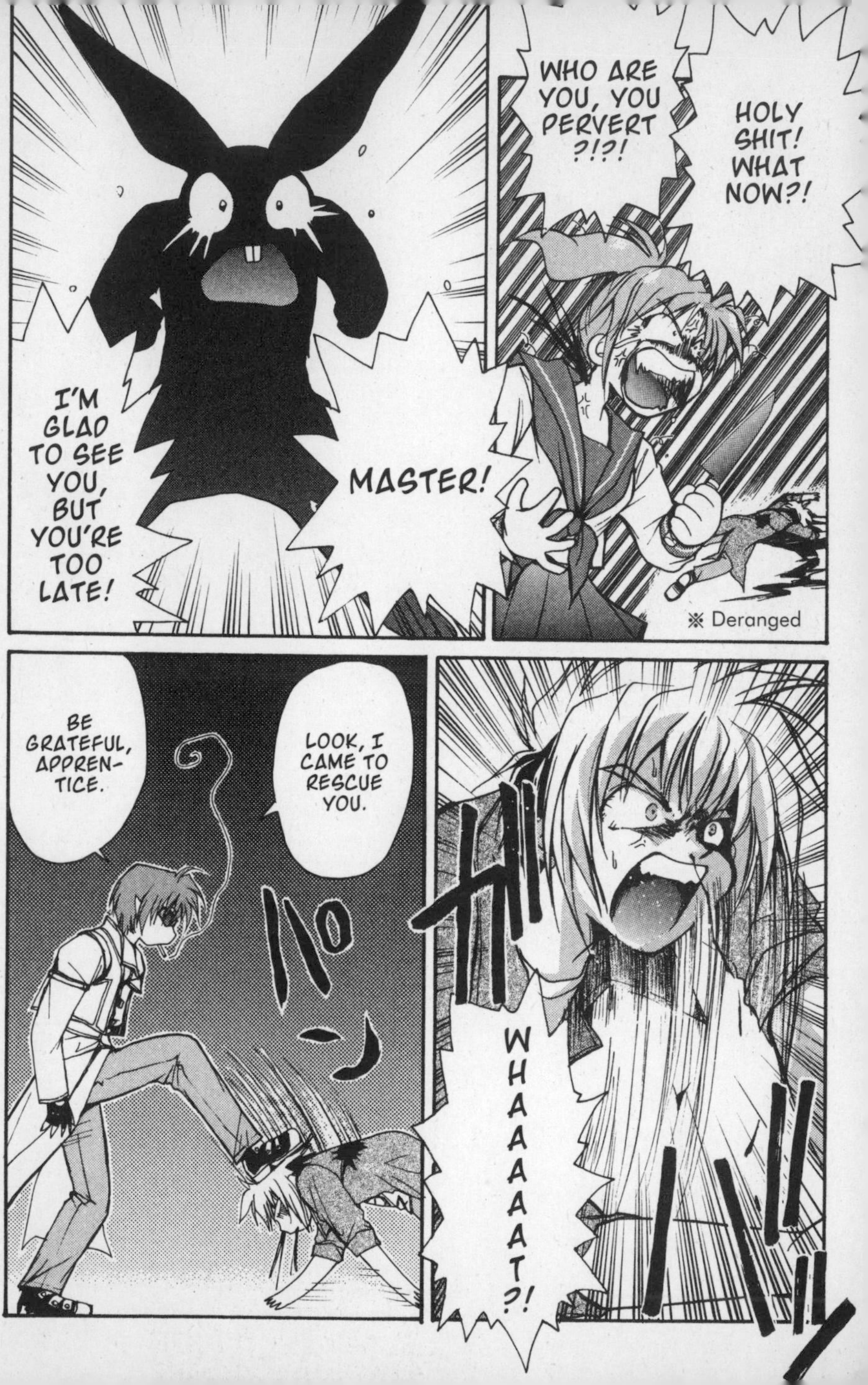
HOLY SHIT! WHAT NOW?!
WHO ARE YOU, YOU PERVERT ?!?!
※ Deranged
MASTER!
I'M GLAD TO SEE YOU, BUT YOU'RE TOO LATE!
WHAAAAAAT?!
LOOK, I CAME TO RESCUE YOU.
BE GRATEFUL, APPRENTICE.

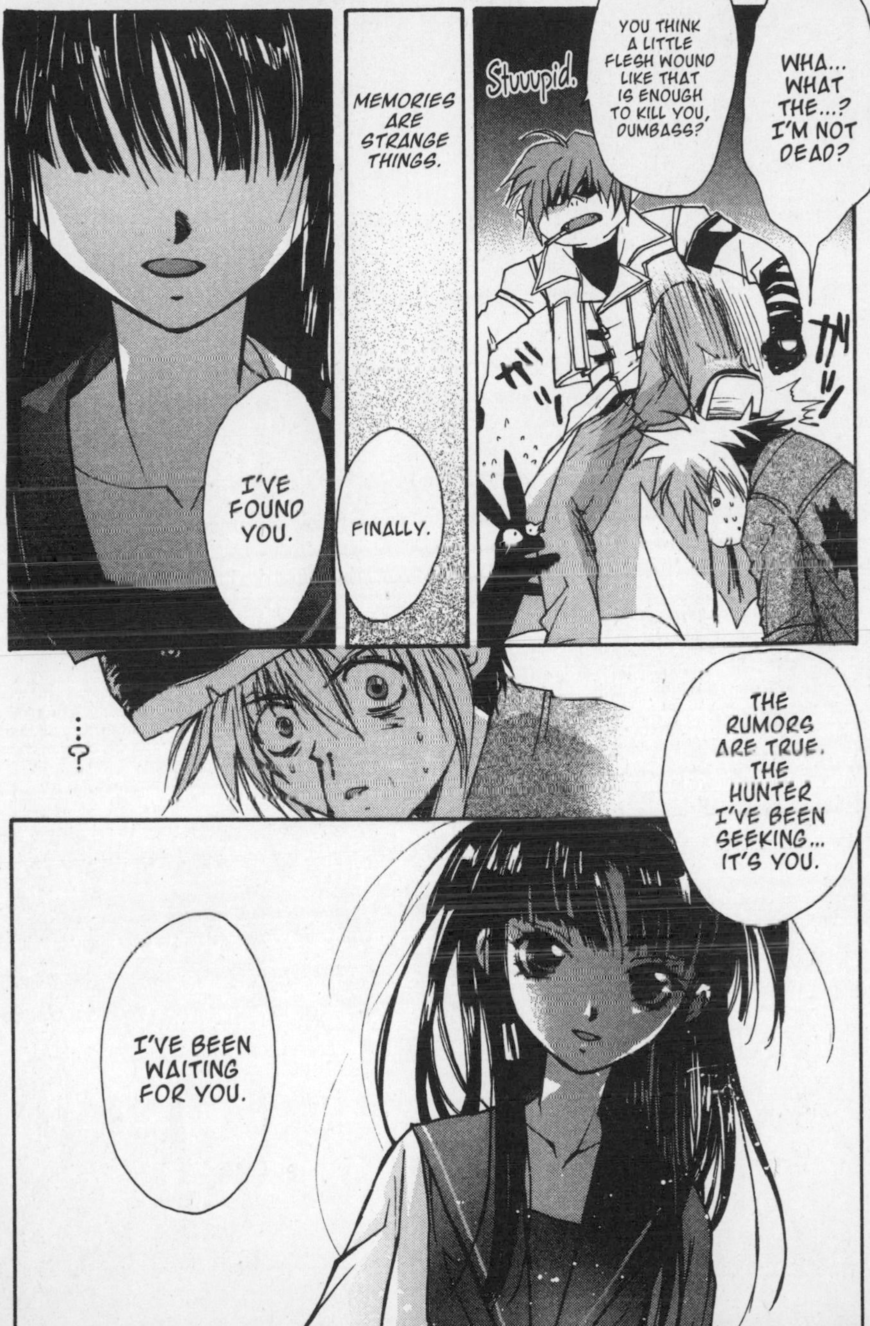
WHA... WHAT THE...? I'M NOT DEAD?
YOU THINK A LITTLE FLESH WOUND LIKE THAT IS ENOUGH TO KILL YOU, DUMBASS?
Stuuupid.
MEMORIES ARE STRANGE THINGS.
FINALLY.
I'VE FOUND YOU.
...?
THE RUMORS ARE TRUE. THE HUNTER I'VE BEEN SEEKING... IT'S YOU.
I'VE BEEN WAITING FOR YOU.

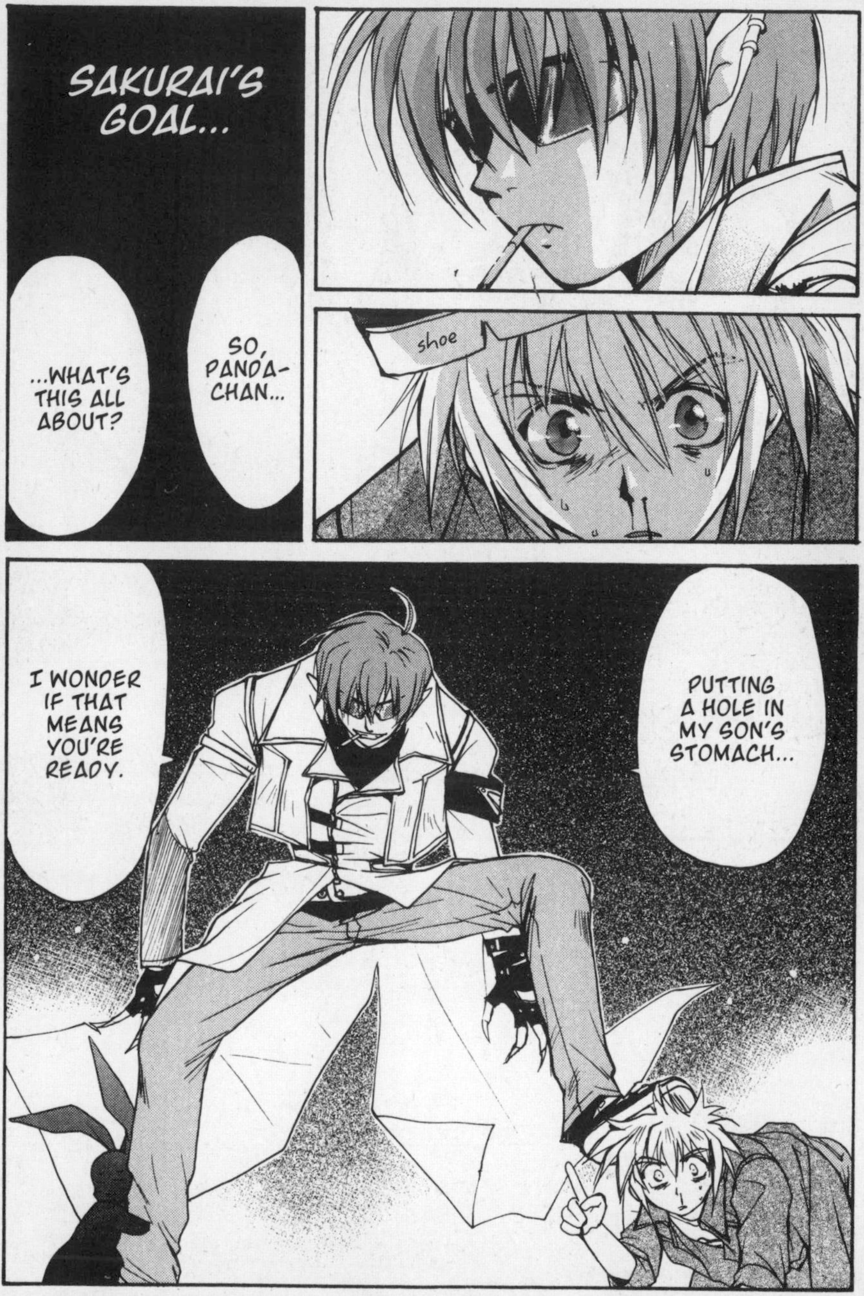
shoe
SAKURAI'S GOAL...
SO, PANDA-CHAN...
...WHAT'S THIS ALL ABOUT?
PUTTING A HOLE IN MY SON'S STOMACH...
I WONDER IF THAT MEANS YOU'RE READY.

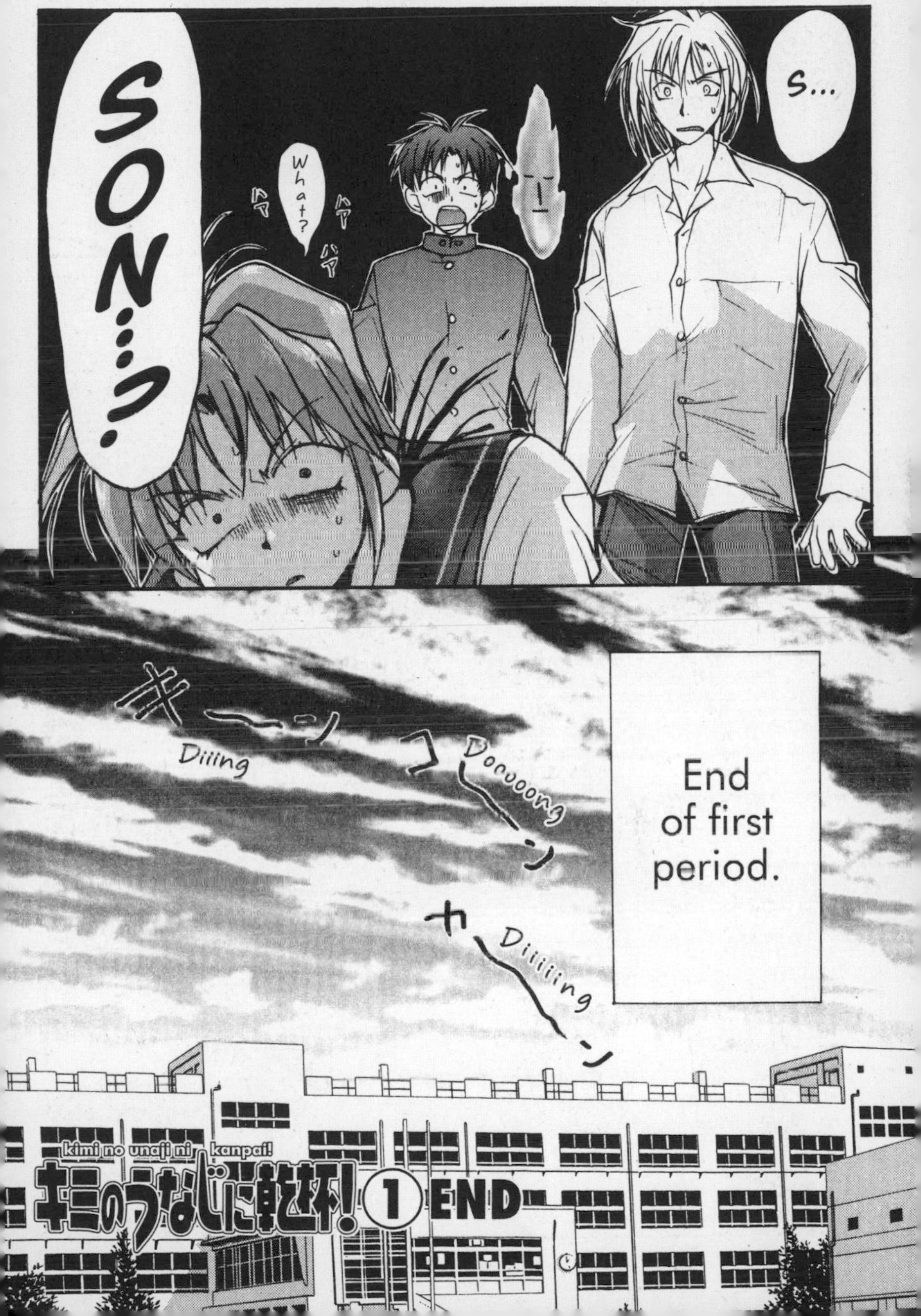
S...
What?
ハァ ハァ ハァ
SON...?!
End of first period.
キーンコーンカーンコーン
Diiing
Doooong
Diiiiing
kimi no unaji ni kanpai!
キミのうなじに乾杯! 1 END

Kanpai!
By Maki Murakami
2
From the Creator of Gravitation
TOKYOPOP

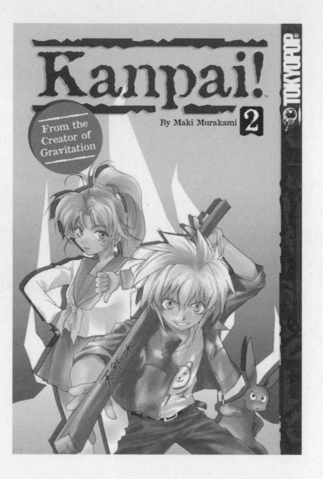

The chaos continues as the fight between Miko and the mysterious man claiming to be Shintaro's father builds to a climax...and then is suddenly over? No one except our fabulous five can remember anything about the insane goings-on at their school, and Nao is especially displeased to find out that she is now Shintaro's wife/permanent snack. Wackiness ensues as Shintaro and Ponta face off against the school Occult Club and a new excorcist, with the ability to control Shintaro's personality and powers, suddenly appears...

TOKYOPOP SHOP

WWW.TOKYOPOP.COM/SHOP

HOT NEWS!
Check out the
TOKYOPOP SHOP!
The world's best
collection of manga in
English is now available
online in one place!

GIRLS BRAVO

RIZELMINE

WWW.TOKYOPOP.COM/SHOP

WAR ON FLESH

War on Flesh and other hot titles are available at the store that never closes!

- LOOK FOR SPECIAL OFFERS
- PRE-ORDER UPCOMING RELEASES
- COMPLETE YOUR COLLECTIONS

SPOTLIGHT TOKYOPOP MANGA SUPPLEMENT

SCRAPPED PRINCESS

BY GO YABUKI, ICHIRO SAKAKI, AND YUKINOBU AZUMI

HER BIRTH FORETOLD THE DESTRUCTION OF THE WORLD!

Fifteen years ago, a set of twins—a girl and a boy—was born to the king of Linevan. Shortly after their birth, a prophecy foretold that when the girl turned 16, she would bring about the end of humanity. To avoid this terrible fate, the king ordered the girl disposed of—scrapped! She miraculously survived and was raised away from the kingdom that would kill her. But now she has turned 15, the king's guards have caught wind that she's still alive...and they set out to finish the job!

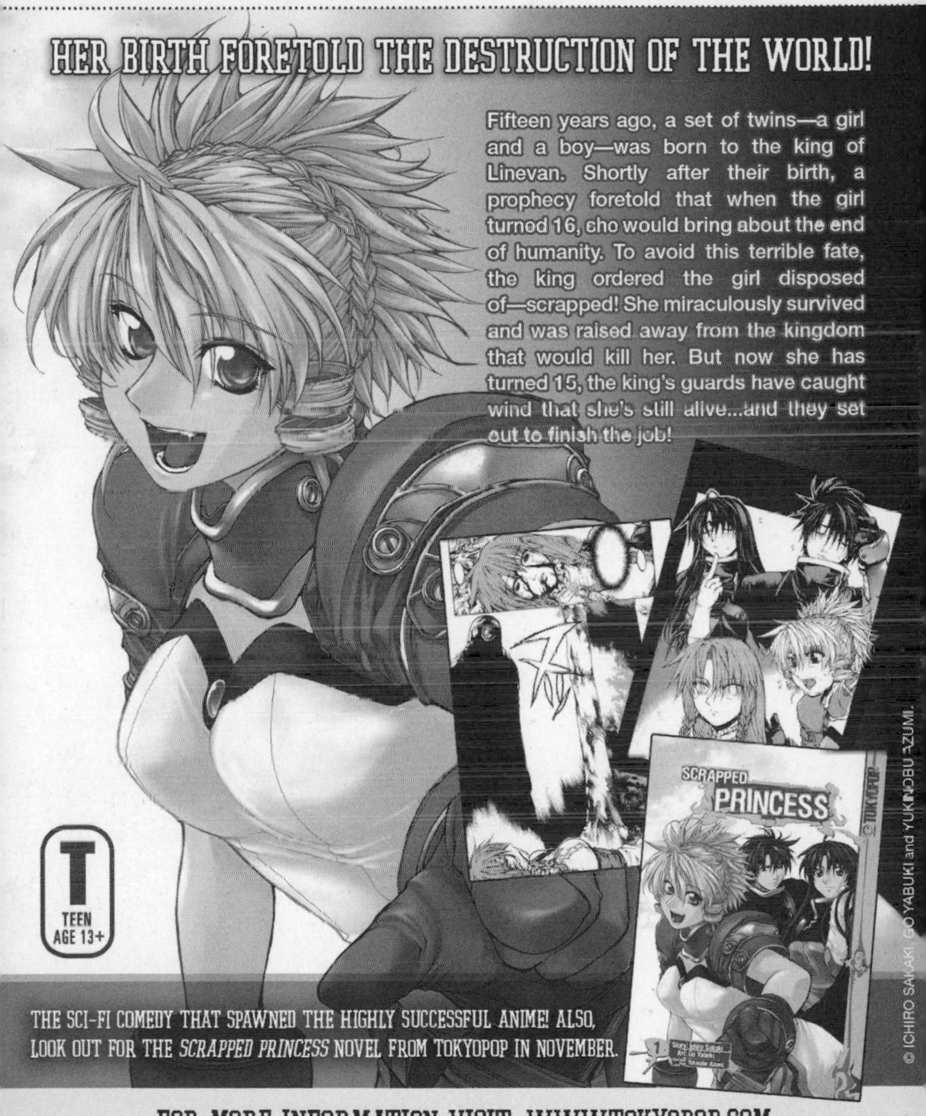
SCRAPPED PRINCESS
TOKYOPOP
1
T
TEEN
AGE 13+

THE SCI-FI COMEDY THAT SPAWNED THE HIGHLY SUCCESSFUL ANIME! ALSO, LOOK OUT FOR THE *SCRAPPED PRINCESS* NOVEL FROM TOKYOPOP IN NOVEMBER.

FOR MORE INFORMATION VISIT: WWW.TOKYOPOP.COM

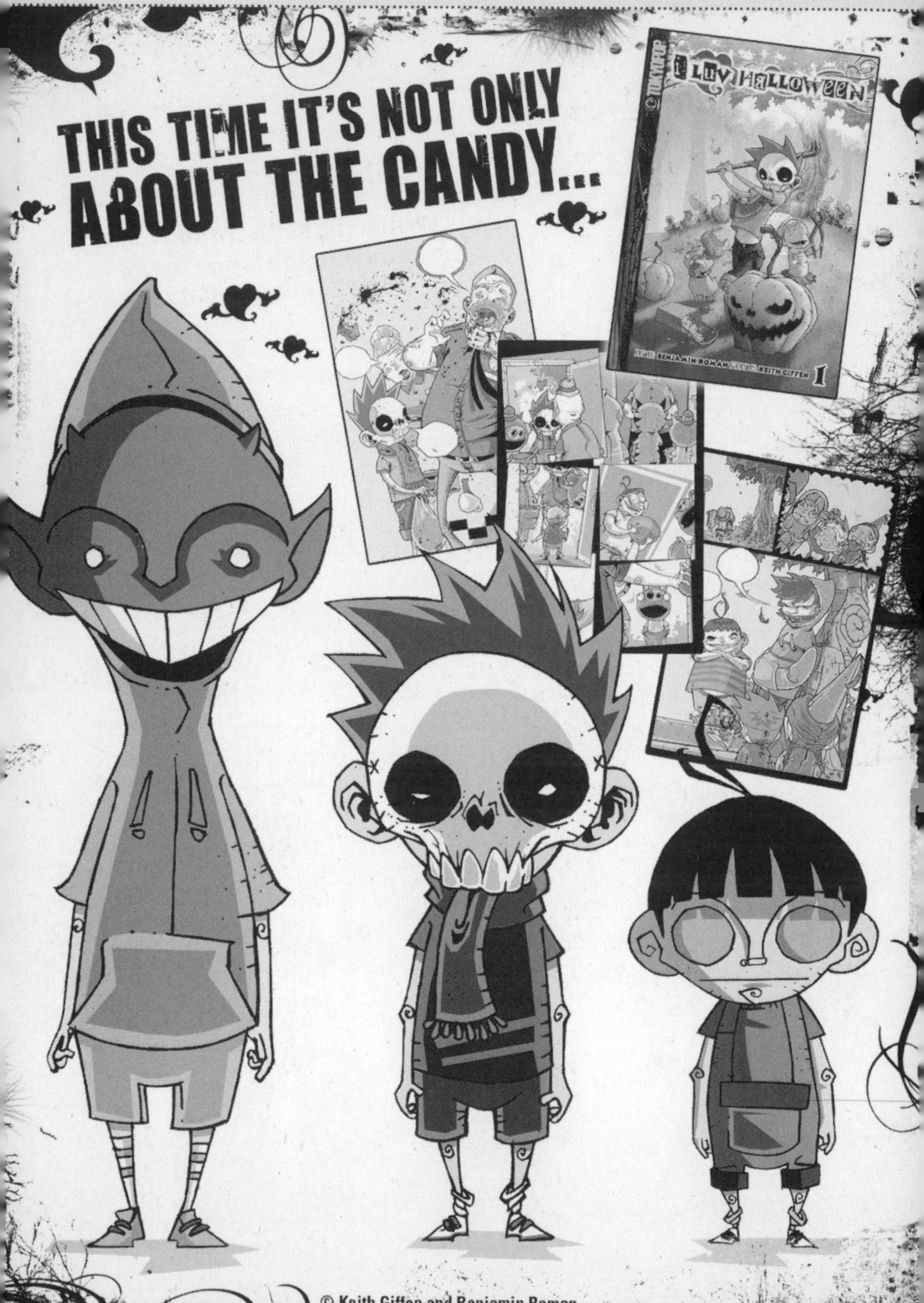
THIS TIME IT'S NOT ONLY
ABOUT THE CANDY...
TOKYOPOP
I LUV HALLOWEEN
BENJAMIN ROMAN
KEITH GIFFEN
1

i LUV HALLOWEEN ™

Written by Keith Giffen, comic book pro and English language adapter of *Battle Royale* and *Battle Vixens*.

Join the misadventures of a group of particularly disturbing trick-or-treaters as they go about their macabre business on Halloween night. Blaming the apples they got from the first house of the evening for the bad candy they've been receiving all night, the kids plot revenge on the old bag who handed out the funky fruit. Riotously funny and always wickedly shocking— who doesn't *love* Halloween?

OT
OLDER TEEN
AGE 16+

STOP!

This is the back of the book.
You wouldn't want to spoil a great ending!

This book is printed "manga-style," in the authentic Japanese right-to-left format. Since none of the artwork has been flipped or altered, readers get to experience the story just as the creator intended. You've been asking for it, so TOKYOPOP® delivered: authentic, hot-off-the-press, and far more fun!

DIRECTIONS

If this is your first time reading manga-style, here's a quick guide to help you understand how it works.

It's easy... just start in the top right panel and follow the numbers. Have fun, and look for more 100% authentic manga from TOKYOPOP®!

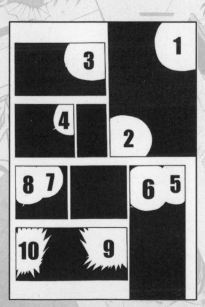